A MIND FOR EVER VOYAGING

A Mind For Ever Voyaging

*Wordsworth at Work
Portraying Newton and Science*

What oft was thought, but ne'er so well exprest

W. K. Thomas and Warren U. Ober

The University of Alberta Press

First published by
The University of Alberta Press
Athabasca Hall
Edmonton, Alberta
Canada T6G 2E8

Copyright © The University of Alberta Press 1989

ISBN 0-88864-135-4

Canadian Cataloguing in Publication Data

Thomas, W. K. (Walter Keith), 1927–
    A mind for ever voyaging : Wordsworth at work portraying Newton and Science

    Includes bibliographical references and index.
    ISBN 0-88864-135-4

    1. Wordsworth, William, 1770-1850—Criticism and interpretation. 2. Wordsworth, William, 1770-1850—Knowledge—Science. 3. Newton, Isaac, Sir, 1642-1727, in fiction, drama, poetry, etc. 4. Science in literature. I. Ober, Warren U.   II. Title.
PR5892.S3T56   1989   821.7   C88-091151-4

All rights reserved.
No part of this publication may be produced, stored in a retrieval system, or transmitted in any forms or by any means, electronic, mechanical, photocopying, recording, or otherwise, without the prior permission of the copyright owner.

Typesetting by The Typeworks, Vancouver, British Columbia

Printed by Hignell Printing Ltd., Winnipeg, Manitoba, Canada

Contents

Preface vii
Acknowledgements xi

1 Elevating the Mind to God   3
2 The Sage as Hero   17
3 What Oft Was Thought   43
4 A Prevailing Practice   59
5 Linking Together   81
6 Strange Seas   98
7 A Kindred Spirit   118
8 But Ne'er So Well Exprest   145

Appendices   181
A: The Myth of Wordsworth's Reading But Little   183
B: Wordsworth's Attitude Towards Cambridge Undergraduates   191
C: Shenstone and Cowper   195
D: Wordsworth's Attitude Concerning Acknowledgements   199
E: The Myth of Wordsworth's Total Originality   202
F: The Availability of Sources for the Hymn to Science   205
G: The Distinctive Cluster of Elements   207
H: Wordsworth's Poetic Expectations in Old Age   213
I: Dating the Last Two Lines on Newton's Statue   217
J: The Availability of Bulwer's Poem   221
K: Further Changes Due to Hamilton   226
L: The Availability of Hunt's Review of Haydon's Painting   234
M: Wordsworth's Acquaintance with Philo   237
N: Further Changes Due to Young   241
O: On the Editing of the Lines on Newton's Statue   244

Abbreviations   255
Notes   259
Bibliography   299
Index   315

Preface

THIS BOOK IS ABOUT THE PROCESS OF POETIC COMPOSItion. If it should happen that you, the reader, are currently of the opinion that the best poetry, certainly the best Romantic poetry, and indubitably the best of William Wordsworth's poetry, has been composed with entire originality and without recourse to previous literature, then you may well find this book unsettling or even troublesome.

That is how a particular Wordsworth scholar who read an earlier version of the book found it, so much so that he was moved to recall what Tennyson had said about his critic, Churton Collins: that he was "a louse upon the locks of literature." And why? Because, as the scholar remembered the incident, Churton Collins, that "hyperactive drudge" and that "misguided literary hack," had delved into Tennyson's sources and had "'proved' that everything the poet ever wrote was stolen from others." Curiously, Tennyson's own grandson presents the incident somewhat differently. Collins had indeed identified Tennyson's borrowings (as we do with Wordsworth's) and had found that, although many of them were from the most famous poets of four nations, many others were from "less conspicuous writers" (as is the case with Wordsworth's borrowings), but he did not accuse Tennyson of theft. Instead, while he "was assiduous in emphasizing Tennyson's pre-eminence among contemporary poets" (as we would with Wordsworth), "he dealt with him as 'not so much a poet of original genius...as one whose mastery lay in assimilative skill and tireless artistry'"—which comes close to how we present Wordsworth.[1]

Actually our principal concern is not with the presumed fact *that* Wordsworth used various sources, but with *how* he used them, reworking them, combining them, fusing disparate elements into one glorious whole. A necessary part of such a study is the close examination of various details, and after a while the accumulation of detail may affect the reader in the way it did our scholar who recalled Collins: although he was supportive and most helpful in his suggestions, he objected that on occasion we "border on the maniacal." Perhaps unfortunately, details are inescapable, and not just because of the nature of this study, but also because of the nature of Wordsworth's sensibility. It is abundantly clear that he could respond to the smallest detail in what he observed, whether the detail was in the landscape (like the shape of the shadow cast by a meadow-flower) or in his reading (like an odd turn of phrase in an out-of-the-way writer). And our study has convinced us that these details, transmuted, find their way into Wordsworth's poetry. In fact, sometimes the smallest, most trifling detail in what Wordsworth observed can, in the process of poetic transmutation, become a major element in a particularly effective piece of poetry, as Wordsworth himself often acknowledged. One simply cannot afford to dismiss details as being unimportant in the study of Wordsworth's poetry.

There is also a further reason for dealing with so many details. The view of Wordsworth's poetry which we have been led to by our study, and which we present in this book, is still a minority view, the exact opposite (it happens) of the majority view. We know, from our own experience in holding to the favoured view on other issues, how easy it is for people in the majority to dismiss the arguments of those in the minority: the details they offer by way of disproving the orthodox view are "minor," "trivial," or "of infrequent occurrence." We know that often the majority have to be inundated with details disproving their view before they will really take notice.

Often they try to dismiss the arguments of the minority by saying that they fail to distinguish between the forest and the trees. This popular figure of speech illustrates the matter nicely. A forest is the sum total of the trees in it, and how can one tell what kind of forest it is without knowing what kinds of trees are in it? And yet the majority have said, in effect, "In the forest of English literature, that particular stand over there—Wordsworth's—is a stand of poplar, of quick and easy growth." We have looked closely at one magnificent tree in particular and we have found that it is no poplar at all; instead it is an oak, of slow and laboured growth and glorious majesty. We have looked far enough into trees near this one to know that some of them are not poplars, but rowan trees. We suspect that others are sycamores, or hawthorns, or still other varieties, which can be identified correctly only after close examination of a myriad of details.

If giving serious consideration to this myriad of details borders on the maniacal, and if showing how Wordsworth used this myriad to create magnificent poetry makes literary parasites of us, then we shall simply have to subscribe ourselves as "Maniacal Lice upon the Locks of Literature," and wear the appellation as a badge of honour.

Acknowledgements

WE SHOULD LIKE TO EXPRESS OUR GRATEFUL APpreciation to Mr. Jonathan Wordsworth and the Dove Cottage Trustees for permission to quote (and to reproduce in facsimile) the lines concerning Newton's statue that appear in the various manuscripts of *The Prelude*; to Mr. John W. Charles, Special Collections Librarian at the University of Alberta Library, for permission to examine the Dove Cottage Papers Facsimiles that are on deposit there; and to the staff of the Rare Book Room of the Olin Library of Cornell University for their courtesy in making available the Cornell copies of the Dove Cottage Facsimiles. We are particularly grateful to Mrs. Anna H. Burgess, Librarian of Caven Library, Knox College, Toronto, for most generously making available to us Thomas Mangey's edition of Philo's works.

To various people we are indebted for kind permission to reproduce photographs: to the Master and Fellows of Trinity College, Cambridge, for the photograph of Newton's statue by Roubiliac; to the Master and Fellows of St. John's College, Cambridge, for the photograph of the portrait of Wordsworth by Pickersgill; to the Rector and Reverend Fathers of the Athenaeum of Ohio, for the detail of Wordsworth from the painting by Haydon of Christ's Triumphant Entry into Jerusalem, which hangs in the foyer of the chapel of the

Athenaeum of Ohio / Mt. St. Mary's Seminary of the West in Cincinnati, Ohio; to Mr. Robert Ober for the photograph itself of that detail; and to the Department of Rare Books and Special Collections, University Library, The University of Michigan, and the Augustan Reprint Society for both their permissions to reproduce illustrations of Veneration and Extasy from Charles Le Brun's *A Method to Learn to Design the Passions* (1734; Los Angeles: Augustan Reprint Society, 1980). To all of these we are most grateful.

To the scholars whose works are cited in our notes we are especially indebted: without their work, of course, we could not even have begun. We hope that we have been able to extend their findings somewhat, and so prepare the way for others to extend ours.

This book has been published with the help of a grant from the Canadian Federation for the Humanities, using funds provided by the Social Sciences and Humanities Research Council of Canada.

A MIND FOR EVER VOYAGING

1 Elevating the Mind to God

WHEN IN AUGUST OF 1829 WORDSWORTH VISITED HIS friend William Rowan Hamilton, who was a leading mathematician and astronomer, the poet found himself gently taken to task for certain uncomplimentary things he had said about science and scientists in *The Excursion*. The particular passage in question (lines 941-78 of Book IV)[1] had begun by comparing modern scientists with more spiritually enlightened pagans of old:

"Now, shall our great Discoverers," he exclaimed,
Raising his voice triumphantly, "obtain
From sense and reason less than these obtained,
Though far misled? Shall men for whom our age
Unbaffled powers of vision hath prepared, [945]
To explore the world without and world within,
Be joyless as the blind? Ambitious spirits—
Whom earth, at this late season, hath produced
To regulate the moving spheres, and weigh
The planets in the hollow of their hand; [950]
And they who rather dive than soar, whose pains
Have solved the elements, or analysed
The thinking principle—shall they in fact

> Prove a degraded Race? and what avails
> Renown, if their presumption make them such? [955]
> Oh! there is laughter at their work in heaven!

The passage proceeded to offer examples of the diving and joylessness:

> Enquire of ancient Wisdom; go, demand
> Of mighty Nature, if 'twas ever meant
> That we should pry far off yet be unraised;
> That we should pore, and dwindle as we pore, [960]
> Viewing all objects unremittingly
> In disconnexion dead and spiritless;
> And still dividing, and dividing still,
> Break down all grandeur, still unsatisfied
> With the perverse attempt, while littleness [965]
> May yet become more little; waging thus
> An impious warfare with the very life
> Of our own souls!

The enormity of what the scientists were doing was then made clearer still:

> And if indeed there be
> An all-pervading Spirit, upon whom
> Our dark foundations rest, could he design [970]
> That this magnificent effect of power,
> The earth we tread, the sky that we behold
> By day, and all the pomp which night reveals;
> That these—and that superior mystery
> Our vital frame, so fearfully devised, [975]
> And the dread soul within it—should exist
> Only to be examined, pondered, searched,
> Probed, vexed, and criticised?"

Wordsworth defended himself to his scientific friend by making a distinction between two kinds of science and scientists. The one kind that was concerned with "a bare collection of facts for their own sake, or to be applied merely to the material uses of life" was the kind that he had attacked in *The Excursion.* The other kind, however, which has as its purpose "elevating the mind to God," he "venerated." Then why had he not spoken of this other kind in *The Excursion?* "What would have been the use of my praising such men as Newton? They do not need my insignificant praise, and therefore I did not allude to such sons of Science." He must have keenly felt the irony of his situation, for he had actually written three passages of poetry praising Newton and Newton's kind of science, but had published none.[2] One, admittedly, had been a schoolboy exercise, but another was a passage he had cancelled from his manuscript of *An Evening Walk*, and the third was a passage of five lines on Newton's statue which he had written in what was to become *The Prelude* but which was not to be published till much later.

Approximately ten years after this discussion with Hamilton, and quite possibly in part motivated by his memory of it, Wordsworth added two final lines to the description of Newton's statue and so completed his tribute to the kind of Science and Scientist that elevates the mind to God. The passage in his manuscript reads thus, with the opening line referring to the clock in Trinity College, Cambridge:

> Her pealing organ was my neighbour too,
> And from my pillow looking forth by light
> Of moon or favoring stars, I could behold
> The Antichapel where the Statue stood
> Of Newton with his prism, & silent face,
> The marble index of a Mind for ever
> Voyaging thro' strange seas of Thought, alone.[3]

The two lines added at the end have been hailed as a most remarkable achievement. Part of the reason is the age at which Wordsworth wrote them. He had for some years been convinced that he was no longer able "to turn to account in verse" images which his mind had received, no matter how rich they might have been.[4] And yet it is to these lines that Ernest de Selincourt was able to point as evidence of the fact that "Wordsworth's poetic inspiration was not so short-lived as is sometimes supposed."[5] But the achievement goes beyond its connexion with the age at which Wordsworth wrote the lines. The three editors of the recent Norton Critical Edition of *The Prelude* acclaim the two final lines as "majestic" in their own right.[6] Mary Moorman describes them as "the most famous 'allusion' ever made to any man of science," and she says further that they supply "in marvellous perfection" whatever may have been lacking in the lines before, by way of tribute to Newton.[7] And Sir Paul Harvey, acclaiming the lines as "glorious," suggests that it may well be because of them that the statue in Trinity College is Newton's best-known memorial, even though he was buried in Westminster Abbey, and there honoured with another statue.[8]

All the passages that Wordsworth wrote on Newton and Newton's kind of science will be a major concern in this study, and especially, of course, the culminating triumph. And we shall be particularly interested in seeing what indication there is in them of how Newton's kind of science "elevates the mind to God." There is certainly a range of meaning possible in Wordsworth's key phrase. At the very least it means something more than Pope's "look[ing] thro' Nature, up to Nature's God," for with Pope the observer remains below, looking up through a phenomenon that is superior to him, up to the Creator of both the phenomenon and its observer.[9] Wordsworth may have implied "elevates the mind to thoughts of God," as Eliza Hamilton believed he did, since she paraphrased him as saying "raised the mind to the contemplation of God in [His] works."[10] Even so, of course, the phrase indicates that the mind has been elevated from its usual position to some kind of vantage point, from which it can contemplate God in his creation: where, then, is that vantage point? There may, at the same time, be something far grander involved than mere contemplating. In the passage of poetry included in the Preface to *The Excursion*, Wordsworth speaks of "the discerning intellect of Man," which, "When wedded to this goodly universe / In love and holy passion"— and presumably also scientific study (in view of the word "intellect")—can produce a "creation (by no lower name / Can it be called)" which, presumably, parallels the original divine creation.[11] In *The Prelude*, likewise, Wordsworth speaks of "a majestic Intellect"

> That feeds upon infinity, that broods
> Over the dark abyss,

and that, in company with other "higher minds"

> from their native selves, can send abroad
> Kindred mutations; for themselves create
> A like existence.[12]

This kind of mind is what Newton had, as his very first eulogist (the astronomer Halley, after whom the comet is named) pointed out, even when Newton was still alive:

> cui pectore puro
> Phoebus adest, totoque incessit Numine mentem:
> Nec fas est propius Mortali attingere Divos.[13]

(Because he was pure of heart, Phoebus [Apollo] came to [him] and infused into his mind all His Divine Power: closer to the Gods may no Mortal approach.)

Obviously involved in our study will be what Newton meant to the English people in general, to poets in particular and especially Romantic poets, and, most of all, to William Wordsworth. Also involved will be the major influence of William Rowan Hamilton, called the Newton of his day, in shaping Wordsworth's later attitude towards science and scientists, for certainly a marked change has been attested to. So great was Hamilton's influence, in fact, that, impelled by it, Wordsworth made changes to a number of passages in *The Prelude*.

The same *Excursion* passage which led to the exchange between the two also illustrates another major theme of our study, for it should not stand alone, isolated from the framework to which it alludes.

Avoiding Disconnexion

It is clear from verbal echoes in Wordsworth's passage that he was consciously writing within the context of a tradition of commentary on the right and wrong kinds of learning. James Thomson, in his *Castle of Indolence*, said approvingly of his hero that "he pryed through Nature's store" outside himself and also "searched the mind" within (cf. lines 946 and 959 in Wordsworth's passage). Pope, in various passages, complained of the wrong kind of learning. In *An Essay on Man*, for instance, he depicted "subtle schoolmen" who were "More studious to divide than to unite" (cf. line 963). In *The Dunciad* he depicts the same schoolmen (or scholiasts) as "poring" while located "dim in clouds," and he has Bentley, his principal representative of learning that degrades, say about his students:

> In ancient Sense if any needs will deal,
> Be sure I give them Fragments, not a Meal;
> What Gellius or Stobaeus hash'd before,
> Or chew'd by blind old Scholiasts o'er and o'er.
> The critic Eye, that microscope of Wit,
> Sees hairs and pores, examines bit by bit:
> How parts relate to parts, or they to whole,
> The body's harmony, the beaming soul,
> Are things which Kuster, Burman, Wasse shall see,
> When Man's whole frame is obvious to a *Flea*.

James Beattie, in three stanzas of his *Minstrel*, followed Pope's example and, besides anticipating Wordsworth in using such words as "dread," "little," and "impious," described "cold-hearted sceptics," who, instead of soaring on Fancy's wing, "creeping, pore / Through microscope of metaphysic lore" and never reach Truth because, "Their powers, inadequate before, / This idle art makes more and more unfit." (Cf. lines 951, 960, 965-66.)[14]

Almost by way of complement to the use of concepts, words, and phrases from his predecessors in the denigration of false learning, Wordsworth drew from a favourite source of his, Milton's poems, for phrases with which to pass judgement on the perverted activities he described. As often, the contexts from which he drew his phrases provide a further comment on the activities. The use of "degraded Race" to describe the persons responsible for misleading humanity (line 954) reminds one of the way in which Milton, in *Paradise Lost*, described "miserable Mankind, to what fall / Degraded, to what wretched state reserv'd!" Wordsworth's condemnation of the practice of "Viewing of objects unremittingly / In disconnexion dead and spiritless" (lines 961-62) recalls two passages in *Paradise Lost*, each concerned with disconnexion from God. Man, "dead in sins and lost," is matched with the rebel angels who have come as close to death as angels can, being "drain'd, / Exhausted, spiritless, afflicted, fall'n." These have reached this sad state by raising "impious War" against God. Wordsworth's perverted scientists have reached their sad state by

>   waging thus
> An impious warfare with the very life
> Of our own souls!
>   (lines 966-68)

That there is an even closer parallel than may at first appear is seen in the fact that Eliza Hamilton recorded Wordsworth as having elaborated on this phrase by saying that the kind of science he detested "waged war with...Imagination in the mind of man," and that faculty for Wordsworth was indeed God-like. In view of the quintessential powers of good and evil involved in the process Wordsworth has described, it is no wonder that his phrase "Our dark foundations rest" (line 970) should derive from both the "dark foundations deep" of the universe as a whole described in Milton's "Nativity Ode" and from the "dark foundations" of Hell, which, in *Paradise Lost*, had likewise been cast deep.[15]

There was another work, virtually a complement to Milton's poems, that Wordsworth would have been familiar with, since at one point he seriously considered entering the Anglican priesthood,[16] and that was, of course, *The Book of Common Prayer*. It would appear that his acquaintance with this book assisted him in producing the closely textured lines that appear near the end of his passage. He provides a threefold illustration of the "magnificent effect" of God's creating "power": the earth, the sky seen in daylight, and "all the pomp which night reveals" (lines 971-73). He then proceeds to "that superior mystery / Our vital frame" (lines 974-75) and thereby raises the question: what preceding "mystery" has he mentioned that would warrant his using the comparative epithet "superior"? The answer can be found in one of the verses of Psalm 88, which was included in *The Book of Common Prayer* for oral reading. Verse 12 reads, in part and referring to God: "Shall thy wondrous works be known in the dark...?" The parallel phrasing of "all the pomp which night reveals" serves as an implicit allusion to the Biblical verse, where, in turn, the phrase "wondrous works" justifies the use of the synonym "mystery" in a comparative way, with the "mystery" of the human body and soul being presented as superior to the "wondrous works" of the night sky alluded to by the "pomp." The pattern is then strengthened by the next allusion, somewhat more recognizable, that Wordsworth makes. "Our vital frame," he says, is "so fearfully devised," and promptly adds to it "the dread soul within it." Verse 13 of Psalm 139 (also included in *The Book of Common Prayer* for oral reading) reads, in part: "I am fearfully and wonderfully made:...that my soul knoweth right well." From this verse Wordsworth has selected certain words and has left simply alluded to the "wonderfully" which matches the "wondrous" of the other Psalm verse alluded to. Then, needing an iambic synonym for "made" in his own verse, it would seem, he was reminded of what appears in the same *Book of Common Prayer*, as the opening words of the section entitled "Concerning the Service of the Church," words that refer to the body's partner and provide the needed synonym: "There was never any thing by the wit of man so well devised." Although this way of proceeding from one of his own verses to the next—by alluding to scriptural verses—may appear rather involved and unusual, Wordsworth actually had a precedent in Sir Philip Sidney, who did much the same sort of thing in his famous sonnet "Leave Me, O Love, Which Reachest But to Dust."[17] As for the epithet "dread," since it clearly implies the Creator of the soul and has to do with something intimately associated with the body, it could well be that Blake's questions "What dread hand? & what dread feet?" prompted its inclusion.[18]

Wordsworth's *Excursion* passage ends by asking the question whether God intended that his Creation

>   should exist
> Only to be examined, pondered, searched,
> Probed, vexed, and criticised?
>
>   (lines 976-78)

The concluding list of six past participles has had a number of precedents in literature, such as this by Bishop Ussher, who said that God's word is compared to "a Rule, Line, Square, Measure, and Ballance, whereby must be framed, ordered, measured, and pondered."[19] When such lists appear in sophisticated authors, there is usually a principle of progression which accounts for the order in which the individual words are placed. With Wordsworth's list, likewise, if it is to be anything more than a piled-up heap of obloquy, it must have an order of progression within it. We can perceive such an order if we bear in mind, as Wordsworth could readily have done, certain lines by Pope, Hartley, and Wordsworth himself.

Could the creator intend, Wordsworth asks, that his magnificent creation—the universe outside and we ourselves—should be only "examined"—a word that denotes a close inquiry and clearly connotes a total lack of admiration? That it should be "pondered"—i.e., as with Ussher, weighed mentally, and here weighed without wonder? "Searched" means both "looked through" (as if nothing extraordinary would hold one's attention) and "probed as by a surgeon"—which leads to the word "probed" itself. This adds the practice of cutting, for it involves exploring with a probe or any sharp instrument. Any cutting involves "dividing" (made much of in line 963) and producing something smaller than before (the "littleness" producing something "more little" of lines 965-66). So far the order of progression has been clear enough: an increase in littleness, both of attitude and of product. How "vexed" and "criticised" continue that order certainly does not appear on the surface, and it is here that bearing in mind previous writings can provide an answer. "Vexed," on its own, means only "agitated," "fretted," "troubled," and "afflicted," but the way Pope used it tied it closely to cutting and reducing things to littleness. Speaking of Envy (which of course relates to the scholars examining both divine mysteries), Pope wrote: "Like a curs'd Cur, *Malice* before her clatters, / And vexing ev'ry Wight, tears Cloaths and all to Tatters." The meaning and association of "criticised" appropriate to its use here derive from another writer Wordsworth had read closely, and from his own writings. David Hartley had observed "we criticize much upon the Beauty of Faces, and upon the Proportion of the several Features to each other," and he had done so in a context which at least suggested that this practice of criticizing helped to destroy the beauty criticized and reduce it to ghastliness. Wordsworth's own view of criticism was to be seen later in two minor poems. In "The Farmer of Tilsbury Vale" Wordsworth refers to "the small critic wielding his delicate pen," clearly continuing the theme of littleness developed in the *Excursion* passage; and in an epigram on Byron's *Cain* he describes critics as presenting "a night-shade wreath," clearly implying the death-dealing effect they can have. But these later references serve mainly to remind us of three lines which he had written several years before *The Excursion* and which clearly relate to the effect of criticism:

> Our meddling intellect
> Mis-shapes the beauteous forms of things:—
> We murder to dissect.

"Criticised" is certainly the right word with which to end the series of increasingly degrading activities. Once the objects being examined without wonder have been weighed, pierced through, and cut to little pieces, they are left dead upon the dissecting table.[20]

The method we have been following is the exact opposite: by restoring lost connexions to broader contexts, we have tried to increase the effect and effectiveness, for present-day readers, of what Wordsworth wrote almost two hundred years ago. We have been able to do this because Wordsworth originally attached his passage to those broader contexts by borrowing from them and by alluding to them. This practice of his will be a major concern of our study. He was trained to use it in his grammar school, as seen in his first surviving poem, a schoolboy exercise on Science, which turns out to be a poem on Newton. As an apprentice poet, writing *An Evening Walk*, he enriched his method by interweaving, in what is virtually a hymn to Science, reworkings of poems by three or four other writers. At the height of his powers, in 1803, when he wrote his original five-line description of Newton's statue, he drew principally on the work of one predecessor, but since that predecessor had already drawn on many earlier writers, Wordsworth in effect drew on them, too. In fact, by the time Wordsworth came to write on Newton, there had been established a corpus of poetic tribute to him. The content had quickly become standardized, and the diction and imagery used to convey that content had, with equal speed, become stereotyped. Wordsworth knew what had "oft been thought" and said about Newton, and he set out, in presenting much the same kind of content and in using much the same kind of diction and imagery, to express what had oft been thought in a way that was superior to any that had been achieved before. In tracing Wordsworth's lines back to their sources and in examining how he used them to create something new with its own integrity, we shall, incidentally, be doing the sort of thing that Wordsworth himself recommended to Sir Walter Scott, when the latter undertook an edition of Dryden's works: the "pointing out passages or authors to which the Poet has been indebted, not in the piddling way of phrase here and phrase there (which [i.e., pointing out "piddling" borrowings] is detestable as a general practice) but where the Poet has really had essential obligations either as to matter or manner."[21] This process will reach its culmination when we examine the two lines which Wordsworth added, in what he considered his old age, to the original five describing Newton's statue and which in themselves constitute the culmination of Wordsworth's own practice. They also constitute the most condensed, succinct, and imagistic expression of the way in which Newton the scientist elevated the human mind to God.

Synthetic Originality

This practice of Wordsworth's, which extended to many of his poems outside those referring to science and scientists, illustrates a concept of the poet which parallels the concept of the man of science who elevates the mind to God.

Sidney had alluded to such a concept when he said that the Greeks called a creative writer "'Poet,' which name has, as the most excellent, gone through other languages. It comes of this word *poiein*, which is 'to make,' wherein (I know not whether by luck or wisdom) we Englishmen have met with the Greeks in calling him a maker."[22] As a maker, or shaper, or creator, the poet does not create *ex nihilo* (out of nothing), but rather he creates, in parallel with the Stoic and Miltonic concept of the divine creation, *de deo* (by the power of God), shaping already existing material to the form the creator desires. As such he is like the Anglo-Saxon *scop* and Eskimo sculptor, who have likewise shaped existing materials into forms they desired. In fact, with the poet, since the material he often uses is poetry which has already been shaped in one form, he may be called a *reshaper*, doing what Coleridge said the secondary Imagination does: "It dissolves, diffuses, dissipates, in order to re-create."[23]

Such a practice, when applied to pre-existing poetry, raises the question of originality: could Wordsworth really have been original? We believe he was, but not in the way many Romantic theorists have believed. His originality lies in re-creating, re-fusing, and re-shaping. The phenomenon is not confined to Wordsworth, by any means. It was noted and commented on, almost casually, in the early poetry of Tennyson, and was commented on, not by a literary critic, but by a friend of William Rowan Hamilton, John T. Graves, who was a mathematician and a lawyer. In writing to Hamilton about poets he had been reading for pleasure, Graves remarked that Tennyson had derived one of his lines from a line in Wordsworth's "Laodamia." He elaborated:

> Tennyson is a most learned poet. I trace him foraging in many modern works as well as in the older Italian poets and the ancient classics. Like Virgil, he seems to like to borrow his own thoughts from others. I suppose the thoughts to be latent in him, and to be welcomed as his

own when he finds them elsewhere. But his is a kind of sympathetic originality.[24]

Like Tennyson, Wordsworth would independently (and in that sense originally) form in his mind an idea of what he wished to say—as with the thought behind "Our vital frame, so fearfully devised" and the use to which it is wrongly put by perverted scholars. He would then go searching through his memory for what other writers had said about the idea he wished to comment on, until he found passages with what he called "identity of thought." These provided him with a place from which to proceed. He could add to them other passages from his memory and, adopting and adapting particular words and phrases, fashion the whole into a new unity with its own integrity. The resulting product could therefore be said to have a synthetic originality. And the product was not confined to his poetry on science: as we shall have the opportunity of seeing, Wordsworth applied the practice of reshaping existing material to several of his best known poems.

As indicated, Wordsworth's memory was of immense importance in that practice. As we shall see, it was most remarkable indeed—the envy of scholars, critics, and creative artists. He had been trained to memorize extensively in school, and he evidently continued to do so throughout his lifetime. As a result he was able, for instance, to quote six lines from Canto II of Thomson's *Castle of Indolence* while writing a letter when far removed from any copy of that work. He wrote to a friend, late in life, that he could still remember several thousand lines of Pope. He recited Beattie from memory, as he did Milton—and to the latter he acknowledged indebtedness in many of the notes he printed with his poetry. His memory also contained within itself an amazing ability to detect parallels between disparate passages which had entered his memory at widely different times—and parallels which even professional editors seeking to find such things had overlooked.[25]

The variety of sources from which he drew for reshaping was exceptionally great: not only major poets, but also minor, even obscure; not only former writers, but also his contemporaries, even very junior contemporaries; and not only verse, but also prose of all kinds. In fact the immense memory Wordsworth called on in the creation of his poetry reveals the peculiar kind of poetic sensibility he had, for his memory shows what sorts of things impressed his sensibility to begin with. Their range is surprising, extending from mighty and majestic aspects of nature and literature (as one would expect) to a dialect word like *rakes* (to describe what a cloud does) and to minutiae tucked away in the introduction to a charter given to a mediaeval abbey. Altogether the testimony provided by Wordsworth's memory about his poetic sensibility affords an eloquent illustration of what Henry James said in his essay "The Art of Fiction": "Experience is never limited, and it is never complete; it is an immense sensibility, a kind of huge spider-web of the finest silken threads suspended in the chamber of consciousness, and catching every air-borne particle in its tissue. It is the very atmosphere of the mind; and when the mind is imaginative—much more when it happens to be that of a man of genius—it takes to itself the faintest hints of life, it converts the very pulses of the air into revelations."[26] This reads almost as if James had read what Aubrey de Vere had said about Wordsworth in writing to his friend Henry Taylor: "It is one of the wonders of the world to hear him talk over his own poetry and give you its secret history. I verily believe that not an object he ever saw or sound he ever heard has been lost upon him."[27]

With Wordsworth the revelations which James speaks of were not confined to the poetry he wrote on science. Altogether, the picture of Wordsworth that will emerge from our study—of a poet with startling intellectual powers, who consciously and deliberately remembered and reworked poetry of his predecessors (and sometimes his contemporaries)—is, of course, directly opposite to what many writers on Wordsworth have affirmed. But even this will not be the most remarkable thing to emerge.

Our study will lead us along many paths, ranging widely through Wordsworth's experience, letters, and poetry, but all these paths will converge in the last chapter. There, in closely examining the final two lines describing Newton's statue, we shall do something that the authors of this book never thought that they, or anyone, would be able to do: we shall enter, cautiously, into Wordsworth's mind and there, by means of a model, witness the processes by which images presumably came together from a wide variety of sources and, being fused in the crucible of his creativity, emerged in a passage of tributary poetry which has been hailed as rivalling, and possibly surpassing, the statue of Newton which it describes. Up to the final chapter, those parts of our study which have been concerned with the final two lines will have acted like the prism held in the statue's hand: they will have separated the individual strands that came together to produce the pure white light of the encomium on Newton. The last chapter will act like a corresponding prism which collects those separated strands and re-fuses them into a single stream of pure white radiance.

These, then, are the closely interrelated themes of our study. They make up the complex which is encapsulated in our subtitle "Wordsworth at Work Portraying Newton and Science" and highlighted in our title *A Mind For Ever Voyaging*. For the Mind referred to is not only the mind of Newton, as it voyages into an elevated relationship with God, but it is also the mind of Wordsworth, as, God-like, it voyages through the vast ocean of pre-existing poetic material and there selects certain elements, recombines and reshapes them into a new unity and integrity reflecting his original design, and so creates worlds of shining splendour.

One of those worlds concerns Newton himself. Let us see why the English in general and Wordsworth, the Romantic poet, in particular, regarded him as worthy of being translated to the stars.

2 The Sage as Hero

THE WAYS IN WHICH SIR ISAAC NEWTON WAS ENshrined as one of the principal heroes of England, and the reasons for that enshrining, can be seen demonstrated in Louis François Roubiliac's statue of Newton in the Antechapel of Trinity College, the very statue which Wordsworth came to describe in later years.

Roubiliac's Statue

A professional connoisseur, Sir Francis Legatt Chantrey, who was a contemporary of Wordsworth's and who in fact made a celebrated bust of the poet, expressed this opinion of the statue: "The Sir Isaac Newton is the noblest, I think, of all our English statues. There is an air of nature, and a loftiness of thought about it, which no other artist has in this country, I suspect, reached. You cannot imagine any thing grander in sentiment, and the execution is every way worthy of it."[1] In particular, the positioning of the statue in Wordsworth's day was well calculated to assist in its striking quality. George Dyer, a friend of Wordsworth's, wrote in that part of his *History* of Cambridge concerned with Trinity College: "The ante-chapel being open and undivided, leaves the view undistracted, nor is it as yet overcrowded with monuments and figures. Hence the few objects are more striking, and as implying more selection, leave an impression of greater character. The statue of Newton strikes immediately every beholder with reverence...."[2]

Well it might, for it stands near the end wall, by itself. Placed on top of a pedestal about five feet high, the life-sized figure of Newton, clothed in academic dress, stands, for the most part, above the observer's eyes. Especially when the observer is close by, he has to look up to see the figure, and what he sees continues the direction of looking upwards. With his prism held in his right hand, Newton looks upwards and to the left, like Bernini's David. Where David looks at his gigantic target, Newton gazes up into the skies, the stars, the heavens, the hitherto unknown. In fact, since the pupils of his eyes have rolled upwards until they touch the upper lids, the impression grows that his mind is likewise searching upwards. This peculiar half-roll of the pupils can also be interpreted as a sign that Newton is lost in adoration of what he has perceived. Coleridge, in a poetic passage that is ostensibly about Newton himself but that presumably derives immediately from the statue instead, is quite explicit:

> hush'd
> Adoring NEWTON his serener eye
> Raises to heaven....[3]

William Selwyn, in describing the statue, is less explicit but beautifully blends the natural and supernatural in Newton's contemplation: "It is a monument to be gazed at in silence and stillness...the philosopher is alone with nature and with God."[4]

On the pedestal below the statue appears the simple inscription: "Newton, qui genus humanum ingenio superavit." One meaning of the Latin is "who in mind surpassed the human race." Because of the case ending of "ingenio," it could also mean "who surpassed the human race by his genius"—which suggests the *use* of Newton's intellect, not simply its nature. Because of a further ambiguity (this time in "superavit"), the Latin can also mean, most fittingly in view of its location on the base of the towering statue, "who because of his intellect rose above the human race."

This appropriate ambiguity in the word "superavit"—meaning both "surpassed" and "rose above"—coupled with its being placed beneath the statue which rises above the viewer's eyes, suggests that a donnish pun is somehow involved. Since donnish puns frequently involved quotations and allusions, one might suspect that the inscription was not newly composed for Newton, but was, rather, a quotation selected from a larger passage originally written for someone else. In making the selection, the selector at the same time would, of course, have invited his reader to bring that larger passage to mind and, in doing so, to compare Newton with whoever was originally praised as being the one and only person who, in relation to all the rest of the human race, *superavit.*

The Risen Sun

That larger passage is, in fact, in Lucretius' poem *De Rerum Natura* (On the Nature of Things), specifically that part of Book III in which the poet reminds his reader of the necessity of dying. Even the best of wise men, poets, and philosophers have died, even, specifically, that philosopher whom Lucretius venerated above all others, Epicurus,

> ipse Epicurus obit decurso lumine vitae,
> qui genus humanum ingenio superavit et omnis
> restincxit, stellas exortus ut aetherius sol.[5]

Russel M. Geer has provided a particularly literal yet clear translation:

> Even Epicurus himself died, when the light of life had run its course, he who surpassed the human race by his genius and dimmed the light of all men as the heavenly sun when it has risen dims the stars.[6]

If, for the moment, one ignores the names of Lucretius and Epicurus, one can regard the context from which the inscription was selected as being as happily appropriate to Newton as the inscription itself. The double reference to light reminds one of his discoveries in optics (memorialized in the prism held in the statue's hand), and the comparison with the sun and the other stars reminds one of his discovery of the gravitational forces at work on all the heavenly bodies.

The context of the line inscribed was, however, written by Lucretius and applied to Epicurus, and these facts make the choice of inscription from this passage particularly odd. Newton himself, a scholar reminds us, attacked, in his religious writings, as enemies of God, "contemporary Deists and atheists, like Hobbes, and their ancient counterparts the theological Epicureans, for whom all was chance" and for whom, it should be added, Lucretius was the principal poetic exponent.[7] When Richard Bentley in 1692 presented the first of the Boyle Lectures, which he entitled *A Confutation of Atheism*, he sought to dispose of "the theory of Lucretius (from whom Hobbes derived) that the cosmic system began with chance bumpings together of descending atoms, each endowed with an innate power of gravity."[8] And yet the person who chose the inscription for Newton's statue selected a line from a poet whom Newton himself, and those of his party, regarded as an archenemy.

That, it turns out, was precisely the reason for choosing the inscription. Newton, who had made celestial discoveries far beyond what Epicurus and Lucretius had thought of, had, in the General Scholium to his *Principia*, professed his belief in a living God.[9] Bentley refuted the Lucretian theory mentioned above by calling on the *Principia*, as the work of "that very excellent and divine Theorist Mr. Isaac Newton."[10] Consequently, by selecting the praise which Lucretius had applied to Epicurus, and applying it to Newton instead, the person responsible for choosing the inscription (presumably Robert Smith, who "placed" the statue in the antechapel)[11] was exercising ecclesiastical one-upmanship. He was reminding the world that, although Lucretius had said that Epicurus, the atheist, was the one who surpassed the human race in intellect, it was actually Newton, the devout believer, who *really* surpassed the human race, including Epicurus, in intellect and so rose above them all, towering over their heads.

The Conquering Hero

England had special reasons to embrace Newton gladly and to enshrine him as a national hero, towering above all observers.

Since the days of Queen Elizabeth there had been very few people who could be recognized as making England pre-eminent in Europe. Oliver Cromwell, through his "pacifying" of Ireland and Scotland and through his military and diplomatic triumphs on the Continent, had made England respected as she had not been for a long time and would not be again for another long time. Both Andrew Marvell and John Dryden had paid him poetic tributes for his prowess,[12] but, for many (perhaps most) Englishmen, Cromwell's having killed his king had tarnished his image as a hero—his eikon was more than a little cracked.

So great was the dearth of real-life heroes, in fact, that the people of the Restoration Court turned, it has been suggested, to the make-believe of heroic tragedy in order to have *somewhere* a figure that could be regarded as heroic.[13] So in place of living Drakes and Raleighs they had "the God-like Heroes" on the stage, the Almanzors and Aureng-Zebes. Fortunately before too long the Duke of Marlborough, beginning with the Battle of Blenheim, provided England with an unparallelled series of military victories which made her, for a while, pre-eminent in Europe. In response, with unprecedented generosity, the government and people of England presented to their national hero the ducal (indeed regal) house of Blenheim Palace and scores of adulatory poems, from Joseph Addison's *Campaign* downwards.[14] Later there were similar outpourings of poetical praise (accompanied with pictorial adulation) as England enshrined still more martial heroes: Wolfe, Nelson, and Wellington.

Along the way, however, there developed a public discussion (in fact, often a controversy) over the question "What makes for the true hero?" Was he "a great man"—a military conqueror or a statesman-politician who won many elections? Or was Alexander the Great more suitably regarded as a monstrous cut-throat and Sir Robert Walpole as a monstrous criminal—as Fielding suggested for both?[15] Was the true hero, instead, more the "good man," who, like Pope's Man of Ross, lived quietly and did good to his neighbours because he was blessed with the wisdom of benign philosophy and Christian charity? Was the sage a better candidate for hero than the general? Interestingly, Wordsworth himself, as a schoolboy, put the answer rather well in a verse exercise he wrote at Hawkshead Grammar School:

> Britain, who long her warriors had adored,
> And deem'd all merit centred in the sword;
> Britain, who thought to stain the field was fame,
> Now honour'd Edward's less than Bacon's name.[16]

And what about Shakespeare or Milton? What about the artist as the sage who creates and builds up instead of the military conqueror who kills and tears down?

To certain Englishmen Sir Christopher Wren was this kind of sage and artist who should accordingly be regarded as a hero. For John Evelyn, Wren

> needs no *Panegyrick,* or other *History* to eternize [his Virtues and Accomplishments], than the *greatest City of the Universe,* which he hath *rebuilt* and *beautified,* and is still *improving*; witness the *Churches,* the *royal Courts, stately Halls, Magazines, Palaces,* and other *publick Structures*;... All of them so many Trophies of his Skill and Industry, and conducted with that Success, that if the whole *Art of Building* were lost, it might be recovered, and found again in *St. Paul's,* the *historical Pillar,* and those other *Monuments* of his happy *Talent,* and extraordinary *Genius*.[17]

The "continued Aim of his whole Life" was, according to his son, "to be (in his own Words) *beneficus humano generi*; for his great Humanity appeared to the last, in Benevolence and Complacency, free from all Moroseness in Behaviour or Aspect." His temperament was admirable: "he was happily endued with such Evenness of Temper, a steady Tranquility of Mind, and christian Fortitude, that no injurious Incidents, or Inquietudes of human Life, could ever ruffle or discompose; and was in Practice a *Stoick*. Such was *Seneca's* good Man...." After having spent more than fifty years "in a continued active and laborious Service to the *Crown* and *Publick*" (during part of which his merits went unappreciated), Wren "betook himself to a Country Retirement...

> in which Recess, free from worldly Affairs, he passed the greatest Part of the *five* last following Years of his Life in Contemplation and Studies, and principally in the Consolation of the *holy Scriptures*; chearful in Solitude, and as well pleased to die in the Shade as in the Light.

> "Heroick Souls a nobler Lustre find
> "Even from those Griefs which break a vulgar Mind;
> "That Frost which cracks the brittle common Glass,
> "Makes Crystal into stronger Brightness pass."[18]

Since Sir Christopher Wren was accorded such adulation, it should not then be surprising that his contemporary and friend, Sir Isaac Newton, was accorded even more. In the cathedral church of St. Paul's, Wren had begun "and compleated...the second greatest Structure in *Europe*."[19] Newton had made achievements no one else in Europe (or any other part of the world) had ever attained: he had discovered the properties of light, he had determined the causes of the tides, and he had revealed the most fundamental law in the entire universe—the function of gravity. In and through him England was pre-eminent throughout the world in the realm of natural philosophy. Nor did his personal achievements end here: his temperament and private virtues were such that he too, like his friend Wren, was the good man, a devout Christian and model citizen. In his scientific discoveries he triumphed over the French, as Marlborough had done in military matters. Francis Fawkes, translating from the Latin of his friend Richard Oakley, wrote:

> Descartes thus, great Nature's wandering guide,
> Fallacious led philosophy aside,
> 'Till Newton rose, in orient beauty bright,
> He rose, and brought the world's dark laws to light,
> Then subtile matter saw, and vanished at his sight.[20]

In his philosophical discoveries, Newton achieved an even greater triumph, for, as indicated in the lines just quoted and as implied in the inscription incised below his statue, he triumphed over the philosophy of mechanistic materialism. Newton's successor at Cambridge, William Whiston, put the matter forcefully when he wrote, basing his remarks squarely on Newton's writings:

> That there is a God, i.e. an Immaterial or Spiritual, Almighty, Omnipresent and Omniscient Being; who, as at first he made the World, so does now continually govern and act in it, is so certain and so next to Mathematick Demonstration, from the Wonderful Discoveries made in Sir Isaac Newton's Works, that he must be a strange Person indeed who is sufficiently acquainted with those Discoveries and is yet unsatisfied in this matter....The

> Universe... is continually supported by nothing else than one Uniform Law of Gravity; or one continued Exercise of a Divine and Immaterial Power, acting by first and constant Rules.... If the Almighty should supersede or suspend this his constant Providential Power for one single Hour, all the World would be dissolved and dissipated....[21]

No wonder James Thomson wrote, about Newton:

> how mild, how calm,
> How greatly humble, how divinely good,
> How firmly stablished on eternal truth....
>
> What wonder thence that his devotion swelled
> Responsive to his knowledge? For could he
> Whose piercing mental eye diffusive saw
> The finished university of things
> In all its order, magnitude, and parts
> Forbear incessant to adore that Power
> Who fills, sustains, and actuates the whole?[22]

Apotheosis

No wonder that poets addressed him in the language used for the heroes of heroic tragedy. "The godlike man now mounts the sky," wrote Allan Ramsay, and Henry Jones praised "godlike NEWTON's all capacious Mind, / (The Glory and the Guide of human Kind)."[23] Richard Owen Cambridge described the effort of a gentleman to "give the demigod a shrine," and Francis Fawkes, this time translating the Latin of Edmund Halley which we quoted earlier, wrote, somewhat more felicitously:

> Newton, by every favouring Muse inspir'd,
> With all Apollo's radiations fir'd:
> Newton, that reach'd th' insuperable line,
> The nice barrier 'twixt human and divine.[24]

No wonder either, especially in view of this kind of language, that Fontenelle, as Wren's son was careful to point out, observed that Sir Isaac "had the extraordinary Fortune *to see his own Apotheosis.*"[25]

More meaningful than his being addressed as "God-like" was the celebration of his various discoveries. His invention of fluxions, an early form of calculus, was lauded by Elizabeth Tollet (who, with her father, was a friend of Newton's) as she wrote "Thy soul th' abyss of numbers could explore; / Though they, like Hydra, multiply their store...."[26] His discovery of how sound is propagated Richard Glover referred to by saying, "he taught the muse, how sound progressive floats / Upon the waving particles of air."[27] His discoveries concerning light—its speed, its source, and its colourful composition—John Hughes in 1720 celebrated by asking Newton to let him, as his companion,

> descry Light's fountain-head,
> And measure its descending speed;
> Or learn how sun-born colours rise
> In rays distinct, and in the skies
> Blended in yellow radiance flow,
> Or stain the fleecy cloud, or streak the wat'ry bow;
> Or, now diffus'd, their beauteous tinctures shed
> On ev'ry planet's rising hills, and ev'ry verdant mead.[28]

The same John Hughes referred to Newton's solving of the tides in one concise couplet, reflecting the physical ebb and flow, the pulling and being pulled:

> Here the pale moon, whom the same laws ordain
> T'obey the earth and rule the main.

His solving of the comets' courses received more wondering praise from Thomson: "He, first of men, with awful wing pursued / The comet through the long elliptic curve."[29] The underlying power of gravity (which controls the tides, the comets, and all physical bodies), along with Newton's crowning discovery of its function, many poets celebrated, perhaps none better than David Mallet, when he said (in 1728),

> This spring of motion, this hid power infus'd
> Through universal nature, first was known
> To thee, great Newton! Britain's justest pride,
> The boast of human race; whose towering thought,

> In her amazing progress unconfin'd,
> From truth to truth ascending, gain'd the height
> Of science, whither mankind from afar
> Gaze up astonish'd.[30]

It seemed, as John Theophilus Desaguliers observed, that "Nature, compell'd, his piercing Mind obeys, / And gladly shows him all her secret Ways."[31] And yet, in all his discoveries, Newton's sole aim and purpose was (like Wren's) to help mankind. As John Hughes put it, "Newton's soul...daily travels here [i.e., in the skies] / In search of knowledge for mankind below."[32]

Since the writers whose poems and poetical passages made up the corpus of praise to Newton all dealt, more or less, with the same kind of content, it is not surprising that they often made use of the same motifs and imagery. As Marjorie Hope Nicolson implies, when "the 'cosmic voyage' of the seventeenth century settled into the 'excursion' of the eighteenth century,"[33] it was only natural to depict Newton, in either his own material person, his soul, or his mind, as travelling through the heavens. John Hughes did so, as already noted, and Elizabeth Tollet described him, as "through the heavens [his] spirit flew, / To trace their motions [the planets'] with a nearer view."[34] James Thomson wrote that "he took his ardent flight / Through the blue infinite," and David Mallet said that, freed from mortality, "he wings his way / Through wondrous scenes."[35] Flight has been the metaphor in these examples; sailing on an endless sea is a natural alternative. Mallet described "this limpid sky" as "Vast ocean without storm, where these huge globes / Sail undisturb'd, a rounding voyage each."[36] Ramsay mingled the intellectual with the physical when he wrote that Newton's "penetration"

> Launch'd far in that extended sea,
> Where human minds can reach no bound,
> And never div'd so deep as he.[37]

And Mallet, again, in the concluding lines of his poem, implied much the same mingling as he described

> th' immensity of space;
> That infinite diffusion, where the mind

>   Conceives no limits; undistinguish'd void,
>   Invariable, where no land-marks are,
>   No paths to guide imagination's flight.[38]

(Together, these last three passages constitute a remarkable prefiguring of Wordsworth's image, but more of that later.)

Since, in order to make his intellectual voyage through the heavens, Newton had used both his mind and his eye, his enshrining poets often praised those parts, those faculties, and called them "piercing" and "penetrating." Moses Browne hailed Newton as "vast mind! whose piercing pow'rs apply'd / The secret cause of motion first descry'd."[39] Earlier, Thomson had referred to his "piercing mental eye," and Ramsay, as noted, to his "penetration."[40] Desaguliers asserted that "Nature, compell'd, his piercing Mind obeys," and Glover increased the praise by saying that Newton's "unbounded thought... even seeks th' unseen recesses dark / To penetrate of Providence immense."[41] As a result of this mental penetration, Newton stood preeminent, alone, towering above all others. Desaguliers hailed his "Tow'ring Genius," Mallet praised his "towering thought" that "gain'd the height / Of science, whither mankind from afar / Gaze up astonish'd," and Thomson said that he "The noiseless tide of time...stemmed alone."[42] Even without the statue placed on high, Newton towered above his observers.

Even the allusion to the sun image made by the inscription incised below that statue had been anticipated. Elizabeth Tollet had written, "Bacon and Boyle thy triumphs but fore-run, / As Phosphor rises to precede the Sun," and Richard Glover had elaborated more, saying that the ancient philosophers "like meteors"

>   In their dark age bright sons of wisdom shone:
>   But at thy Newton all their laurels fade,
>   They shrink from all the honours of their names.
>   So glimm'ring stars contract their feeble rays,
>   When the swift lustre of Aurora's face
>   Flows o'er the skies, and wraps the heav'ns in light.[43]

Robert Smith was not the only one who had read Lucretius and remembered.[44] The particular reason for this praise lay, of course, in what Newton's penetrating eye beheld, which has already been hinted at in Glover's reference to the "unseen recesses...of Providence immense." Jane Brereton was more explicit. First she described plainly, as she said that Newton

> Sublimely on the Wings of Knowledge, soars;
> Th' establish'd Order of each Orb unfolds,
> And th' omnipresent God, in all, beholds....

Then she borrowed an image from landscape gardening with its penchant for views that terminated in a small building (often like a temple) or a statue:

> If to the dark Abyss, a bright Abode
> He points; the View still terminates in God.[45]

Mark Akenside was less confining in his imagery. Though he is describing what his own soul beholds, it is no doubt similar (in view of the imagery used) to what Newton beheld: "the unfathomable gulf / Where God alone hath being."[46] Mallet likewise describes what the soul (this time, Newton's) can behold, but again the imagery suggests that what it beholds is what Newton on earth came close to beholding while still in mortal flesh: "For God himself shines forth immediate there."[47] These images already suggest a great deal about what is meant by Wordsworth's "strange seas" and "silent face," and we have not yet mentioned a few other tribute-writers who preceded Wordsworth.

Unweaving the Rainbow

But no doubt some questions have been building, which must be answered first. These tributes to Newton have been of the eighteenth century, many of them penned close to his death: was there not a change in the view of Newton that took place between the time of these tributes and the time when Wordsworth wrote? Was the situation not that as described by the modern philosopher E. A. Burtt, when he said that

> now the great Newton's authority was squarely behind that view of the cosmos which saw in man a puny, irrelevant spectator (so far as a being wholly imprisoned in a dark

room can be called such) of the vast mathematical system whose regular motions according to mechanical principles constituted the world of nature.... The world that people had thought themselves living in—a world rich with color and sound, redolent with fragrance, filled with gladness, love and beauty, speaking everywhere of purposive harmony and creative ideals—was crowded now into minute corners in the brains of scattered organic beings. The really important world outside was a world, hard, cold, colorless, silent and dead; a world of quantity, a world of mathematically computable motions in mechanical regularity. The world of qualities as immediately perceived by man became just a curious and quite minor effect of that infinite machine, beyond.[48]

Did not William Blake see Newton as rationalistic and deistic, a prime enemy of poets, one who, in reducing the universe to a material mechanism, warranted being linked with Bacon and Locke in an unholy trinity?[49] Did not Shelley in his notes to *Queen Mab* remark that "the consistent Newtonian is necessarily an atheist"?[50] To move closer to Wordsworth, did not his friend Coleridge shift in his view of Newton from commending him, for having given comfort to the pious, to condemning him as a Lockean, a mechanistic philosopher, and a contributor to atheism?[51] And as for Wordsworth himself, was he not a party to the "immortal dinner" held in Benjamin Haydon's painting-room on 28 December 1817, and did not the conversation at that dinner make it inescapably clear that English poets regarded Newton as their enemy?

Let us recall the circumstances, as Haydon himself recorded them.[52] The host had gathered together Wordsworth, Lamb, Keats, and Monkhouse and had set them down to feast in front of the colossal canvas of his which was still in the process of being finished, *Christ's Triumphant Entry into Jerusalem*. Into that painting he had inserted portraits (clothed in the dress of their own day) of Newton, Voltaire, and Wordsworth. As Lamb "got delightfully merry," he chided Wordsworth for calling Voltaire dull. Lamb then, Haydon records,

> in a strain of humour beyond description, abused me for putting Newton's head into my picture—"a fellow," said he, "who believed nothing unless it was as clear as the

three sides of a triangle." And then he and Keats agreed he had destroyed all the poetry of the rainbow, by reducing it to the prismatic colours. It was impossible to resist him, and we all drank "Newton's health, and confusion to mathematics." It was delightful to see the good-humour of Wordsworth in giving in to all our frolics without affectation, and laughing as heartily as the best of us.

Is this not sufficient evidence that English poets, at least English Romantic poets, were not inclined to pay tribute to Sir Isaac Newton, the man who "had destroyed all the poetry of the rainbow," who had, as Keats was to remark in his *Lamia* (2:237), unweaved the rainbow?

Yet, as Miss Nicolson has reminded us,[53] Shelley certainly admired Newton and used his "reductive" discovery about light (in reverse) for the crowning image in his *Adonais* (lines 462-64):

> Life, like a dome of many-coloured glass,
> Stains the white radiance of Eternity,
> Until Death tramples it to fragments.[54]

Certainly the view which Keats and Lamb held about the rainbow was not shared by the earlier, tribute-bearing poets. Glover had celebrated Newton's prismatic analysis as particularly magnificent:

> But, O bright angel of the lamp of day,
> How shall the muse display his greatest toil?
> Let her plunge deep in Aganippe's waves,
> Or in Castalia's ever-flowing stream,
> That reinspired she may sing to thee,
> How Newton dar'd advent'rous to unbraid
> The yellow tresses of thy shining hair.
> Or did'st thou gracious leave thy radiant sphere,
> And to his hand thy lucid splendours give,
> T' unweave the light-diffusing wreath, and part
> The blended glories of thy golden plumes?[55]

Thomson likewise celebrated what Newton had done with the rainbow:

> Even Light itself, which every thing displays,
> Shone undiscovered, till his brighter mind

> Untwisted all the shining robe of day;
> And, from the whitening undistinguished blaze,
> Collecting every ray into his kind,
> To the charmed eye educed the gorgeous train
> Of parent colours.
> . . . .
>   Did ever poet image aught so fair,
> Dreaming in whispering groves by the hoarse brook?
> Or prophet, to whose rapture heaven descends?
> Even now the setting sun and shifting clouds,
> Seen, Greenwich, from thy lovely heights, declare
> How just, how beauteous the refractive law.[56]

Mark Akenside, writing seventeen years later and not involved in presenting a tribute to Newton, still attested to the increase in poetic beauty which, for him, had accrued to the rainbow because of what Newton had discovered:

>   Nor ever yet
> The melting rainbow's vernal-tinctur'd hues
> To me have shone so pleasing, as when first
> The hand of Science pointed out the path
> In which the sun-beams gleaming from the west
> Fall on the watery cloud...
>   through the brede
> Of colours changing from the splendid rose
> To the pale violet's dejected hue.[57]

What then happened in between these eighteenth-century poets and the Romantic poets who held such a different view of Newton? Professor Lee M. Johnson has pointed to the practice, in the eighteenth century, whereby commentators separated the bulk of the *Principia* from the "General Scholium" and so ignored Newton's own statement of his philosophy.[58] F. E. L. Priestley has pointed to a series of events: Locke's interpreting of Newton (while greatly influenced by Hobbes), the seizing on his interpretation by French materialists, and the consequent emergence of a materialistic and mechanistic view of Newton's universe that was totally unlike Newton's but that was still presented as if it were Newton's.[59] This is how, presumably, such a view as that presented by E. A. Burtt in the twentieth century came to be possible: Newton was falsely read through the eyes of Locke and Hobbes and was misleadingly yoked with them.[60]

The situation was like that in Spenser's *Faerie Queene*, in which the false Una, "that ydle dreame" shaped by Archimago, passed herself off as the true Una, and fooled even the Redcrosse Knight.[61] Evidently all five of Blake, Shelley, Coleridge, Keats, and Lamb were, at one time or another and to whatever degree, taken in by the false Una. But it is equally evident that Wordsworth's scientific friend, William Rowan Hamilton, was not taken in; he had met and admired the real Una, the real philosophy of Sir Isaac Newton. Wordsworth himself, then, may also have come to know the real Newton, and "in giving in," at the immortal dinner with his friends, "to all [their] frolics without affectation, and laughing as heartily as the best of [them]" as, along with the rest, he "drank 'Newton's health, and confusion to mathematics'," he may simply have been humouring the tipsy Lamb and have been unwilling to interrupt their merriment.

What, then, was Wordsworth's own, individual attitude towards Sir Isaac Newton?

Ethereal Self

Even by the time he left Hawkshead School, Mary Moorman says, "Wordsworth had conceived a veneration for the name of Newton which amounted to worship." Such a claim may well be only a little exaggerated, for Wordsworth's headmaster, William Taylor, had been second Wrangler at Cambridge, at a time when "only proficiency in Newtonian science could secure high honours for a B.A. degree candidate." In addition, one day while he was still at Hawkshead school, Wordsworth was discovered, on his own initiative and to his master's amazement, "poring over Newton's *Opticks*."[62]

Yet it is surprising that Wordsworth, a prolific letter-writer on a great variety of topics and almost a non-stop talker during his waking hours,[63] has left on record very few explicit references to Newton. Only once in his surviving letters does he mention him, and that is to use his name, admittedly as an exemplar of surpassing genius (as we would that of Einstein), in what is little more than a political squib.[64] In the Preface to *Lyrical Ballads* Wordsworth uses Newton's name in much the same way, as the paradigm of genius.[65] In his poetry he mentions Newton only three times by name. In one passage in *The*

Prelude (7:162-67), Newton is one of several people the pictures of whose heads are used on signs for public houses. In another (3:269-70) Wordsworth refers to "Newton's own etherial Self" as representative of "spiritual men."[66] The third is the passage on Newton's statue. Fortunately what Wordsworth is recorded as having said in conversation provides something of a corrective. To James Patrick Muirhead he remarked that Newton's discoveries were the grandest ever known.[67] And of course we have the account which Eliza Hamilton gave of the conversation between Wordsworth and her brother, from which it is clear that Wordsworth regarded Newton as one, probably the pre-eminent one (perhaps with Hamilton himself), of those "sons of Science" who pursued their endeavours so as to contemplate God in his works.[68]

These remarks which Wordsworth made in private conversation suggest a great deal about how we should read the phrase in *The Prelude* concerning "Newton's own etherial Self" (3:270). The context for the phrase is this: Wordsworth felt that the "spiritual men" who had preceded him to Cambridge (and of whom Newton's own ethereal self was the most eminent) seemed "humbled" in the precincts of the University. Their memories, like their persons (which in their portraits were clothed in unchanging academic dress—"the accustomed garb of daily life"), "Put on a lowly and a touching grace / Of more distinct humanity."[69] Thus a contrast is established between their more lowly humanity and that higher quality characterized as "ethereal" (or "etherial" as in Owen's reading text) and "spiritual." Consequently, guided by the *Oxford English Dictionary*, we might be tempted to read "ethereal" as meaning "of unearthly delicacy" and "spiritual" as "exhibiting a high degree of refinement of thought or feeling." But, in view of these "spiritual" predecessors' having been the intellectual giants of Cambridge, it is much more likely that "spiritual" here means "having higher moral qualities" and having a remarkable "intellect or higher faculties of the mind" as well as "having souls acted on by God." Similarly "ethereal" is more likely to have the older poetic meaning (as used by Milton, Dryden, and Pope) of "heavenly, celestial."

But there is an even more specific meaning to "ethereal" which is probably operative in this particular phrase concerning Newton. That meaning is related to the general one of "resembling the ether, the lightest and most subtle of elements." Newton was particularly concerned with the nature of ether and saw it as the material medium through which worked the various laws of the universe that he had discovered.[70] Of the many passages Newton wrote concerning ether, this one, in his Second Paper on Light & Colours, is probably the most revealing:

> Perhaps the whole frame of nature may be nothing but various contextures of some certain aethereal spirits, or vapours, condensed as it were by precipitation, much after the manner, that vapours are condensed into water, or exhalations into grosser substances, though not so easily condensible; and after condensation wrought into various forms; at first by the immediate hand of the Creator; and ever since by the power of nature; which, by virtue of the command, increase and multiply, became a complete imitator of the copies set her by the protoplast. Thus perhaps may all things be originated from aether.[71]

(Parenthetically, one might observe how completely this passage refutes Lamb's claim that Newton was "a fellow who believed nothing unless it was as clear as the three sides of a triangle.") The paper from which this passage is quoted was reprinted in Thomas Birch's *History of the Royal Society of London* (1757), and the passage itself was reprinted in "The Life of the honourable Robert Boyle," which appeared in the first volume of the second edition of *The Works of the Honourable Robert Boyle* (1772); so Wordsworth could easily have encountered it either at Hawkshead or at any place afterwards.[72]

Accordingly, when the poet came, in the lines on the "spiritual men" of Cambridge, to seek a single epithet which would best sum up the nature, achievement, and significance of Sir Isaac Newton, what more appropriate word could he have been prompted to use than the adjectival form of that noun which pointed to the substance through which worked all the fundamental laws which Newton had discovered and which Newton himself thought was the very essence of material creation at the hand of God? No other word could have better summed up the way in which Newton had penetrated to the heart of the mechanism by which the universe works and the way, likewise, in which he had "pursued" science "for the elevation of the mind to God."

Some illumination (and possibly confirmation) concerning the likelihood of Wordsworth's having intended the Newtonian meaning of "ethereal" in this particular passage can be provided by a review of how some of Wordsworth's predecessors in the group of tribute-bearers used the word. When Francis Fawkes wrote, "Learn hence the mind's etherial powers to trace, / Exalted high above the brutal race," and when Mallet in one passage wrote, "rais'd aloft, / Fir'd with ethereal ardour," they both probably had in mind the older meaning of "heavenly" or "celestial."[73] But Hughes clearly had the Newtonian meaning in mind when he wrote:

> Mount me sublime along the shining way,
> Where planets, in pure streams of ether driv'n,
> Swim thro' the blue expanse of heav'n.
> . . . .
> New solid globes their weight, self-balanc'd, bear
> Unpropp'd amidst the fluid air,
> And all around the central sun in circling eddies roll'd.[74]

And Mallet in two other passages clearly refers to the Newtonian ether. In one he describes how the sun is "A shoreless sea of fluctuating fire, / That deluges all ether with its tide."[75] In the other passage, he unmistakably has in mind precisely what Newton himself had said about the ether. The reader will remember that Newton had written, "Perhaps the whole frame of nature may be nothing but various contextures of some aethereal spirits...condensed...at first by the immediate hand of the Creator...." Mallet in turn describes Newton's soul, "a pure intelligence," as after release from mortality it enjoys

> clear vision from all darkness purg'd,
> For God himself shines forth immediate there,
> Through those eternal climes, the frame of things,
> In its ideal harmony, to him
> Stands all reveal'd.

The Excursion, Mallet's poem in which these passages appear, was reprinted in volume 9 of Anderson's *Works of the British Poets* which Wordsworth's brother John left with him in September of 1800.[76] The opportunity for influence certainly existed.

A Brooding Presence

So far the references which Wordsworth made to Newton have been explicit. There are also a number of implicit references to him in Wordsworth's poetry that may be even more revealing because they are only implicit. The first appears in that schoolboy exercise already quoted from, the earliest surviving poem from Wordsworth's hand, written when he was fourteen years old. In that poem, dating from 1784-85, he has the Power of Education describe the result when "immortal Science reigns":

> Fair to the view is sacred Truth display'd,
> In all the majesty of light array'd,
> To teach, on rapid wings, the curious soul
> To roam from heaven to heaven, from pole to pole,
> From thence to search the mystic cause of things,
> And follow Nature to her secret springs....
>
> (lines 70-76)[77]

In view of what we have already seen about the ways in which the earlier poetic tribute-bearers described Newton's achievements, is it not clear that when Wordsworth referred to "sacred Truth," "majesty of light," "heaven to heaven," "pole to pole" (not the earth's, but the universe's), "mystic cause," and especially the "secret springs" of Nature, he could count on his reader realizing that he was referring to Newton as the exemplar of "immortal Science"? In fact he has "immortal Science" reigning, while "throned in gold" on the "Elysian plains." Since it was not abstractions but the souls of human heroes who inhabited the Elysian plains, is this not further evidence that Wordsworth is actually talking about Newton and that he sees Newton as the embodiment of Science? It is probably worth noting that Mark Akenside, in the 1744 version of his poem *The Pleasures of the Imagination*, had likewise written of Science as a guide and had clearly implied, from the aspects of Science that he mentioned, that Science and Newton were virtually synonymous.[78] (Still further evidence that Wordsworth equated Newton with Science in this passage will appear in the next chapter.)

Some years later, presumably in 1794, when Wordsworth was revising *An Evening Walk*, he again, it is evident, had Newton in mind, as the exemplar par excellence of

> those to whom the harmonious doors
> Of Science have unbarred celestial stores,
> To whom a burning energy has given
> That other eye which darts thro' earth and heaven,
> Roams through all space and [ ] unconfined,
> Explores the illimitable tracts of mind,
> . . . .
> And proud beyond all limits to aspire
> Mounts through the fields of thought on wings of fire.
> But sure with tenfold pleasure they behold
> The powers of Nature in each various mould,
> If like the Sun their [ ] love surrounds
> The various world to life's remotest bounds....[79]

B. R. Schneider, Jr., in writing about the influence on Wordsworth of his Cambridge education, sees the *Prelude* passage on Newton as "an echo of these [lines] from *An Evening Walk*" and says that "it seems clear that Wordsworth, when he wrote 'celestial,' 'earth and heaven,' and 'roams through all space,' had Newtonian science in mind."[80] As further evidence of the "echo" relationship, one can of course also point to the "illimitable tracts of mind," the mounting "through the fields of thought," and the action extending "to life's remotest bounds." In view of the echo relationship, not only between these lines and those on Newton's statue, but also between these and many passages of the tribute-bearers, it is evident that Wordsworth admired Newton for what his far-ranging spirit had been able to perceive.

When, a few years later (in 1797 and 1798), Wordsworth came to write the first drafts of what was later to evolve into Book One of *The Excursion*, he ascribed to his pedlar certain activities which parallelled his own. One of these was meditating on a waterfall.

> I have heard him say
> That at this time he scann'd the laws of light
> With a strange pleasure of disquietude
> Amid the din of torrents, when they send
> From hollow clefts, up to the clearer air
> A cloud of mist which in the shining sun
> Varies its rainbow hues.
>
> (lines 229-35)[81]

If Wordsworth had simply described the "cloud of mist which in the shining sun / Varies its rainbow hues," he would probably have been drawing only on observed nature; but when he introduces his description with the phrase "the laws of light," it is evident that Newton and his spectral analysis have proved exceedingly influential. (Nor Newton alone, for here are echoed the response of Akenside to the scientific analysis of the rainbow and the feeling of Thomson when he exclaimed, "how beauteous the refractive law.")

In 1805 Wordsworth wrote, for the fifth book of *The Prelude*, the story of the Arab which, with modifications, he retained throughout later revisions. In that story he tells of a dream he had. While musing, beside the sea,

> On Poetry, and geometric truth,
> And their high privilege of lasting life,
> From all internal injury exempt,
>
> (5:65-67)[82]

he fell asleep and dreamed of being met on a desert by an Arabian equivalent of the Don Quixote he had been reading about before musing. In one hand the Arab bore a shell, and under his arm on the other side he carried a stone. The shell is revealed as the power of poetry (which prophesies of doom), and the stone (the Arab says) is "Euclid's Elements" (5:86-88): it

> held acquaintance with the stars,
> And wedded Soul to Soul in purest bond
> Of Reason, undisturbed by space or time....
>
> (5:104-06)[83]

The otherwise strange proceeding from a stone to geometry and from there to the stars is readily explained by the prism held in the hand of Newton's statue. It is itself stone, but shaped as a prism, which is a shape of geometry and which (when made of glass—itself a product of refined stone) refracts light received from the stars. As B. R. Schneider remarks, "...the phenomena of the heavens most stimulated Wordsworth's imagination, as his poetry testifies. Moreover, the relation of geometry to those phenomena was abundantly clear to any reader of Newton's *Principia*, for that book was no more than geometry set in motion, the motion of the sun, planets, and comets. The geometrically expressed laws of nature were another form of the 'brooding presence'."[84] As that "brooding presence" suggests, for Wordsworth the astronomical geometry did more even than explain the physical operations of the universe: it also "wedded soul to soul in purest bond / Of reason." And again Newton is the implicit exemplar, for it was he (he who is depicted holding the prism) who had, in that same eminently rational *Principia,* testified to the living God who, being omnipresent, joined soul to soul.[85]

That in all four of the Wordsworth passages Newton should remain nameless, though clearly alluded to, says a great deal. Newton evidently meant so much to Wordsworth, and to his countrymen in the poet's own day, that there was no need to mention him by name. He was himself a brooding presence whenever discoveries in science were mentioned, especially discoveries which further elevated the mind to a contemplation of God.

Newton's influence in other important passages of Wordsworth has already been detailed by scholars. In fact a number of them have suggested that Newton provided the framework for much of Wordsworth's description of the grander aspects of the universe. J. W. Beach has taken Newton's statement concerning the fixed stars—that it is divine law which prevents them from falling upon one another—and has shown how it is relevant to the line in "Ode to Duty" that proclaims grandly, "Thou dost preserve the stars from wrong."[86] He has also shown how Newton's description of God, in his omnipotence, omniscience, and omnipresence, may well have contributed to the lines, in "Tintern Abbey," describing the spirit Wordsworth felt as "something far more deeply interfused." B. R. Schneider, Jr., and Geoffrey Durrant have both demonstrated close parallels between this same passage in Wordsworth's poem and certain key passages appearing in the final paragraph of Newton's *Principia.*[87] And Professor Schneider suggests an even more pervasive influence: "Newton's Cambridge is probably in part responsible for the fact that Wordsworth's poetry is haunted by the sun, moon and stars. The sea also is ever present with these, perhaps because, by explaining the tides, Newton had linked the sea to the solar system." Other, parallel, influences, such as those of "Young's and Thomson's passionate but inaccurate interest in the stars and planets," also no doubt worked on Wordsworth, but "his residence in Newton's starhaunted Cambridge certainly did much to foster and more to refine his appreciation of astronomical phenomena."[88] Need it be added that it was in accounting for those phenomena that the philosophical Newton had elevated his mind, and the mind of those who followed his gaze, to God?

Kinship

With that philosopher it would appear that Wordsworth felt a certain kinship. Such a comment may well seem strange, in view of the humility with which Wordsworth asked, "What would have been the use of my praising such men as Newton? They do not need my insignificant praise...."[89] Such humility appears, however, to have been uncharacteristic. Closer to reflecting his view of himself was the claim he made to descent from King Alfred. William Rowan Hamilton, who had been a close friend and correspondent of Wordsworth's for many years, wrote to a woman who had published a book on Alfred, "It may not be known to you, that Mr. Wordsworth, the Poet,... claimed to be a lineal descendant of Alfred...."[90] A particular line in a pair of poems provides reciprocal confirmation for Hamilton's statement. The poems are addressed, in part, to the poet's granddaughter Jane, and in one of them Wordsworth says that Alfred was her "great Progenitor." Admittedly, if read only by themselves, these poems would allow for the descent to have come through the girl's mother, or Wordsworth's wife, or Wordsworth himself, but the two statements, taken together, serve to confirm each other.[91] Such a sublime sense of status appears to be behind the passage in Book Twelve of *The Prelude* in which Wordsworth refers to

> the elevation which had made me one
> With the great Family that still survives
> To illuminate the abyss of ages past,
> Sage, Warrior, Patriot, Hero....
>
> (12:61-64)[92]

Interestingly, the thought of illuminating the abyss of ages past had appeared before, in William Tasker's "Ode to the Spirit of Alfred," in the form "dispel the mists, which Time / Hath spread round Glory's lucid clime." More interestingly, Wordsworth's line "Sage, Warrior, Patriot, Hero" had a precedent in the line "'Mid heroes, sages, patriots, old" of the same Ode, in which the word "warrior" appeared a few lines later.[93] With Tasker, all four nouns were applied to Alfred;

Wordsworth, accordingly, may have had that ancestor in mind when he, in turn, listed the same nouns associated with the "great Family" in which he claimed membership. At the same time, however, from boyhood Wordsworth would have been keenly aware of the fact that no Englishman was more obviously a "Sage" (and indeed a "Hero") than Newton, and, again, Wordsworth claims to be of his company.

In fact that feeling of kinship must have been strengthened when Wordsworth realized that Newton had used an image closely similar to one that Wordsworth had used to illustrate the essence of his own existence. "Sir Isaac Newton," Joseph Spence remarked in his *Anecdotes*, "a little before he died, said: 'I don't know what I may seem to the world, but as to myself, I seem to have been only like a boy playing on the sea shore, and diverting myself in now and then finding a smoother pebble or a prettier shell than ordinary, whilst the great ocean of truth lay all undiscovered before me.'"[94] In view of Wordsworth's manifest and great admiration for Newton, it is unlikely that he would not have encountered this passage in Spence's *Anecdotes*. He could have come across it at almost any time, for the Anecdotes were well known and widely quoted in the eighteenth century, even though they had not yet been published. Even if he had not encountered it earlier, he would have been invited to do so by a thirty-five page article in the *Quarterly Review* of 1820 on the two versions of Spence's *Anecdotes* then published, and on another book much concerned with the poetry of Pope.[95] There are in fact extraordinary parallels between Newton's image and two of Wordsworth's pictures, the one of his Quixotic Arab holding (on the seashore) both a Euclidean stone and a poetic shell, and the other, in his Intimations Ode, of himself as a boy sporting upon the shore "of that immortal sea / Which brought us hither" (lines 164-67). These parallels emphasize even more the further parallel, as Wordsworth would have seen it, between the two sages and heroes of England.

Nor does the parallel stop here. What Newton said, in his *Principia*, about the omnipresence of God was echoed by his follower James Foster in a way which would have impressed the parallel on Wordsworth even more directly: "God," Foster said (paraphrasing Newton), supports "the frame and order of the material world, in every part, and instant, of its duration.... His eternal omnipresent spirit pervades both mind and matter everywhere—the operations of the human mind as well as the motions and operations of matter."[96] Similarly Roubiliac, in his statue of Newton, has shown that sage and hero responding to the might and omnipresence of his Maker's mind as if keenly aware of the way Foster expressed those qualities, and responding, moreover, in much the same way as Wordsworth describes himself, in "Tintern Abbey," as responding to an experience closely similar. In fact, Wordsworth's lines on himself can equally well articulate the stance and expression of Newton's statue:

> I have felt
> A presence that disturbs me with the joy
> Of elevated thoughts; a sense sublime
> Of something far more deeply interfused,
> Whose dwelling is the light of setting suns,
> And the round ocean and the living air,
> And the blue sky, and in the mind of man;
> A motion and a spirit, that impels
> All thinking things, all objects of all thought,
> And rolls through all things.
>
> (lines 93-102)[97]

3 What Oft Was Thought

THE ENSHRINING OF ENGLAND'S STAR-GAZING SAGE and meditating hero which the tribute-bearers of the eighteenth century had performed was marked, as we saw in the last chapter, by a frequent recurrence of certain motifs and imagery. The recurrence raises an important and pertinent question: did it result from coincidence or a conscious reworking, by later poets, of earlier poets' material?

Through Every Maze

The sea image used by many of the poets (e. g., Mallet and Ramsay) to describe the heavens and the realm of astronomical thought could readily have occurred to the individual poets independently. After all, the eighteenth century was an era of great nautical exploration, and this activity would readily offer the image of a ship sailing on the sea for that other kind of exploration which wandered the heavens—especially when Newton himself had offered the opinion that connecting all the heavenly bodies was the ether, which many took to be a form of fluid.

The piercing eye and penetrating mind which many of the poets attributed to Newton could also have been simply, with each of them, an extension of physical reality. Newton had indeed "seen" farther and more clearly than anyone else. In addition, his nephew, John Conduitt, had said that Newton, in his own physical person, "had a lively and piercing eye."[1] Since, however, Bishop Atterbury gave quite the opposite description ("In the whole of his face and make, there was nothing of that penetrating sagacity which appears in his compositions...."), we mention this description, not to suggest that it was accurate in itself, but to remind the reader that a piercing eye was a commonplace of facial description at the time. Its appearance in Pope's poetry indicates as much, for not only did the heroic Hector have piercing eyes *(Iliad* 13:1015), but also Ulysses' dog, Argus *(Odyssey* 17:384), and even the hen in "The Capon's Tale" (line 7).[2] The tribute-bearers need not have created the extension from the meaning of physical sharp-sightedness, for, as the *OED* reminds us, "piercing" had the denotation, from at least the end of the sixteenth century, of being able to "see into" a thing. We would add that there existed at least two particularly appropriate precedents. Ben Jonson had written of Inigo Jones that he had "Eyes, that can pierce into the mysteries / Of many colours."[3] And Pope, in *The Temple of Fame* (1714), had written, of "the mighty *Stagyrite,"* that, while he "Sate fix'd in Thought,"

> His piercing Eyes, erect, appear to view
> Superior Worlds, and look all Nature thro'.
>
> (lines 233-37)[4]

Although the commonplace use of "piercing eyes" may have been the source for each of the tribute-bearers who made use of it, the possibility begins to emerge that some of them may have been reworking literary material, such as Pope's, which lay outside the corpus of poetic praise for Newton.

This independent use of external literary material can already be seen in certain other elements of the praise. The heroic terms with which the God-like Newton was saluted by such poets as Ramsay, Cambridge, Jones, and Fawkes, presumably resulted, not so much from one poet's imitating another, as from all of them being moved to look to the same source—the heroic tragedy which flourished in the Restoration period but which continued to be performed on the stage throughout much of the eighteenth century.[5] Similarly, when Tollet, Glover, and Fawkes all made use of the eclipsing sun image, presumably they all had the same source in mind—Lucretius' lines on Epicurus. That all their minds should turn to the same source is really not surprising in view of the remarkable degree of homogeneity in the classical authors studied at school and university—and in view of the extensive memorizing required of students, especially at the grammar schools.[6] Parallel to this kind of common source would have been the corpus of poetry employing the image of cosmic voyaging— poetry which flourished in the latter part of the seventeenth century and continued into the eighteenth.[7] Presumably it was to this corpus that Tollet, Hughes, and Thomson turned, independently, for the pictures we have seen them draw of Newton's soul voyaging through the heavens. Likewise, the similarity in the depiction of what Newton ultimately gazed upon can be accounted for by the fact that all the poets concerned (Glover, Brereton, and Akenside so far) would presumably have remembered what Newton had written in the General Scholium of his *Principia* and in Queries 28 and 29 of his *Opticks.*

One must, of course, still be careful about assuming a literary source. In 1731 there appeared, in the *Gentleman's Magazine* for April (page 169), a copy of verses designed for Newton's monument, which included this couplet describing Newton,

> Who, in the Eye of Heaven, like *Enoch,* stood,
> And thro' the Paths of Knowledge, walk'd with God.

This couplet, which nicely combines the innocence of the Garden of Eden with the paths and avenues of Georgian landscaped gardens, was followed in 1733 by the lines of Mrs. Brereton quoted in the last chapter, in which she said that Newton

> th' omnipresent God, in all, beholds:
> If to the dark Abyss, a bright Abode
> He points; the View still terminates in God.[8]

One might assume that the later poet has chosen to rework the material provided by the earlier, but the likelihood is diminished considerably when one remembers that the title of Mrs. Brereton's poem reads *On the Bustoes in the Royal Hermitage.* Since she was writing about sculptured busts placed in a landscaped garden, the image she used of Newton's view still terminating in God could readily have derived directly from her subject.

But with the following example one is almost compelled to conclude that one poet has deliberately reworked the material of another, so as to draw attention to both the similarity and the difference between the original and his reworking. The first passage is one already quoted in part—Pope's lines, in his *Temple of Fame,* on Aristotle, "the mighty *Stagyrite.*" The whole passage reads thus:

> Here in a Shrine that cast a dazling Light,
> Sate fix'd in Thought the mighty *Stagyrite*;
> His Sacred Head a radiant Zodiack crown'd,
> And various Animals his Sides surround;
> His piercing Eyes, erect, appear to view
> Superior Worlds, and look all Nature thro'.
> (lines 232-37)[9]

The other passage, on Newton, has also been quoted in part (it appeared in Desaguliers' *Newtonian System of the World* of 1729). It begins in such a way as to direct attention to Pope's poem, for in it the earlier poet had celebrated various sages in addition to Aristotle, and he had prefaced the poem with an advertisement referring to Chaucer's "Third Book of Fame,"[10] while Desaguliers wrote:

> Newton the unparallel'd, whose Name
> No Time will wear out of the Book of Fame,
> Coelestiall Science has promoted more,
> Than all the Sages that have shone before.[11]

Desaguliers then continued by paraphrasing the last two of Pope's lines on Aristotle:

> Nature compell'd his piercing Mind obeys,
> And gladly shows him all her secret Ways.

Desaguliers has done what Robert Smith was to do later in his choice of inscription for Roubiliac's statue: he is saying that what was said before about an ancient sage can be said about Newton—and much more appropriately. Desaguliers then proceeded to indicate what Newton had used in order to surpass Aristotle and how, through its conclusion, his discovery far surpassed the Greek's. In the process he used a phrase ("His Tow'ring Genius") which was to reappear in

Smith's quotation from Lucretius and which may well have been an equally conscious allusion:

> 'Gainst Mathematics she has no Defence,
> And yields t' experimental Consequence;
> His Tow'ring Genius, from its certain Cause
> Ev'ry Appearance *a priori* draws,
> And shews th' Almighty Architect's unalter'd Laws.

These have been instances, for the most part, in which poets paid their tribute to Newton by drawing on literary sources that existed outside the body of poetic praise for Newton: heroic tragedy, Lucretius, cosmic voyages, Newton's own writings, and Pope's lines on Aristotle. What about the use made of passages already existing within the body of poetic praise itself?

Marjorie Hope Nicolson has already pointed out that Edmund Halley's Latin poem, which was prefixed by way of summary to the first edition of the *Principia* and which Francis Fawkes later translated into English verse, served as a model for the organization of many later poems on Newton, including part of Thomson's elegy, and that Thomson's poem then, along with Glover's, served as a model for succeeding poems.[12]

The practice of following models extended to components as well as to organization. When Allan Ramsay, in his "Ode to the Memory of Sir Isaac Newton" (1728), said that "The godlike man now mounts the sky, / Exploring all yon radiant spheres," and that later Newtons would "bring down knowledge from the skies, / To plant on wild barbarian climes," he appears to have been elaborating on John Hughes's lines which read, referring to "The great Columbus of the skies," "'Tis Newton's soul! that daily travels here / In search of knowledge for mankind below."[13] Another idea Ramsay appears to have taken, not from Hughes, but from Thomson's elegy. Thomson had written that Newton, after death,

> wanders through those endless worlds
> He here so well descried, and wondering talks,
> And hymns their Author with his glad compeers.[14]

Ramsay, likewise pointing to Newton's ascent, after death, into the skies, says that now the "godlike man...with one view can more descry, / Than here below in eighty years." (It may be that Ramsay was so pointed and succinct with his verb "descry," because he presumed that his readers, on recognizing the allusion, would remember what it was that Newton had "descried.") Still another apparent echo concerns the image of the sea, which both Ramsay and Thomson use. Since the sea was readily available to both from commonplace experience outside literature, the test for a possible echo must be the epithet used to describe the sea. Thomson had referred to "vast eternity's unbounded sea,"[15] and Ramsay elaborated, referring to "that extended sea, / Where human minds can reach no bound."

Ramsay himself was alluded to when he wrote, a few lines later, "Thro' ev'ry maze he was the guide." Mark Akenside, whose poetry in Wordsworth's day was highly enough regarded for a friend to give a volume of it to Dorothy in 1795, began a passage in the 1744 version of his *Pleasures of the Imagination* that dealt with scientists by repeating Ramsay's image of the maze:

> Speak ye, the pure delight, whose favour'd steps
> The lamp of Science through the jealous maze
> Of Nature guides, when haply you reveal
> Her secret honours....
>
> (2:126-29)[16]

Akenside continued his passage, in part:

> whether in the sky,
> The beauteous laws of light, the central powers
> That wheel the pensile planets round the year....
>
> (2:129-31)

In these lines he appears to allude to works of two other poets. The last line and a half, with its "pensile" (i.e., hanging) planets, reflects these lines by John Hughes, who is likewise describing the planets:

> New solid globes their weight, self-balanc'd, bear
> Unpropp'd amidst the fluid air,
> And all around the central sun in circling eddies roll'd.
>
> (lines 123-25)

Akenside's preceding lines, about "The beauteous laws of light," closely parallel Thomson's line, referring to "the setting sun and shifting clouds," which exclaims: "How just, how beauteous the refractive law."[17] Such a borrowing, so little altered in its phrasing, was presumably meant to be recognized as an allusion. So, too, could the other borrowings have been, from Ramsay and Hughes. What Akenside is doing, in his six lines, is giving a brief, succinct catalogue of Nature's "secret honours" that have been revealed to Science. He can afford to be succinct, because, by alluding to other, more elaborated, passages by his predecessors, he can count on his readers (or at least those of them who were familiar with the poetry of the time) filling out, from their memory, the details of the earlier celebrations of these "secret honours."

It should also be noted that, in the lines of Akenside with which we have been concerned, the poet, although he has been talking about "Science" and Nature's "secret honours," has actually been describing Sir Isaac Newton and his discoveries. So much was Newton the principal exemplar of scientists, that Akenside could regard Newton and Science as virtually synonymous. In 1731 the copy of verses referred to earlier as appearing in the *Gentleman's Magazine* included in its praises of Newton the phrase "That Soul of Science!"[18] In 1744 Akenside put the implied identification into practice and wrote of Science as if synonymous with Newton. In 1784 Wordsworth did precisely the same thing.

The Hawkshead Exercise

In fact, it will be well worth our time to take another look at the passage on Science, part of which we quoted in the last chapter, from the earliest poem we have from Wordsworth's pen, "Lines Written as a School Exercise at Hawkshead." Z. S. Fink has reproduced an "Outline of a Poem" drafted, in manuscript, by Wordsworth's brother Christopher, while he was at Hawkshead Grammar School.[19] W. J. B. Owen describes the "Outline" as "a fairly continuous draft, in English prose, for a Latin poem on Lake District scenery, with fragments of, and reference to, Latin verse...and likewise references to English poets whose images might be useful."[20] Since presumably William underwent the same kind of training and wrote the same kind of exercise, Professor Owen concludes: "The Wordsworths, then, were trained in the art of writing poetry out of their own thoughts in other men's words. And if in Latin, then (as Christopher's outline more or less indicates) in English too." With the phrase "in other men's words," we should presumably not take "words" too literally: as we have seen with the tribute-bearers, later poets chose to rework the concepts and images of their predecessors, as well as, occasionally, to repeat their exact phrasing. Consequently, as we take another look at the relevant part of Wordsworth's Hawkshead exercise, we shall have a sense of a slightly blurred *déjà vu.* At Hawkshead, Wordsworth has the Power of Education say,

>   immortal Science reigns;
> Fair to the view is sacred Truth display'd,
> In all the majesty of light array'd,
> To teach, on rapid wings, the curious soul
> To roam from heaven to heaven, from pole to pole,
> From thence to search the mystic cause of things,
> And follow Nature to her secret springs....
>   (lines 70-76)[21]

With the roaming of the curious soul from heaven to heaven, we have parallels with Tollet's lines on Newton—"through the heavens thy spirit flew, / To trace their motions with a nearer view"—and Hughes's lines, also on Newton, in which "Newton's soul... travels... thro' all th' unbeaten wilds of day...from orb to orb."[22] Ramsay's lines likewise come to mind, in which it is said, of Newton, that

>   none with greater strength of soul
> Could rise to more divine a height,
> Or range the orbs from pole to pole,
> And more improve the human sight.[23]

In Thomson's elegy on Newton, also, many parallels can be found. With Thomson, Newton, while living, "took his ardent flight / Through the blue infinite" and pursued the comet "with awful wing"; and after death, "mounted on cherubic wing," his "swift career is with the whirling orbs."[24] Nor do Wordsworth's parallels stop with the "curious soul on rapid wings": his searching "the mystic cause of things" calls to mind Thomson's description of Newton's "penetrating eye" which, "The mystic veil transpiercing, inly scanned / The rising, moving, wide-established frame." And Wordsworth's "majesty of light" in which "sacred Truth" is displayed recalls Thomson's "light / So plenteous rayed into thy mind below / From Light Himself." Any or all of these earlier passages could have served as sources for Wordsworth at Hawkshead, or any of them could have served to reinforce the choice of phrases from yet another source.

There is another source available, which does indeed appear to have provided the principal influence on Wordsworth's choice of ideas, images, and phrasing. It is a poem referred to briefly in the previous chapter and written by Francis Fawkes. Called "An Eulogy on Sir Isaac Newton," it is actually a translation (sometimes free, sometimes close) of the Latin poem by Edmund Halley the astronomer, referred to earlier. There is no doubt that Wordsworth's masters at Hawkshead, all Cambridge trained,[25] would have known of Halley's poem, which had been prefixed by way of summary to the first edition of the *Principia*. The translation, written by Fawkes, another Cantabrigian, first appeared in Benjamin Martin's *General Magazine of Arts and Science*, which might possibly have been available to Wordsworth, inasmuch as Hawkshead Grammar School made available to his brother Christopher the *European Magazine*.[26] The poem also appeared in Fawkes's collection of original poems and translations, which, when published in 1761, was assisted by the unusually large number of nearly eight hundred subscribers; it should be noted that under the headship of Thomas Bowman "a fine collection of books" was added to the Hawkshead library.[27] In addition Bowman made a practice of lending Wordsworth all sorts of books—especially poetry—from his own personal collection.

Thought for thought, an echo can be traced to Fawkes's translation of the poem on Newton from Wordsworth's passage on Science. Wordsworth's couplet about "Truth display'd, / In all the majesty of light" echoes Fawkes's line "And truth breaks on them in a blaze of day."[28] Wordsworth's couplet on the "curious soul" roaming "from heaven to heaven" echoes Fawkes's lines "But now, admitted guests in Heaven, we rove / Free and familiar in the realms above." Wordsworth's next couplet, about searching "the mystic cause of things," echoes Fawkes's next couplet—"The wonders hidden deep in Earth below, / And nature's laws, before conceal'd, we know"—and the second line in the succeeding couplet but one: "Lend your sweet voice to warble Newton's praise, / Who search'd out truth through all her mystic maze." Any doubt that the schoolboy Wordsworth, in writing about Science, was paraphrasing what Francis Fawkes had written about Newton should be removed by a comparison of the couplet with which Wordsworth introduced his passage on Science with the couplet of Fawkes that appears between the two sets of lines about Newton's discoveries. Wordsworth introduced his passage by having the Power of Education say that she loved, at Hawkshead,

> To lead the mind to those Elysian plains
> Where, throned in gold, immortal Science reigns....
> (lines 69-70)

What the Elysian plains have to do with Science and the discoveries of Science is accounted for by the way Fawkes translated his original:

> Lend, lend your aid, ye bright superior powers,
> That live embosom'd in Elysian bowers....

The original Latin makes no mention of Elysian bowers: these were Fawkes's geographic gaffe as he translated lines which called upon those "who now upon heavenly nectar fare."[29]

This practice of paraphrase which Wordsworth learned at Hawkshead he applied to a revision of one of the two poems he published separately in 1793.

A Hymn to Science

As with the passage from the Hawkshead exercise, the pertinent passage from a revision of *An Evening Walk* we have already examined in part—within the context of seeing what Newton meant to Wordsworth. But, again as with the Hawkshead exercise, this later passage on Science is also of importance in demonstrating Wordsworth's use of preceding poets. In the ten years that passed between the writing of the schoolboy exercise and the revising of *An Evening Walk*, Wordsworth had understandably progressed in the finesse with which he adapted earlier poets to his purpose. Where in the schoolboy exercise he had, for the most part, followed a single source, with the later passage, admittedly considerably longer than the first, he evidently borrowed his building blocks from several different poems and proceeded to erect a structure of his own.

The design of that structure he appears to have adapted from Mark Akenside's "Hymn to Science." As Akenside ranges through the various areas ("disciplines" we would say nowadays) in which science had made discoveries, so does Wordsworth, and often in the same order.³⁰ Wordsworth begins by saying that of the "favoured souls" the chief are

> those to whom the harmonious doors
> Of Science have unbarred celestial stores. . . .³¹

Especially when we remember that, in the eighteenth and nineteenth centuries, Science and Natural Philosophy were synonymous, we can see, in Wordsworth's lines, a paraphrase of these lines from Glover's "Poem on Sir Isaac Newton":

> O happy he, whose enterprising hand
> Unbars the golden and relucid gates
> Of th' empyrean dome, where thou enthron'd
> Philosophy art seated.³²

Wordsworth then turns to his first area of scientific discovery, and says, providing a clause parallel to the one we have looked at:

> To whom a burning energy has given
> That other eye which darts thro' earth and heaven,
> Roams through all space. . . .

Once more synonyms point us to a source, and, as we remember that "ardour" derives from the Latin word for "burn" and at least implies a form of energy, we can see behind these lines of Wordsworth the following ones from Mallet's *Excursion:*

>   Or, rais'd aloft,
> Fir'd with ethereal ardour, to survey
> The circuit of creation, all these suns
> With all their worlds. . . .³³

This first area of Wordsworth's was also the first area with Akenside, and as Akenside in his ode moved from that area, the heavens, to the human mind, so did Wordsworth. Akenside wrote:

> The busy, restless human mind
> Through every maze pursue;
> . . . .

> Say from what simple springs began
> The vast, ambitious thoughts of man,
>   Which range beyond control. . . .

Wordsworth wrote more succinctly:

>   and [ ] unconfined,
> Explores the illimitable tracts of mind. . . .

Akenside continued:

> Which seek eternity to trace,
> Dive through the infinity of space.

Wordsworth combined the two concepts and produced an image that could also have been influenced, as several of his phrases were, by Milton's "gulf profound," for Wordsworth wrote "And piercing the profound of time...."[34] The area of discovery he turns to with this phrase is Akenside's second next area, an area the earlier poet phrased thus:

> The plan, the genius of each state,
> Its interest and its powers relate,
>   Its fortunes and its rise.

With Wordsworth the thought is essentially the same, but the phrasing is different:

> And piercing the profound of time can see
> Whatever man has been and man can be,
> From him the local tenant of the shade
> To man by all the elements obeyed.

The phrasing of this clause appears to derive from various sources. One of these is Ramsay, who, in his "Ode to the Memory of Sir Isaac Newton," urged future Newtons to

> bring down knowledge from the skies
> To plant on wild barbarian climes,

> Till nations, few degrees from brutes,
>   Be brought into each proper road,
> Which leads to wisdom's happiest fruits,
>   To know their Saviour and their God.[35]

It is interesting to note that, just as Wordsworth omits the religious aspects which constitute an important part of Akenside's ode, so does he present a *telos* for states considerably different from Ramsay's. The phrasing of both the primitive state and the perfected one appears to be influenced by Pope. Wordsworth's "local tenant of the shade," besides suggesting—through its parallel to *locum tenens*—that man's residency in the primitive state was only temporary, is too close to Pope's "joint tenant of the shade" (describing man in his state of nature) not to have been a borrowing and adaptation.[36] The content of the line "To man by all the elements obeyed"—and perhaps some of its phrasing as well—reflects the situation of Prospero in *The Tempest*. In that play the Boatswain says to his noble companions, "If you can command these elements," and we learn, ironically, that Prospero actually does command them. Moreover, they obey: Prospero says of his elemental minions: "My spirits obey," and even the reluctant, earthly Caliban confesses, "I must obey."[37] A much closer bringing together of the words "elements" and "obeyed" appears in a couplet in Pope's *Windsor Forest:*

> What could be free, when lawless Beasts obey'd,
> And ev'n the Elements a Tyrant sway'd?
>
>   (lines 51-52)[38]

At least two kinds of linkages could have prompted Wordsworth to remember these particular lines from the "much" of Pope he had memorized.[39] Both sets of Wordsworth's phrases run in exactly the opposite direction from Pope's: Wordsworth's tenant of the shade is inferior to his successor, while Pope's is superior to his; and Wordsworth is commendatory about being obeyed by the elements, while Pope is not. The other linkage is through rhyme: "shade," which is the rhyming word for both Wordsworth and Pope, could have prompted the matching word "obeyed," which in turn could have called to Wordsworth's mind that couplet of Pope's in which "obeyed" was one of the rhyming words.

As will have become evident, when Wordsworth proceeded into political history with his "local tenant of the shade," he passed out of the areas of scientific discovery with which Newton was identifiable, apart, of course, from his *Chronology* of ancient kingdoms. At the same time, Wordsworth passed out of the corpus of poems written by the tribute-bearers and into a vastly larger body of poetry from which he could borrow and adapt. For this reason we do not offer the parallels with Pope and *The Tempest* as the probable sources for the particular lines of Wordsworth: we merely offer them as possible sources, being convinced, from his practice in the rest of these lines, that in all likelihood he did continue, in these few, to borrow and adapt. The same observation holds for his next couplet:

> With them the sense no trivial object knows,
> Oft at its meanest touch their spirit glows. . . .

These lines appear to anticipate the more famous ones at the end of his *Intimations Ode:*

> To me the meanest flower that blows can give
> Thoughts that do often lie too deep for tears.[40]

Since de Selincourt offers as a source for these lines in the *Ode* four lines from Gray's *Ode on the Pleasure arising from Vicissitude*, we would offer them as at least a possible source and influence for the lines on Science:

> The meanest floweret of the vale,
> The simplest note that swells the gale,
> The common sun, the air, the skies
> To him are opening Paradise.[41]

For Wordsworth, great height and great depth were often interchangeable; consequently it is not surprising to find that, in response to the "meanest," Wordsworth in one poem proceeds to great depths and in the other to great heights.[42]

It is to the heights that he proceeds in the lines on Science, and in doing so he returns to areas of scientific discovery identifiable with Newton and to the corpus of poetic tribute paid him. Wordsworth says of the "spirit" that it "glows"

> And proud beyond all limits to aspire
> Mounts through the fields of thought on wings of fire.

Mrs. Brereton had written that Newton "Sublimely on the Wings of Knowledge, soars,"[43] and so may have influenced Wordsworth's phrasing, but a more likely candidate is Glover, again, who wrote two pertinent passages:

> But chiefly Newton let me soar with thee
> . . . .
> And waft aloft my high-aspiring mind,

and

> O Newton, whither flies thy mighty soul,
> How shall the feeble muse pursue through all
> The vast extent of thy unbounded thought. . . .[44]

(Glover's influence, through these last lines, need not have been confined to this particular couplet of Wordsworth's: the "illimitable tracts of mind" of a few lines earlier could well reflect this part of Glover.) Wordsworth then leaves Glover, at least for the space of a couplet, and returns to Akenside for content as well as design. The earlier poet had addressed himself to "the fair scale," the "progressive order" that extends "from the dead, corporeal mass...To Instinct, Reason, God." Wordsworth phrases the thought thus:

> But sure with tenfold pleasure they behold
> The powers of Nature in each various mould. . . .

He continues:

> If like the Sun their [ ] love surrounds
> The various world[s] to life's remotest bounds. . . .

Glover again provides a parallel as he urges the immortalized Newton

> E'en to th' extremest bounds of knowledge reach,
> To those unknown innumerable suns,
> Whose light but glimmers from those distant worlds,

> Ev'n to those utmost boundaries, those bars
> That shut the entrance of th' illumin'd space
> Where angels only tread the vast unknown.

Akenside, too, in his hymn had not ventured beyond the realm of Reason; instead he turned to "social nature's ties," to "private life," and asked Science there to help him "form the life, and rule the will." Wordsworth follows his direction:

> Yet not extinguishes the warmer fire
> Round which the close domestic train retire,
> If but to them these forms an emblem yield,
> Home their gay garden and the world their field,
> While that more near demands minuter cares
> Yet this its proper tendance duly shares.

And so ends Wordsworth's virtual hymn to Science, patterned after an earlier hymn and adapting, for his own reconstituting purpose, ideas, images, and phrases from several earlier poets.[45]

But this virtual hymn to Science was part of *An Evening Walk*, part of his early period and early way of writing, a period and way he put behind him when he wrote and published the revolutionary *Lyrical Ballads*. Did he not say, to a correspondent who asked him in 1801 whether he had "always thought so independently," that *An Evening Walk* shows "how very widely different my former opinions must have been from those which I hold at present"?[46] Would he not, with the *Lyrical Ballads*, have ceased to use earlier poets as he had used them at school and in *An Evening Walk*?

4 A Prevailing Practice

AS W. J. B. OWEN HAS POINTED OUT, WORDSWORTH, while at school, was trained to write poetry, out of his own thoughts, but in the words and images of other poets, English as well as Latin.[1] As we have seen, he continued this practice in the writing of at least part of *An Evening Walk*. That this practice continued into his mature writing—and, in fact, throughout his literary career—appears from several of the letters which he and Dorothy wrote, separately and together.

Nourishing His Mind

While William was preparing for *The White Doe of Rylstone*, Dorothy wrote to a friend that her brother was "greedily devouring" two of Dr. T. D. Whitaker's histories and had "found all the information which he wanted for the prosecution of his plan."[2] A few months later, and concerning the same poem, she wrote to another friend: "My Brother has seized upon the Book [Walton's *Compleat Angler*] for his own reading this night, as he fancies that the imagery and sentiments accord with his own train of thought at present, in connection with his poem, which he is just upon the point of finishing."[3] When Wordsworth was working on *The Recluse* in 1805, Dorothy wrote that "he is very anxious to get forward with [it], and is reading for the nourishment of his mind, preparatory to beginning."[4] In 1815, when Wordsworth was again working on *The Recluse*, Dorothy wrote that, "as he intends completely to plan the first part of the Recluse before he begins the composition, he must read many Books before he will fairly set to labour again."[5]

Wordsworth's own letters confirm his heavy reliance on other writers. In 1798, while writing about his work on *The Recluse*, he remarked to a friend: "If you could collect for me any books of travels you would render me an essential service, as without much of such reading my present labours cannot be brought to a conclusion."[6] In 1815, while defending *The Excursion*, he wrote a sentence which implies a great deal concerning our subject: "Had my Poem been much coloured by Books, as many parts of what I have to write must be, I should have been accused as Milton has been of pedantry, and of having a mind which could not support itself but by other mens labours."[7] Notice that, although he insists that *The Excursion* is not "much coloured by Books," he readily admits that "many parts" of his poetry *are* "much coloured by Books." In 1844 he made an allusion which likewise implies a great deal. On thanking Alexander Dyce for sending him his edition of Skelton's works, Wordsworth offered his sincere thanks "with unavoidable regret that, being so advanced in years, I cannot make that profitable use of your labours, which at an earlier period of life I might have done. I am much in the same situation as Pope when Hall's Satires were first put into his hand."[8] De Selincourt, in a note to these lines, has directed us to a passage in Johnson's *Life of Pope*, where the meaning is made clear. Johnson wrote of Pope: "How he obtained possession of so many beauties of speech, it were desirable to know. That he gleaned from authors, obscure as well as eminent, what he thought brilliant or useful, and preserved it all in a regular collection, is not unlikely. When, in his last years, Hall's *Satires* were shewn to him, he wished that he had seen them sooner."[9] The parallel with regard to gleaning is, of course, intended, but even the "regular collection" has its parallel—in Wordsworth's prodigious memory.

Certain of Wordsworth's letters likewise make it clear that he assumed that other poets, also, composed in the same way, drawing on their memory of what their predecessors had written. What he wrote to Scott about the latter's editing of Dryden encapsulates the matter. Among the things which an editor (in general) has to provide,

Wordsworth placed ("last" and "of less importance" than a correct text and explanatory notes) "notes pointing out passages or authors to which the Poet has been indebted, not in the piddling way of [a] phrase here and phrase there (which is detestable as a general practice) but where the Poet has really had essential obligations either as to matter or manner."[10] He obviously took for granted that a poet would have such "obligations." When Wordsworth sent a group of his new sonnets to Crabb Robinson, he asked that he not show them to any other verse writers. Why? Because "We are all in spite of ourselves a parcel of thieves."[11] We should not allow the comic mockery in the mock-harshness to prevent us from seeing that he clearly implied that all poets frequently borrow from one another and rework one another's writings. This, evidently, had been his experience. As Frederick A. Pottle has observed, "...The fact is (though this is doctrine little heard of among men) that Wordsworth made grateful use of prefabricated material whenever he could get it of the right sort."[12]

Over the years Wordsworth acquired, through reading, an exceptionally wide and varied range of material from which to borrow. Leaving the details to an appendix, we shall here simply point to the highlights.[13] In his father's library he read the classics of English literature. At Hawkshead school he read Ovid "voraciously" and was supplied by his master with "the latest books from Kendal every month." During his holidays from Hawkshead, when he had the opportunity to range the outdoors at will, he would frequently lie down with a book, instead, "devouring as I read, / Defrauding the day's glory, desperate!" *(P(1850)* 5:488-89). Instead of looking to Nature in the woods and fields, he turned to

> the great Nature that exists in works
> Of mighty Poets. Visionary Power
> Attends the motions of the viewless winds
> Embodied in the mystery of words:...
> *(P(1850)* 5:596-99)

At University he read poetry and history and other subjects in Italian, Spanish, French, Greek, and Latin in addition to English. In 1807 Dorothy had occasion to remark that he was "greedily devouring" a couple of histories, and he read literally dozens and dozens of travel books. He asked for a particular volume of "Bell's forgotten poetry" and was able to suggest to the anthologist Anderson that he add, to his collection of English poetry, work from obscure authors whom specialists of today would be hard pressed to elaborate on. They ranged from the fourteenth century to the early eighteenth, and within these he developed a special interest in the works of female authors. Moreover, he felt a particular affection for the works sent to him by Cambridge undergraduates and their counterparts.[14] He picked out individual lines for praise and paid to one such junior contemporary the second highest compliment possible: he would memorize his poetry. To another he paid the highest: "I may be tempted to steal from you."

"They End, I Remember, Thus"

When Wordsworth came to write and wished to borrow from what he had read, there was evidently little need for him to turn to the actual books he had read, for his amazingly retentive memory was able to supply him with what he had read. This fact is illustrated particularly well in his practice of quoting literary passages from memory in writing to his correspondents. When in 1805 he referred to certain lines by Bishop Corbet, he did so thus: "There are some pleasing verses (I think by Corbet Bishop of Norwich) on the death of Francis Beaumont the elder, they end I remember thus, alluding to his short life:

> 'by whose sole death appears,
> Wit's a disease consumes men in few years'."[15]

Thirty years later, he wrote, just as casually, "Tell Mr. Mitford that the passage in King John is at the close of the 4th Act—the words these, or something like it—

> *Vast Confusion waits as* doth a Raven *on*, etc.
> The imminent decay—

near the commencement of the fifth act you meet the word *Amazement* — all shewing that Gray when he wrote his Ode was fresh from the perusal of these scenes."[16]

A particular album which Wordsworth prepared for a friend reveals even more about the extent both of Wordsworth's reading and of his memory. This album, which runs to ninety-two pages, is entitled

Poems and Extracts Chosen by William Wordsworth for an Album Presented to Lady Mary Lowther, Christmas, 1819, and, as its title indicates, its contents were selected with the particular recipient in mind.[17] Presumably for this reason, it contains no Milton, no Spenser, no Dryden, no Gray (all of whom Wordsworth had read and memorized extensively), only three sonnets of Shakespeare (nothing from his plays), and only two pages of Pope. Many familiar names appear (we give the number of pages after each): Akenside (7), Armstrong (2), Beattie (1), Carew (1), Cowper (2), Dyer (3), Marvell (3), Smart (1), Thomson (4), Waller (2), Webster (1), and Wither (9). It is not surprising that four other favourites of Wordsworth should appear: Sir John Beaumont (2), Daniel (8), Mickle (2), and Winchilsea (31). But the remaining names indicate even more clearly how extensive Wordsworth's reading was: Philip Doddridge (1), John Langhorne (1), Anne Killigrew (1), Laetitia Pilkington (2), Jane Warton (2), and three pages of "Lines Written by Capt. [Thomas] James upon his leaving Charlton Island, where many of his Ship's Crew had died during the winter, which they passed there A. D. 1631-2." The album contains misquotations: in one of the Shakespearean sonnets and in two of the passages from Waller.[18] As its editor remarks, the fact of misquotations suggests that the passages had been dictated from memory. The recipient recorded that Sarah Hutchinson had done the actual writing, as Wordsworth "dictated in the winter evenings" of 1819.[19] Is it likely that Wordsworth would have read from the printed texts, while Sarah wrote? Or, if printed texts were involved at all, would it not be more likely that Wordsworth would have marked the passages and have handed them over to Sarah to copy? Actually one of Wordsworth's letters provides a definitive answer. Writing to Haydon on 16 January 1820, and referring, evidently, to a succession of preceding months, he said that, because of recurring inflammation in his eyes, "I neither write nor read by Candle light."[20] Since he "dictated" the contents of the album "in the winter evenings"—and did so with the occasional misquotation—he must have dictated all ninety-two pages from memory.

The misquotations in the album found parallels in some of his letters, and these also reflect his sense of assurance in quoting from memory instead of looking the passages up in his library. Spenser he modified somewhat when he quoted two lines from the second book of *The Faerie Queene*.[21] More surprisingly, he misquoted Byron, even though he had the pertinent passage close at hand.[22] But most revealing of all is what Wordsworth did, in a letter he wrote to a friend in 1803, with two passages from Petrarch, one of four lines and the other of seven: he misidentified them—which indicates that he had not bothered looking them up—and then quoted them, in Italian.[23]

His quoting of Petrarch was not, moreover, exceptional for him. He had evidently been trained to memorize at school. Presumably the system of education at Hawkshead was basically the same as that at Winchester College during the eighteenth century, and the system there has been described thus:

> [it] consisted of translation, composition, and "standing-up." The boys read Sophocles, Homer, Virgil, Horace, Cicero, Livy, Juvenal, Phaedrus, Pindar, Barton's Plutarch, the *Encheiridion* of Epictetus, and the *Metamorphosis* of Ovid. . . . They learnt vast quantities of Latin and Greek verse. One boy repeated the whole *Iliad* for standing-up, another astonished the Posers by presenting them with a complete translation of Lucan's *Pharsalia*. They wrote thousands of "vulguses" and "varyings" [a "vulgus" was an exercise in which a short passage in English was translated into Latin or Greek verse, and a "varying" added the task of expressing the original content in different words] and at election time performed these feats extempore. Despite its imperfections there is something to be said for the system. The boys construed a large amount of classical literature, and their memories were stored with its choicest treasures.[24]

As a result of required memorizing for "standing-up" and voluntary additions, Wordsworth had committed to memory, as well as the thousands upon thousands of classical verses, all of Milton's sonnets, "large portions" of Shakespeare and Spenser, and "much" of both Dryden and Pope.[25] Nor did he confine himself to English poems that were considered classics. The whole of *Sir Martyn*, a poem of over 1200 lines by William Julius Mickle, he quoted from memory, and a frequent companion of Wordsworth's reported that he "used to quote much" from Virgil, Horace, and Lucretius—all, of course, in Latin.[26] Evidently whatever pieces of literature Wordsworth wished to memorize, he did, and consequently had them available to him whenever he wished to make use of them.

How retentive his memory could be is well illustrated by what he wrote to his friend Alexander Dyce in 1830, about a poem he recommended by Sneyd Davies. He called it "an exceedingly pleasing poem with a very original air. It begins 'There was a time my dear Cornwallis, when'. I first met with it in Dr Enfield's Exercises of Elocution or Speaker, I forget which."[27] We have supplied the learned doctor's name in place of the guess made by the editors of Wordsworth's letters, because presumably Wordsworth is referring to an episode recorded in Dorothy's *Journal* for 15 April 1802. She and William had stopped at an inn to change into dry clothes and to have dinner. While waiting for the dinner to be prepared, William "made his way to the Library piled up in a corner of the window. He brought out a volume of Enfield's Speaker" and two other books.[28] Since Wordsworth gave Dyce no other help in locating Davies' poem, which he said "well merits preservation," he must have been calling on his memory of this event which had happened twenty-eight years before, and from that memory he was able to quote the opening line.[29]

Insights from Cowper

To that kind of memory Wordsworth was able to add an uncanny ability to detect similarities in two otherwise disparate passages, each encountered at widely different times. When he wrote to John Peace about the parallelisms which that editor had noted between passages in Cowper's *Task* and the writings of other authors, he said: "Though I can make but little use of my eyes in writing, or reading, I have lately been reading Cowper's 'Task' aloud, and in so doing was tempted to look over the parallelisms, for which Mr. Southey was, in his edition, indebted to you. Knowing how comprehensive your acquaintance with poetry is, I was rather surprised that you did not notice the identity of the thought, and accompanying illustrations of it, in a passage of Shenstone's 'Ode upon Rural Elegance', compared with one in 'The Task'. . . . " Wordsworth then provided, in a note, the parallel which had escaped both Southey and Peace, each of whom had turned as professionals to the job of finding parallels: "Book IV, 'It is a flame', &c., compared with Shenstone's 'Ode to the Duchess of Somerset', 'Her impulse nothing may restrain.'" The passages so referred to appear to be lines 232-63 of Shenstone's "Rural Elegance: An Ode to the late Duchess of Somerset" and lines 743-801 of Book IV of Cowper's *Task*.[30] We have reproduced these in Appendix C:

Shenstone and Cowper, and it is instructive to compare the two passages so as to see what Wordsworth meant by "parallelisms," "identity of thought," and the way in which Cowper had presumably used Shenstone.

The image of the "flame" is certainly one of the "parallelisms" which Wordsworth would have observed, although it is notable that the image itself is so common that most people would have missed the specific parallels between Cowper's use of it and Shenstone's, especially since with Cowper it appears at the beginning of his passage while with Shenstone it is almost buried two-thirds of the way through his Ode. Nor is there a complete identity of thought between the two. With Cowper the "flame" is clearly "the love of Nature's works" (line 731), but with Shenstone one is rather hard pressed to specify, for he is much more vague in phrasing and one would have to interpret his "flame" as referring to values arising from and connected with the beauties of Nature's works (lines 244-52). The function of the flame likewise differs. With Cowper it leads to the growing of plants within the confines of the city (lines 753-59), while with Shenstone it is designed "To sift Opinion's mingled mass, / Impress a nation's taste, and bid the sterling pass" (lines 253-54). As partial and incomplete as this "identity of thought" may be, however, Wordsworth spotted it and concluded that, on the basis of the degree of identity, Cowper had reworked Shenstone's content and phrasing. Or, to put the matter from the point of view of the borrower and reworker, Wordsworth concluded that Cowper had noted Shenstone's image of the flame and had recognized that, while the use to which Shenstone had put it was not precisely what he himself needed, still he could use the image, applying it effectively to a somewhat different subject.

Since Wordsworth specified plural "illustrations" of the "identity of thought," he must have felt that others were important as well. Presumably one of these would have been what Cowper did with this line of Shenstone's, referring to heaven: "Her impulse nothing may restrain" (line 232). Cowper, in speaking about his "flame," says

> nothing feeds it: neither business, crowds,
> Nor habits of luxurious city-life
> (Whatever else they smother of true worth
> In human bosoms) quench it, or abate.
>
>   (lines 744-47)[31]

Cowper split Shenstone's phrase, providing the "nothing" with a new verb and assigning a new (and rather involved) subject for the verbs that parallel "restrain," namely the phrase "quench it or abate." The "identity" or "parallelism" can be found within considerable nonparallel material, and that, presumably, is what Wordsworth did, taking the synonyms as fully equivalent to the original. This is what he did in the two poems of his on Science we have already examined, and presumably this is also what he did later when he went looking for parallels in other writers' works which he could turn to his own poetic purpose. This certainly appears to be what Cowper did with a number of Shenstone's words. On reviewing the earlier Ode, Cowper would have frequently encountered a word (say, a verb) that was coupled with another (say, a noun); Cowper himself was not currently concerned with what the noun referred to, but he realized that the verb would do well in conjunction with a different noun, with which he *was* concerned. Shenstone's "soothe," for instance, had taken for an object "some vapour'd fair" (line 242); Cowper made it govern "the rich possessor" of a garden (line 754). Shenstone's "breathless," which had modified "flowers" (line 235), with Cowper becomes "stifling" and modifies the "bosom of the town" (line 753). And Shenstone's almost heroic "shrubs fuliginously grim" (line 236) is reduced to a specific example in Cowper's "mournful mint" (line 756). Presumably Wordsworth would have been as much prepared to modify any useful phrases he found in his reading.

More extensive modifying can be found in a few other of Cowper's phrases, and again it is presumably the sort of thing which Wordsworth himself was also prepared to do. Cowper took Shenstone's word "luxury" and reversed the value judgement associated with it: Shenstone had written approvingly of "that rich luxury of thought" which the lovers of nature enjoy (line 248); Cowper turned the thought to his customary condemnation of the "habits of luxurious city-life" (line 745). This kind of reversing of values we have seen in Wordsworth's sally into social theory in his virtual hymn to Science. Updating became necessary when Cowper chose to use Shenstone's visual form through which the concept of the rural as ideal was expressed. Shenstone had written of a pictorial representation which "trace[d] the dun far distant grove" (line 238): this choice of a grove and this way of presenting verdure in brown tones were both the fashion in aristocratic art when Shenstone wrote,[32] but Cowper lived in a period closer to actual nature, and so he provided, instead, a "glimpse of a green pasture" (line 751). Similar updating occurred when Cowper took Shenstone's abstract phrase "To mimic rural life" (line 242) and provided instead the specific example of a broken pitcher and a spoutless tea-pot both pressed into service as planters for flowers (lines 775-79). In each of these instances the second artist, potentially a borrower and reshaper, recognized something in his predecessor's work that he himself could improve upon for his own purpose.

So Pervasive

One predecessor in particular Wordsworth turned to almost instinctively. The admiration he had for Milton's poetry is reflected instructively in the account Felicia Dorothea Hemans gave of evening rides she took with Wordsworth "through the lovely vales of Grasmere and Rydal." She particularly noted "his beautiful, sometimes half-unconscious recitation in a voice so deep and solemn, that it has often brought tears into my eyes. His voice has something quite breeze-like in the soft gradations of its swells and falls. . . . We had been listening during one of these evening rides, to various sounds and notes of birds, which broke upon the stillness; and at last I said, 'Perhaps there may be still deeper and richer music pervading all nature than we are permitted, in this state, to hear.' He answered by reciting those glorious lines of Milton's:

> 'Millions of spiritual creatures walk the earth,
> Unseen, both when we [wake] and when we sleep,' etc.

and this in tones that seemed rising from such depths of veneration! His tones of solemn earnestness, sinking, almost dying away into a murmur of veneration, as if the passage were breathed forth from the heart, I shall never forget."[33]

It is not so surprising, then, that as one reads the notes in the standard edition, one comes upon a borrowing from Milton every twenty lines or so. As an almost random example, we would offer two lines from the sonnet "Spanish Guerillas," written during the Peninsular War. These lines (3-4) say of the guerillas that "they have learnt to open and to close / The ridges of grim war." One might think that the terrain fought over provided the image, but the source turns out to be Milton's warring angels, who were likewise "expert / When to...open...and when to close / The ridges of grim Warr."[34] Shakespeare is not far behind in the frequency of levy, and, after him, Gray. Nor are two other expected sources hard to find: the Bible and Wordsworth himself.

Not all of the borrowings were made consciously. In several of their notes to the standard edition, Ernest de Selincourt and Helen Darbishire describe Wordsworth's indebtedness in a way remarkably similar to that Wordsworth himself used about his young disciple who reproduced "several lines" of Wordsworth's poetry "word for word or nearly so": Wordsworth observed, "—the Author being probably altogether unconscious of it."[35] His editors come close to this phrasing when they say, as they do at least twice, that Wordsworth "had at the back of his mind" a certain phrase, usually of Milton's.[36] They use the phrase itself when they say that line 17 of "The Sparrow's Nest" was "an unconscious borrowing from Churchill's *Independence*," that line 2 of "In a Carriage, Upon the Banks of the Rhine" was "an unconscious reminiscence of Milton," and again that a line in *The Excursion* (6:1005) was "an unconscious reminiscence of the last line" in *Paradise Regained*.[37] They use a variant of the phrase (without, we are sure, any Freudian or Jungian connotation) when they say that line 22 of "She Was a Phantom of Delight" was "perhaps due to a subconscious recollection of a passage in Bartram's *Travels*," and that line 10 of number XXIV of the River Duddon Sonnets was "a subconscious reminiscence of Keats's *Ode to a Nightingale*."[38] Their choice of phrasing indicates that, on the basis of their intensive and exhaustive study of Wordsworth's poetry, they had come to the conclusion that, so pervasive was Wordsworth's practice of making levy on his poetic predecessors, he on occasion did so without even being aware of it.

We would add a particularly poignant example of his borrowing from Milton, presumably instinctive and possibly unconscious, which is to be found in the sonnet "Surprised by Joy," written in relation to the death in 1812 of his three-year-old daughter, Catherine. She had been a most delightful child, whom Wordsworth had celebrated in a poem written a year before, in which he said, "Light are her sallies as the tripping fawn's / Forth-startled from the fern where she lay couched."[39] In lines 11 and 12 of "Surprised by Joy," he referred to the time when he realized that she was dead: "when I stood forlorn, / Knowing my heart's best treasure was no more."[40] Most readers have undoubtedly pictured Wordsworth standing at the side of the little girl's bed, stricken by the reality of what he had just witnessed. This would be the normal public reading of the phrase; for Wordsworth, however, it meant something else, for he had been away in Essex when Catherine died, and it was there that he received the news. Consequently the parallel that can be seen between the way in which Wordsworth describes his situation and similar situations presented in certain lines of Milton suggests that Wordsworth himself was aware of the parallel and sought to allude to it by making use of key words in Milton's lines. Just as Wordsworth had heard that he had lost his family paradise, so Adam was told that he would be expelled from his. As a result,

> Adam at the newes
> Heart-strook with chilling gripe of sorrow stood....

This description would readily call to mind another, parallel one, in which the speaker responds to learning that the heroine is in dire peril:

> Amaz'd I stood, harrow'd with grief and fear.

And the single word summing up the emotion expressed in both these passages was available in another parallel description, that one depicting Eve's response to the news that Adam might be taken from her:

> forlorn of thee,
> Whither shall I betake me, where subsist?[41]

Reinforcing these parallels, which would probably have forced themselves upon Wordsworth's attention from his well-stocked memory, could easily have been this memorable couplet from Cowper, with whose works Wordsworth was also familiar: it describes Virtue as she

> Stands in the desert, shiv'ring and forlorn,
> A wintry figure, like a wither'd thorn.[42]

It is worth noting that the phrase "I stood forlorn" would consequently provoke two different responses in two different groups of readers. The general public would respond by picturing the deathbed scene. Because of the allusions to Milton (and possibly Cowper),

Wordsworth and his circle of family and intimate friends would respond by appreciating the implication that, for Wordsworth, the loss of his daughter Catherine, with all her paradisal innocence, was fully equivalent to what Adam experienced when he was driven from Eden.

Another private allusion is to be found in "Tintern Abbey," one which allowed Wordsworth to solve a particular problem he had created for himself. It is generally agreed that in speaking of "sensations," Wordsworth was following the philosopher Hartley, but when it came to the route which sensations follow, Wordsworth departed from his mentor. Hartley had written that sensations produced by external objects proceed along the ether in the nerves to the brain, but Wordsworth, speaking of the "beauteous forms" of natural objects, said that he "owed to them"

> sensations sweet,
> Felt in the blood, and felt along the heart;
> And passing even into my purer mind,
> With tranquil restoration. . . .
> (lines 22-30)[43]

Wordsworth evidently wished to depart from the clinically accurate route described by Hartley and sought, instead, to involve the heart and what it stood for. He knew a writer who had celebrated sensations and who had associated them with the heart.

In 1791 he remarked on having read Sterne's *Tristram Shandy*, and in fact he was later to borrow from it, without acknowledgement.[44] He would accordingly have noticed what Sterne had Yorick say about preaching, that, instead of parading learning before his audience, he "had rather direct five words point blank to the heart."[45] St. Paul, in the King James Version of 1 Corinthians 14:19, had remarked that, instead of speaking in unintelligible tongues before his audience in church, he "had rather speak five words with [his] understanding." Sterne had changed the governing organ from the head to the heart, just as Wordsworth changed the route which the sensations followed from Hartley's (along the nerves to the brain) to a more sentimental one, in the blood and along the heart, before finally arriving in the mind. Sterne had more to say about the relative roles of the head and heart, and the importance of the blood, in his *Sentimental Journey*, a book which Wordsworth does not mention having read but which one must assume he had read, from his liking for Sterne's writings and from his having gone on his own sentimental journey through France.

Of the many descriptions in *A Sentimental Journey* of Yorick's holding a woman's hand, and even taking her pulse to feel the blood beating, there is one in particular which appears to have a bearing on Wordsworth's lines. It concerns the lady whom Yorick met by chance in Calais.[46] It mentions "a subtle sensation" felt in the palm; it describes the pain which Yorick's heart suffered when the lady disengaged her hand; and it records her comment that he had had reason to thank Fortune: "the heart knew it, and was satisfied: and who but an English philosopher would have sent notice of it to the brain to reverse the judgment?" And, most tellingly, it contains Yorick's explanation: "The pulsations of the arteries along my fingers pressing across hers told her what was passing within me." Yorick's phrase, "along my fingers," is an expression of acute sensibility that is exceeded in its graphic nature only by Wordsworth's peculiar phrase "along the heart." Thus did Hartley's poetic disciple correct the excessive rationalism of his mentor.

In the Intimations Ode, likewise, there is evidence for concluding that Wordsworth borrowed from a predecessor in order to solve a difficulty he had created for himself. When he first published the Ode in 1807, he put as its title the single word "Ode." Many years later, when providing Isabella Fenwick with the material for her notes, Wordsworth expressed great concern about the pain given "to some good and pious persons" by the conclusion they had drawn that Wordsworth, in the Ode, sought to inculcate a belief in the prior existence of the soul.[47] Presumably in 1815 he felt some concern about the possibility of such an effect, especially since he himself had moved considerably closer to an orthodox position in religion. Certainly in 1815 he was aware of attacks made on his poetry by members of the orthodox community, and in particular, it is clear from a letter he wrote to Catherine Clarkson, he was smarting from the "monstrous" remarks that had been made about him by Mrs. Clarkson's friend: "To talk of the offense of writing the Ex[cursion] and the difficulty of forgiving the Author is carrying audacity and presumption to a heigth of which I did not think any *Woman* was capable."[48] Presumably he would have wished to prevent any renewal of such attacks, and he could do so by diverting the attention of his readers away from the discussion of pre-existence, which was objectionable, to the ideas hinted at in the poem of post-existence, which was perfectly acceptable to the orthodox.

The most efficient way of directing his readers' attention would be to provide a title which would precondition them not to look for pre-existence but rather to look for and interpret everything in terms of post-existence, or immortality. Part of a new title he had available to him in his letter to Mrs. Clarkson: the phrase "recollections of childhood." What he needed now was an appropriate phrase dealing with immortality. In later life, at least, and quite possibly in 1815, he had in his library a book which contained two relevant passages, passages, moreover, which he had probably committed to memory years before.[49] One of these is the opening speech from Act V of Addison's tragedy *Cato*, which was very well known throughout the eighteenth century and which, appearing in the edition of *Elegant Extracts* used at Hawkshead, could easily have been required for a "standing-up." The other was the last essay that had appeared in the *Spectator*, one written by Henry Grove and concerned with the immortality of the soul—another prime candidate for memorizing somewhere in his school career (even the dame school Wordsworth attended provided its pupils with copies of the *Spectator* for study—and quite possibly for memorizing).[50]

Grove's essay contains a tribute to Sir Isaac Newton, which in itself would have rivetted Wordsworth's attention, as Newton is described beholding the works of the Creator with the transport of the philosopher (a description that could also, later on, be applied to Newton's statue). In the paragraph preceding the one in which Newton appears, Grove elaborates at some length on the large variety of intelligent Beings which God must have created in various parts of the universe, all for the pleasure which He derives from seeing their satisfaction. Without further preparation he then remarks, "Is not this more than an Intimation of our Immortality?"[51] Nothing that could be called an intimation, let alone an intimation of immortality, has been mentioned before: why would Grove insert such a singularly irrelevant remark? Wordsworth and many other readers of the eighteenth and early nineteenth centuries would have known, for they would have recognized his question as an allusion to the particularly notable speech of the hero in Addison's play, which had first been uttered a year before Grove's rhetorical question.

At the beginning of Act V of *Cato*, the hero is revealed with a drawn sword on the table beside him and a copy of Plato's book on the Immortality of the Soul in his hand. He soliloquizes:

> It must be so—Plato, thou reason'st well—
> Else whence this pleasing hope, this fond desire,
> This longing after immortality?
> Or whence this secret dread, and inward horror
> Of falling into nought? Why shrinks the soul
> Back on herself, and startles at destruction?
> 'Tis the divinity that stirs within us;
> 'Tis Heav'n itself that points out an hereafter,
> And intimates eternity to man.[52]

In this speech the two crucial words "intimates" and "immortality" appear to be six lines apart, but actually, through the word "eternity," they appear together, for the context makes quite clear that in this line "eternity" means "immortality."[53] Certainly Grove took it to mean that, for he remarked that his own argument was "more than an Intimation of our Immortality." There, in all its mellifluousness, was the chrysalis of Wordsworth's title, and he had only to decide whether Grove's belittling of "Intimation" detracted from its usefulness for him. Obviously he decided that the word would do nicely, especially in the plural, and possibly because he liked understatement anyway and also possibly because the root of both "intimate" and "intimation" was *intimus*, which meant "inmost" or "innermost," and for Wordsworth the intimations of immortality had come to him from innermost promptings, from deep within his psyche.

In *The Prelude*, likewise, are to be found passages in which the expression is typically and distinctively Wordsworthian and yet is drawn from phrasing used by earlier writers. W. J. B. Owen has examined three of these passages. The first of these describes "old Grandame Earth" as grieving to find that "the play-things which her love designed" for the boy are instead "Unthought of: in their woodland beds the flowers / Weep, and the river sides are all forlorn" (5:339-42). The phrasing in the last two lines, in particular, Owen shows, derives, for all its Wordsworthian sound, from the language of classical and neo-classical pastoral elegy—and especially from passages in Dryden's Virgil, in Spenser, and in Milton.[54] The second *Prelude* passage is the scene from the top of Snowdon, where Wordsworth found himself "on the shore /... of a huge sea of mist" and where "A hundred hills their dusky backs upheaved / All over this still Ocean" (13:42-46 in the 1805 version). Again the expression is typically Wordsworthian, and again it derives from Milton, from the passage in *Paradise Lost* in which, in response to the command of God at creation, the mountains "thir broad bare backs upheave / Into the Clouds" above "a hollow bottom broad and deep, / Capacious bed of Waters" (7:282-90). The third passage is more surprising still. At the beginning of *The Prelude*, Wordsworth describes himself (in lines 6-7 of the 1805 version) as a "captive...coming from a house / Of bondage" (the city); wondering "what sweet stream / Shall with its murmur lull [him] to [his] rest" and finding that "the earth is all before" him, he says,

> I look about, and should the guide I chuse
> Be nothing better than a wandering cloud,
> I cannot miss my way.
>
> (1:13-19)[55]

As Owen comments: "This looks like an ordinary Wordsworthian image: the nature-lover trusting to Nature to guide him." But as Owen goes on to demonstrate, Wordsworth is drawing on Israel's experience in Egypt (the "house of bondage") and their escape from it, guided by a Providential cloud, and on the close of *Paradise Lost:* "The World was all before them, where to choose / Thir place of rest, and Providence thir guide" (12:646-47).

The fourth passage was examined by Lane Cooper many years ago. It is Wordsworth's vision of the ideal setting for a seat of learning, "a Sanctuary for our Country's Youth." That setting is "a primeval grove" whose "countenance"

> should wear a stamp of awe:
> A habitation sober and demure
> For ruminating Creatures; a domain
> For quiet things to wander in; a haunt
> In which the heron should delight to feed
> By the shy rivers, and the Pelican
> Upon the Cypress spire in lonely thought
> Might sit and sun himself.
>
> (3:431-44)

Lane Cooper showed that much of the phrasing in this passage derives from the description of a scene on the banks of the Altamaha in Georgia, provided by the Quaker botanist, William Bartram, in his *Travels Through North and South Carolina, Georgia, East and West Florida*....[56] Bartram presented "groves" and "fresh scenes of grandeur and sublimity." His "deep forests and distant hills re-echoed the cheering social lowings of domestic herds" (Wordsworth's "ruminating Creatures"). Bartram has a "sharp-sighted crane," which Wordsworth has transformed to a "heron." But Bartram's pelican is virtually unchanged, except for the purpose of its activity: "Behold, on yon decayed, defoliated cypress tree, the solitary wood pelican, dejectedly perched upon its utmost elevated spire; he there, like an ancient venerable sage, sets himself up as a mark of derision, for the safety of his kindred tribes." Bartram's "solitary" has become Wordsworth's "lonely" (synonyms, again); the cypress spire has remained virtually unchanged; and the "ancient venerable sage" (shades of both Newton and Wren) has become, with Wordsworth, the overt "lonely thought." Again, as with the passages Owen examined, so pervasive was Wordsworth's practice that in this passage, too, in order to express ideas closest to his heart, Wordsworth searched his memory for the phrasing which other writers had used and which he could reshape to his own purposes.

The same holds true for the five-line description of Newton's statue which Wordsworth wrote in 1803.

I Could Behold

One year after Roubiliac's statue was put in place, there appeared in Number 200 of *The World* (the issue for 28 October 1756) an anonymous poem which was entitled "An Ode on Sculpture" and which had been supplied to the editor by "a very ingenious correspondent at Cambridge."[57] The writer, in talking about the achievements of Sculpture (personified), says that

> She, like *Prometheus*, grasps the fire;
> Her touch revives the lambent flame;
> While, Phoenix-like, the statesman, bard, or sage,
> Spring fresh to life, and breathe through ev'ry age.

He then illustrates this statuary tribute to the tripartite hero ("statesman, bard, or sage") by referring to "A noble statue of Sir Isaac Newton, erected in Trinity-college chapel, by doctor Smith," which he describes thus:

> Hence, where the organ full and clear,
> With loud hosannas charms the ear,
> Behold (a prism within his hands)
> Absorb'd in thought, great *Newton* stands!
> Such was his solemn, wonted state,
> His serious brow, and musing gait,
> When, taught on eagle-wings to fly,
> He trac'd the wonders of the sky;
> The chambers of the sun explor'd,
> Where tints of thousand hues are stor'd;
> Whence ev'ry flow'r in painted robes is drest,
> And varying *Iris* steals her gaudy vest.

Within the text of this description, the reader will have noticed the presence of a phenomenon we have seen before in the corpus of tribute poems: the reworking of material supplied by earlier poets writing in the tradition. The almost requisite flight into the heavens is here expressed in terms of the eagle image. The "chambers of the sun... / Where tints of thousand hues are stor'd" appear to be derived from John Hughes's "sun-born colours," and the phrase "Absorb'd in thought" is precisely the one Elizabeth Tollet used for the statue she foresaw being created:

> Soon shall the marble monument arise,
> And Newton's honour'd name attract our eyes:
> The finish'd bust, in curious sculpture wrought,
> Shall seem to breathe alone, absorb'd in thought.[58]

What is even more noteworthy, however, is that now the entire description of Newton—everything that is said about him—is firmly attached to his statue.

In 1791 the whole of the "Ode to Sculpture" was reprinted, under the author's name (James Scott, D.D.), as Ode XL in volume 13 of *Bell's Classical Arrangement of Fugitive Poetry*.[59] Two facts associated with this publication are worth mentioning: in 1795 Wordsworth asked a friend to provide him with volume 10 of that same collection, and Scott's passage on Newton was still, in Wordsworth's day (according to his friend George Dyer), "often quoted"; in fact, Dyer quoted it from memory in his history and got some of the lines twisted.[60] More importantly, when, probably in 1803, Wordsworth was at work on the first surviving draft of the *Prelude* passage on Newton's statue, he finished his sentence about "Trinity's loquacious Clock" and wrote:

> Her pealing Organ was my neighbour, too;
> And, from my Bed-room, I in moonlight nights
> Could see, right opposite, a few yards off,
> The Antechapel, where the Statue stood
> Of Newton, with his Prism & silent Face.[61]

Soon after, on the opposite side of the page (in a form that has come to be designated as A²), Wordsworth enlarged the sentence to read as follows:

> Her pealing Organ was my neighbour, too;
> And, from my Pillow, when the Moon shone fair
> Or even by dimmer influence of the stars,
> In wakeful vision rapt I could behold
> Solemnly near and pressing on my sight
> The Antechapel, where the Statue stood
> Of Newton, with his Prism & silent Face.[62]

That part of the enlargement which reads "In wakeful vision rapt" appears to reflect a reinforcing source, the passage on Newton in Grove's *Spectator* essay on the immortality of the soul. There Grove had written, referring to Newton's exploration of the laws of the universe: "while with the Transport of a Philosopher he beholds and admires the glorious Work."[63] The description of transport that had been applied to Newton, as he beheld the work of the Creator, Wordsworth, using the synonymous concept of rapture, applied to himself, as he beheld the statue of Newton. In the second copy of the original version (what is called MS. B), the enlargement disappeared, and the lines as a whole underwent at least four revisions: in three of these the word "solemnly" appears, while in all four "mark" replaces "behold" as the alternative to "see."[64] In the single revision made to this passage in MS. C (which de Selincourt dated some time in 1817-19), "behold" reappears and is linked with "solemnly":

> And from my Pillow when the silver Moon
> Shone fair I could behold solemnly near
> The Antechapel. . . .[65]

The parallels between Scott's passage and Wordsworth's drafts are indeed striking. Scott's "organ full and clear" reappears as Wordsworth's "pealing Organ" and offers a reason why Wordsworth included Trinity's organ in the same sentence in which he describes Newton's statue. Also parallel is the emphasis placed on the prism, which gives it equal importance with the expression on the statue's face. That expression, described by Scott as "Absorb'd in thought," implies that Newton is depicted as being silent, and so at least parallels Wordsworth's "with his...silent Face." It is of course only to be expected that each author would describe Newton as standing, but it is worth noting that Wordsworth echoes Scott's "solemn state" in his own "solemnly near," which he introduced in his first revision and held to, almost consistently, up to the penultimate form of the lines. In these same revisions Wordsworth introduced, discarded, and then returned to and kept the phrase "I could behold," which echoes Scott's injunction "Behold!" In fact the entire direction of all the drafts and the final form of these lines (whether the particular phrase is "behold," "see," or "mark") appears to derive from Scott's lines, just as Wordsworth's virtual hymn to Science derived its direction from Akenside's Hymn. In answer to Scott's injunction about Newton's statue (an injunction still "often quoted" in Cambridge) Wordsworth, especially for the benefit of his fellow Cantabrigians, replies, I did behold, precisely there and in the stance described. In other words, as he had done in "Surprised by Joy," he created a semi-private allusion, which would have been beyond the recognition of the general public.

If Wordsworth had acknowledged his use of James Scott's poem, more people would have been able to appreciate fully what he was doing, but such full appreciation by as many readers as possible was evidently not a goal. His attitude and practice concerning acknowledgement of sources ranged widely, and there is no clear reason why, on one occasion, he would choose to acknowledge (as he often did) and why, on another, he would choose not to (which happened more often than the other).[66] The degree to which he made use of other writers' material says something, of course, about the myth of his being entirely original, and the complexity of such use can reach astonishing proportions.[67]

5 Linking Together

WHEN WORDSWORTH CAME TO ADD TO HIS DESCRIPtion of Newton's statue, he drew from at least seven or eight sources and blended his borrowings together into one brief passage of two lines. This achievement marked the culmination of a long development in the art of blending varied borrowings and compacting them into a unified passage of great concentration.

Streams Innumerable

For many years it has been recognized that, in writing "The Solitary Reaper" (which has 32 lines), Wordsworth joined to his own experience in Scotland the reading of an account by Thomas Wilkinson, from which he derived his own last line verbatim.[1] And in 1953 Professor Charles Norton Coe demonstrated that, in all likelihood, Wordsworth also drew from a second description of Scotland, by Robert Heron.[2]

The central thirty lines in the *Prelude* passage describing Wordsworth's climbing of Mt. Snowdon (13:36-65 of the 1805 version) derive from a number of sources in addition to the passage in *Paradise Lost*. Jonathan Wordsworth has shown that, in composing these lines, Wordsworth also drew upon two of his own earlier writings and upon "Kubla Khan" and that, in the composition of those two earlier works of his, three further sources were involved.[3] The "Light upon the turf," which "Fell like a flash" on Mt. Snowdon (lines 39-40), revealing the sea of mist at the climbers' feet, derives from the "pleasant instantaneous light" of "A Night-Piece" (line 6). As in the earlier poem the light "Startles the musing man whose eyes are bent / To earth," so in the Snowdon passage it is preceded by a brightening of the ground at the feet of the meditative Wordsworth.[4] The "huge sea of mist" revealed by the light in the Snowdon passage, and the "hundred hills" whose "dusky backs" are "upheaved / All over this still Ocean" (lines 43-46), derive, not only from *Paradise Lost* as pointed out by W. J. B. Owen,[5] but also from Wordsworth's earlier *Descriptive Sketches*, where

> A mighty waste of mist the valley fills,
> A solemn sea! whose vales and mountains round
> Stand motionless, to awful silence bound.
>   (lines 495-97)

These lines in turn derived from "th' enormous waste of vapour / ... / with mountains now emboss'd" appearing in Stanza 23 of Part 1 of *The Minstrel* by James Beattie.[6] In the midst of Wordsworth's "sea of mist" appears "a blue chasm..., / A deep and gloomy breathing-place" (lines 56-57). In its blueness, depth, and gloominess, this chasm derives from three sources. One, as pointed out by Jonathan Wordsworth, is the "gulf of gloomy blue, that opens wide / And bottomless" in the same passage from *Descriptive Sketches* (lines 498-99).[7] Another, we would suggest, in view of Wordsworth's habit of interchanging great depth with great height, can be found in "A Night-Piece," where the moon is displayed in "a black-blue vault" (lines 10-11), and the third is the work where Wordsworth found that "black-blue vault"—Dorothy's Journal.[8] The phrase characterizing the chasm as a "breathing-place," Jonathan Wordsworth has pointed out, derives from "Kubla Khan," where a "deep romantic chasm" suggests that the earth itself is "breathing" (lines 12, 17-18).[9] Through Wordsworth's chasm ascends "the roar of waters, torrents, streams / Innumerable, roaring with one voice" (lines 57-59). The phrase "streams Innumerable" derives from the "Unnumbered streams" whose roar ascends through the gulf in *Descriptive Sketches* (lines 504-05), and their "one voice" arises, it can be conjectured, from Wordsworth's antithetic response to the claim that James Clarke made, in his *Survey of the Lakes,* that in such a situation the sounds of various waters are heard, each one distinct from the others.[10] Certainly the two lines summing up the scene, "The universal spectacle throughout / Was shaped for admiration and delight" (lines 60-61), are, as Jonathan Wordsworth observes, "quite un-Wordsworthian" and catch the tone exactly of Coleridge's pleasure dome: "It was a miracle of rare device."[11] They also serve to cap the achievement of integrating a remarkable number of sources into a mere thirty lines.

The opening twenty lines of Book 9 of *The Excursion* likewise bear witness to a number of sources. Alerted by the work of S. G. Dunn and Newton P. Stallknecht,[12] we can see Newton and Shaftesbury intermixing repeatedly as sources, both of thought and of expression, for the first fifteen lines. Both thinkers described the "active Principle" Wordsworth discusses, as he indicates how, "removed / From sense and observation, it subsists / In all things, in all natures."[13] About this spirit Shaftesbury said that "no Place is empty, no Void which is not full,"[14] and Wordsworth, using synonyms for varying, described it as knowing "no insulated spot, / No chasm, no solitude." Newton said that God governs, "not as the soul of the world, but as Lord over all,"[15] and Wordsworth echoes, speaking about the spirit and changing the negative to positive: it is "the Soul of all the worlds." When in the next five lines Wordsworth declares that "This is the freedom of the universe," most apparent "in the human Mind," Professor Stallknecht has shown that he paraphrases Jakob Boehme and may also have been influenced by another German thinker, Schelling.[16] Certainly behind the entire passage there can also be seen works which Wordsworth would have memorized. Anchises' speech in the sixth *Aeneid,* about the spirit that sustains all matter, bears directly on the subject, as do sections in Cicero's *De Natura Deorum.*[17] Lines from Thomson's *Spring,* describing God as, although "concealed," he "pervades...the whole" while "water, earth / And air attest his bounty" would probably have come to Wordsworth's mind, as would those lines of Pope's *Essay on Man* which speak of God's being the soul of Nature.[18]

Wordsworth's sonnets could also reflect multiple sources. His "Ecclesiastical Sonnet XVIII. Apology," for instance, derives many of its details, as A. F. Potts has shown, from the Venerable Bede, and parallels, in five of its lines, three passages from Milton, two from *Paradise Lost* and one from *Samson Agonistes.*[19] The Miscellaneous

Sonnet known as "The World Is Too Much With Us" derives from even more varied sources. Line 5 ("This Sea that bares her bosom to the moon") in effect, as John Robert Moore pointed out, combines a number of variations Ossian made on the same image (via Macpherson),[20] and the next two lines, about howling winds up-gathered like flowers in sleep, have an Ossianic flavour as well. The concluding five and a half lines derive in thought, as Douglas Bush has pointed out, from Plato through Proclus as translated by Thomas Taylor, and in expression from one passage in *Paradise Lost,* one in *Comus,* one in *The Faerie Queene,* and three in Spenser's *Colin Clout's come home again.*[21]

Enter William, Solus

But the simple little lyric—so typically Wordsworthian—"I Wandered Lonely As a Cloud" outdoes all these. It seems so straightforward: Wordsworth saw the host of golden daffodils, he enjoyed the sight, and he enjoyed it again in his reveries.

> I wandered lonely as a cloud
> That floats on high o'er vales and hills,
> When all at once I saw a crowd,
> A host, of golden daffodils;
> Beside the lake, beneath the trees, [5]
> Fluttering and dancing in the breeze.
>
> Continuous as the stars that shine
> And twinkle on the milky way,
> They stretched in never-ending line
> Along the margin of a bay: [10]
> Ten thousand saw I at a glance,
> Tossing their heads in sprightly dance.
>
> The waves beside them danced; but they
> Out-did the sparkling waves in glee:
> A poet could not but be gay, [15]
> In such a jocund company:
> I gazed—and gazed—but little thought
> What wealth the show to me had brought:

> For oft, when on my couch I lie
> In vacant or in pensive mood,   [20]
> They flash upon that inward eye
> Which is the bliss of solitude;
> And then my heart with pleasure fills,
> And dances with the daffodils.[22]

Scholars have already discovered a number of sources for the poem and have examined how Wordsworth used them in creating it. Wordsworth began, of course, with his own experience and then, Frederick Garber would argue, added to his experience the philosophical import of flowers dancing in the wind as presented by Sir John Davies in his *Orchestra* and, with regard to the dance image, by Plato in his *Timaeus* and by Milton in three of his passages.[23] For his expression he drew from even more varied sources. From a passage in Dorothy's *Journal* describing the same incident he took and modified these lines in particular (about the daffodils): "the rest tossed and reeled and danced, and seemed as if they verily laughed with the wind, that blew upon them over the lake; they looked so gay, ever glancing, ever changing." Lines 21 and 22 ("They flash upon that inward eye / Which is the bliss of solitude") his wife Mary wrote, *in toto*.[24] The opening line, in view of Wordsworth's frequent borrowing from Ossian, could well have been shaped by the Celtic poet's image "like the shade of a wandering cloud," just as part of the description of the daffodils "fluttering and dancing in the breeze" could well, in view of his frequent borrowings from William Bartram's *Travels*, have been partially shaped by a passage in that work.[25] The metrical shape and rhythm, Hanspeter Schelp has argued, parallel those of Charles Wesley's hymn "When quiet in my house I sit" so closely that one is inclined to see influence.[26] The inclination is strengthened by a remarkable parallel between certain lines. Wesley's line "Oft as I lay me down to rest" appears parallelled by Wordsworth's "For oft, when on my couch I lie," and each of these lines is in close conjunction with another two which also appear to parallel one another. Wesley wrote about the result of converse with the Lord:

> So shall my heart His presence prove,
> And burn with everlasting love.

Wordsworth wrote about the result of converse with the daffodils:

> And then my heart with pleasure fills,
> And dances with the daffodils.

Certain difficulties remain, however, with some of the scholarly findings. Frederick Garber, for instance, argues for reading the dance in the poem as "a marriage dance, celebrating the nuptials of earth and sky."[27] But it is far from clear that we are invited to see only two elements in the poem, earth and sky. Instead, four are discernible, even in the first and incomplete version of 1807, which did not have the present second stanza. Land is represented by the daffodils growing beneath the trees; water is present in the lake, whose waves figure prominently in the dance; air is present in the breeze; and the cloud in the 1807 version could have represented the sky. (Certainly in the 1815 version the cloud is closer to representing the air, and the stars clearly make the sky fully present.) Furthermore, as Garber remarks, Plato's image of the dance, appearing in *Timaeus* 40 C-D, is confined to the heavenly bodies. Milton, he notes, had extended the dance downwards (in *Comus*) to the seas (and to tipsy revellers).[28] But here, in Wordsworth's poem, the dance is extended further yet, to all the elements (the air dances in the movement of the breeze) and to the heart of the human observer. Plato's image also, it should be noted, is involved and prosaic:

> "But the choric dances of these same stars and their crossings one of another, and the relative reversals and progressions of their orbits, and which of the gods meet in their conjunctions, and how many are in opposition, and behind which and at what times they severally pass before one another and are hidden from our view, and again reappearing send upon men unable to calculate alarming portents of the things which shall come to pass hereafter,—to describe all this without an inspection of models of these movements would be labour in vain."[29]

There is a much more forthright and poetic passage which is more likely to have served as a stimulus to Wordsworth. It is the poem "Wings," written about 300 BCE by Simmias Rhodius, which presents Heavenly Love as speaking:

> *I'm not that Wanton Boy,*
> *The Sea-froath Goddess's only Joy.*
> *Pure Heavenly Love I hight, and my*
> *Soft Magick Charms, not Iron Bands, fast tye*
> *Heaven, Earth and Seas. The Gods themselves do readily*
> *Stoop to my Laws. The whole World daunces to my Harmony.*

This poem (the translation quoted and the Greek original) appeared on page 122 of Ralph Cudworth's massive study *The True Intellectual System of the Universe*, which was recommended reading at Cambridge and a copy of which Wordsworth himself owned; so the poem could readily have come to his attention at any time over a number of years.[30]

Another ancient writer, known in Wordsworth's day as Philo Judaeus, offered, in his treatise on the creation of the world, a number of passages which provide a still closer parallel to many aspects of Wordsworth's poem. Philo said, for instance, that "man is at home" in all four elements: "land and water and air and sky." With each of these elements dance is closely associated, as it is with the human observer also.[31] More importantly, the basic situations in both writers run parallel. With Wordsworth, the speaker, wandering alone, comes all at once upon a very great number of daffodils dancing. They outdo their neighbouring waves in their dancing, and as a result the speaker's heart is prompted to dance with them. With Philo, in answering the question why God created man last of all, the author compares God to the perfect host who, before inviting a guest, will prepare fully for a twofold entertainment: a banquet and a theatrical performance by contending athletes. He prepares an abundance and a plenitude of things for enjoyment, so that when man, living alone, enters on the scene, he should at once light upon a lavish spectacle complete with movement and dance worthy of admiration. As a result of experiences like this, God's guest, man, is able to join in the dance.[32]

There is a slight problem with Philo, inasmuch as no mention is made of him in any of Wordsworth's poems, in any of his notes to his poems, or in any of his extant letters. Nor is any book of Philo's included in the sales catalogue of Wordsworth's library. But undoubtedly Wordsworth would have had many opportunities and promptings to become acquainted with the writings of the Hellenistic Alexandrian: Cambridge was a centre, in Wordsworth's day, for the study of Philo, and there was considerable scholarly publication on him.[33] The real test, however, of whether Wordsworth would have read him is the extent and closeness of the parallel between their works, and we trust that, as we proceed in our examination, our readers will agree that Wordsworth must, in fact, have read Philo and have used him—in the form most readily available to him, the edition prepared by Thomas Mangey, in which the Greek text is matched in parallel columns with Mangey's translation in Latin.[34]

Intellectual Daffodils

As we work our way through the parallel between Wordsworth's poem and passages in Philo's treatise, it will appear more and more likely that Wordsworth's poem resulted, not so much from his personal experience in seeing the daffodils, even when that experience was reinforced by Dorothy's account of it in her journal, as from the parallel which Wordsworth saw between his personal experience and what Philo said in his treatise. More specifically, the parallel he saw allowed him to regard and to present his encounter with the daffodils as a particular and personal illustration of the overflowing generosity with which God entertains his invited guest, man.

Not surprisingly, Wordsworth often borrowed from Philo's phrasing as well as his ideas. One example can be seen in the way in which the four elements are characterized. It need not, of course, be anything more than coincidence that both writers describe the human being moving about on the ground, but the way of presenting that person's relation to the air is striking. Philo remarks that insofar as man's body ascends and is raised aloft from the earth, he would justly be said to be "a traverser in the air" (ἀεροπόρον) or, as Mangey translated it, "an inhabitant of the air" *(aëricola)*.[35] Wordsworth, in turn, "wandered...as a cloud / That floats on high" (lines 1-2). Less striking, but still noteworthy, is the parallel in the description of the stars inhabiting the sky. Philo refers to both the fixed stars and the wandering stars. Mangey translated Philo's πλανήτων ("wandering") as *erraticarum*, which means, not only "wandering," but also "erratic." If one were to express "fixed" and "erratic" in terms of emitting light, what words would one use but those which Wordsworth used: "the stars that shine / And twinkle" (lines 7-8)?

To see a parallel in the way the two writers describe water requires a more detailed argument. In order to show how much at home man is in the water, Philo offers a number of aquatic activities, one of which is fishing for "purple-fish." The word for "purple-fish" (πορφυρεῖς) is the same word for the purple dye obtained from the fish. Wordsworth described the waves as "sparkling"—which, admittedly, has no immediately apparent connexion with "purple," but one will emerge before long. It is almost certain that the waves he saw beside the daffodils he encountered were, in fact, *not* sparkling. It has, of course, long been realized that, at the time of the encounter, Wordsworth was, in fact, not "lonely"—Dorothy, whom he referred to as his eyes and ears, was with him. Nor was the wind a mere breeze. Dorothy described it as "furious," and because of it the two had to stop many times. The day, according to Dorothy, started out "threatening," the wind blew furiously all the time, and shortly after they saw the daffodils, the rain came on.[36] So it is altogether likely that, when they saw the daffodils, there was no sunlight showing, to make the waves sparkle. It would appear, consequently, that in all three details—the being "lonely," the wind being but a breeze, and the sparkling of the waves—Wordsworth was not attempting to represent what he had actually observed, but rather was incorporating literary elements for a purpose other than literal reporting. "Purple," he would know well, had been used throughout much of the eighteenth century (and earlier) to mean "brilliant" (instead of the colour we now associate with the word)—witness Ariel's "purple pinions" and Dryden's couplet "White Lillies in full Canisters they bring, / With all the Glories of the Purple Spring."[37] So "sparkling," clearly at odds with the physical fact he had observed, would serve as a synonym for the "purple" Philo had used, a synonym that also emphasized the vitality of the dancing waves.

Many of the details concerning the daffodils themselves appear to be drawn from Philo's passages. As already mentioned, there is a close match between the guest's lighting upon the entertainment "at once" and Wordsworth's coming upon the daffodils "all at once" (line 3). The word Philo used, εὐθύς, means "straightway, immediately, at once," and the Latin word Mangey used, *continuo*, means the same things, but it also means "without interruption, continuously," which leads, of course, to Wordsworth's description of the daffodils as "Continuous" and stretching "in never-ending line" (lines 7 and 9).[38] It is interesting to note that in his manuscript Wordsworth began the new second stanza by writing "As numerous as the stars." He then tried "Close crowding, like the stars" and changed that to "Close crowded, like the stars." His settling then on "Continuous" is at least consonant with his having paused and recalled to mind the source on which he had drawn when first writing the poem and so become aware of the double duty to which Mangey's *continuo* could serve.[39] The number of things for enjoyment provided beforehand by God for his guest is described by Philo as "an abundance and a plenitude," which pair of synonyms is matched by Wordsworth's monosyllabic pair "a crowd, / A host" (lines 3-4).[40] These English words, in fact, are both translations of the word πλῆθος, which Philo uses a few lines later. The configuration of the daffodils Dorothy described as "a long belt... about the breadth of a country turnpike road." Philo described the elements of the spectacular display as being "in an order" (ἐν τάξεσιν); Mangey translated this as *ordine*, which can mean, not only "in an order," but also "in a line"; and Wordsworth's daffodils "stretched in never-ending line" (line 9).[41] The relationship between the daffodils and the neighbouring waves Dorothy was really unconcerned with; she simply said that the "wind blew directly over the lake to them," and the only mention she makes specifically of the waves is to the effect that she and William "heard [them] at different distances." Philo, on the other hand, refers twice to the athletes as contending with one another, once in the phrase "gymnastic contest" and the other time in the phrase "a crowd of contenders."[42] Wordsworth says that the dancing daffodils "Out-did the sparkling waves" (line 14).

Other key words in the third stanza also appear to derive from Philo. The banquet or entertainment to which man is invited—συμπόσιον with Philo—Mangey translated as *convivium*: since both these words were also used for the company assembled for a banquet or an entertainment, it is not surprising to see Wordsworth using the word "company" to describe the waves and the dancing daffodils, and the epithet "jocund" used with it of course accords with the conviviality derived from *convivium* (line 16).[43] The word which Philo uses to describe the magnificent display which the invited guest looks upon is θεαμάτων, which Mangey translates as *spectacula*: both words mean "performances, especially of combatants, devised for entertainment," "theatrical spectacles," or, more simply, "shows," which is of course the word which the English poet uses to describe the display put on by the daffodils (line 18).[44] In gazing on the show, Wordsworth acquired considerable benefit. His "gazed—and gazed" (line 17) reflects the word θεωρία used by Philo, for that means "the beholding or the viewing."[45] The "show" and Wordsworth's gazing on it brought him "wealth" (line 18): with this phrase Wordsworth does not translate a particular word in the Greek or Latin, but instead he summarizes the account which Philo gives when he says that, as a result of beholding the divine display, man's mind develops a love and longing for the knowledge of heavenly things, and from this longing arises philosophy, by which, in turn, "man, mortal though he be, is rendered immortal."[46]

How the ascent into immortality takes place, Philo has explained a few lines earlier. As the mind examines its homes in the various elements, one after another and climbing higher each time, it finally joins in the dance of the heavenly bodies, and then, "carrying its gaze beyond the confines of all substance discernible by sense, it comes to a point at which it reaches out after the intelligible world."[47] What Philo calls "intelligible" others have called "intellectual," or "noumenal," or "spiritual"—all words indicating a kind of reality apart from the physical reality. This kind of language would not be foreign to Wordsworth, for in *The Prelude* he used "intellectual" with the meaning "spiritual," and his comment, in "Tintern Abbey," about the weight of "all this unintelligible world" appears to be an ironic play on Philo's phrase.[48] For Philo in the passage we are concerned with, one approaches the nonphysical through the physical until, at a certain point, the mind leaves the physical and comes into contact with the nonphysical, the intellectual, the "intelligible."

Is there anything of this thought in Wordsworth's poem on the daffodils? Yes, at various points in the fourth stanza. The "vacant" used to describe the mood (line 20) can, of course, mean all kinds of ludicrous things, but if it is to have a meaning that is in accord with what has been described in the other three stanzas, it will have to be the one presented thus by the *Oxford English Dictionary* as referring to the mind: "Abstracted from (the body, etc.) in contemplation or reverie." The most helpful illustration is drawn from a paragraph by the Cambridge Platonist Henry More which elaborates, in a paraphrastic manner, on verse 10 of chapter 1 of the Book of Revelation. This reads, in large part: "...*I was in the spirit on the Lords day*, actuated and impressed upon in my inward man, my mind being vacant from this earthly body, and external senses, and wholly seised by this Divine or Angelical Power...: *And* when I was thus in the Spirit, and had as it were left the body in this ecstasie, *I heard behind me a great voice as a Trumpet.*"[49] More's thought certainly parallels Philo's, and his phrase "inward man" comes close to Wordsworth's "inward eye" (line 21), which in turn parallels Philo's thought, for Philo indicated that the mind or intellect is to the soul what the physical eye is to the body: as the physical eye perceives things of sense (physical reality), so the intellect perceives things beyond sense (the nonphysical reality). In fact the word "vacant" appears to be a one-word synonym for the phrase, already quoted, in which Philo said that the mind, "carrying its gaze beyond the confines of all substance discernible by sense," reaches out after the intelligible world.[50] In other words, it would appear that, in order to express one of Philo's thoughts, Wordsworth turned to still another author for the phrase that would serve best.

Certainly in arriving at the "inward eye" (another manifestation of the nonphysical), it would appear that Wordsworth took the thought of Philo and searched his memory (perhaps with the assistance of Mary) for a phrase from some other writer to express it. His search for "identity of thought" could easily have taken him to the context which Ralph Cudworth provided for his quoting of the "Wings" poem by Simmias Rhodius.[51] There Cudworth remarked that the Love which Simmias described was "Intellectual Love" and was equatable with God, and that phrase in turn could easily have taken Wordsworth to two poems by Spenser, his "Hymn of Heavenly Love" and his "Hymn of Heavenly Beauty." In the latter of these he would then have found precisely the phrase he used. Those beings, Spenser says, who have perceived Heavenly Beauty can delight in "nought else" but "that felicitie, / Which they haue written in their inward ey."[52]

Matching the "vacant" in describing the kind of mood in which the "inward eye" perceives reality of the nonphysical kind, is the epithet "pensive," and again it appears that Wordsworth, in order to find a phrase to express Philo's thought, has gone to another author, this time the English author from whom he draws the most. Fitting perfectly the context of perceiving reality while the mind is out of the body, is the address Milton makes to Melancholy in *Il Penseroso*: "Com pensive Nun, devout and pure, /... / Thy rapt soul sitting in thine eyes"—with "rapt" referring to the same state as More's "ecstasie" and "vacant" referred to.[53] Actually it would appear, on reexamination, that Wordsworth announced a series of borrowings from Milton in his opening lines, for, as the hero of *Il Penseroso* said "I walk unseen / On the...Green" and then "Oft on a Plat of rising ground," so Wordsworth says, "I wandered lonely...o'er vales and hills." Wordsworth's description of the daffodils as "dancing in the breeze" (line 6) has parallels, not only in *Il Penseroso*, where the "rocking Winds are Piping loud," but also in the companion poem *L'Allegro*, where "The frolick Wind...breathes the Spring," and where "many a youth, and many a maid" are "Dancing in the Chequer'd shade." This company of dancers perform while "the jocond rebecks sound," offering still another parallel. Two further allusions can be seen: the otherwise unnecessary mention specifically of a poet (line 15) alludes to "Such sights as youthful Poets dream" in *L'Allegro*, and the emphasis on "gazed" (line 17) parallels, at least, the description "Streit mine eye hath caught new pleasures," also in *L'Allegro*. Wordsworth evidently combines allusions to both the companion poems and thereby suggests that, just as *L'Allegro* leads to *Il Penseroso* and the pursuits of the one lead to the pursuits of the other, so too does his physical encounter with the daffodils lead to the ecstatic contact with a reality beyond the physical.[54]

An English Corybant

Obviously a considerable gap is opening between the public reading of "I Wandered Lonely As a Cloud" and the private one which emerges when allusions to various writers are seen to be at work in the poem. The gap is at its largest in the last stanza, and is perhaps best illustrated in the opening of that stanza. The public reading would picture Wordsworth stretched out on his couch, indulging in reverie, in the midst of which there would flash upon his mental (but physical) screen a remembered picture of the daffodils, and as a result he would experience pleasure, probably much the same kind of pleasure as he experienced when he first saw them. Hartley's associationism is obviously at work: both the sight and the accompanying pleasure enter Wordsworth's memory, and when the sight is recalled, the accompanying pleasure re-emerges with it. But when "vacant" and "pensive" are read as indicating that the mind has left the body, and when the "inward eye" is read as perceiving a nonphysical reality, one is left wondering about the couch. Again the kind of parallel which Wordsworth would have noticed between his own experience and what he read in Philo would account for the phrasing. Certainly Wordsworth would relax on his couch and think back to his original encounter with the daffodils, and as he did so, he would remember that he had seen a parallel between that encounter and the encounter Philo described in which God's invited guest appears at the banquet He has prepared for him. And how were guests at a Hellenistic banquet arranged? They lay on couches and helped themselves to the viands provided. How appropriate, then, that when Wordsworth prepared to re-experience the intellectual banquet he had first encountered beside the lake, he should recline upon a couch. There, as with Philo's invited guest of God, Wordsworth, in contemplating his remembered daffodils, would again proceed from them, in his perception, to the nonphysical reality beyond.

The resulting pleasure which fills his heart reflects the pleasure which the hero of *Il Penseroso* experiences when he says that his perceptions "Dissolve me into extasies, / And bring all Heav'n before mine eyes." Philo expressed much the same idea when he said that the sight of the solar dance "produced in his soul ineffable delight and pleasure." That pair of words of course finds its parallel in the "bliss" and "pleasure" of Wordsworth's poem (lines 22 and 23). The concluding lines to Spenser's "Hymne of Heavenly Love" also parallel the thought and may possibly have contributed its "fill":

> all thy spirits shall fill
> With sweete enragement of celestiall loue,
> Kindled through sight of those faire things aboue.[55]

It is noteworthy that, although all his models speak of soul or spirit, Wordsworth, being a man of his period, held to his "heart" as that part of him which filled with pleasure—just as he insisted, in "Tintern Abbey," on saying that his sensations are "felt along the heart." The "celestial love" Spenser referred to, and the divine love which Cudworth saw in the poem of Simmias, together provide the reason for the dance in Wordsworth's poem. He describes the daffodils and waves as dancing, he implies that the stars are dancing ("twinkle"), and perhaps he implies that the cloud likewise is dancing as it floats; and, most importantly, his heart dances. But nowhere does he explicitly say why the daffodils are dancing, or why the waves are dancing. Nowhere does he mention divine love, let alone the name of God. It is, however, not surprising that in 1804 he would avoid using the name of God, since in 1798, in "Tintern Abbey," although clearly referring to the deity, the closest he came to a name was "something far more deeply interfused." As for the reason for the dance, he may well have felt that, since his presentation of the nonphysical reality in the poem was indirect and implicit, operating through allusions to other writers' works, he could present the reason for the dance in the same way. After all, Milton had written in *Il Penseroso*, "Where more is meant then meets the ear."[56]

Information about the kind of dance is provided in Philo's treatise, and Wordsworth may well have alluded to it there, privately. The soul, rising in contemplation (Philo says), "is whirled round with the dances of planets and fixed stars..., following that love of wisdom which guides its steps." (It is the sage who is caught up in the celestial dance.) When the soul, Philo continues, descries the patterns and ideas of things which sense reflects, then "it is seized by a sober intoxication, like those filled with Corybantic frenzy." Translated into the terms Wordsworth has been alluding to, especially in the final stanza, this means that the sage, on seeing the nonphysical reality behind and beyond the physical, is in a state of ecstasy, in which his soul dances with the kind of divine inspiration ascribed to the priests of Cybele. And why he is able to dance with the daffodils, specifically, is also explained by Philo, and probably alluded to. While man (without woman) was still leading "a life of solitude," God planted a park for him in which all the plants were endowed with soul or reason.[57] There is the explanation: the One Life. Recognizing the One Life, nonphysical as well as physical, in all parts of creation, Wordsworth's heart responded by joining in the dance by which all parts of creation celebrated what the bountiful Creator had done for them. No wonder his concluding lines echo the rhythm of Wesley's hymn, and no wonder also that in his manuscript he should have spelled the kind of dance in which the daffodils tossed their heads as "spritely," for the basic meaning of "sprite" is, of course, "spirit."[58]

Wordsworth's use of Philo allows the dance to be read as an image of the One Life, as Frederick Garber reads it, and Wordsworth's use of Philo allows the daffodils to become transfigured, as Frederick A. Pottle sees them. They remain, as he remarks, the physical daffodils, while at the same time serving as symbols for Hartleian theopathy, the exultant response to the loving kindness of the Creator.[59] "I Wandered Lonely As a Cloud" is a poem about science, about natural philosophy, about the way in which the universe functions and the way in which it is perceived. Through it Wordsworth presents his comments on science in such a way as to elevate the mind to God.

The poem has two levels of meaning, public and private, and

Wordsworth was evidently quite content for there to be two and for them to be radically different. The private meaning—which Wordsworth and his close associates would be aware of—derived from the allusions he made to many other writers and from the way in which he interwove his numerous borrowings from them. It was not for nothing, after all, that he had remarked in the Preface of 1802, "Poems to which any value can be attached, were never produced on any variety of subjects but by a man, who being possessed of more than usual organic sensibility, had also thought long and deeply." Some of the more important sources from which he borrowed—and which he interwove—were prose, and again it was not for nothing that he had remarked, "some of the most interesting parts of the best poems will be found to be strictly the language of prose, when prose is well written." A major reason why much of the private meaning has not been detected before this is that much of the poem is understated, and again it is not for nothing that Wordsworth indicated, in the same Preface, that he sought to counteract the "outrageous stimulation" he found in contemporary literature.[60]

In a note appended to the 1815 version of "I Wandered Lonely As a Cloud," Wordsworth said, "The subject of these Stanzas is rather an elementary feeling and simple impression (approaching to the nature of an ocular spectrum) upon the imaginative faculty, than an *exertion* of it."[61] The word "spectrum" in Wordsworth's day had two or three meanings which are not current with us but which appear to be operative in Wordsworth's sentence. Having recently come into currency, according to the *Oxford English Dictionary*, was the meaning "an image retained for a time on the retina of the eye when it had turned away after gazing fixedly for some time at a brightly coloured object" (the implication for the physical meaning of Wordsworth's "gazed—and gazed" is obvious), and a submeaning included the seeing, in that after-image, of colours complementary to those seen when looking at the object. Since Wordsworth said that the impression he experienced "approached to the nature of an ocular spectrum," it would appear that he meant that the image appearing on the physical screen inside his brain when he remembered the original incident reproduced the original sight but in an enhanced way: all discomfort had vanished and the gale had become a breeze; the sun had come out and made the waves sparkle. When this refurbished and enhanced image appeared on his mental screen, his heart filled with a pleasure closely akin to the pleasure he had felt on first viewing the daffodils—a situation that would be almost parallel to what he described happening when he recollected emotion in tranquillity: "an emotion, kindred to that which was before the subject of contemplation, is gradually produced, and does itself actually exist in the mind."[62] This, then, was the public meaning of his note.

At the same time, the primary meaning of "spectrum" continued current: "apparition or phantom; a spectre." Since "spectre" is "a visible, incorporeal spirit," it would appear that Wordsworth was also alluding, privately, to the fact that, when the image of the daffodils recurred in his mind, since he had superimposed on them the dancing contestants of Philo's treatise, what he perceived was the almost visible spirits of those daffodils as they danced for the benefit of God's guest; as a very understandable result, his heart then filled with pleasure and joined in that dance. Such a reading accords with the use of "spritely" to describe the dance of the daffodils and with Wordsworth's comments, recorded in the Isabella Fenwick note on the Intimations Ode, about "immaterial nature" and the falling away and vanishing (he had experienced) of outward things, leaving, presumably, the nonphysical open to the inward eye.[63] This, then, would be the private meaning of his note, and so the two levels of meaning present in the poem itself were thus extended into the note on it—spectrally.

Wordsworth was not always so private about his use of sources, especially multiple sources, for the ultimate (and amusing) extension of the practice appeared in a poem Wordsworth published in 1835. It was a cento he had made entirely from passages in poems of other authors: "a fine stanza of Akenside, connected with a still finer from Beattie, by a couplet of Thomson."[64] It illustrated, Wordsworth explained, the "practice, in which [he] sometimes indulges, of linking together, in his own mind, favourite passages from different authors."

6 Strange Seas

When, in his 69th year, Wordsworth came to review and revise that part of the *Prelude* manuscript which described Newton's statue, he probably felt a number of promptings that encouraged him to add to that description.[1] One was, no doubt, his remembering the gentle chiding he had received from his scientist friend William Rowan Hamilton, for having presented an erroneous picture of science to his readers. Another would have been his desire to serve God. All study, Wordsworth was convinced at this stage in his life, should be for the honour of God. Speaking at the laying of the foundation stone for the new elementary school in Bowness, Windermere, for instance, Wordsworth insisted that even elementary instruction in grammar, writing, and reading should be "for *the honour of God*."[2] Education thus became, "not for time but for eternity." In his own writing, then, he would be anxious to take advantage of any legitimate opportunity for elevating the mind to God, and the opportunity to remind his readers, in a striking way, that this is precisely what the national hero, Newton, had done would be too good to pass by. There may even have been the matter of kinship at work. As he read his original five lines, he could well have felt that he could do better by way of honouring the memory of the man with whom he had felt such a close kinship. Possibly his having been yoked, by Haydon, in his painting, with Newton and Voltaire had something to do with his decision, also, for Voltaire had honoured Newton in verse, and, if the French sceptic could do that, why should not the English believer do at least as much—and do it better?[3]

Patterns

Whatever nonartistic promptings he may have felt, there were probably two artistic ones, at least, which moved him to add to the original five lines.

One is the pattern that can be seen in the immediate context for the lines on Newton's statue. At first sight the verse paragraph which ends with the description of the statue appears to contain a passing strange mixture of things. Wordsworth begins the paragraph with domestic trivia:

> The Evangelist St. John my Patron was;
> Three gothic Courts are his, & in the first
> Was my abiding-place, a nook obscure;
> Right underneath the College kitchens made
> A humming sound less tuneable than bees
> But hardly less industrious; with shrill notes
> Of sharp command & scolding intermixed.
>
> (3:46-52)[4]

Wordsworth then turns to the neighbouring Trinity College and says,

> Near me hung Trinity's loquacious Clock
> Who never let the quarters, night or day,
> Slip by him unproclaimed, & told the hours
> Twice over with a male & female voice.
>
> (3:53-56)

Then comes the passage quoted at the beginning of this study, concerning the organ and the statue:

> Her pealing organ was my neighbour too,
> And from my pillow looking forth by light
> Of moon or favoring stars, I could behold

> The Antichapel where the Statue stood
> Of Newton with his prism, & silent face,
> The marble index of a Mind for ever
> Voyaging thro' strange seas of Thought, alone.
>
> (3:57-63)

At first there may appear to be a simple contrast between the description of St. John's College and that of Trinity, but actually the pattern is more complex, and more significant. The lines describing the clock illustrate. On first reading they appear to record, ruefully, the interfering noisiness of Trinity's clock (like St. John's kitchen) in insisting on noting every quarter hour, day and night, regardless of whether a person wished to sleep, and then announcing the hours, not simply once, but twice over, with different "voices." In temporary revisions Wordsworth made to these lines, in what de Selincourt refers to as MSS. A^2, A^3, and B^2, there is evidence to support the first part of this interpretation, for there Wordsworth described the clock as a monitor "importunately" or "superfluously" strict.[5] But Wordsworth's description of the clock's double tone as "a male & female voice" must give pause, as must his proceeding, without any indication of a change in direction, to the "pealing organ" with its connotations of beauty and delight.

Wordsworth had a peculiar view of machinery, and what he says in *The Excursion* about a piece of machinery (a water mill), ostensibly much grander than a clock, may provide a gloss to the description of the clock. In Book Eight the Wanderer says that, regardless of certain grave disadvantages,

>   yet do I exult,
> Casting reserve away, exult to see
> An intellectual mastery exercised
> O'er the blind elements; a purpose given,
> A perseverance fed; almost a soul
> Imparted—to brute matter.[6]

What is "almost a soul" appears to be reflected in "a male & female voice" and at least helps to account for the shift in tone from the loquacity of the clock to the pealing of the organ. For Wordsworth that organ would have had connotations of both Milton and Dryden, the one a graduate of Christ's, the other of Trinity. Milton's hero, in *Il*

Penseroso, sought out (as we have seen) "the studious cloysters pale," there to "let the pealing Organ blow"

> As may with sweetness, through mine ear,
> Dissolve me into extasies,
> And bring all Heav'n before mine eyes.[7]

And Dryden's "bright *CECILIA*," in his poem "A Song for St. Cecilia's Day, 1687,"

> rais'd the wonder high'r;
> When to her ORGAN, vocal Breath was giv'n,
> An Angel heard, and straight appear'd
> Mistaking Earth for Heaven.[8]

No wonder Wordsworth was able to proceed, in the same sentence, from Trinity's pealing organ to the statue of Newton gazing into the heavens, an index of his mind "Voyaging thro' strange seas of Thought."

In fact there is, throughout the entire verse paragraph, a pattern of ascension. It starts in the darkness, the confusion, and the shrillness of St. John's Gothic courts, and it proceeds, in the degree of order, harmony, and presence of soul, through the clock, the organ, and the statue of Newton to the mind of Newton and to what that mind contemplates. Without the last two lines of the revised description of the statue, however, there would be no mention of mind and no mention of what that mind contemplates: the pattern, in other words, would not have been complete. We would suggest that, when he came to reread his original verse paragraph, Wordsworth would have recognized the incompleteness and would have sought to supply what was missing.

It should be noted, almost parenthetically, that this pattern of ascension and the place in it which Newton's mind enjoys (immediately next to the highest) both provide added reason why Wordsworth, in the later passage in Book Three, should have chosen to refer to Newton's "own Self" as "etherial." In its amazing penetration, Newton's mind, in effect, stood right next to "the power of nature," indeed next to "the immediate hand of the Creator" himself (to use Newton's own words), as these shaped, out of ether, "the whole frame" of creation. Traditionally this particular shaping power, whether of God or of nature, has been referred to as spiritual. Hence again it is only appropriate that Wordsworth, in the passage describing Newton's self as "etherial," should present him as the pre-eminent exemplar of the "spiritual men" who preceded the poet to Cambridge. These epithets, in their stressing some kind of spirituality, of course support our seeing Newton's being alluded to implicitly in the Arabian dream passage about soul being wedded to soul in purest bond of reason. But they also suggest that there is probably something specifically spiritual present in the description of Newton's statue as well. And this has to do with another pattern.

Edward A. Armstrong, in his study entitled *Shakespeare's Imagination*, has pointed to an image cluster recurring in Wordsworth's poetry similar to those found in Shakespeare's poetry, and he has further suggested that the appearance of nakedness and sunlight, water and bathing, in one occurrence of Wordsworth's cluster throws some light on their meaning when they appear in another.[9] In a somewhat similar way we turn for illumination to other passages in Wordsworth's poetry, where a pattern of elements can be found similar to that in the Newton passage.

These elements are seven in number: solitariness ("alone" in the Newton passage), quiet or silence (the "silent face"), stars ("by light / Of moon or favoring stars"), height or its counterpart, depth (the implicit elevation of both the stars and the statue above the observer, and the implicit depth of the "strange seas of Thought"), eternity ("for ever"), an exceptional perceiver (which Newton clearly is), and what is perceived (here represented by the "strange seas of Thought").

In each of (at least) five other major passages in Wordsworth's poetry the same cluster of seven elements appears. These passages are the description of "the hidden nook" in *The Excursion* (3:50-112); the description, in early drafts of what was to become Book One of *The Excursion*, of the influences at work on the pedlar (1:202-59); the passage in Book One of *The Prelude* beginning "Fair seed-time had my soul" (1:301-475); the whole of the Intimations Ode; and the whole of "Lines Composed a Few Miles above Tintern Abbey."[10] Each of these passages is discussed in detail in an appendix; here we would simply draw two conclusions.[11] Without the final two lines, the passage on Newton's statue would leave implicit at best the solitariness of Newton and his status as an exceptional perceiver, and it would lack altogether the sense of eternity and any indication of what it was that Newton perceived. In other words, we would suggest, as before, that Wordsworth, on rereading the original five lines, would have recognized that the pattern was incomplete. Having become accustomed to grouping the seven elements together, he would have felt the absence of those missing and would have realized the need to complete what he had to say about Newton by including those elements that had hitherto been absent.

The other conclusion relates to the nature of one of those elements. In the other five passages we have cited, it is clear that what the exceptional perceiver perceived was a spiritual power virtually indistinguishable from the creating and sustaining power of God. When the same cluster appears in the sixth passage, the description of Newton's statue, is it not likely, then, that what is perceived is the same almighty power? When Newton is presented, through his high-placed statue, as alone in the presence of the moon and stars, as for ever gazing upwards with his silent face while his Mind voyages through strange seas of Thought, are the chances not rather great that, for Wordsworth at least, what Newton perceived on those strange seas of Thought was that ineffable power which "impels / All thinking things, all objects of all thought, / And rolls through all things"?

Those chances are made even greater by the implication, again for Wordsworth at least, of certain specific words in the Newton passage as seen in the light, not only of the clusters just examined, but also of Wordsworth's practice elsewhere. As John Jones has pointed out, Wordsworth's heroes—the perceptive ones at least—are invariably solitary.[12] As Herbert Lindenberger has suggested, the solitaries include not only the soldier, the leech-gatherer, and Lucy, but also Wordsworth's intimates—Michel Beaupuy, Dorothy, and Coleridge—and those he admired, such as William Taylor, his schoolmaster, and John Milton, the speaker of truth.[13] As A. C. Bradley has observed, "What is lonely is a spirit. To call a thing lonely or solitary is, with [Wordsworth], to say that it opens a bright or solemn vista into infinity."[14] Consequently when Wordsworth presents Newton as voyaging "alone," one knows, paradoxically, what company he is in.

Similarly with the word "silent." In view of the virtual gloss provided by the other five lengthy passages, it would seem likely that, in ascribing to Newton's statue a "silent face," Wordsworth implied that the statue represents Newton standing in the presence of a supernatural power and that, having been made silent by the power of harmony, Newton was absorbed in meditating upon the eternal deep. Observations offered by R. D. Havens about Wordsworth's practice elsewhere would appear to support this reading: Havens cites many passages in which silence connotes a proximity to the divine, and of these the "grave and steady joy" experienced by the star-gazers is for us especially apropos, since this joy felt by the amateur Newtons is "not of this noisy world, but silent and divine."[15] Havens concludes: "To Wordsworth silence was a Power; it partook of the nature of the permanent; in a world of flux it belonged with those eternal things wherein only we can find the joy and rest for which we were created."[16]

In the light of these meanings implicit in "silent" and "alone," it would appear only reasonable to conclude that the way "strange" is used in the *Excursion* passage and in the "fair seed-time" passage (from Book One of *The Prelude*) provides a further gloss to its use in the Newton passage. Just as the "loud dry wind" blew through the young Wordsworth's ears with "strange utterance" *(P(1850)* 1:337-38) as it impregnated perception of the divine, and just as the rocks and stones of the hidden nook "bear / A semblance strange of power intelligent" *(Excursion* 3:82-83), so the "strange seas of Thought" through which Newton voyages have much to do with that divine intelligence. Not surprisingly, then, since those "seas of Thought" bear witness to the Almighty's creativity, Newton will have to voyage "for ever" as he meditates upon the eternal deep.[17]

Further illumination is cast on the inherent meaning of the Newton passage by certain specific things said in the parallel passages already cited and in other related passages. We have implied that there is a great deal of understatement in the Newton passage, as that philosopher's gazings into the innermost recesses of God's creating mind are conveyed through such simple phrases as "silent," "alone," and "strange seas of Thought." A parallel example is found, of course, in "Tintern Abbey," where Wordsworth substitutes for the word "God," or any of his usual titles, the equally understated phrases "presence," "something...interfused," and "a motion and a spirit" (lines 94-102). Another parallel instance of understatement occurs in the fourth book of *The Prelude* where Wordsworth describes how he was plucked from the pursuit of social gaiety and in "one particular hour" transformed into Nature's lifelong devoted celebrant, and expresses that transformation in these simple words:

> I made no vows, but vows
> Were then made for me; bond unknown to me
> Was given, that I should be, else sinning greatly,
> A dedicated Spirit. On I walked
> In thankful blessedness which yet survives.
>
> (4:334-38)[18]

Corpus

As Wordsworth set about the task of completing the lines on Newton's statue, he would undoubtedly have called to mind parts of the corpus of poetic tribute to Newton that were not nearly so understated.

It would, of course, have been only natural for him to recall the poem he had borrowed from in writing the initial five lines, and James Scott's Ode could have offered Wordsworth some material for his enlargement of the description. From Scott's lines introducing the principal description, the word "sage" may have helped Wordsworth to his "Thought," and the idea of "through ev'ry age" could have reappeared in Wordsworth's "for ever." From the description itself the "wonders of the sky" and the "chambers of the sun" could have helped to account for the significant strangeness of the "strange seas of Thought." In lines closely following his description, Scott addressed Newton—"Hail, mighty mind! Hail, awful name!"—and asked Science, "bright ethereal guest," to come and lead him "Through *Wisdom's* arduous paths, to fair renown!" Here, certainly, are further thoughts that could be reflected in Wordsworth's concluding lines. But perhaps the most important influence Scott could have exerted in 1839 was the example of his image about the eagle. Scott, in describing Newton's flight through the heavens, was reworking material that had already been worked over several times before— just as Wordsworth was in turn to set about reworking it. What Scott achieved provided an object lesson: he took an image, albeit initially trite, and elaborated it in such a way as to revivify material that would otherwise have remained old and tired. He made Newton's flight that of an eagle:

> When, taught on eagle-wings to fly,
> He trac'd the wonders of the sky;

> The chambers of the sun explor'd,
> Where tints of thousand hues are stor'd....

An eagle, of course, flies higher than any other creature and, moreover, was reputed to be able to stare right into the sun unblinkingly (as Newton did with light in a way that had not been equalled). Once his image had taken him into the sun, Scott was able to expand seamlessly into the related image of a storehouse with many chambers, each chamber containing a separate colour. The much greater effectiveness provided by the image, compared to abstract or rhetorical description such as, even, the "beauteous laws of light," would not have been lost on Wordsworth.

Scott's Ode, however, is not the only candidate for having influenced Wordsworth in his writing of the Newton passage. In fact, a fairly large number of antecedents should be considered, especially since, by the time Wordsworth came to make his revision, he had had more than sixty years of reading and memorizing to nourish his mind. That his memory continued sharp can be seen from two letters that he wrote. In March of 1844 he finished a letter to Gladstone with this presumably spontaneous recollection:

> "But as my departed Friend Southey said long ago,
> Onward in *faith*, and leave the rest to Heaven."[19]

Southey had written that line fifty years before. And in writing to the son of George Crabbe, Wordsworth said, "I first became acquainted with Mr Crabbe's Works in the same way, and about the same time, as did Sir Walter Scott"—which means that he encountered extracts from *The Village* (in particular) in Dodsley's *Annual Register*, also about fifty years before, or possibly earlier. Wordsworth continued his letter to Crabbe's son: "The extracts made such an impression upon me, that *I* can also repeat them. The two lines

> 'Far the happiest they
> The moping idiot and the madman gay'

struck my youthful feelings particularly...."[20]

Many years ago Emile Legouis suggested, with regard to the last two lines of Wordsworth's tribute, that the "beautiful lines on Newton seem to be inspired by the equally happy lines of [James] Thomson" that appear in his elegiac poem "To the Memory of Sir Isaac Newton."[21] His suggestion has been quoted by de Selincourt and has thereby received his imprimatur, and the three editors of the Norton Critical Edition of *The Prelude* have likewise given their imprimatur.[22]

There certainly appears to have been good reason for their doing so. Wordsworth maintained a lifelong interest in Thomson and even contemplated editing a selection of his poetry.[23] He publicly acknowledged indebtedness to him for lines 190-91 of *An Evening Walk* and alluded to him in another book of *The Prelude*.[24] Oswald Doughty has drawn attention to a further parallel between a passage in *The Prelude* and one in Thomson's poetry, and Doughty's observation has been repeated by de Selincourt and R. D. Havens.[25] In addition, de Selincourt has pointed to two further Thomson echoes in *The Prelude*, and Havens to still another two.[26] Abbie Findlay Potts has offered evidence of a pervasive verbal influence in certain books of *The Prelude* and has argued for a Thomsonian influence on Wordsworth's ordering of his content.[27]

Wordsworth had Thomson's poetry readily to mind and available for him to draw on at any time he wished to do so. Particularly when he came to write about the statue of Newton holding a prism in his hand, there would have been two reasons within Thomson's elegy on Newton for Wordsworth to think of that poem. Thomson had described at length, and vividly, the spectral analysis of light Newton had achieved when with his prism he had "Untwisted all the shining robe of day" (lines 96-118), and immediately after that memorable passage he had asked (lines 119-20), "Did ever poet image aught so fair, / Dreaming in whispering groves by the hoarse brook?"—a question which many a poet, especially one who *had* dreamed by the hoarse brook, would regard as a challenge.

In the lines quoted and referred to by Legouis and his successors there appear certain elements which would undoubtedly have been of interest to Wordsworth. The entire passage, which extends beyond the point at which Legouis finished quoting ("He stemmed alone"), reads thus:

> The noiseless tide of time, all bearing down
> To vast eternity's unbounded sea,
> Where the green islands of the happy shine,
> He stemmed alone; and, to the source (involved
> Deep in primeval gloom) ascending, raised
> His lights at equal distances, to guide
> Historian wildered on his darksome way.[28]

Up to this point in his elegy, Thomson has celebrated the various labours and discoveries of Newton: what was contained in and signified by his complex *Principia* (published in 1687), and the same for his *Opticks* (published in 1704-06). There then appears the passage we are concerned with, followed by the rhetorical question, "Who can number up his labours? who / His high discoveries sing?" After this, Thomson turns to Newton's private virtues, forecasts continuing fame for him, and pictures him wandering "through those endless worlds / He here so well descried." In other words, the passage we are concerned with would appropriately address itself to Newton's last labour and discovery. This was *The Chronology of Antient Kingdoms Amended*, which he spent the last three years of his life working on and which was left to his nephew Conduitt (mentioned in Thomson's elegy) to publish in 1728.[29] This work sought to assist historians by establishing an accurate timetable of events, in both human and natural history, stretching back to the creation of the world. Hence another reason for seeing this work as being what is referred to in Thomson's lines: the "tide of time" (chronos, of course) Newton alone was able to make headway against and to trace to its source, deep in the gloom that existed before God said, "Let there be light," and so began the process of time. The historian, hitherto lost in the murk of ancient history, would, by following Newton, be able to relate events in their proper order.[30]

The metaphor through which this content is presented would certainly have interested Wordsworth. Newton is depicted as a singularly successful navigator who journeys, alone, into waters fraught with uncertainty, leading the way for those who might wish to follow him. The emphasis placed on Newton's having proceeded "alone" of course parallels Wordsworth's own, later emphasis. Thomson's one "vast...unbounded sea" parallels Wordsworth's plural "seas." The lights raised at equal distances and so guiding followers along the course which Newton pursued could, conceivably, be seen as a luminary index to his mind and so could, possibly, have suggested to Wordsworth the "marble index" represented by the statue. And the statement that Newton stemmed the tide of time could be read as a way of saying that he was immortal, that he would continue on his journey for ever. But such a reading would be a distortion: seeing the lights as an index would be rather recherché, the sea that Thomson described is one of time (not Thought), and his navigator does not even set sail on it—instead, he sets his back to it and ascends the river away from it.

Not much, in short, of the imagery in these particular lines of Thomson's elegy would have likely served as a source for Wordsworth. Other parts of the elegy, however, could have supplemented this passage. The equivalent of Wordsworth's "Mind" and "Thought" can be found, for instance, in lines 139-41 of the elegy, where Thomson described Newton's mind as a "piercing mental eye diffusive" which saw "The finished university of things / In all its order, magnitude, and parts." And, earlier, it was Newton's "mind," which, brighter than "Even Light itself," had "Untwisted all the shining robe of day" (lines 96-98). Nor did Thomson confine Newton's movement to proceeding away from the "unbounded sea." In lines 57-58 of the elegy Newton "took his ardent flight / Through the blue infinite," and now, after his death and elevation, "he wanders through those endless worlds / He here so well descried" (lines 187-88). By linking these various passages from Thomson's elegy in his mind, and there meditating on them, Wordsworth could, admittedly, have been brought fairly close to the metaphor he actually came to use.

But, as we have already seen, there were many other poems which could have provided Wordsworth with his metaphor, without the need to piece its elements together in this way. Nor were they all from preceding generations.

A contemporary of Wordsworth's nephew in 1825 wrote a poem, entitled "Sculpture," which won the Cambridge Chancellor's Gold Medal for an English poem and which would have assured Wordsworth that the corpus of poetic tribute to Newton not only was still alive, but also was being actively added to. The young poet was E. G. Lytton Bulwer, who was to go on to greater literary fame under the augmented surname Bulwer-Lytton. Wordsworth could have encountered his prize poem in either of two ways. He could have read it in the same 1828 edition of *Cambridge Prize Poems* that contained his nephew's prize poem, or, since there is some evidence that Bulwer visited Rydal Mount in 1824 and since he did in fact send Wordsworth a copy of his book *Siamese Twins and Other Poems* (1831) with an autograph presentation addressed to the "Illustrious Wordsworth," there is the distinct possibility that Bulwer could have sent him a copy of his prize poem.[31]

If Wordsworth had in fact read Bulwer's poem, the lines in it on Newton's statue would have appealed to him for a particular, compelling reason. They included a more elaborate expression of the thought Wordsworth had conveyed to William Rowan Hamilton in 1829, when he said that he venerated science when it was "legitimately pursued for the elevation of the mind to God." Concerning Newton, Bulwer wrote:

> Nature drew
> Her secret veil from his undazzled view—
> For him, her glowing depths had solemn speech,—
> And myriad worlds—life—glory—GOD in each,
> Hymning high joy through Heaven's eternal dome,
> Blazed from the darkness round Jehovah's Home![32]

A further source of interest to Wordsworth would have been observing how Bulwer made use of Scott's Ode, just as Wordsworth himself had done.[33] Of more immediate interest to us, however, is the fact that in Bulwer's poem appears a passage that in many ways parallels Wordsworth's culminating lines on Newton's statue:

> Lo! where, through cloister'd aisles, the soften'd day
> Throws o'er the form a "dim religious" ray,
> In graven pomp, and marble majesty,
> Stands the immortal Wanderer of the sky—
> The sage who, borne on Thought's sublimest car,
> Track'd the vague moon, and read the mystic star. . . .

Here is the "marble" of Wordsworth's lines, here in "the immortal Wanderer" is the one "for ever / Voyaging," and here in the "sage" and "Thought" is Wordsworth's "Thought"—a parallel further strengthened by a later couplet in which Bulwer says that the Sculptor "o'er each feature's lofty beauty wrought / The deep intense pervading soul of thought." More significant even than these verbal parallels is, of course, the fact that these lines of Bulwer's—alone of all the possible sources examined so far—provide a verbal link between the statue and Newton's intellectual voyaging.

That statue, with the Latin inscription beneath it, requires further consideration.

The Silent Stone

That Wordsworth could respond profoundly and vividly to a work of art is evidenced, of course, by the description he wrote of the statue. But if confirmation were needed, it could be found in another passage in *The Prelude*. In the ninth book of that poem Wordsworth records that during his visit to Paris he went to see what was left of the Bastille, that evocative symbol of the Revolution. At the time, he was to record later, he was a radical supporter of the Revolution and "pretty hot in it."[34] Yet, on looking at that emotion-charged rubble, he found himself less moved, "however potent [the] first shock," than by

> the painted Magdalene of Le Brun,
> A beauty exquisitely wrought, with hair
> Dishevelled, gleaming eyes, and rueful cheek
> Pale and bedropped with everflowing tears.
> *(P(1850)* 9:75-80)

Roubiliac's statue of Newton evidently meant even more to Wordsworth, as attested to by the story told by Isabella Fenwick in a letter she wrote to Henry Taylor. During a visit to Cambridge in 1835, Wordsworth went with friends to see the room in St. John's College that he had occupied as a student. Isabella Fenwick writes, referring to the manuscript of *The Prelude* she had been allowed to read: "I remembered the description of it in his autobiographical poem, and most faithful it was; one of the meanest and most dismal apartments it must be in the whole University; 'but here' (he said in showing it) 'I was as joyous *as a lark.*' There was a dark closet taken off it for his bed. The present occupant had pushed his bed into the darkest corner, but he [Wordsworth] showed us how he drew his bed to the door, that he might see the top of the window in Trinity College Chapel, under which stands that glorious statue of Sir Isaac Newton. This, too, he has recorded in his poem."[35] The original moving of the bed, and the re-enactment of the moving, both say much about Wordsworth's continuing emotional attachment to the statue of Newton.

The way people close to Wordsworth responded to the statue would have reinforced his regard for it. Two such people have recorded their personal response. A few years before Wordsworth added the magnificent conclusion, Sara Hutchinson described the statue as being "expressive of the peaceful & quiet thought so deep as if one dared [not] breathe when looking upon it—I am sure I held my breath & would not have spoken above a whisper for the world."[36] Long before the composition of the concluding lines, but after the rest of the description had been drafted, Dorothy Wordsworth, writing to Lady Beaumont, 14 August 1810, said that she stood in Trinity Chapel "for many minutes in silence before the Statue of Newton, while the organ sounded. I never saw a Statue that gave me one hundredth part so much pleasure—but pleasure, that is not the word: it is a sublime sensation, in harmony with sentiments of devotion to the divine Being, and reverence for the holy places where he is worshipped."[37]

As mentioned earlier, the statue does not exist by itself. It has, incised on the pedestal below it, the inscription which is equally affecting. It reads, "Newton, qui genus humanum ingenio superavit." With its various ambiguities, this Latin statement proclaims that Newton surpassed or rose above the human race and did so either in mind or, indeed, by his mind, his genius.

Taken together, the statue in its location of lonely grandeur and the inscription under it could easily have helped bring to Wordsworth's mind at least five of the phrases in his description. Since the statue concentrates attention on what is represented as going on inside the head, in itself it could have suggested the "marble index." The look on the face, joined with the prism held in the hand and the "ingenio" inscribed below, could likewise have suggested the "Mind" engaged in "Thought." These promptings would have been immediate: the others would follow from meditation. On realizing that the statue would continue gazing into the heavens for as long as Wordsworth lived and, presumably, for many centuries after, Wordsworth could readily have been prompted to think of Newton himself as "for ever" pursuing his thought.

Certain writings about the statue which we have already quoted could also have served as sources for some of the phrases in Wordsworth's passage. Francis Chantrey, the leading English sculptor of his day, emphasized the grandeur of the statue: "[It] is the noblest...of all our English statues," "There is...a loftiness of thought about it," and "You cannot imagine any thing grander in sentiment...."[38] Coleridge emphasized a holy stillness:

inly hushed,
Adoring Newton his serener eye
Raises to heaven. . . .³⁹

From this hush could have come both Wordsworth's "silent" and his idiosyncratic "strange." William Selwyn explained the silence and strangeness: "the philosopher is alone with nature and with God."⁴⁰

To these must be added a description appearing in the work which quoted Chantrey's comment, a detailed history of British art by Allan Cunningham. Cunningham wrote:

> Newton is represented standing, holding up a prism, and between his hand and the thought stamped upon his brow there is a visible connexion and harmony. He exhibits a calm colossal vigour of intellect, such as we have reason to believe was the character of the living man—touched too, and that not a little, with those amenities enumerated by his friend Thomson. . . . On looking upon this noble statue—the worthy image of one of the loftiest of human beings—we may ask with the poet of the Seasons, when dwelling on the greatness of Newton's discoveries, and pointing out the wondrous harmony of their combinations,
> "Did ever poet image aught so fair?"⁴¹

Here is the equivalent matching of the prism held in the hand with the expression on the face. Here is the emphasis put on mind ("intellect") and thought. Here is the link between the statue itself and the mind, a link expressed in abstract terms: "the worthy image." And here is repeated the invitation, indeed the challenge, to the poet to express that link, not in abstract terms, but in an image: "Did ever poet image aught so fair?"

There can be no doubt that Wordsworth had read this passage of Cunningham's. He knew Cunningham, he corresponded with him, and he spoke admiringly of his Scots poetry.⁴² That relation, coupled with his passionate interest in Newton, would assure that he had read this passage, and, as we have seen, reading it would ensure remembering it and being able to call upon his memory of it.

Associated with Newton's statue would have been the simile, mentioned earlier, that Newton had used about himself, when he said: "I don't know what I may seem to the world, but as to myself, I seem to have been only like a boy playing on the sea shore, and diverting myself in now and then finding a smoother pebble or a prettier shell than ordinary, whilst the great ocean of truth lay all undiscovered before me."[43]

This image of Newton about himself, so much like the image Wordsworth had used about his own boyhood in the Intimations Ode, would have been of considerable assistance to Wordsworth when he sat down to enlarge on his lines about the statue. The statue itself, the various descriptions about it, and Thomson's image of the explorer would together have emphasized the towering, solitary nature of Newton's genius, but they all lacked something related to movement: most of them were completely static, and Thomson's image turned Newton's back on the eternal sea and sent him off in the wrong direction. At least Newton's own image put him back by the sea and it also, just as importantly, made that sea the right kind of sea: "the great ocean of truth [which] lay all undiscovered before [him]." The germ of discovery is there, in the word "undiscovered," but there is still no overt action, no sending of Newton out on to that ocean.

There was, however, another description of an artistic representation of Newton that could have provided Wordsworth with the impetus in the right direction over that very sea. The description he could have found in a rather unlikely place (though no more unlikely than the introduction to the foundation-charter of an abbey).

Other Worlds

A lengthy review appeared in the *Examiner* of Benjamin Robert Haydon's colossal painting of "Christ's Triumphant Entry into Jerusalem," the one in front of which Keats and Lamb said such disparaging things about Newton. It is also the painting in which Haydon placed Wordsworth and Voltaire in company with Newton. (Hazlitt remarked that Wordsworth's head in the painting "is the most like his drooping weight of thought and expression.")[44] When the painting was put on public display in the Great Room of Bullock's Egyptian Hall in Piccadilly, beginning in late March 1820, it caused a great commotion and brought large crowds to see it.[45] Wordsworth himself was so impressed by the painting that he was prompted to add a stanza, alluding to it, to the 1820 version of *Peter Bell* and, in a note, to call his readers' attention to "Mr. Haydon's noble picture."[46]

On Sunday, May 7, 1820, not long before one of Wordsworth's visits to London,[47] the review appeared, running from pages 297 to 300 of the *Examiner* and signed with the initials "R. H.," the usual designation of Robert Hunt, the brother of Leigh and John, founders of the *Examiner*. In the midst of an otherwise thoroughly laudatory account of the painting, there appeared, in a parenthesis on page 300, a complaint about Haydon's depiction of Newton, "which certainly presents nothing of that deep abstraction of mind which travelled through the immensity of the planetary regions, and brought back an account of their relative and magnificent situation and courses."[48]

The complaint is remarkably irrelevant, for in the painting Newton is depicted as looking attentively at Christ, who is no more than twenty feet away and is approaching even closer on the back of an ass. But the very irrelevancy could have fixed the verbal description of Newton even more firmly in Wordsworth's memory, and at least implicit in Hunt's description of Newton's "deep abstraction of mind" is the vehicle of a metaphor—an intrepid explorer (such as Captain Cook) who ventures forth on uncharted seas and returns to civilization with a detailed description of the hitherto unknown territories that he has discovered. In addition, then, to the explicit use of the word "mind" (an element missing from Thomson's passage on the navigator), Hunt added, by implication, a voyaging on strange seas (something Thomson's navigator turned his back on) and expressed that voyaging in such terms—"brought back an account of their relative and magnificent situation and courses"—that the concept "Thought" comes readily to mind. Here is intellectual exploration that is of the highest order and that proceeds visually in the right direction—all applied to Newton and all available together in one brief passage.

Admittedly Newton's own image set him, as a boy and still essentially static, on the shore beside "the great ocean of truth," but Hunt's image of the intellectual explorer voyaging through the immensities of space, in conjunction with Newton's, would have changed the boy into the man and would have released him from the shore, sending him voyaging, as the great explorer, through strange seas of Thought.[49]

But the same review could have served an even more important function. It could well have activated Wordsworth's propensity for following up "identity of thought" and parallels in phrasing, and have taken him to a passage in Philo's treatise on dreams.[50]

There Philo writes of the man who sets out on a journey from the region of scientific knowledge, which is without boundaries and is illimitable in its vastness.[51] Such a man can make two kinds of voyage or voyaging: if his mind remains within his body and hence impeded by his senses, he will make only the second-best kind of voyage and perceive only the world of the senses, the physical reality. But if his mind escapes from his body and proceeds by itself alone, he will make the best kind of voyage and perceive the intelligible world, the intellectual world, the nonphysical reality.[52] Here, in Philo's passage, are several elements which reappear in Wordsworth's lines: here is the immensity of knowledge or understanding (akin to thought), and here is even the mind voyaging, and voyaging alone. But, even more importantly, here is a pattern of thought and words that could be superimposed on Hunt's statement. Just as Philo provided a pattern that could be superimposed on Wordsworth's encounter with the daffodils and so afford another, nonphysical dimension, so here, again, Philo provided a pattern that, by being superimposed, could afford another, nonphysical dimension that would parallel and greatly enrich the original physical dimension.

Either Hunt's journey through intergalactic space or Philo's disembodied voyage to the intelligible could readily have called to Wordsworth's mind certain lines of Edward Young's *Night Thoughts*. Referring to a person freed from the bounds of mortality and making a journey through space, these lines read:

> How shall the stranger man's illumined eye,
> In the vast ocean of unbounded space,
> Behold an infinite of floating worlds
> Divide the crystal waves of ether pure,
> In endless voyage, without port![53]

Here, curiously, are the seven elements (five explicit, two implied) that figure in Wordsworth's distinctive cluster of elements and that reappear in the final, fleshed-out description of Newton's statue. Both extreme height and extreme depth are in the "vast ocean of unbounded space"; stars voyage on this ocean; an exceptional observer ("the stranger man") is observing something most exceptional, "an infinite of floating worlds"; eternity is present in the "endless voyage"; both the solitary nature of the observer and the silence of the whole scene are clearly implied. In view of this degree of parallel, it would be only natural for Wordsworth to consider Young's passage for phrases he himself could use.

He had already publicly acknowledged borrowing from Young (in "Tintern Abbey"),[54] and there is also reason for believing that he borrowed from him again, to make changes in another passage in the *Prelude* at much the same time as when he added to the passage on Newton's statue.[55] Here, in the passage quoted, with its "endless voyage" through a "vast ocean" full of strange sights, perceived by an observer who is even "stranger," he had a model for his own description.

But these various passages are not the only ones that could have supplied much of the material and phrasing for the lines which Wordsworth added to the description of Newton's statue. There remains yet another candidate, a candidate even more significant and with influence even more pervasive, but one to whom Wordsworthian scholars have so far paid but little attention.

7 A Kindred Spirit

WHEN WILLIAM ROWAN HAMILTON FIRST MET Wordsworth, in September of 1827, he was already a most extraordinary young man. In each term of his first year at Trinity College, Dublin, he won both of the two examination prizes offered—in Science and in Classics.[1] He also received two Chancellor's Prizes for poems and was awarded the very rarely given judgement of *optime* for his answering examination questions in Homer. Before entering university, he had detected a flaw in the reasoning Laplace had used in his celebrated *Mécanique Céleste,* and while still in his final year as an undergraduate he presented, to the Royal Irish Academy, a paper on a system of rays which was highly acclaimed and which contributed to his being chosen, while still an undergradute and over impressive competitors, as Professor of Astronomy to the University and superintendent of its observatory. And this man wrote poetry, fluently and copiously. Moreover, he was convinced that Science shared with Poetry the ability to reveal beauty in its most sublime aspects and to ascend even into "the counsels of Creation."

No wonder he and Wordsworth took to each other on first acquaintance.[2]

Kinship

Their first meeting is recorded by both. Shortly after receiving his Professorship and then his baccalaureate, Hamilton undertook a trip to England. There, with a party of friends, he made a visit to Wordsworth. When the visit was completed (after nightfall), Wordsworth walked back with the party to the friends' house near Ambleside. Having bid the others goodnight, Hamilton then offered to walk back to Rydal with Wordsworth. "This offer," Hamilton recorded, "he accepted, and our conversation had become so interesting that when we arrived at his house, a distance of about a mile, he proposed to walk back with me on my way to Ambleside, a proposal which you may be sure that I did not reject; so far from it, that when he came to turn once more towards his home, I also turned once more along with him. It was very late when I reached the hotel after all this walking...."[3] And what were they talking about during this *"midnight walk together for a long, long time, without any companion* except the stars and our own burning thoughts and words"? Presumably, about Poetry and Science, Beauty and God, for these subjects they had intensely in common.

Wordsworth himself expressed almost as much pleasure, though not at such length. In a letter answering Hamilton's, Wordsworth said about their parting, "Seldom have I parted—never I was going to say with one whom after so short an acquaintance, I lost sight of with more regret."[4] R. P. Graves, Wordsworth's close friend for many years, recorded, about this meeting, that he had "more than once heard" Wordsworth "refer in terms of pleasurable reminiscence to the midnight walk in which the two oscillated between Rydal and Ambleside, absorbed in converse on high themes, and finding it almost impossible to part."[5]

The letter which Hamilton sent to Wordsworth, in response to the latter's hospitality, contained a poem about Hamilton's recent severe disappointment in love. He had set all his hopes for happiness on the prospects of marrying a certain young lady to whom he had been attracted for some time, but when she delicately hinted that he should not propose marriage, he delicately withdrew and then turned, for assistance in overcoming his bitter disappointment and dejection, to the memory of his principal hero. From him and his example he sought strength in devoting himself entirely to Science, particularly to his duty of excelling in astronomy. That hero was, of course, Newton, whom he addressed this way in the poem (the reader will notice echoes of Scott's Ode):

> And THOU too, mighty Spirit! whom to name
>   Seems all too daring for this lowly line;
> Thou who didst climb the pinnacle of Fame,
>   And left'st a memory almost divine!
> To whom the heavens unbarred their inner shrine,
>   And drew aside their sanctuary's veil,
> While Nature's self disclosed her grand design,
>   And smiled to see thee kindle at the tale,
>   And before Science' sun thine eagle eye not quail:
>
> All reverently though I deem of thee,
>   Though scarce of earth the homage that I pay,
> Forgive, if 'mid this fond idolatry
>   A voice of human sympathy find way;
> And whisper that while Truth's and Science' ray
>   With such serene effulgence o'er thee shone,
> There yet were moments when thy mortal day
>   Was dark with clouds by secret sorrow thrown,
>   Some lingering dream of youth—some lost beloved one.
>
> If then thy history I read aright,
>   O be my great Example! and though above,
> Immeasurably above, my feeble flight,
>   The steep ascent up which thy pinions strove,
> Yet in their track *my* strength let me too prove;
>   And if I cannot, quite, past thoughts undo,
> Yet let no memory of unhappy love
>   Have power my fixèd purpose to o'erthrow,
>   Or Duty's onward course e'er tempt me to forego![6]

The "history" of Newton which Hamilton felt he had "read aright" was presumably a brief anecdote about Newton's early disappointment in love that had appeared twenty years before in a history of the town of Grantham. That work had reproduced a letter, written in 1727, which contained the following passage:

> Mrs. Vincent is a widow gentlewoman living here, aged 82. Her maiden name was Storey, sister to Dr. Storey a physician of Buckminster near Colsterworth.... Sir Isaac and she being thus brought up together, 'tis said that he entertained a love for her; nor does she deny it: but her portion being not considerable, and he being a fellow of a college, it was incompatible with his fortunes to marry; perhaps his studies too. 'Tis certain he always had a kindness for her, visited her whenever in the country, in both her husbands [sic] days, and gave her forty shillings, upon a time, whenever it was of service to her.[7]

That from this sketchy, indeed shadowy, account Hamilton could see vivid and strong resemblances between his plight and Newton's says much about his eagerness to see further parallels between himself and his idol. Wordsworth's comment on the stanzas which delineated the parallels in blighted love is also revealing about Wordsworth. These stanzas, he wrote to Hamilton, "affected me much, even to the dimming of my eye, and faltering of my voice while I was reading them aloud. Having said this, I have said enough."[8] Well might his eye dim and his voice falter, and not simply because Wordsworth could respond in artistic and impersonal sympathy to the past plight of his young friend and that of the dead Newton. Can anyone doubt that there came flooding to his mind memories of Annette Vallon and the wrenching decision he had to make to forgo the love of his youth? And can anyone doubt that he was forcefully struck with this further evidence of kinship shared among the three sages who elevated their minds to God?

Kinship extended beyond personal, amatory experience to their guiding philosophies. In the "General Scholium" to his *Principia*, Newton said that "to discourse of [God] from the appearances of things, does certainly belong to natural philosophy."[9] In the first of his four letters to Dr. Bentley, he said, "When I wrote my Treatise about our System, I had an eye upon such principles as might work with considering men, for the belief of a Deity; and nothing can rejoice me more than to find it useful for that purpose."[10] In his *Opticks*, likewise, he said, about Science, "Though every true Step made in this Philosophy brings us not immediately to the Knowledge of the first Cause, yet it brings us nearer to it, and on that account is to be highly valued."[11] All these statements find their parallel in Alexander Pope's summary statement, about the student of Nature who "looks thro' Nature, up to Nature's God."[12]

Hamilton on occasion referred to Newton, by way of illustrating how the study of science leads to a recognition of God and the active role He plays in the universe. In a lecture on astronomy he remarked that Newton saw attraction as a law given to matter by God at the time of creation, and projection as something that comes more directly from God, being still "an immediate impulse from the Omnipotent arm."[13] When he remarked that Science was able "to penetrate the counsels of Creation," he was, in effect, alluding to the passage in the General Scholium in which Newton had said, "This most beautiful system of the sun, planets, and comets, could only proceed from the counsel and dominion of an intelligent and powerful Being."[14] This matter of the study of science providing evidence for the activity of God was a recurring motif in what Hamilton wrote, whether in lectures, letters, or poems. Newton, he said, derived "an additional pleasure from the perception of the observed conformity between the work of his finite intellect and the Creation of the Eternal Mind."[15] In continuing Newton's study "we walk through the temple of Creation, awed but not bewildered, with reverence but without confusion; and stand beside the altar of astronomy as by a pyramid of fire, composed of earth's least earthly substance, and burning upward to heaven." Science has, as its ultimate end, he said in another lecture, "restoring and preserving harmony between the various elements of our own being; a harmony which can be perfect only when it includes reconciliation with our God."[16] To Wordsworth himself, Hamilton wrote, "Science, as well as Poetry, has its own enthusiasm, and holds its own communion with the sublimity and beauty of the Universe." As a result, a study of Science will unfold "the external works of God, and the magnificent simplicity of Creation."[17] In a poem to Wordsworth he put the parallel even more clearly. In thanking Wordsworth for the "commune" he had experienced at Rydal Mount, he said:

> Whether my joy was heightened and refined
> By impress of thy meditative mind,
> Which, long to Beauty and to Nature vowed,
> Not less could hear their still voice than their loud;
> Or I, who love to tread the sister-fane,

> Where Science worships with her solemn train,
> Would tell how also there from little things
> To the purged eye a sight of wonder springs;
> Or whether soared we, as these walks we trod,
> From Beauty and from Science up to God.[18]

Little wonder that a frequent image in Hamilton's writings is the golden chain, climbing from earth up to the heavens: in his Lecture of 1831, for instance, he said, "Astronomy is man's golden chain between the earth and the visible heaven. It is a Science, but it is more than a Science, for it is woven of feeling as well as of thought, and it pervades not the mind only, but the soul."[19] And in another poem to Wordsworth he referred to the "golden chain whose summit is in heaven."[20]

Hamilton's kinship with Newton would have appeared to extend, most strikingly, even into the areas of his professional research. As Newton invented a form of algebraic calculus, so Hamilton extended the field of algebra, and, even by the time Wordsworth came to revise his Newton passage, Hamilton had produced a number of "Metaphysical Remarks on Algebra as the Science of Pure Time."[21] More strikingly, as Newton had pioneered work in optics, so Hamilton devised a mathematical theory predicting that "under particular circumstances a ray of light must be refracted into a conical pencil."[22] The prediction was confirmed by experiment and in 1833 was hailed by Hamilton's colleagues as a work of genius: "In the way of such prophecies, few things have been more remarkable than [this] prediction," said one, and "Perhaps the most remarkable prediction that has ever been made," said another. Hamilton himself recorded in a letter he drafted to Coleridge an observation that he probably made to Wordsworth in person during his visit a little later, in 1834: "My aim has been...to remould the Geometry of Light, by establishing one uniform method for the solution of all problems in that science, deduced from the contemplation of one central or characteristic relation....my chief desire and direct aim being to introduce harmony and unity into the contemplations and reasonings of Optics, considered as a portion of pure Science."[23]

Hamilton's professional kinship with Newton was recognized by his colleagues. When the British Association (of leading scientists) held its meeting of 1835 in Dublin, the Lord Lieutenant of Ireland arranged for an appropriate ceremony. At the formal banquet held in the imposing hall of the Library of Trinity College, the Lord Lieutenant cleared a space in front of him and summoned Hamilton to him.

> "I am," said his Excellency, "about to exercise a prerogative of royalty, and it gives me great pleasure to do it, on this splendid public occasion, which has brought together so many distinguished men from all parts of the empire, and from all parts even of the world where Science is held in honour. But, in exercising it, Professor Hamilton, I do not confer a distinction. I but set the royal, and, therefore, the national mark on a distinction already acquired by your genius and labours." He went on in this way for three or four minutes, his voice very fine, rich, and full; his manner as graceful and dignified as possible; and his language and allusions, appropriate, and combined into very ample flowing sentences.
>
> Then, receiving the State sword from one of his attendants, he said, "Kneel down, Professor Hamilton;" and laying the blade gracefully and gently first on one shoulder, and then on the other, he said, "Rise up, Sir William Rowan Hamilton."[24]

In making his arrangements, the Lord Lieutenant presumably had in mind a similar happening when Queen Anne of England made a detour from her trip to Newmarket in order to visit Cambridge. Certainly Professor Whewell of Trinity College, Cambridge, saw the similarity, for when, during the banquet, this prominent mathematician returned thanks for a toast, he made a point of adding the words: "'there was one point which strongly pressed upon him at that moment: it was now one hundred and thirty years since a great man in another Trinity College knelt down before his sovereign and rose up Sir Isaac Newton.' The compliment was welcomed by 'immense applause.'"[25]

The Star Flower

No wonder Wordsworth held Hamilton in high regard. In January of 1839, referring to the poem "Recollections," in which Hamilton had summed up the visits he had shared with his friend, Wordsworth wrote: "Be assured, my dear Sir William, that without the help of these interesting lines I should retain a most lively remembrance of our first meeting, and of the hours so pleasantly and profitably spent in your Society, both in Ireland and at Rydal."[26] A few months earlier, Isabella Fenwick had reported that Wordsworth had said that Hamilton "resembles Coleridge more in his intellectual character than any one else he has ever known."[27] What this remark implied is made clear by Graves, who recorded that Wordsworth "has said in my hearing that Coleridge and Hamilton were the two most wonderful men, taking all their endowments together, that he had ever met."[28] In two letters to Hamilton himself, Aubrey De Vere confirmed this observation of Graves'. In one he reported that Wordsworth "used to say you were the only man who had ever reminded him of Coleridge"; and in the other he said, "Whenever I have seen [Wordsworth] he has spoken much of you, and in higher terms than of anyone else except Coleridge."[29]

This high regard is reflected in one of Wordsworth's later lyric poems, the one that begins "So fair, so sweet, withal so sensitive." The background to its writing incorporates a variety of circumstances. Hamilton's Introductory Lecture on Astronomy of 1832 contained two motifs that are particularly pertinent. One is the assertion, frequently reiterated, of the close analogy he often drew between science and beauty, between the scientific spirit and the poetical spirit, between what produces "a *Principia*" and what produces "a *Paradise Lost*," between the respective powers that placed on their "kindred thrones...the spirits of Milton and Newton."[30] The other motif is the compliment, also frequently reiterated, that Hamilton paid to Wordsworth. He paraphrased lines from *Tintern Abbey* when he described the ability of the "scientific imagination..., in the trivial and everyday changes which are witnessed around us on this earth [to] perceive the indications of a mighty power, extending through all space, and compelling [the planets] to their proper orbits...."[31] He referred to Wordsworth as "a great living poet" and twice quoted directly from his poetry, from *The Excursion* and from the Immortality Ode, altogether making it clear that he felt Wordsworth belonged in the company of the "immortal Milton."[32]

A few years after Hamilton wrote his Lecture, he composed the poem recollecting the various times he had been with Wordsworth and, of course, sent a copy to Wordsworth himself. In the poem he recalled one of the more recent visits with Wordsworth, when Hamilton went from a conference of astronomers and proceeded to Rydal Mount. In doing so, he left behind men of Science, some of whom loved "her Beauty," and went to visit

> With him who still had cleaved unfalteringly
> To the better part, and ever truly served
> Beauty, which breathes at times the "charm severe
> Of line and number," and the minds inspires
> Of meditative men to science vowed,
> Through stars, or flowers, or harmonies of thought,
> And linkings of the many into one
> By golden chain whose summit is in heaven;
> But oftener fills the gentle Poet's heart,
> Musing on Nature and Humanity...."[33]

The quotation "charm severe / Of line and number" further magnified the compliment, for it was taken (with some distortion of memory) from *The Excursion* (1:254). Receiving such compliments undoubtedly created a desire to be able to repay.

An opportunity for repayment occurred in August of 1844. In that month Hamilton was again visiting Wordsworth at Rydal Mount, and on one of the days he was there, he and Wordsworth, in the company of R. P. Graves, Professor Archer Butler, and Julius C. Hare, set out to walk to Loughrigg Tarn. On the way they paused at a particular point to enjoy the magnificent view. Then, as Graves tells the story, Wordsworth, in looking "for new beauty in the flower-enamelled turf at his feet," had his attention "attracted by a fair, smooth stone, of the size of an ostrich's egg, seeming to imbed at its centre, and, at the same time, to display a dark star-shaped fossil of most distinct outline. Upon closer inspection this proved to be the shadow of a daisy projected upon it with extraordinary precision by the intense light of an almost vertical sun. The poet drew the attention of the rest of the party to the minute, but beautiful phenomenon, and gave expression at the time to thoughts suggested by it."[34] Julius Hare observed, "We shall have a sonnet upon it."[35] They had, indeed, a poem, but not a sonnet: instead a poem in triplet measure, the first of this kind Wordsworth had attempted and so even more strikingly an example of "line and number" providing a "charm severe."

More significantly for us, however, Wordsworth, presumably remembering Hamilton's line "Through stars, or flowers, or harmonies of thought," began the poem thus:

> So fair, so sweet, withal so sensitive,
> Would that the little Flowers were born to live,
> Conscious of half the pleasure which they give;
>
> That to this mountain-daisy's self were known
> The beauty of its star-shaped shadow, thrown
> On the smooth surface of this naked stone![36]

Then as if (at least) he remembered Hamilton's succeeding lines ("And linkings of the many into one / By golden chain whose summit is in heaven"), Wordsworth continued:

> And what if hence a bold desire should mount
> High as the Sun, that he could take account
> Of all that issues from his glorious fount!
>
> So might he ken how by his sovereign aid
> These delicate companionships are made;
> And how he rules the pomp of light and shade;
>
> And were the Sister-power that shines by night
> So privileged, what a countenance of delight
> Would through the clouds break forth on human sight!

Having appropriately elaborated from the star to the sun and then to the moon, and having thereby demonstrated the affinity between astronomical Science and poetic Beauty, Wordsworth concluded with an address to a "Thou" which is usually interpreted, no doubt, as being the reader in general, but which, in view of the circumstances mentioned, can now be seen as being initially Hamilton himself (another instance of public and private meanings):

> Fond fancies! whereso'er shall turn thine eye
> On earth, air, ocean, or the starry sky,
> Converse with Nature in pure sympathy;

> All vain desires, all lawless wishes quelled,
> Be Thou to love and praise alike impelled,
> Whatever boon is granted or withheld.

And so the compliment was returned.

Such a compliment suggests, of course, that Hamilton as a person could exert considerable influence upon Wordsworth's poetry, in both its content and its expression. There is reason, indeed, to believe that his influence was more than considerable.

Sons of Science

To Hamilton himself Wordsworth wrote that his sister Dorothy and his friend Coleridge "are the two Beings to whom my intellect is most indebted," and the extent of that indebtedness is well known.[37] Dorothy with her conversations and her Journal, and Coleridge with his conversations and his writings, affected Wordsworth's mind profoundly, modifying his attitudes, providing him with ideas, and supplying him with phrases for his poems. Various lyrics would probably not have come into being if it had not been for Dorothy, and certainly the whole of *The Prelude* would not have existed, had it not been for Coleridge's prodding. And it was with Coleridge, this man of immense influence on him, that Wordsworth paired Hamilton. He did so, moreover, at a time when, as he remarked to Hamilton, both Coleridge and Dorothy were "proceeding as it were pari passu along the path of sickness, I will not say towards the grave but I trust towards a blessed immortality."[38] In other words, at the time when Coleridge and Dorothy had ceased being able to provide fresh influence on Wordsworth, Hamilton came along to take their place, especially the place of Coleridge.

On occasion at least Hamilton would have impressed Wordsworth as manifesting much the same philosophical concerns and as expressing them in much the same way as Coleridge had done. Hamilton was fond of describing how the imaginative and perceptive scientist viewed the universe and how he went about trying to discover its fundamentals. The scientist would, of course, observe the appearance of the physical world and would record the facts he had observed. "...By the application of reason and of the scientific imagination to carefully recorded facts, we ascend to an hypothesis, a theory, a law, which includes the particular appearances, and enables them to be accounted for and foreseen."[39] But the scientist does not stop there. From "familiar facts" and "obvious laws" he proceeds "to the observation of facts more remote, and to the discovery of laws of higher order."[40] These higher laws reveal "the more intellectual world of living spiritual energies," with which are associated, not only Beauty, but also Power.[41] (Note, in passing, the close relation of "intellectual" and "spiritual.") To Hamilton "the Newtonian, no less than the Platonic, Philosophy appears...to be...an architectural edifice" that exhibited the way in which the Deity continues to energize his Creation.[42] As Wordsworth listened to Hamilton expound these views, as presumably he did on more than one of their visits together,[43] he must have been struck with the parallel, in both content and expression, between what Hamilton said to him and what Coleridge had written to him in that letter in which he had explained why he had complained of *The Excursion* to Lady Beaumont. He had complained, he said, because Wordsworth had not put into the poem what he thought he would have written about the universe: "Facts elevated into Theory—Theory into Laws—& Laws into living and intelligent Powers—true Idealism necessarily perfecting itself in Realism, & Realism refining itself into Idealism."[44] In view of these and other similarities, one would accordingly look for signs of Hamilton's influence in much the same areas as those in which Coleridge influenced Wordsworth.

The Reverend Charles Graves, a close associate and personal friend of Hamilton, and likewise a friend of Wordsworth, reported that, by pointing out to Wordsworth the kind of imaginative faculty required for scientific discovery, Hamilton provided to the poet "an entirely new revelation, and had the effect of raising his conception, which had before been unduly depreciatory, of the dignity both of science itself and of its most eminent votaries."[45]

In astronomy in particular, Hamilton made clear to Wordsworth, imagination was "an essential element," and Newton's representation of the Solar System, arrived at by the exercise of the highest imagination, was thereby analogous to "a beautiful representation of nature in poetry, painting, or sculpture."[46] This argument, and the phrases placed in quotation marks, appeared in Hamilton's Introductory Lecture on Astronomy delivered in 1831. In all likelihood Hamilton sent Wordsworth a copy of it, for he made a practice of sending him copies, not only of his poetry, but also of those of his prose works which he thought Wordsworth would be able to understand.[47] In addition, Hamilton would have had ample opportunity of expressing these views, in this phrasing, during any of the four visits which he paid to Wordsworth before 1839, as well as during the visit Wordsworth paid him at the Observatory. In the same kinds of vehicle, Hamilton also made clear that what Newton, Hamilton himself, and other imaginative scientists used their imagination for greatly increased the value of what they did. They observed individual facts closely and analyzed them minutely so as to arrive at the laws which operated through the observed facts. Indeed their imagination led them "from familiar facts to obvious laws, then to the observation of facts more remote, and to the discovery of laws of higher orders."[48] Kepler, for instance, had connected observed facts about the orbits of Mars and Jupiter and had thereby discovered the law that made for those orbits; Newton had then analyzed that and other, related laws and found the much higher (and simpler) law which allowed *them* to operate.[49] And what, he asked Francis Edgeworth in a letter and could well have repeated to Wordsworth in person, "have we gained by knowing that Nature operates by the simplest laws...? We are, or may be, led by this knowledge to elevate ourselves above the corporeal region of dead, though beautiful, forms, into the more intellectual world of living spiritual energies. The universal *meaning* which you would give to natural objects...is attained...by showing (so far as it can be shown) how the Deity continues to energise in each...."[50]

In the prose works of Hamilton that are extant, all the illustrations of examining individual details imaginatively so as to arrive at fundamental laws are drawn from astronomy and mathematics. Wordsworth would, of course, have been much more interested in botany, and Hamilton would, in fact, have had an opportunity of using plants as illustrations on the walks he took with Wordsworth through the garden of the Observatory during the poet's visit. R. P. Graves testified about himself and, by implication, about others: "Often was the Observatory garden the scene of the private lectures I enjoyed at that time and afterwards; there teacher and learner were more than peripatetics, for frequently both drove hoops abreast round the walks, as they carried on talk about astronomy or optics; and flowers and poetry, reminiscences of Brinkley [the astronomer] and Wordsworth (from each of whom a walk was named) relieved agreeably the severer subjects."[51]

Even if Hamilton had not alluded to plants for illustration during

Wordsworth's visit, a sonnet he wrote in 1837 would have served the purpose, for undoubtedly he would have sent Wordsworth a copy:

BOTANY

> O, do not say that with less loving heart
> The beauty of a flower is gazed upon,
> For ever after, and by everyone,
> If once the eye enact the scholar's part
> To that wood-wandering honey-laden Art,
> Which, with the bee, doth every flower explore,
> And gather, out of many, one sweet lore,
> From blossom'd bank or bower slow to depart.
> The sense of beauty need not sleep, though mind,
> With its own admiration, wake, and yield
> Its proper joy—with feeling thought entwined:
> Considering the lilies of the field,
> Whose rare array, and gorgeous colouring,
> Outshone the glory of the Eastern King.[52]

In the winter of 1842-43 Wordsworth dictated to Isabella Fenwick a lengthy note by way of annotating a short lyric that he had written in 1829 and first published in 1835.[53] The poem, "This Lawn, a carpet all alive," is about dancing shadows on a lawn and the emblem they provide for "Worldlings revelling in the fields / Of strenuous idleness." The note begins by being tied, appropriately, to the actual lawn which inspired the poem, but, as it proceeds, the connexion of the note to the lawn becomes more and more tenuous, until finally Wordsworth mentions "the laws whereupon, as we learn by research, [the inexhaustible treasures of Nature] are dependent." He then refers to the process of intellectual dissection, which, in "The Tables Turned," he had referred to as murder:

> Some are of opinion that the habit of analysing, decomposing, and anatomizing is inevitably unfavourable to the perception of beauty. People are led into this mistake by over-looking the fact that such processes being to a certain extent within the reach of a limited intellect, we are apt to ascribe to them that insensibility of which they are in

> truth the effect and not the cause. Admiration and love, to which all knowledge truly vital must tend, are felt by men of real genius in proportion as their discoveries in natural Philosophy are enlarged; and the beauty in form of a plant or an animal is not made less but more apparent as a whole by more accurate insight into its constituent properties and powers. A *Savant* who is not also a Poet in soul and a religionist in heart is a feeble and unhappy Creature.

Hamilton had obviously made his point well, and how amusing it is that Wordsworth should have used scientific wording ("analysing, decomposing, and anatomizing"), while it was Hamilton who used the beautifully appropriate image of the bee who, by exploring every flower, gathers, "out of many, one sweet lore."

Bowing Their Heads

When Wordsworth came to revise the lines, in Book VI of *The Prelude*, which he had written about his experience with geometry, he made certain interesting changes. In the thirteen-book version he had written (lines 143-49) that he had meditated

> Upon the alliance of those simple, pure
> Proportions and relations with the frame
> And laws of Nature, how they could become
> Herein a leader to the human mind,
> And made endeavours frequent to detect
> The process by dark guesses of my own.[54]

On a wafer in MS. D Wordsworth replaced the "alliance" of the "Proportions and relations" with the simpler statement (lines 123-24 in the fourteen-book version): "On the relation those abstractions bear / To Nature's laws...."[55] Behind this change can be seen the many descriptions which Hamilton provided of how a scientist abstracts principles from observed facts. One such description, typical of the others, appeared in his Lecture of 1832:

> in order to derive from phenomena the instruction which they are fitted to afford, we must not content ourselves with the first vague perceptions, and obvious and common

appearances. We must discriminate the similar from the same—must vary, must measure, must combine—until, by the application of reason and of the scientific imagination to carefully recorded facts, we ascend to an hypothesis, a theory, a law, which includes the particular appearances, and enables them to be accounted for and foreseen.[56]

Clearly he is here talking about abstractions. He then proceeds to say: "Then, when the passive of our being has been so far made subject to the active, and sensation absorbed or sublimed into reason, the philosopher reverses the process, and asks how far the conceptions of his mind are realised in the outward world." These conceptions being realized in the outward world could certainly have given rise to Wordsworth's phrase "the relation those abstractions bear / To Nature's laws."

Continuing in the same MS., Wordsworth proceeded to make a radical change to the phrase, concerning Nature's laws, "how they would become / Herein a leader to the human mind" (lines 146-47 in the thirteen-book version). On a wafer in MS. D (lines 124-26 in the fourteen-book version) this became:

> & by what process led
> Those immaterial agents bowed their heads
> Duly to serve the mind of earth-born Man....[57]

The living and intelligent nature of the laws has been brought much more to the fore, and the laws themselves have been shifted to a subservient role, serving rather than leading. This is indeed a startling change in role, all the more remarkable because, as Helen Darbishire has pointed out, the older Wordsworth, in revising other parts of *The Prelude*, reduced the status of the human mind from what he had expressed in the earlier version, when he claimed for it "majesty" and "sovereignty within." "In his revision," Miss Darbishire observed, "these phrases are thrown out, or their fangs drawn."[58] Yet here the status of the human mind is enhanced, for no longer is it led by the laws of Nature, but rather those, now seen as living and intelligent agents, humbly bow their heads and serve their superior, "the mind of earth-born Man." Interestingly enough, both these new (or newly emphasized) concepts regarding the laws of Nature—their being alive and intelligent and at the same time serving the mind of man—can be seen foreshadowed in Hamilton's Lecture of 1832. The climax of the scientist's increasingly more profound process of observing, abstracting, theorizing, and testing will come, if it can ever come, "when the mind of man shall grasp the infinity of nature, and comprehend all the scope, and character, and habits of those innumerable energies which to our understanding compose the material universe."[59] To ascribe "habits" to "energies" certainly suggests that those "energies" have some kind of life and intelligence. Hamilton continued by saying that we have already come close to seeing a prototype of the kind of "mind of man" that can indeed comprehend the habits of these energies, for Newton, "by one great stride of thought, placed theory at once so far in advance of observation, that the latter has not even yet overtaken the former." Here is reason for expressing the thought that the "immaterial agents" bow their heads "to serve the mind of earth-born Man."[60]

Wordsworth then, in MS. D, removed the reference to his own "dark guesses" and replaced it with two new lines (lines 127-28 in the fourteen-book version) referring (grandly, but somewhat vaguely) to the whole process of discovering the laws of Nature and to those laws, as "immaterial agents," serving "the mind of earth-born Man":

> From star to star, from kindred sphere to sphere,
> From system on to system without end.[61]

In the introduction to his Lecture of 1832, just before he quoted seven lines from Wordsworth (referred to as "a great living poet"), Hamilton had given particularly forceful expression to a favoured idea of his, that on other worlds there exist beings with higher intelligence than ours. (In this belief, incidentally, Hamilton provided yet another parallel with Sir Isaac Newton, who likewise gave the impression, at least, of believing in such creatures.)[62] These beings are, he believed,

> akin to us—members of one great family—beings animated, thoughtful, loving—susceptible of joy and hope, of pain and fear—able to adore God, or to rebel against him—able to admire and speculate upon that goodly array of worlds with which they also are surrounded. And often

> this deep instinct of affection, to the wide family of being, to the children of God thus scattered throughout all worlds, has stirred within human bosoms; often have men, tired of petty cares and petty pleasures, fretting within this narrow world of ours, seeking for other suns and ampler ether, gone forth as it were colonists from earth, and become naturalized and denizens in heaven.[63]

Behind this particular description of Hamilton's is undoubtedly that of Edward Young, who, in his *Night Thoughts*, described the flight his soul made through a succession of worlds, increasingly advanced, the nearer he approached to the throne of God.[64] While Wordsworth's word "system" probably derived from Young (for it was a favourite with him), the word "kindred" in similar manner probably derived from Hamilton, for it was a favourite with him, especially in his Lecture of 1832.[65] Wordsworth himself, of course, had used the word before,[66] but it appears that this time he was encouraged to do so by the example of Hamilton. In fact, the adding of these two lines about systems of stars and spheres could readily have been offered as a compliment to Hamilton himself, by way of compensating for the indulgent smile with which Wordsworth had greeted Hamilton's statement of his favoured idea during their conversation at the Observatory outside Dublin.[67]

Feeding on Infinity

More significant was the change Wordsworth made to the description of the scene at the top of Mt. Snowdon, a scene which marks the culmination of *The Prelude*. In the thirteen-book version, after describing the Moon, naked, "at height / Immense" above his head, and the "still Ocean" of mist at his feet, Wordsworth concluded thus (13:52-65):

> Meanwhile the Moon look'd down upon this shew
> In single glory, and we stood, the mist
> Touching our very feet; and from the shore
> At distance not the third part of a mile
> Was a blue chasm; a fracture in the vapour,
> A deep and gloomy breathing-place thro' which

>   Mounted the roar of waters, torrents, streams
>   Innumerable, roaring with one voice.
>   The universal spectacle throughout
>   Was shaped for admiration and delight,
>   Grand in itself alone, but in that breach
>   Through which the homeless voice of waters rose,
>   That dark deep thorough-fare had Nature lo[d]g'd
>   The Soul, the Imagination of the whole.[68]

In this immensely evocative picture, the focus is divided between two objects: the Moon looking down in single glory and, on a level with the speaker's feet and distant from him a third of a mile, the blue chasm, the breach, the deep and gloomy breathing-place in which Nature had lodged the "Soul, the Imagination of the whole." In the fourteen-book version, Wordsworth made a radical change. Bringing forward revisions he had made in MS. A^3 (sometime between 1816 and 1819), he first enlarged upon the function of the moon on a wafer in MS. D (14:51-56):

>   only the inferior stars
>   Had disappeared, or shed a fainter light
>   In the clear presence of the full-orbed Moon,
>   Who, from her sovereign elevation, gazed
>   Upon the billowy ocean, as it lay
>   All meek & silent. . . .

Then he abbreviated the description of the chasm, but maintained the description of the roar of waters rising through it (lines 56-60):

>   save that thro' a rift
>   Not distant from the shore whereon we stood,
>   A fixed abysmal, gloomy, breathing-place
>   Mounted the roar of waters—torrents—streams
>   Innumerable, roaring with one voice![69]

In the earlier version, this roar had nowhere to go: it simply rose, and the reader's attention was focussed on what it had risen through. In the later version, that part of the description is eliminated, and in its place appear two lines, added on a wafer in MS. E, which follow the rising roar (lines 61-62):

>   Heard over earth & sea, & in that hour,
>   For so it seemed, felt by the starry heavens.[70]

The focus of the picture is now unified, for "the starry heavens" would include, pre-eminently, "the full-orbed Moon," which, in Wordsworth's day, would have been regarded as a "star," certainly the largest "star" in the sky, beside which all the others were indeed "inferior."[71] Evidently the destination of the rising roar is phrased as "the starry heavens" so as to combine the visual aspect of the Moon and the philosophical aspect of heaven. Now the reader's mind is elevated, in the company of the rising roar, to a contemplation of God in his glorious works, and the total impression is reinforced by that part of the description of the mind that "feeds upon infinity" which Wordsworth added to the final version (lines 71-74), the fact that it

>   broods
>   Over the dark abyss intent to hear
>   Its voices issuing forth to silent light
>   In one continuous stream....[72]

In his conversation with Hamilton at the Observatory in 1829 Wordsworth had been prompted to become more emphatic in expressing the need for science, especially that part of it which analyzed parts of Nature, to elevate the mind of the student to God. Presumably the same would hold for poetic descriptions of Nature: they, too, should "look through Nature, up to Nature's God." Over the years Wordsworth had frequent reminders of this principle in the image of the golden chain which Hamilton kept using in his lectures, letters, and conversations. In Hamilton's Lecture of 1832 Wordsworth had before him the insistence on the "close connexion," the "unity," and the "harmony" in the frame of earth and heaven.[73] Wordsworth also had at hand in that Lecture (and applicable to the "full-orbed Moon") a description of the "stars," which, "from their thrones of glory and of mystery, excite and win toward themselves the heart of man;...the golden chain has [not] been let down in vain....The heart, because it is human—say rather because it is not wholly not divine—lifts itself up in aspiration, and claims to mingle with the lights of heaven; and joyfully receives into itself the skyey influences, and feels that it is no stranger in the courts of the moon and the stars." In Hamilton's address to the British Association in 1835,

Wordsworth had available another passage of considerable relevance. Hamilton there spoke of the "very silence and solitude" of the meditations of genius and how that genius will "penetrate gloom after gloom into those Delphic depths, and force the reluctant Sibyl to utter her oracular responses. Or if we look 'from Nature up to Nature's God,' we may remember that it is written—'Great are the works of the Lord, sought out of all them that have pleasure therein'."[74] With such reminders before him, is it any wonder that Wordsworth chose to follow the soaring flight of the roaring voices?

Or is it any wonder, in view of Wordsworth's association with Hamilton, that, as he came to revise *The Prelude*, he added Hamilton as an exemplar of the "majestic intellect"? Is it even any wonder that in introducing that phrase, "majestic intellect," he evidently chose to reverse the process Helen Darbishire pointed to his pursuing elsewhere in *The Prelude*, generally of toning down the claims for the human intellect and specifically of replacing "majestic intellect" with "unfolding intellect"?[75] In the original version it is clear that Wordsworth had Coleridge in his thoughts as the "mighty Mind" of which the vision granted from the top of Snowdon was a perfect image (13:69-73). The alternative draft which Wordsworth wrote in MS. A makes the parallel with Coleridge even clearer than does the official 1805 version. The alternative reads, about the scene from Snowdon:

> and to my thoughts it gave
> A shadowy image of a mighty Mind
> That while it copes with visible shapes hears also
> Through vents and openings in the ideal world
> The astounding chorus of infinity
> Exalted by an underconsciousness
> Of depth not faithless, the sustaining thought
> Of God in human Being.[76]

Coleridge's attempts to deal with both the material world and the ideal have been well enough documented, and these lines from his poem "The Eolian Harp" provide an explanatory parallel to the "astounding chorus of infinity," the blending of the many into one:

> And what if all of animated nature
> Be but organic Harps diversely fram'd,

> That tremble into thought, as o'er them sweeps
> Plastic and vast, one intellectual breeze,
> At once the Soul of each, and God of all?[77]

When Wordsworth came to revise *The Prelude* for the last time, he had met the second of the two men in his life "whose powers had impressed him with wonder,"[78] and so he chose to add a second exemplar of the superior mind. To the mind that "feeds upon infinity" (the official phrasing of both versions), Wordsworth added, on a wafer in MS. E, the observation (14:66-69) that the vision from Snowdon

> appeared to me, the type
> Of a majestic Intellect, its acts
> And its possessions, what it has & craves,
> What in itself it is, & would become.[79]

This passage certainly raises a number of questions: What are the acts of a majestic intellect? What are its possessions? What does it have? What would it become?

The observations that Hamilton chose to make about Newton in his Introductory Lecture on Astronomy for 1833 (the successor to the Lecture to which we have already paid considerable attention) provide the answers to most of these questions. They also explain why Wordsworth used "intellect" at this point instead of "mind": in his description of what Newton did, Hamilton used the word "intellect" three times in six sentences.[80] This intellect, with its fire, fused a number of basic laws of Nature into one more fundamental law, the principle of gravitation. This is what it has: what does it crave? Newton desired "a wider dynamical theory" that would account for all phenomena on earth and in the heavens. If such understanding were to be granted to such an intellect with its present powers ("majestic" does appear an appropriate epithet), what in time would that intellect become? "Even then we may be sure that new [intellectual] desires would arise, the intellect would find something to do;...from the seemingly finished work there would rise up a new and growing enterprise, an unexplored and unimagined world of genius."

The final remaining question, "What are the possessions of this majestic intellect?," is answered in Hamilton's address to the British Association, already quoted. In that address Hamilton referred to "that rapture solemn and sublime, with which a human mind, possessing or possessed by some great truth, sees in prophetic vision that truth acknowledged by mankind."[81] This same reference appears to be behind a phrase which Wordsworth added, presumably in MS. D, to his description of the higher minds creating a "like existence." Whenever that existence, he wrote in the thirteen-book version (13:95-96), is "Created for them," they "catch it by an instinct." This he changed to (14:95-97):

> wheneer it dawns
> Created for them, catch it,—or are caught
> By its inevitable mastery.[82]

Possessing an understanding of the whole universe, craving an understanding of God himself, catching these projections of intellect, and caught by their mastery—such was the intellect of Sir William Rowan Hamilton, and such, behind him and above him still, was the intellect of Sir Isaac Newton. No wonder that the type of such a majestic intellect is figured in the roaring with one voice of innumerable streams, rising triumphantly to encompass even the starry heavens.

A paradox can certainly be seen in these lines about the majestic intellect and in those about its poetic type, the streams innumerable, roaring with one voice. Wordsworth appears to have done what Thomas Gray did in those lines in his *Elegy* addressed in particular to Ambition and Grandeur:

> The boast of heraldry, the pomp of pow'r,
> And all that beauty, all that wealth e'er gave,
> Awaits alike th' inevitable hour.
> The paths of glory lead but to the grave.[83]

Gray presumably had in mind the pomp-filled proceedings he had witnessed within the grandeur of Westminster Hall, at which three Scottish lords who had supported Bonnie Prince Charlie were tried for treason. They had contributed all they had of privilege, prestige, and power for glory, and had found, at last, that the paths of glory lead but to the grave.[84] Gray's witnessing of the proceedings had been his private experience; when he came to make a public statement about them, he chose to leave behind the specifics of what was private and to use only the abstractions that would be understood in public.

So with Wordsworth; although he presumably had in mind his private experiencing of the specifics of Hamilton's intellect, and Newton's too—what those intellects were like, what they achieved, and what they still sought to achieve—when he came to make a poetic statement about their kind of intellect, he chose to use abstractions, presumably in the belief that they would be better understood by his public audience.[85] The result is, paradoxically, the opposite of what he probably intended. Without Hamilton and Newton present (at least implicitly) as exemplars, when such lines as the following are read as a public statement—

> its acts
> And its possessions, what it has and what it craves,
> What in itself it is, and would become,

they appear remarkably empty, as they have done to Jonathan Wordsworth. For him they provide only "irrelevant aspects of the mind that [Wordsworth] would like his poetry to conjure up."[86] But when read as a private expression, addressed to a much smaller audience and dependent on a recollection of the achievements and aspirations of Hamilton and Newton, the lines are suitably rich in majestic implication. So, too, with the roaring voices rising to the full-orbed Moon in the starry heavens. As long as these lines, too, are read as a strictly public statement, they will appear to be prettily literary, in the manner of Swinburne's "A Forsaken Garden"—as, again, they appear to have been read by Jonathan Wordsworth. But when the private experience of the insistence on linking earth to heaven and on ascending the golden chain is borne in mind, when one remembers the need to emphasize the harmony of creation and to elevate the mind to God, then the philosophical import becomes clear. One may reject that import as far as one's own view of the universe is concerned, but one can no longer regard the lines as prettily flimsy or conventionally tawdry.

This discussion of private and public has, however, been something of an interruption; let us return to our main concern. We have examined a number of passages in which Wordsworth made changes that have to do with things which Hamilton had talked or written about—usually things, too, about which Hamilton had already altered Wordsworth's attitude. In these and still other passages,[87] the changes Wordsworth made bear a remarkable relation to what Hamilton said or wrote, both in the ideas conveyed and in the peculiar expression given to them. Wordsworth's new phrasings read as if he had examined Hamilton closely, accepted his ideas, and also accepted many of his phrases, to the extent that Wordsworth either used them directly or substituted synonyms for them. In the process Wordsworth usually condensed what Hamilton had said, summarizing and rearranging to suit his own context. He may well have done the same when he came to revise the passage on Newton's statue.

Favoring Stars

As one traces the revision of the Newton passage through the various manuscripts, one comes to notice the stars blinking in and out. In MS. A (the thirteen-book version), lines 56-57 read in part, "I in moonlight nights / Could see" the Antechapel.[88] This was then changed, in the same MS., to read: "... from my Pillow, when the Moon shone fair / Or even by dimmer influence of the stars." MS. B likewise began by referring only to moonlight, but was changed to read: "By glimmering starlight, or with mellow gleams / Of moonshine on the branchy windows playing." MS. C saw the expulsion of the stars altogether, with only moonlight being described ("when the silver Moon / Shone fair"). In MS. D, on the wafer pasted over the initial text of the MS., the stars are restored, with a new kind of epithet added: "looking forth by light / Of moon or favoring stars."

Wordsworth's decision to restore the stars and once more to couple them with the moon could well have been influenced by Hamilton's image which introduced his Lecture of 1832. There the depiction of the stars on "their thrones of glory and of mystery" and the culminating assertion that the human heart "is no stranger in the courts of the moon and the stars" would certainly encourage such a restoration, and Hamilton's further assertion that the human heart "lifts itself up in aspiration, and claims to mingle with the lights of heaven; and joyfully receives into itself the skyey influences" would encourage a presentation of the stars as having a benign influence.[89] Nor was this the only passage in Hamilton's Lecture which would encourage such a presentation. In another equally poetic passage, one (moreover) which deliberately parallelled celebrated lines in "Tintern Abbey," Hamilton spoke of the scientific imagination which divines from the falling of an apple the law of gravitation and which in trivial and everyday things round about perceives "the indications of a mighty power, extending through all space, and compelling [heavenly bodies] to their proper orbits"; "such divinations" are received "by the favoured discoverer himself."[90] From the past participle "favoured," applied to the person receiving the favour, to the present participle "favoring," applied to the symbol of the power bestowing the favour, is but a short and natural transition.

The "discoverer" himself, who is so "favoured" in Hamilton's Lecture, could provide the concept of Wordsworth's "voyaging," for in Wordsworth's day—and especially in his library—most discoveries were made by means of voyaging, which, when undertaken at night, was pursued with the assistance of favouring stars. Astronomy, in fact, Hamilton continued within a few paragraphs, by "binding in so close connexion the earth with the visible heaven, and mapping the one in the other, has guided through wastes, which else were trackless, the fleet and the caravan, and made a path over the desert and the deep."[91] The other kind of deep, which Wordsworth had in mind and which he characterized as "strange seas of thought," is also present in Hamilton's writings. Whenever he speaks of discoveries in astronomy, one is aware of the profound and venturesome kind of thought into which the discoverer had to launch himself. In a letter to Francis Edgeworth he put the concept in a way he could easily have done to Wordsworth orally: we are led, he wrote, by the knowledge of Nature's simplest laws "into the more intellectual world of living spiritual energies."[92] And in his Address to the British Association he used a modification of Newton's own image when he referred to "those treasures which wave after wave may dash up on the shore of the ocean of truth."[93] Precisely whose truth was involved he also made clear. In the same letter to Francis Edgeworth he indicated that it is the Deity who "continues to energise," with living, spiritual energies, each natural object. And in a somewhat later letter to Viscount Adare he indicated that he was "well inclined to adopt the opinion" of Berkeley "that the *immediate cause* of all our sensations is the Supreme Spirit, in Whom we live and move and have our being, acting on subordinate minds according to rules which He has allowed them to discover."[94] These concepts and phrasing are, of course, what Hamilton would have had ample opportunity, and indeed occasion, to discuss with Wordsworth in their lengthy conversations during any of his visits with the poet. They are also such as would prompt Wordsworth to use the epithet "strange"—a word which, when used in conjunction with the other elements of the image cluster, would indicate to him (as we have suggested) that the observer stood in the presence of divine thought, the thought of God himself.

Obviously it is the mind, with Hamilton, that makes the discoveries in the ocean of truth. This is always abundantly clear in what he writes; and in the peroration to his Lecture of 1833, which we have quoted before, he celebrated, in memorable phrasing, the "mind," the "intellect," of Sir Isaac Newton himself, which sought to understand all the forces of Nature, all the energies emanating from God himself.[95] This same mind, in the same peroration, is said to be "for ever" in action, seeking to acquire greater and greater understanding. Inevitably that mind functioned alone. Again this concept is clear in any of Hamilton's writings, but is emphasized repeatedly in his Address to the British Association. "We meet, we speak, we feel *together now*, that we may afterwards the better think, and act, and feel *alone*.... It is the individual man who thinks and who discovers.... The humblest student of astronomy...must...go over for himself, in his own mind,...that process of induction which leads from familiar facts to obvious laws, then to the observation of facts more remote, and to the discovery of laws of higher orders. And if even this study be a personal act, much more must that discovery have been individual. Individual energy, individual patience, individual genius, have all been needed to tear fold after fold away which hung before the shrine of Nature; to penetrate gloom after gloom into those Delphic depths, and force the reluctant Sibyl to utter her oracular responses."[96]

So consistent are Hamilton's remarks about astronomy that whatever he writes on one occasion can easily trigger one's memory of what he wrote about the same aspect on another occasion. The Lecture of 1832, which Wordsworth acknowledged receiving and finding "philosophical and eloquent, and instructive,"[97] contained, in concept, all the elements of Wordsworth's "Mind for ever / Voyaging thro' strange seas of Thought, alone." Many of the phrasings were also available in that Lecture. It would then have been reinforced by the Lecture of 1833 and the Association Address of 1835, each of which also provided an additional exact parallel to Wordsworth's phrasing: the Lecture offering the "for ever" during which the mind of Newton functioned, and the Address emphasizing that discoveries like Newton's are achieved "alone."

But of course there were other candidates as well, which could also have provided many of the concepts and even the phrases which Wordsworth used in revising his passage on Newton's statue. Could they and Hamilton's writings have operated together in the process of poetic creation?

8 But Ne'er So Well Exprest

EVEN FOR WORDSWORTH, THE ORIGINAL FIVE LINES OF the description of Newton's statue were remarkably understated, especially the concluding lines: "where the Statue stood / Of Newton with his prism, & silent face." There is certainly not much excitement expressed in "stood" or "prism" or "silent face," especially when the phrasing is compared to what we know was Wordsworth's response to the statue. His re-enactment, many years later, of pulling his bed to the door where he could see the outside of the Chapel, which enclosed the statue and shut it off from his outward eye, says much. So does Isabella Fenwick's exclamation: "that glorious statue of Sir Isaac Newton." Philo has a passage about a particular pillar or monument which expresses the kind of feeling that Wordsworth must have felt about the statue (which was also a monument), and that also could easily have pointed out to Wordsworth the way in which he could begin to enlarge his original description.

Turned to Stone

Philo's pillar, described in his treatise on dreams, was "surpassingly beautiful and long-lasting" (in Mangey's Latin, *pulcherrimum & firmissimum*). What would also have associated it, in Wordsworth's mind

145

with Newton's statue was that it had to do with a person whose mind had acquired strength and vigour that was insuperable, the key words (again, in Mangey's Latin) *mens...insuperabile* parallelling the key words in the inscription on Newton's statue: *mens...superavit.*[1] On the same page in Mangey's edition appears a startling image about another pillar described in the Bible, the pillar of salt into which Lot's wife was transformed. This pillar, Philo said, was "set up in public" (ἀνετέθη in the Greek), a phrase which closely parallels the *posuit* that appears in the inscription on the back of Newton's monument, saying that Robert Smith had "set up and put" the statue "in its position." The transformation of Lot's wife came about in such a way that the "soul...was turned to stone, like a monument" (in Mangey's Latin, *anima...velut columna, defixa*).[2] In Philo's context, of course, the turning to stone was undesirable, but Wordsworth showed in his Hymn to Science that he could take a concept or an image and reverse the value judgement associated with it. What the stone bodied forth was the soul, not the figure of the person, not the kind of person she had been in general, but the soul. In the same way Wordsworth depicts the statue of Newton as being an index, not of the figure which Newton presented, nor the kind of person he had been in general, but his mind. Even if one wishes to distinguish, as Philo did on occasion, between mind and soul, when one sees the mind as that part or aspect or mode of the soul which is concerned with thought, the parallel between the image in Philo's passage and the image in Wordsworth's appears even closer.

Just as Philo provided the model of an image that would link the beginning of Wordsworth's enlargement with the original lines, so Hunt's phrase provided a model for the size, shape, and direction of the enlargement—as indeed the poems of Fawkes, Akenside, and Scott had done for the three poetic passages Wordsworth had already written on Newton. Hunt had drawn attention to "that deep abstraction of mind which travelled through the immensity of the planetary regions, and brought back an account of their relative and magnificent situation and courses." This brief description included thought ("that deep abstraction of mind"), travelling for the purpose of discovery, what was discovered, and the vastness of space, and it attached all these to an artistic representation of Newton's face. The comment failed to include the vastness of time and the source of Nature's laws, but the latter of these, especially, Wordsworth was so accustomed to emphasizing, he would have added almost automatically.

Most importantly, Hunt's comment did all this in two or three lines of prose and so indicated that the same could be done in two or three lines of verse. Hunt had used prose and abstractions: Wordsworth as a poet would use verse and imagery. The challenge to be succinct and encapsulating was his to meet.

Obviously we have been considering various thoughts that probably were going through Wordsworth's mind as he set about revising his lines on Newton's statue. Especially since we shall soon embark on a consideration of the roles which various sources likely played in the revision itself, it is no doubt prudent to pause and assess our assumptions. For the past generation or more, have we not been warned about the Intentional Fallacy, and have we not been repeatedly assured that it is impossible to get inside another person's mind?

But the entire *Prelude* is about the development of a particular poet's mind. We have been invited to notice carefully what went into its making and to examine how it operates. The published notes which Wordsworth provided for many of his poems, along with multitudinous remarks made in his letters, have indicated that Wordsworth often made use of sources in writing his poems and have, furthermore, pointed to the ways in which he used them. We have also had left to us, as far as *The Prelude* in particular is concerned, the various manuscripts on which are recorded the results of what went on in the poet's mind during each stage of creation and revision. Many of the materials for reconstructing the various poetic processes clearly exist.

With particular regard to the passage on Newton's statue, we know enough of the relation between Wordsworth and Hamilton to be reasonably certain that, as Wordsworth set about describing what it was that Newton's mind had achieved, he would have, front and centre in his own mind, the conversations and writings of the man who had given him insight into the workings of Newton's mind. We know that at other times, when writing on Newton, Wordsworth had put into practice the lesson he had learned at Hawkshead: of selecting ideas, images, and phrases from other writers' works, of paraphrasing some of their expressions and using others unchanged, and of putting his borrowings (along with his own original contributions) into a new whole, whose structure he also, at least on occasion, adapted from another writer. We know, further, that for the two lines he added to his Newton passage he had available to him certain sources. He had vivid recollections of the statue itself, its inscription, and its location. Undoubtedly he had available Hamilton's writings and the memory of conversations with him. He had available in that prodigious memory of his massive amounts of Thomson's poetry, including (presumably) the relevant lines from his elegy on Newton. Also in that same memory he would have had available whatever other passages, such as Newton's own image about himself, that he had encountered over a lifetime of reading. And here we move out of the realm of reasonable certainty.

Clearly caution, great caution, is required. We could never know *all* the thoughts that were in Wordsworth's mind as he wrote, nor *all* the sources on which he might have drawn. (As authors we should certainly wish to avoid giving the impression that we believe that *all* the sources have now been found for the lines on Newton's statue—or any other passage in Wordsworth: further sources will undoubtedly continue to be discovered, as will the ways in which Wordsworth used them.) While about some of his sources we can be certain, about some others we can conclude only that he was probably indebted to them. And about the actual thought processes, especially the particular stages through which they evolved, we can make only informed guesses.

Actually we are in a position remarkably analogous to that of scientists who study the operation of the human mind in general. They know that certain things happen during the process of human thinking, but as for *how* those things happen, they can only offer models—schemes of the various ways in which they believe the processes probably take place. We too shall offer models (some with variations)—models of the ways in which we believe the numerous elements in Wordsworth's lines probably came together. Very rarely has one the opportunity of entering, even imaginatively, the sensorium of a major poet and there observing as the rays of creativity flash upon treasures offered by the memory and fuse them into a new and startling unity. We have found the opportunity too tempting to decline.

Marble Index

When Wordsworth decided to enlarge on the original five lines, he could readily have allowed what Philo had said about pillars—words that could as appropriately be applied to Newton's statue—to provide him with the means of letting the enlargement develop out of the preceding description. The concept of the statue representing or reflecting the very mind (or soul) of Newton would serve nicely: all that was needed was to find English words with which to express the concept most effectively.

Actually Mangey's Latin translation of Philo and Wordsworth's own broad knowledge of Latin would have helped him to find the right English words. Philo had said that his στήλη (monument) was a σύμβολον (sign, token, symbol), and Mangey translated this by saying that the column *significat* (indicates, signifies, gives a sign), and very evident in that word was the root *signum*, meaning "sign."[3] Curiously, the Latin phrase *marmore signum* meant "a marble statue" (and so was used at least three times by Ovid),[4] and since *index* also meant "sign," the transfer of "marble" from "sign" to "index" could easily occur. More curiously still, the sixth edition of the *Concise Oxford English Dictionary* does not list "sign" as one of the meanings for the English word "index," nor does it provide any of the other principal meanings which Wordsworth probably counted on conveying.

There was a proverb current in Wordsworth's day that ran either, "The face is the index of the heart," or, "The face is the index of the mind."[5] Coleridge, in his youthful "Monody on the Death of Chatterton," had used a modified form of it when he wrote, "The quick emotions struggling in the Face / Faint index of thy mental Throes."[6] And in 1837 the Irish novelist and song-writer Samuel Lover, in his popular novel *Rory O'More*, had used the form closer to Wordsworth's: "The face is the index of the mind:...it is a true saying."[7] Certainly, in Wordsworth's passage, "face" has the best claim to being the governing word for the appositive "index," and so it would appear that the initial meaning of the phrase is that the face of the statue is the index of Newton's mind, with "index" meaning "that which points out or reveals," from the Latin *indicare*, meaning "to point out," "disclose," at times even "betray." The simple apposition was, in Wordsworth's day, commonplace and prosaic. The surprise and the poetry are in the "marble," providing the alliterative paradox that something "marble" should reveal a "Mind," and such a mind. In part the paradox is a tribute to Roubiliac's surpassing skill in being able to carve marble so that it actually does indicate, graphically and movingly, the quality of mind that Newton had. In part, too, the paradox reflects the wonder of the fact that insensate marble should be able to point to the most penetrating intellect and even to suggest what it was that that intellect penetrated to. Thanks to the skill of the sculptor, stone, the lowest link in the Great Chain of Being, was brought, through the mind it indicated, to the highest point in the Chain, the very presence of God.

With almost equal grammatical propriety, the word "statue" can also claim to be the governing word for the appositive "index." Certainly it is the statue as a whole, with its stance provoking the phrase "absorb'd in thought," and with its inscription and its location, that more adequately serves as the index to Newton's mind.[8] The same complimentary and marvelling paradox is conveyed as when "face" is taken to be the governing word, and certain other meanings become operative as well. Cunningham had used a similar apposition when he wrote: "This noble statue—the worthy image of one of the loftiest of human beings."[9] Wordsworth himself, when writing, in the various manuscript versions of the last book of *The Prelude*, about the higher kind of mind, the "mighty Mind," the "great Intellect," and the "majestic Intellect," says that the "scene" or "vision" he had beheld at the top of Mt. Snowdon was a number of things (all roughly synonymous): "the image," "the type or image," "the emblem," "a shadowy image" ("shadow" being synonymous with "emblem"), and "the perfect image" of that mind.[10] The question consequently arises, why did Wordsworth not write "The marble image of a Mind"? The word "image" could have come from Cunningham or his own writing, and "marble" could have come from Bulwer's "marble majesty" or from his remembering the statue itself; and many a poet would have been delighted with the witty ambiguity of the phrase, with "image" in the context meaning both a concrete statue and an abstract representation. But evidently Wordsworth felt "index" had more to offer, in addition to its having come to him in the phrase "the face is the index of the mind."

For one thing, for Wordsworth and his contemporaries, "index" would bring to mind the first meaning which Johnson listed for the word (and a prominent meaning of the original Latin word): "discoverer."[11] How appropriate to be used with regard to Newton, especially when he is presented as voyaging! In fact, if the word "index" had not come to Wordsworth through the proverb, Hamilton's key use of the phrase "favoured discoverer himself" could have called it up for him, through association.[12] "Index" also makes use of the second phrase Johnson lists: "pointer out." This meaning distinguishes the statue from the vision on top of Mt. Snowdon. That "vision" or "scene" was an "image," or a "type," or an "emblem," because it had to be interpreted as to how it represented the higher mind. The statue, on the other hand, is so successful in pointing out the "Mind" that no interpretation is needed. Somewhat parallel is Wordsworth's other use of "index" in *The Prelude*. In the eighth Book he describes a shepherd whose form was glorified by refracting fog, by being set against the distant sky, and "By the deep radiance of the setting sun."[13] Hence, he says,

> the human Form
> To me became an index of delight,
> Of grace, and honor, power, and worthiness.

Like the statue, the shepherd's form, so glorified, had functioned directly, had pointed out so clearly the qualities listed, that no interpretation was needed—hence "index" rather than some other word. Roubiliac had competed successfully with the elemental powers of Nature and their abilities to reveal the qualities within a human form.

In addition to these meanings of "index" that were immediately applicable to Wordsworth's passage, there were also two others which at first would have appeared irrelevant but which, on meditation, would become astonishingly appropriate. One of these meanings was that of the gnomon of a sun-dial, the vertical pin or plate whose shadow pointed to the symbol of the hour placed on the circumference. Thomas Love Peacock, in his satirical novel *Melincourt* (1817), had used it this way: "There was a sun-dial in the centre of the court; the sun shone on the brazen plate, and the shadow of the index fell on the line of noon."[14] The entire statue, rising on its pedestal and receiving, on its right side, the sunlight as it sloped through the south windows of the Antechapel, would function as a gnomon— exactly as the actual gnomon did on the sun-dial located just outside in the courtyard. At a particular hour on each sunny day (as Wordsworth would be well aware), the statue-cum-index would point its prophetic shadow North-Northwest towards a room in the neighbouring St. John's College where resided another man, kindred in spirit to Newton, whose "Mind" would some day likewise go "Voyaging thro' strange seas of Thought, alone."

Nor was sunlight the only kind of light that sloped through the window. Every time on a moonlit night when Wordsworth would return from visiting a friend in Trinity or some other college and would look into the Antechapel, there he would see (without the diminishing distraction of electric light) the marble statue glowing white in the shadows of the night. Bathed in moonlight, it would gleam like a ship's lamp hung out to point the way through the encircling gloom. And so Thomson's lines do become relevant, after all, in this rather indirect way. The strange seas of thought through which Newton voyaged need not, of course, be confined to his discoveries in space; they apply just as readily, even to the import of "strange," to his charting (in his *Chronology of Antient Kingdoms Amended*) of the ways in which God, in his Thought, had intervened in human history.[15] To this voyaging the statue, bathed in moonlight, would indeed serve as a luminary index, similar to the lights which Thomson described Newton as raising "to guide / Historian wildered on his darksome way," and to lead him, with Newton, "to the source" of time, "involved / Deep in primeval gloom."[16]

For ever voyaging

We have used the word "voyaging," but that is not the word which most of the sources available to Wordsworth had used. Hunt had said "travelled": Hughes likewise had said "travels," Ramsay "ranges," and Fawkes "roves." Many of the other tribute-bearers had used the figure of flight: Tollet, Thomson, and Scott had all depicted Newton, or his soul, flying in his own person (at times with "cherubic wings"), and Bulwer had presented him "borne on Thought's sublimest car" as he tracked the heavenly bodies. Wordsworth himself, in his Hawkshead exercise, had presented the unnamed Newton as he "roam[ed] from heaven to heaven," "search[ed] the mystic cause of things," and "follow[ed] Nature to her secret springs." In his virtual Hymn to Science, Wordsworth had used the phrases "Roams through all space," "Explores the illimitable tracks of mind," "Piercing the profound of time," and "Mounts through the fields of thought on wings of fire." In his "Star Gazers" he had depicted the Souls of those who peered through the telescope as making a long "journey."[17]

Clearly something different was needed, a phrase or, preferably, a single word which would combine the ideas of travelling, exploring, tracking to the source, and revealing to human sight. What assistance could Wordsworth's friend and resident expert on Newton, Sir William Rowan Hamilton, provide? In his Address to the British Association, Hamilton emphasized "the discovery of laws of higher orders," and shortly after (on the second next *Athenaeum* page) he used the image (from Newton) of "the ocean of truth."[18] And in his Lecture of 1832, immediately after his paraphrase of lines from "Tintern Abbey" (sure to catch Wordsworth's attention), he had referred, with Newton clearly in mind, to "the favoured discoverer himself," and four paragraphs later he described how astronomy "has guided through wastes, which else were trackless, the fleet and...made a path over... the deep."[19] No doubt this conjunction of phrases, especially with their applicability to Newton, would call to mind Newton's own image, in which "the great ocean of truth lay all undiscovered before me."[20] The key word is, of course, "discovered," not so much for itself as for the word it would have led to in Wordsworth's mind. In his library, and frequent in his reading (as Lane Cooper and C. Norton Coe have pointed out), were many books on voyages of discovery, made over the seven seas to the several parts of the world.[21] Even the titles of many of these books had the word "voyages" in them, such as the Rev. W. Mavor's *Collection of Voyages, Travels, and Discoveries.*[22] And there was *le mot juste:* "voyaging." For Wordsworth it would be confirmed by the use the poets had already made of it in contexts that could be applied to Newton: Mallet had written of the "Vast ocean without storm, where these huge globes / Sail undisturb'd, a rounding voyage each"; and Young had referred to the same "floating worlds /... / In endless voyage, without port." Even more pertinently, Philo had spoken of a mind, indeed the sovereign mind, on a voyage (Mangey's translation *navigatio* could even have been read as "a voyaging") in close association with the boundless and illimitable region of scientific knowledge.[23]

The verbs which the other tribute-bearers (including the younger Wordsworth) had used, such as "travelling," "wandering," "flying," "tracing," "ranging," and "roaming," all indicated movement, and a movement that is open to discovery, it is true, but a discovery that is, nonetheless, haphazard. "Voyaging" through strange seas of thought implies, especially because of its association with voyages of discovery, a purpose, a predetermined goal, a discovery to be found in a specific direction and by following a specific course—precisely what it is appropriate for us to believe Newton had in mind as he set out on his intellectual voyage. Notice, too, that Wordsworth was careful to take the noun "voyage," which he found in his sources, and to change it into the more forceful verb-form "voyaging"; in fact, the choice of the present participle ensured the connotation of a movement that continues.

That continuation is, of course, emphasized by the phrase "for ever." The idea of eternity was, of course, to be found in the poems of the tribute-bearers: elegies dealing with the afterlife are bound to incorporate the idea, and the favoured image (for space) of a boundless sea likewise implied eternity. Wordsworth himself, in his Hawkshead exercise, had used the phrase "immortal Science reigns," and in his virtual Hymn to Science he had referred to "piercing the profound of time." Not to be forgotten, either, was the element of eternity present in his fully-developed cluster of elements associated with his special perceivers. As mentioned earlier, the statue of Newton itself could easily have impressed upon Wordsworth the fact that, being an inanimate work of art, it would live on virtually for ever (a fine Keatsian touch). In fact Scott, in his Ode, had remarked that the subjects of sculpture "breathe through every age." Bulwer had blended the eternity of the statue with the person it commemorated when he wrote: "In graven pomp, and marble majesty, / Stands the immortal Wanderer of the sky." Here Newton's kind of movement was also blended with eternity, and Young, as noted, had effected a similar blending with regard to planets in their "endless voyage, without port."

But it was Hamilton who used the very words "for ever"—about Newton, and especially about Newton's mind. Having by "the fire of intellect" fused a number of the higher laws of Nature "into one glowing whole," even then "he did not think that the intellect must for ever rest": he sought, instead, to discover a still more fundamental principle, and when even that would be discovered, his "intellect would find something to do," "a new and growing enterprise, an unexplored and unimagined world of genius."[24] So Wordsworth wrote of the "Mind for ever / Voyaging." A lesser poet might have chosen to follow Young and to write "a Mind endlessly / Voyaging"; but that phrasing, especially with its suggestions of the Wandering Jew, would have implied that the voyager was denied an end to his labours, denied the rest he most needed. "For ever," on the other hand, implies a divine gift, set free of the confines of mortality. There was also a further reason, associated with the kind of thought through which Newton voyages for ever, that made the choice of "for ever" even more appropriate, and it is to that consideration we turn in a moment, pausing only to savour the skill of Wordsworth's positioning of the phrase. He could have arranged the lines to read "a Mind / Voyaging for ever," which would have achieved emphasis for the word (and concept) "Mind" and for its activity, "Voyaging," but it would have put the "for ever" into an unemphasized position in the middle of the line. Such an arrangement would have much to commend it, and again would have satisfied a lesser poet. But Wordsworth's positioning dares to emphasize, not the word (and bare concept) "Mind," but rather its distinguishing characteristic, its "for ever" (emphasized by being placed at the end of the line, before a slight pause) / "Voyaging" (emphasized by being placed at the beginning of its line and, of course, starting with a stressed syllable). And voyaging where?— "thro' strange seas of Thought."

"Thro' Strange Seas"

Actually MS. D shows that Wordsworth began his last line of revision somewhat differently. It is often difficult to tell whether certain changes in MS. D are in Wordsworth's hand or Mary's, and, especially when the new lines are crowded in between existing manuscript lines, it is wise to be cautious in declaring who held the pen. So let us say simply that Wordsworth directed the writing hand to begin the last line of revision by inscribing "Voyaging in." He then evidently changed his mind and instructed the hand to write over the word "in" *(over:* there was no room *above* it) the "th" of "through," to continue with the word "through," and to finish the line so that the whole line read, "Voyaging through strange Seas of Thought, alone."[25]

What he originally intended to appear after "in" becomes a question of some interest. Presumably it was *not* "Seas of Thought," for one rarely travels *in* seas: one travels *on* them or *through* them or *over* them, but rarely *in* them. Just possibly an indication of what was intended may be found in what happened when Mary came to transcribe the Newton passage on to the wafer which was then pasted over the part of the page on which the changes had been made. As she began transcribing the last line, she evidently misread the messy original and wrote "Voyaging in thought," and then crossed out "in thought," wrote "thro' strange" above it, and completed the line. Her action may well have resulted from a simple (and very understandable) misreading, but it is also possible that, being of a parallel mind with her husband, she had originally sensed that he would have written "in thought"—or he may originally have uttered the word "thought" before giving the instruction to stop and write over what had been written. At any rate, "Voyaging in thought" is what would readily have come to Wordsworth's mind as he reworked the relevant parts of the corpus of tribute paid by his predecessors to the British sage.

These predecessors frequently referred to "thought" in connexion with Newton, and, when they did, it is, of course, Newton's own thought that they meant, whether the phrase was "absorb'd in thought" (as with both Tollet and Scott) or "unbounded thought" (Glover) or "towering thought" (Mallet), or simply mental "penetration" (Ramsay). Likewise, when Hunt referred to "that deep abstraction of mind," he obviously meant Newton's own thought. Even when Bulwer described the sage (Newton) as "borne on Thought's sublimest car," he probably was using a personified abstraction for Newton's own thought, especially since he went on to say that the sculptor had, on each feature of Newton's statue, "wrought / The deep intense pervading soul of thought."

More importantly, Hamilton, in much of his writing about Newton, used the word "thought" in much the same way. Repeatedly he emphasized that the philosophical scientist (represented especially by the astronomer and pre-eminently by Newton) seeks to find the connexion between his thought and the things of the outward world which he has observed.[26] Incidentally this representation parallels the statue of Newton: in its hand is held the prism, representing observed phenomena, and its gaze upward is the thought, searching for the connexion between the phenomena and the theory. When induction is finished (as with the prism), Hamilton continued, when sensation has been absorbed by the reason, then "the philosopher reverses the process, and asks how far the conceptions of his mind are realised in the outward world."[27] In other words, the philosophical scientist's mind goes out in thought, to find the connexions. This concept Hamilton then expressed in an image of his own: "Newton, who in astronomy, by one great stride of thought, placed theory... so far in advance of observation...." Essentially, of course, this image describes Newton's mind as making a great movement in thought. It appears that Wordsworth took the essence and, prompted by the word "discoverer" and its chain of thought, simply changed the form of movement; he kept the meaning of the mind moving in its own thought, and presumably directed the writing hand to set about inscribing "a Mind for ever / Voyaging in thought."

But voyaging where, especially to what destination—if eternal voyaging can have a destination? Again his predecessors had made that ethereal destination clear. Brereton had written: "If to the dark Abyss, a bright Abode / He points; the View still terminates in God."[28] Glover had said that the "vast extent" of Newton's "unbounded thought /... even seeks th' unseen recesses dark / To penetrate of Providence immense."[29] Mallet had used the other side of Milton's image "dark with excessive bright" and depicted Newton proceeding, after death, to where "God himself shines forth immediate" (and where, accordingly, "the frame of things, / In its ideal harmony, to him / Stands all revealed").[30] Akenside had likewise used Miltonic imagery in passages in two separate poems not ostensibly about Newton but inescapably with him in the background as an exemplar: to Science, he said, "Nor dive too deep, nor soar too high, / In that divine abyss"; that same abyss Imagination found to be "the unfathomable gulf / Where God alone hath being."[31] Samuel Boyse had gone to a different source for his imagery: writing about the omnipresence of God, he said, "Systems enclos'd in his perception roll, / Whose all-informing mind directs the whole."[32] This, of course, reflects Newton's own metaphor that space is God's sensorium.[33] And it is of course through space that the tribute-bearers picture Newton as travelling. Bulwer had recently added traditional Biblical imagery to that already used by his predecessors; this imagery, which was more in keeping with Wordsworth's later views and which describes the climax of Newton's discoveries, he had attached implicitly to the statue itself and thereby had supplied what Hunt's comment had lacked:

>   Nature drew
> Her secret veil from his undazzled view—
> For him, her glowing depths had solemn speech,—
> And myriad worlds—life—glory—GOD in each,
> Hymning high joy through Heaven's eternal dome,
> Blazed from the darkness round Jehovah's Home![34]

Coleridge had put much of this scene a lot more simply when he wrote, obviously influenced by the statue itself: "inly hushed, / Adoring Newton his serener eye / Raises to heaven."[35] And William Selwyn had encapsulated even more: "The philosopher is alone with nature and with God."[36] The most succinct encapsulation was, of course, to be found in the statue itself, the silent stone which, by its stance and location, provoked the thoughts expressed by Bulwer, Coleridge, and Selwyn. Could Wordsworth match, or surpass, that succinctness, that encapsulation of where Newton's mind led the daring mortal? As Cunningham had asked, quoting Thomson: "Did ever poet image ought so fair?"[37]

Again Hamilton provided the answer. He showed how the concept of thought (in or through which Newton was to voyage) and the concept of being in the immediate presence of God could be combined—in a vivid and succinct manner. It derives from the relation he described between perceiver and perceived, an exceptional perceiver and a perceived that was even more exceptional—a relation not without bearing on Wordsworth's use of his cluster of elements. In his Lecture of 1831 Hamilton referred to the "conformity between the work of [Newton's] finite intellect and the Creation of the Eternal Mind."[38] (The parallel with Coleridge's Primary Imagination of man continuing the act of creation initiated by the Divine Imagination will not escape notice.)[39] In his Lecture of 1832 he elaborated somewhat as he referred to the time "when the mind of man shall grasp the infinity of nature, and comprehend all the scope, and character, and habits of those innumerable energies which to our understanding compose the material universe."[40] What he meant by "those innumerable energies which...compose the material universe" is made clear in the notes he recorded for a letter to Francis Edgeworth, which could readily have been parallelled in conversation with Wordsworth directly. Speaking, in those notes, of the "world of living spiritual energies," Hamilton asserted that "the Deity continues to energise in each [natural object]."[41] In other words, the innumerable spiritual energies, which compose the material universe, are divine, emanating from the Eternal Mind of God. They are, in short, God's Thought. And God's Thought is what was parallelled, conformed to, by Newton's finite intellect.

Here is an even more exalted concept than voyaging in thought to behold God in his inner sanctum. Here, in Hamilton's description, is the concept of Newton's mind voyaging within the very mind of God and discovering that his own finite, human mind and God's infinite, creating mind, though different in scale, still conformed in the thoughts sent forth and the thoughts perceived. In another part of his lecture, Hamilton reinforced his description of the relation between the two minds, human and divine, by quoting Bacon's image of the "nuptial chamber of the mind [of man] and of the universe."[42] This image of a union so close as to be called a marriage implies at least as much mental activity in the universe as in the mind of man. Here again is the *idea* of God's Thought, but not the phrase itself. Hamilton did not use the word "Thought," but Bulwer did. Although, as we have remarked, Bulwer undoubtedly meant Newton's thought when he referred to "Thought's sublimest car," the way in which he phrased his image can certainly set the reader's imagination going in the opposite direction. "The sage who [is] borne on Thought's sublimest car" is conveyed to his ultimate destination: "the darkness round Jehovah's Home!" For Wordsworth, who had already conceived "a Mind for ever / Voyaging in thought" and who then wished, remembering Hamilton's more exalted argument, to change to the polar and reciprocating relation of Newton's mind and the living, spiritual energies emanating from the Creative and Eternal Mind of God, Bulwer's phrasing would have provided a most useful parallel. His "sage" (parallel to Mind) was proceeding on a conveyance (the particular form of which was readily changeable) to behold the ineffable source of all the mystery about the operation of the universe that he had penetrated. And there, associated with "sublimest" and spelled with a capital "T," was the word "Thought." Bulwer's phrasing, then, could easily have served as a catalyst that worked on Hamilton's concepts and produced the precipitate which took the form of the single word "Thought." The appropriateness of the word could then have been immediately confirmed by Wordsworth's remembering what he himself had called God, the "Wisdom and Spirit of the Universe": "Thou Soul that art the eternity of thought, / That giv'st to forms and images a breath / And everlasting Motion."[43]

Wordsworth accordingly reversed the role of thought in his image. Newton no longer voyages *in* thought, his own thought, but rather he now voyages *through* Thought, a phrase which has the capacity of suggesting that the Thought is now, not Newton's, but someone else's. For Wordsworth, in the process of composing, there would of course be no question but that the Mind (of Newton) and the Thought (of God) stood in a polar and reciprocating relation— Hamilton's "conformity." These two forms of intellect and their functions—God's creation through his Thought and Newton's perceiving and understanding of it through his Mind—gradually move closer and closer together, the further and further Newton's Mind voyages through the seas of Thought.

But something more was needed to indicate more explicitly that the seas of Thought were those of God. Wordsworth may well have been prompted by his memory of Young's lines about the floating worlds in "endless Voyage, without port," which began with the line "How shall the stranger man's illumined eye." Or he may not have needed that word "stranger" to be reminded of his own use of the word "strange" in the passage on the hidden nook in *The Excursion* and the passage on the fair seed-time of his soul in *The Prelude*. In those passages "strange" had been used in conjunction with the seven elements that made up his cluster and had served to indicate the presence of the divine, of God being perceived. Here, too, in the Newton passage, the word "strange," associated with the seven elements, could be used to describe the Seas of Thought and so indicate, privately, that it was in fact the Thought of God himself that Newton's mind perceived.

It may well be objected that, in making the change, Wordsworth merely chose to elaborate on the metaphor inherent in the word "voyaging," and that the "seas of Thought" are "strange" merely because Newton had not ventured on them before—or, to put the matter prosaically, the thoughts are "strange" merely because Newton had not cerebrated them before: they are still *his* thoughts, simply newly formed. They can, indeed, be "strange" also in the sense that no one else had ever thought of them, either; but they are still Newton's. Let us, however, explore what is implied in the image of voyages of discovery in Wordsworth's day. Such voyages, like those of Captain Cook, would proceed over the shoreless high seas to the seas surrounding hitherto undiscovered lands, and through those seas to the lands themselves. Which set of seas would "strange" describe more appropriately: the high seas, those shoreless stretches of ocean that look basically alike, or the seas surrounding lands not seen before? And while the high seas, being international waters, belonged to no one, would not the seas surrounding Fiji and Hawaii be regarded as belonging to the rulers of those islands? But we already know, from the use of "strange" in association with Wordsworth's cluster of elements, that, for Wordsworth himself, those particular "strange seas of Thought" would belong to a ruler mightier than those mortal chieftains.

So the word "strange" in the "strange seas of Thought" would have two levels of meaning: public and private (as would certain phrases about the higher mind in the final Book). To Wordsworth's contemporaries at large, "strange" would mean, at least, "new" and hitherto "unknown," and probably to many of them it would convey what the *Oxford English Dictionary* describes as its tenth meaning:

"exceptional to a degree that excites wonder or astonishment"—a meaning that catches the essence of what Scott had conveyed in his Ode when he wrote that Newton "trac'd the wonders of the sky; / The chambers of the sun explor'd." A fair number of Wordsworth's contemporaries would also have been reminded of a more recent use of the word "strange" with that particular meaning, for Byron had used it in a notable stanza of *Don Juan*, a stanza, moreover, which in a number of other ways offers suggestive parallels to Wordsworth's passage. "'Tis strange,—but true;" Byron had said, "for Truth is always strange— / Stranger than fiction," and then had gone on to illustrate by showing what would happen "If some Columbus of the moral seas / Would show mankind their Souls' antipodes."[44] For Wordsworth privately—and for those few of his readers who would have understood what "strange" meant for him when he used it in conjunction with the seven elements in the cluster—"strange" (when applied to the "Seas of Thought") would mean even more: it would indicate that Newton's mind was voyaging on the seas of Thought in the very mind of God. And to a more rarefied level than that neither Newton nor Wordsworth could possibly elevate the human mind, in either the study of Nature or the writing of Poetry.

Little wonder, then, that Newton's mind will go voyaging "for ever," for, since (as Hamilton asserted) God continues to energize each natural object with his creative Thought, the "strange seas of Thought" will continue growing for ever. And since those "strange seas of Thought" represent God's continuing creation, there was further reason still for the phrase "for ever"—it calls to mind the ending traditionally added to the Lord's Prayer: "for Thine is the Kingdom, the Power, and the Glory, for ever and ever, Amen."

His Silent Face

But in this reading have we not gone too great a distance, in only two lines of verse, from the statue which simply "stood" with a "prism" and a "silent face"? And have we not made Wordsworth excessively idiosyncratic in his view of Newton, voyaging into the very mind of God? Actually there is a phrase in the original five lines which shows that Wordsworth, in the concluding two, was working out implications already contained in the earlier lines. The same phrase also shows that Wordsworth was not alone in what he had implied. That phrase is "his...silent face."

Why would Wordsworth specify the face as being silent? The mouth, or lips, or tongue, could be silent, but how could the face? A possible answer is, indeed, that by "silent" Wordsworth meant "quiet": that from the statue's face there issued no sound. Such an answer, however, would be bland at best and virtually tautological, and, in view of Wordsworth's penchant for understatement, it would probably not do justice to the phrase.

There is a lot of understated paradoxical irony in the whole of the Newton passage. In the final version there is, pre-eminently, the paradox that what is standing (stone still) points to what is always in motion, for ever voyaging. Even in the early versions, those without the completing couplet, there is a paradox about light and seeing. By the light of the moon or the favouring stars, the speaker could behold the prism, which, however, could not refract light, and the eyes which, likewise, could not see.[45] (Stone statuary makes it painfully obvious that the eyes are blind, and the sculptors' convention of reaming out a circle for the pupil only reinforces the impression.) At the same time, this stone statue, unrefracting and unseeing, represents a prism that revealed the secrets of light and eyes that perceived something far beyond what anyone else had seen before. Those eyes had seen the ideas within the light and within something else, too: within the motion of the midnight moon and the tides it affects and within the motion of the favouring stars.

Our attention is directed to these eyes by the word "silent," applied, not to the eyes directly, but to the face. One meaning of "silent" provides another paradox, that of speaking silently, through the eyes. The poet Daniel had used the word in this meaning, when he wrote "Sweet silent Rhetorique of perswading eyes," and Sir Walter Scott in 1819 would demonstrate that this particular meaning was still current, when he wrote, "The younger knights told each other with their eyes, in silent correspondence."[46] Newton's "silent face" would likewise bespeak his eloquent eyes.

Now that our attention is on the eyes, another meaning of "silent" can come into play. It is the one listed by the *Oxford English Dictionary* as "not shining" (referring to the moon) and by Johnson in his *Dictionary* as "wanting efficacy." It is illustrated in the speech of Milton's Samson:

> The Sun to me is dark
> And silent as the Moon,

When she deserts the night,
Hid in her vacant interlunar cave.

(Another phrase of Milton's—"silent, and in face / Confounded long they sate, as struck'n mute"—could, in its close conjunction of the two words, have helped to produce Wordsworth's "silent face": with regard to both of Milton's phrases, the pejorative value judgement would not, as we have seen, have kept Wordsworth from using them with a favourable connotation.)[47] Most remarkably, Newton himself had used the word "silent" with precisely this lunar meaning. "The Jews," he had written, "referred all the time of the silent moon, as they phrased it, that is, of the moon's disappearing[,] to the old moon."[48] It should be noted that Newton used, not the static noun "disappearance," but the active gerund "disappearing." On the silent face of Newton's statue, as the observer gazes up at it, the moon-like eyes, rolling up, seem to be on the point of disappearing under the upper lids. The imagined eyes they represent had looked to the ideas within, to the non-physcial within the physical. In fact they had become blind to the physical world (as Samson's had—and as Wordsworth's had when he entered his own "vacant" mood), and thereby allowed Newton's mind to voyage free.

Milton's linking of "silent," "Hid," and "vacant" can point us to something similar in Wordsworth's lines. The meaning of "Hid" is clear, and "silent" has been explained (by way of the moon) as meaning "having disappeared from physical sight." "Vacant" remains a puzzle. How likely is it that it means "unoccupied" when the Moon is described as occupying it? There is available the meaning in a definition offered by the *Oxford English Dictionary:* "Devoid of all material contents or accessories." Especially if one emphasizes the word *material*, one can read "vacant" as being in accord with both "silent" and "Hid" as meaning "removed from the realm of physical sight." Not only are all three of Milton's words in accord with one another, but also they are in accord with Wordsworth's "silent," as it directs our attention to the philosopher's eyes disappearing from the physical and material world, and with his "vacant" in the poem on the Daffodils, as it leads us from the physical scene to that which flashed on the poet's "inward eye." As being "vacant" or withdrawn from the physical world in the poem on the Daffodils led to a "pensive" state, so, in the lines on Newton's statue, being "silent" or withdrawn from the physical world allowed Newton's Mind (and for Philo the mind was the eye of the soul) to voyage through strange seas of "Thought."[49]

In Wakeful Vision Rapt

To return to the outward eyes of Newton's statue and to approach them from a different direction: they are certainly at variance with the rest of the statue. Although the eyes roll up, the head is not tilted back far enough to allow the face to look up: instead the legs, body, hands, and head are all consonant with a stationary musing or meditation, in which one gazes straight ahead. Why would the eyes differ so radically?

Two codes appear to be at work with the statue. One we are familiar with, the verbal code of literary allusion, whereby Robert Smith (presumably) was able to indicate, through the inscription, that Newton was superior to all philosophers outside the Judeo-Christian tradition. There was also operative, at the time the statue was erected and for at least close to a hundred years afterwards, another code, a visual code of gesture and expression. In fact there were variations within the code, as indicated by James Elmes in his book, *A General and Bibliographical Dictionary of the Fine Arts*, under the entry "Expression." It was the presence of this code which allowed the same scholar to remark that "To consider a picture aright is to *read it*"—as one would read a poem or a play.[50] Presumably one could read a statue in the same way and for the same reason. Charles Le Brun (whose painting of the Magdalene had moved Wordsworth profoundly) produced the most influential code of the meanings of expressions and gestures, and John Williams provided an English translation of his work, along with illustrative drawings, in 1734. J. J. Engel produced another work, in German, which was translated into French and was adapted by Henry Siddons into an English version.[51]

That the code was taken seriously and applied in works of visual art is seen most eloquently in the painting by Haydon of Christ's triumphant entry into Jerusalem we have mentioned before. There Wordsworth himself, although Christ is depicted as approaching him from no farther away than twenty feet, appears to look, not at Christ, but downwards at his own feet. Actually his eyes are completely shut, and his anomalous posture is explained by the way Le Brun described that kind of veneration which requires our faith: a person filled with this kind of veneration will have "all the parts of the face...

Veneration
From Charles Le Brun's *A Method to Learn to Design the Passions* (1734; Los Angeles: Augustan Reprint Society, 1980).

Wordsworth
Detail from Haydon's painting, *Christ's Triumphant Entry into Jerusalem,* used by permission of the Rector and Reverend Fathers of the Athenaeum of Ohio.

profoundly inclined" and "the eyes and mouth will be shut."[52] Haydon was simply demonstrating Wordsworth's veneration with faith. A comparison of Haydon's Wordsworth and Williams' Veneration will quickly confirm this.

What Le Brun said about rapture (or ecstasy or transport—the terms were interchangeable) indicates that the eyes of Newton's statue, along with other aspects of its face, probably signify such an emotion. For Le Brun rapture (or ecstasy) was the last in a series of four emotions, in which the succeeding one rose above the preceding: admiration led to esteem, which led to veneration (the kind that did not require faith), and that in turn led to "extasy." With all four emotions the mouth is partly open. With admiration the eyebrows are raised and the pupils are fixed in the middle between the two eyelids. With esteem the pupils rise and the cheeks gently fall about the jaws. With veneration the pupils rise higher, as the soul is elevated towards the object contemplated. With ecstasy, which is "caused by an object above the knowledge of the Soul, as the Power and Greatness of

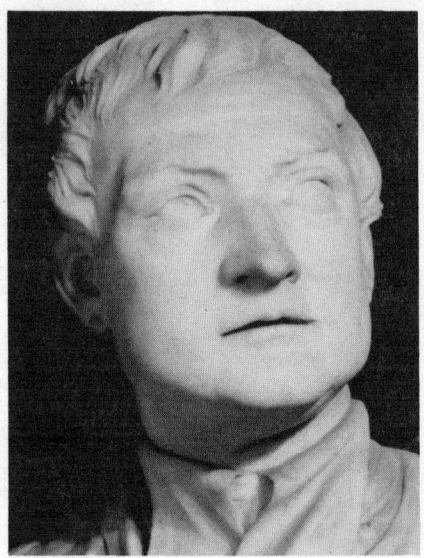

Newton
Detail from statue of Newton by Roubiliac, used by permission of the Master and Fellows of Trinity College, Cambridge.

Extasy
From Charles Le Brun's *A Method to Learn to Design the Passions* (1734; Los Angeles: Augustan Reprint Society, 1980).

GOD," both the eyebrows and the pupils are "lifted up towards heaven, where they seem fixed to discover the mysteries which the Soul cannot attain to." "The Mouth being half open, and the corners a little rising, intimate a kind of Extasy and Transport."[53]

Evidently there were two kinds of rapture. The erotic kind, which Le Brun seems to have in mind with some of his description, caused the head to decline, while the eyes were lifted up towards heaven, and the mouth was half open, with "the corners a little rising." Bernini, in his statue of the Ecstasy of St. Theresa, displays these characteristics to the detail, gently declining the saint's head to the left. There was also, we were reminded by William Rowan Hamilton in his address to the British Association, a "rapture solemn and sublime." This quality appears to be mixed in Newton's statue with what Henry Siddons called "admiration and sublimity," in which state a person is depicted with the head and body thrown back a little, the whole figure straight, and all of the feet, hands, and "traits of the visage" in repose.[54]

Equipped with these details of the code, we can now begin to read the statue of Newton. His whole body is straight, rising up and tilted slightly back, as if he had been suddenly arrested by an elevating thought. The head is tilted slightly to the meditative and intellectual right (as distinct from the sensual left). The face itself bears a startling similarity to the drawing John Williams provided to illustrate what Le Brun had written about ecstasy. The square-set jaws in each probably reflect the gentle fall of the cheeks about the jaws. On close examination, the lines of the mouth can be seen to be similar, with the ends just beginning to rise in a smile. The eyebrows are lifted in similar ways, with a sharp angle in the middle. And the eyes especially are similar, not only in their upward roll, but also in the fact that the left pupil is slightly higher than the right and is already beginning to disappear under the eyelid. In view of this extraordinarily close parallel, it may be that Roubiliac, whether on his own or at the behest of Robert Smith, deliberately reproduced what Le Brun and Williams together had presented as the characteristics of rapture. At the very least, it appears inescapable that the "silent face" depicts a "rapture solemn and sublime."[55]

Not only were there two kinds of rapture: there were also two attitudes current about what rapture meant. One held that rapture was the sudden access of extreme emotion, during which one remained very much in the realm of physical reality. The other held that rapture involved the mind's leaving the body, removing itself (or being removed) from the realm of physical reality, and entering into an apprehension of the intellectual, intelligible, spiritual, or nonphysical kind of reality.[56] The way in which Hamilton went on, in his address, to describe "that rapture solemn and sublime" suggests that he held to this latter view, for he said that, in that state, "a human mind, possessing or possessed by some great truth, sees in prophetic vision that truth acknowledged by mankind." The matter of being "possessed" calls to mind, of course, the classical view of rapture occurring when a deity entered a human being and seized the mind, lifting it up into a perception of supraphysical reality. We can take for granted that, during at least one of his many trips to England, Hamilton made a pilgrimage to the Antechapel of Trinity College, there to revel in the extraordinary felicity with which Roubiliac had represented his idol. He could, consequently, have had the statue in mind when he described the state of rapture in the way he did. (He may even have been influenced by Wordsworth's oral response to the statue during one of their conversations.) At the very least, the existence of the visual code accounts for the anomaly in Newton's stance, between his eyes and the rest of his body, just as it accounts for the anomaly of Wordsworth's stance in Haydon's painting. And if the concept of rapture as being lifted into a supraphysical reality were taken seriously, as Hamilton appears to have taken it, then it would be clear that Wordsworth was not alone, or even idiosyncratic, in his acceptance of two dimensions, aspects, or modes of reality.[57]

This kind of rapture Wordsworth depicted in two other sets of poetic lines. The first set represents a temporary version of the lines on Newton's statue. Reconstructed from Wordsworth's manuscript, and usually referred to as MS. A^2, that version reads:

> Her pealing Organ was my neighbour, too;
> And, from my Pillow, when the Moon shone fair
> Or even by dimmer influence of the stars,
> In wakeful vision rapt I could behold
> Solemnly near and pressing on my sight
> The Antechapel, where the Statue stood
> Of Newton, with his Prism & silent Face.[58]

These lines contain many striking parallels to the account which Agamemnon gave of the vision which came to him in his sleep, as set down in Homer's original Greek *(Iliad,* 2:56-59) and in the translations of the passage made by Chapman, Pope, and Cowper. It is only appropriate that there should be so many parallels, since the vision appeared in the shape of Nestor, the "sage, with whom," in Cowper's translation, "In Agamemnon's thought might none compare," and since, in Chapman's translation, the vision "stood," Agamemnon said, "above my head" (as, of course, Newton's statue does for anyone standing on the floor and looking at it).[59] Homer used two words for the kind of phenomenon the figure was: ὄνειρος (dream) and ἐνύπνιον (vision in sleep), for which reason translators vary between "dream" (Cowper and Pope) and "vision" (Chapman and Pope), and for which reason, presumably, Wordsworth was careful to write "wakeful vision" so as to distinguish his vision, experienced while he was awake, from the vision which came to Agamemnon while he was asleep.[60] In Pope's version Agamemnon said, "A Dream Divine appear'd before my Sight" (2:72), and Wordsworth's line reads "Solemnly near and pressing on my sight." The figure, in Homer's original, was compared to Nestor in three aspects, but with Pope it was in two ("in Habit, and in Mien") and with Chapman it was in four, two of which were "habite [and] forme of face": these two aspects parallel Wordsworth's "prism" as characteristic of the astronomer's accoutrement and, of course, his "silent face."

Homer has Agamemnon say that the vision came ἀμβροσίην διὰ νύκτα, which the Loeb author translates as "through the ambrosial night." Liddell and Scott note that, especially when used to describe night, ἀμβρόσιος means "divine," and undoubtedly the word carried reverberations from the other word from which it derived, ἄμβροτος (immortal). Translators have ranged widely in their attempts to suggest something adequate. Among twentieth-century translators, Richmond Lattimore has written "through the immortal night," E. V. Rieu "through the solemn night," and Robert Fitzgerald "in the starry night."[61] Of the translators Wordsworth would have known, Chapman wrote "In this Night's depth," and it is worth noting that a line which MS. A^2 replaced read "And in deep midnight when the Moon shone fair." More significantly, Cowper wrote "Amid the stillness of the vacant night" (2:68). If it were not for the Greek words Cowper was translating, "vacant" (that word again) could simply indicate the lack of activity in the night, but since it does seek, along with "stillness," to offer something parallel to ἀμβροσίην, it would appear that it carries the meaning Wordsworth used in his poem on the Daffodils: "abstracted from the physical realm." In view of these various attempts at translation, it is little wonder that Wordsworth wrote "by the dimmer influence of the stars," and especially in view of Cowper's "vacant," it is probable that Wordsworth's "rapt" in his phrase "In wakeful vision rapt" bore its full, basic meaning of being carried away in spirit, of being in a state of rapture.[62]

In this particular, temporary version, Wordsworth indicated that it was while he was awake and in a state of rapture that he beheld the vision in the shape of Newton, with his prism and silent face. And there lies the answer to the question that must have been forming: why, in view of its superb appropriateness, accurate down to the smallest detail, did Wordsworth abandon this version which applied Agamemnon's vision of Nestor to his own vision of Newton? We would suggest that Wordsworth came to realize that what he had said about himself, about his being "In wakeful vision rapt," he had already said about Newton, in that one, single word "silent."

Philo explains how. In a passage which runs parallel to ones we have already looked at and which appears in his treatise on the migration of Abraham, Philo wrote something that provides an explanation of why Agamemnon and other ancients like him accepted dream visions as conveyors of truth. "In deep sleep," Philo wrote (such as Agamemnon experienced), "the mind quits its place, and, withdrawing from [sense] perceptions and all other bodily faculties"—it sounds like "vacant" again, does it not?—"...it is filled with Divine frenzy and discerns in dreams absolutely true prophecies concerning things to come."[63] The same happens, Philo wrote, in "wakeful" hours—the same word Wordsworth used to distinguish his "wakeful vision" from one that comes in dreams.[64] When the mind is "possessed by some philosophic principle" and when it has "divested itself of body, sense-perception, [and] speech" and spends its time "in darkness and solitude" (which is how Wordsworth envisaged the statue), then it can perceive the "intelligible," the nonphysical reality.[65] If you were to choose one word to sum up the state in which, according to Philo, a person can achieve that kind of perception, would not that word have to reflect the properties of speechlessness, darkness, and solitude, and would not that single word be "silent"?

That Wordsworth thought so appears in a crucial stanza in his poem "Star Gazers." That stanza begins with noticeable parallels to "I Wandered Lonely As a Cloud" with its "pensive mood," its "bliss of solitude," its "inward eye," its phrase "I gazed—and gazed," and its "pleasure" which fills the heart:

> Does, then, a deep and earnest thought the blissful mind employ
> Of him who gazes, or has gazed? a grave and steady joy,

It continues and ends with obvious parallels to the lines on Newton's statue:

> That doth reject all shew of pride, admits not outward sign,
> Because not of this noisy world, but silent and divine.[66]

Of even greater interest is the close parallel these four lines bear to the passage of Philo we were considering a moment ago, and to other passages of Philo like it. Wordsworth's first line, "Does, then, a deep and earnest thought the blissful mind employ," puts into the active voice what Philo phrased in the passive: "when the mind, possessed by some philosophic principle, is drawn by it." (Philo's word for "possessed"—κατασχεθείς—carries with it connotations of being possessed by a god.)[67] And whose blissful mind is it? With Wordsworth it is "Of him who gazes, or has gazed"; with Philo it is of φιλοθεάμοσι (those who are fond of gazing)—or, as the Loeb translators phrase it, "those who find happiness in beholding." What does this mind do? With Philo it repels the assault of the senses, closing the eyes and stopping up the ears.[68] With Wordsworth it "doth reject all shew of pride, admits not outward sign"—which certainly sounds like a selective paraphrase of Philo's wording.

Early in the treatise of Philo's that is printed immediately after the one on the migration of Abraham appear lines concerned with the effect on the Sage (Abraham) when he received from God the oracle concerning his posterity. One would expect, Philo wrote, that he would have been struck "mute and speechless in amazement at the majesty and greatness of the Giver of the oracle, if not for fear, at any rate for exceeding joy. For men are [silenced] by overwhelming joy, as well as by violent grief."[69] Wordsworth has likewise provided two phrases for his joy, the second stronger than the first, when he wrote "the blissful mind" and followed it with "a grave and steady joy." The matter of being rendered speechless he reduced from Philo's three words to the one "silent" and associated with it the reason, again in one word, "divine," summarizing what Philo had expressed in "the majesty and greatness of the Giver of the oracle."[70] Balanced over against the "silent and divine" he set its opposite, "this noisy world," which parallels neatly the phrase "noisy pack of the senses" which Philo used in another, closely related, treatise.[71] It was from this noisy pack that the mind, shutting out sense-impressions, escapes into a presumably silent contemplation of the "intelligible." Noise and the physical go together; so do silence and the nonphysical, the spiritual and divine.

The whole of "Star Gazers" can be read profitably as an allegory, on two related levels. One, in the manner of Philo himself, considers the noisy crowd as representing the physical senses and sense-perception, and the mind, with its joy silent and divine, representing the eye of the soul which perceives the nonphysical reality.[72] The other level brings us back to the passage in *The Excursion* with which this study began, for here in "Star Gazers" those who "pry and pore" and go away "dissatisfied" (lines 29-32) parallel those scientists in the *Excursion* passage who, by confining themselves to sensual observation, "pry far off" and "pore" but remain "unsatisfied" and continue to wage their "impious warfare with the very life / Of our own souls!"[73] The difference is that in "Star Gazers" there is one astronomer (and which astronomer would qualify more than Newton?) who left behind mere sense impression and with his mind entered into communion with the divine.

Of special relevance to the lines on Newton's statue is the way in which Wordsworth crafted the stanza in "Star Gazers" which is inescapably about Newton. It would appear that Wordsworth called to mind three closely related passages in Philo and selected from them the key phrases that would suit his purpose, often summarizing even those phrases. In "Star Gazers" he summed up the positive characteristics of Newton's mind and what it was associated with in two words, "silent" and "divine." In the early lines on Newton's statue, he summed up in one word: "silent." That word was fraught with meaning for him. It summarized the quality of Philonic darkness and solitude in which Wordsworth envisaged the statue (somehow Cowper's line "In the stillness of the vacant night" comes to mind); it summarized the effect of the upward roll of the statue's eyes, about to shut out the physical world; and it summarized the Philonic and Le Brunian effect of being overwhelmed, rapt and transported, by the sight of the majesty and greatness of the Divine Creator.[74]

The Uncreated

Wordsworth may not have been the only one to combine the concepts of Philo and Le Brun and to apply them to Newton. Robert Smith may well have been behind the use of the visual code in the depiction of Newton, just as he was behind the use of the verbal code, and he may well have intended to indicate, by the visual code, something analogous to what was indicated by the verbal. Smith would probably have known of Philo. He was a reader in Greek at Trinity (as well as the Plumian professor of astronomy), and he quoted Greek writers in his book on harmonics. He was present at Trinity when Mangey would have examined the manuscripts of Philo housed in the library there. And he was in fact Master of Trinity and acting vice-chancellor of the University in the year when Mangey's edition of Philo was published. He would probably also have known of the visual code: he was greatly interested in the fine arts, donating a number of art works to the College and himself becoming proficient in playing the violoncello. He had the kind of mind required to perceive how a suitable statement could be made through using the visual code, for the French translator of his treatise on optics applauded the neatness and order with which he had brought together all the discoveries in optics—discoveries to which he himself had in fact added. That neatness, order, and ability to see a step beyond is what was needed to use the code with dramatic simplicity.[75] Just, then, as Smith used the verbal code to indicate Newton's rising above the philosophers outside the Judeo-Christian tradition, so he (as Professor of Sacred Theology) could have used the visual code to indicate Newton's position vis-à-vis those philosophers who were within the Judeo-Christian tradition, especially one in particular, for whom the claim had been made that he was pre-eminent over all other philosophers.

In his treatise on the allegorical interpretation of the Bible, Philo described what "a mind more perfect and purified" does. It, evidently alone, rises up above all creation (Mangey's Latin runs remarkably parallel to the Lucretian clause inscribed on Newton's statue: *emergens supra creata omnia*). In that solitary position, this mind not only sees the whole world, which is the shadow of God, but also obtains a clear vision of the Uncreated One Himself.[76] This mind, Philo says, is Moses. What he means, clearly, is that Moses symbolically represents this kind of mind, but it is also clear that Philo believed Moses, and Moses alone, possessed this kind of mind, for Moses alone beheld God face to face.[77] Note the three elements involved: Moses rises above all creation, he sees all the physical world (the shadow of God), and he sees God Himself. Compare these with the corresponding three elements that are predominant in the statue of Newton: the inscription, which indicates that Newton rose above all others; the prism held in his hands, which alludes to his *Opticks* and to his discovery of the nature of light (and light's being the shadow of God Milton attests to in his famous description of the skirts of God as "Dark with excessive bright");[78] and his eyes, which in their rapturous roll upwards indicate that Newton saw God and thereby allude to the General Scholium of his *Principia*, where he insisted that it was God who maintained the law of gravity. The implication certainly appears to be that the statue, taken with its inscription, asks the question: who was it, alone among human beings, both those outside the Judeo-Christian tradition and those within it, who rose above creation, saw the shadow of God (i.e., light) clearly, and saw God Himself clearly? In the same way the statue answers the question: it was Newton.

That this was, in fact, the reading of the statue intended to be achieved by those capable of achieving it is indicated, we would suggest, indirectly by William Selwyn's description of the statue. The principal paragraph reads as follows:

> It is a monument to be gazed at in silence and stillness; for such is the expression of the whole figure: the countenance is full of patient thought and calm self possession; the philosopher is alone with nature and with God. He holds in his hand the prism of glass with which he separated the sunbeam, "offspring of heaven first-born," into its seven distinct rays. But the statue represents far more than the circumstances of this particular discovery; it is an excellent impersonation of the whole philosophic character of the man, answering admirably to the description which he gives of his own habits of investigation: "I keep the subject of my enquiry constantly before me and wait till the first dawning opens gradually, by little and little, into a full and clear light." Some may observe a slight expression of pleasure in the countenance, indicating that the light has dawned upon the enquirer and that he is rejoicing to follow his guidance. And perhaps there is even more than this; something beyond the philosophic character. The eye uplifted to heaven, the happy serenity which pervades the features, may well persuade us (and in this hallowed place who can refuse to believe?) that in this outward form was enshrined a spirit full of immortality; a soul touched with "the tender mercy of our God, whereby the dayspring from on high hath visited us."[79]

First, it will be noted, Selwyn, too, associates silence with the presence of the divine: "in silence...alone...with God." More importantly, Selwyn makes a reading, or interpretation, of the statue: "the statue represents far more than the circumstances of this particular discovery....And perhaps there is even more than this; something beyond the philosophic character." Selwyn makes his reading by focussing on the aspects of the statue on which we have focussed: the prism, the expression of pleasure or happy serenity (which would derive from the lips), and the uplifted eye. Selwyn likewise sees rapture, although he does not use the word: "the eye uplifted to heaven" and the "happy serenity which pervades the features" derive from the fact that the soul has been visited by the "dayspring from on high"—which is a Christian expression of the classical concept of a person's being possessed by a deity. No wonder Newton rejoices to follow "his" guidance. There are also signs that Selwyn was aware of the claim being made that Newton rose above Epicurus. His quotation from Newton himself, about early light being eclipsed by the full and clear light, parallels the image in the context from which the inscription below the statue was taken, of stars being eclipsed by the sun; and the quotation from Luke 1.78, of the dayspring, points to the sun and the source of light it represents. Selwyn also says, outright, that Newton went "beyond the philosophic character"; so he must have surpassed Epicurus. The reason Selwyn supplies for Newton's superiority, however, provides a piously passive corrective to the view expressed in the inscription: it was not by his own doing that Newton excelled, but rather, as Newton himself pointed out, because the divine dayspring visited him and provided him with the guidance needed.

There are even implications in the paragraph that are consonant with Selwyn's having been aware of the reading of the statue which claimed that Newton surpassed, not only Epicurus, but also Moses. Selwyn had graduated, like Wordsworth, from St. John's College, next door to Trinity, and in fact his father had "migrated" from St. John's to Trinity itself. The son was an outstanding classical scholar, winning the Chancellor's medal in classics and going on to edit Origen's treatise *Contra Celsum*.[80] Especially in the light of his scholarship, it is a curious thing that he misapplied Milton's phrase "offspring of heaven first-born." Milton had described in these terms, not the sunbeam, but the holy Light, the second person of the Trinity.[81] Actually, since Milton went on to offer the alternative view that the second person was, not created, but Coeternal with the Eternal, Selwyn appears to have accepted this alternative and to have used Milton's phrase "first-born" to refer to the first part of the universe to be created, the light which issued forth at the command "Let there be light!" In this reading, light, being the first-born, represents the whole of creation, and it is the nature of this which Newton has discovered. Where Moses (according to Philo) rose above creation, Newton did more: he perceived what it is; clearly, then, Newton is superior.

Following on Newton's statement that he waited for the light to grow full and clear, Selwyn could have used any number of Biblical quotations concerning the divine source of light, such as 1 Peter 2.9: Christ, "who hath called you out of darkness into his marvellous light." But instead he chose Luke 1.78. That particular verse, like the inscription beneath the statue, has a context which appears to be relevant. Zacharias prophesies concerning his son John:

> 76 And thou, child, shalt be called the prophet of the Highest: for thou shalt go before the face of the Lord to prepare his ways;
> 77 To give knowledge of salvation unto his people by the remission of their sins,
> 78 Through the tender mercy of our God; whereby the dayspring from on high hath visited us,
> 79 To give light to them that sit in darkness and in the shadow of death, to guide our feet into the way of peace.

Selwyn refers to the last phrase of the context when, in the sentence immediately following the description of the statue, he addresses "all the sons of Alma Mater, who desire to follow Newton's steps in Newton's spirit." The beginning of verse 79 Selwyn would certainly appear to expect his readers to have in mind, for its reference to giving light to them that sit in darkness fits both John and Newton as receivers and transmitters of light. Consequently it is at least noteworthy that the reference to John as "the prophet of the Highest" (verse 76) would establish a parallel, not only between John and Newton, but also between John and Moses and hence Newton and Moses, for it was common to refer to Moses as the chief prophet.[82] With that parallel established, a striking difference would then emerge. Although Philo claimed that Moses had seen God clearly, in Exodus 33.20-23 God is presented as saying that Moses cannot see him face to face, for, if he did, he would die. Instead, God granted him the sight only of his "back parts." John, on the other hand, according to Zacharias, will "go before the face of the Lord." The parallel between John and Newton would suggest that, whereas Moses saw only the back parts of God, Newton saw his face. If such an implication was, in fact, intended by Selwyn, he still sought, as with the reference to Newton's relation to Epicurus, to correct the reading that was current, and did so in the same way. Newton achieved the sight of God, not through his own doing, but because God, in his tender mercy, condescended to visit him and to provide him with the light whereby he could see. Nonetheless, of course, a desire to correct a reading confirms the existence of that reading.

Wordsworth's final, complete description of Newton's statue focusses on the same three elements as did the statue and the reading of it. The prism reflects Newton's having seen clearly into those aspects of nature which no one else had seen before. The silent face, bespeaking the eloquent eyes, indicates Newton's having seen God in the workings of nature more clearly than any had before, and this indication is elaborated on in the strange seas of Thought, the flood of Ideas issuing from the Mind of God. Newton was able to voyage on those seas and to behold God at work because, as is suggested by one meaning of the culminating word "alone," his mind had been able to slip free of the senses and to venture into the intelligible unimpeded. And the same culminating word, in another meaning, indicates that it was only Newton, alone of all creation, who was able to make that voyage.

Alone

From many sources Wordsworth would have been moved to emphasize the solitary nature of Newton's undertaking and the uniqueness of his achievement. A number of predecessors had shown him that "alone" would be much more effective than any of its synonyms— sole, single, solitary, apart, and lone—for it combines various useful advantages: it is brief, its second syllable is emphasized, thereby providing an iambic foot, and that same second syllable resonates most effectively.

But how could he present the word for maximum effectiveness? Tollet's placing of the word, in the middle of a line, almost hid it from sight. Thomson ended a clause with it, but in the middle of a line, and he continued his sentence for another three lines and a half—still, the germ of the idea could have been implanted. Wordsworth's friend Coleridge, in a remarkably parallel passage in "The Rime of the Ancient Mariner," had tried two other ways of emphasizing, actually combining the two (repeating the word and placing it at the beginning of the line) when he had his Mariner say of himself: "Alone, alone, all, all alone, / Alone on a wide wide sea!"[83] This was certainly emphatic, but neither restrained nor succinct. Was there still another way?

Of course there was, as Wordsworth well knew, for on at least eleven previous occasions he had placed "alone" at the end of both a sentence and a line. It was as if he had been practising for more than forty years for this particular opportunity. On one occasion he showed signs of imitating his friend Coleridge, for, in writing about a persevering gold-miner and his colleagues, he said: "they tried, were foiled— / And all desisted, all, save him alone."[84] More serious, and restrained, was his Hermit, in "Tintern Abbey," who "by his fire" sat "alone."[85] A number of other "alone's" served to intensify pathos. There was the ineffable Goody Blake, who, "poor Woman! housed alone."[86] There was the narrator who, while riding in a coach, heard a cry; he alighted, "And there a little Girl I found, / Sitting behind the chaise, alone."[87] Another narrator (or was he the same?) saw "A healthy man, a man full grown, / Weep in the public roads, alone."[88] It is clear from these last two examples that, as early as 1798, Wordsworth had learned of the added effect that could be achieved, when ending both a sentence and a line with "alone," by putting a comma before the "alone." But the word "alone" had to be justified, as he remarked to Hamilton, when commenting, as the resident expert in closing with "alone," on lines that Hamilton's friend Francis Edgeworth had written:

> There was nought there
> But those three antient hills, *alone*.
>
> Here the word "alone," being used instead of "only," makes an absurdity like that noticed in the *Spectator*— "Enter a king and three fiddlers, *solus*."[89]

All these examples, except for the solitary gold-miner and the Hermit, appeared in something less than pentameter and so did not provide much insight into what would have to be done to the roomier pentameter setting of the *Prelude* passage in order to gain full effect from ending with "alone"—after the dramatic comma pause. But two other passages, each in pentameter, *do* provide insight, in one way or another, for us, and one of them undoubtedly did for Wordsworth. In *The Borderers* Oswald declaims, "Solitude!— / The Eagle lives in Solitude!", and Marmaduke replies:

> Even so,
> The Sparrow so on the house-top, and I,
> The weakest of God's creatures, stand resolved
> To abide the issue of my act, alone.[90]

The difference between posturing, with Marmaduke, and taking a natural stand, with Newton, is abundantly clear, but we can see the mechanics required to gain maximum effect beginning to emerge, however misdirected they may be. The other passage does a better job of matching content with tone. It addresses a mountain shepherd, such as him whose form, in *The Prelude*, is glorified:

> Up, hardy Mountaineer!
> And guide the Bard, ambitious to be One
> Of Nature's privy council, as thou art,
> On cloud-sequestered heights, that see and hear
> To what dread Powers He delegates his part
> On Earth, who works in the heaven of heavens, alone.[91]

While closer in tone to the Newton passage, these lines are, of course, hortatory and so are elaborated (instead of encapsulating and succinct), but still their mechanics, like the preceding, give a helpful clue. In addition to placing a comma before the final "alone," both passages gain from having enjambement between the penultimate and final lines. But, to consider negative lessons as well, in each passage the final major movement begins some distance before the penultimate line, with only a faint pause (if any) between the third last and second last lines, and in each passage the final major movement, within the last two lines, is interrupted, before the penultimate pause. As a result, the movement sounds, and looks, both serpentine and halting. The peculiar thing is that, although the passage addressing the Mountaineer was written before the concluding lines of the Newton passage, the other passage (or, more accurately, the part of it found in Marmaduke's speech) was written *after*, while Wordsworth was revising *The Borderers* for publication in 1842.[92] Taken together, both suggest that what was needed in the *Prelude* passage was a straightforward, uninterrupted progression, almost like a march, to reflect the purposefulness of the subject's undertaking. Obviously Wordsworth found a source, or model, for that kind of progression and applied it in the Newton passage, but the fact that he was not able to duplicate it, or even come near to equalling it, in Marmaduke's speech indicates that his model must have been almost uniquely well suited for the Newton passage.

For the kind of effect desired, the architecture of the lines is all important. It is noteworthy that as one stands at the communion rail in the Chapel of Trinity College, Cambridge, and looks down the long nave—the long, articulated, but unbroken nave (so remarkably like a stately double line of run-on iambic pentameter)—one's eye proceeds at a measured pace, between rank on rank of serried stalls, pauses at the distant open doorway leading to the Antechapel, and then leaps to the marble index as it floats grandly, just in front of the end wall of the Antechapel, all by itself, alone.[93] And there, of course, it stood, floating grandly, in Wordsworth's day, drawing to itself his physical eye, and drawing to itself his inward eye, as he looked out from his pillow. There it stood, towering above the observer, silent and fixed in penetrating thought, receiving, on its upturned eyes, the light of the moon and favouring stars. There it stood, with its prism and silent face,

> The marble index of a Mind for ever
> Voyaging thro' strange seas of Thought, alone.

Appendices

A The Myth of Wordsworth's Reading But Little

AN IMPRESSION HAS GOT ABROAD THAT WORDSWORTH had few books and was disinclined to read those he had. There are several grounds for that impression. In 1805 Dorothy Wordsworth complained that it was difficult to see a certain new book because of the isolation she and Mary and William endured at Grasmere: "Any new Book in our neighbourhood passes from house to house, and it is difficult to come at it within any reasonable time."[1] Thomas Hutchinson remarked that Dr. Robert Anderson's *Corpus* of the British poets "was for many years the only edition of the older English poets within W[ordsworth]'s reach."[2] Even as late as 1836 Wordsworth referred to his library at Rydal Mount as "My little Library," and in 1841 he remarked to J. P. Muirhead that he preferred to spend his money on travelling rather than buying books: in fact he thought that he could find books enough "in *the running brooks*, or even at a pinch, *make them himself.*"[3] In 1845 Wordsworth's close observer, Isabella Fenwick, remarked that Wordsworth "hardly deserves [receiving] a book—he so seldom reads one."[4] Wordsworth's maid evidently agreed with part of this sentiment, for, when, in 1838, a group of visitors asked her to show them Wordsworth's study, she "showed them the parlour where the books are, saying, 'This is his *library*, but his *study* is out of doors.'"[5] Even Wordsworth's nephew

Christopher agreed, for in his *Memoirs* he remarked that Wordsworth was a "reader of nature rather than books."[6]

Underpinning all such evidence of Wordsworth's being disinclined to read books, and providing a poetic foundation for it, are of course two famous Lyrical Ballads, "The Tables Turned" and "To My Sister." In the first poem the speaker urges his friend to quit his books, to "Close up those barren leaves... of Science and of Art" (lines 29-30). The reason?

> Books! 'tis a dull and endless strife:
> Come, hear the woodland linnet,
> How sweet his music! on my life,
> There's more of wisdom in it.
>
> And hark! how blithe the throstle sings!
> He, too, is no mean preacher:
> Come forth into the light of things,
> Let Nature be your Teacher.
>
> She has a world of ready wealth,
> Our minds and hearts to bless—
> Spontaneous wisdom breathed by health,
> Truth breathed by cheerfulness.
>
> One impulse from a vernal wood
> May teach you more of man,
> Of moral evil and of good,
> Than all the sages can.
>
> (lines 9-24)[7]

In "To My Sister" Wordsworth twice bids Dorothy to

> Put on with speed your woodland dress:
> And bring no book: for this one day
> We'll give to idleness.
>
> (lines 14-16; cf. lines 38-40)

The reason? "It is the first mild day of March" (line 1), and

> Love, now a universal birth
> From heart to heart is stealing,
> From earth to man, from man to earth:
> —It is the hour of feeling.
>
> One moment now may give us more
> Than years of toiling reason:
> Our minds shall drink at every pore
> The spirit of the season.
>
> (lines 21-28)[8]

As overwhelming as all this evidence may at first appear to be, one should still note certain qualifications about it. Dorothy's complaint about the difficulty in borrowing books referred to *new* books: the family still had their old books available, and, it should be added, her very complaint indicates that there *was* a system of borrowing new books in place in their neighbourhood: they were available in time. Dr. Anderson's *Corpus* was a massive twelve-volume collection: it was, after all, available, and if it were in fact the only source available for many years, it could have been referred to frequently, so frequently as to make its contents well known. Wordsworth described his library at Rydal Mount as "little" presumably in comparison to Sir Walter Scott's library at Abbotsford: Muirhead reported in 1841 that "Wordsworth said that his Library was very different from that of Scott, immeasurably smaller...." Muirhead continued in the same sentence: "—although he has books in every room of the house, and in every nook and cranny where they can be put...."[9] Here is part of the reason why Wordsworth preferred, after acquiring these books, to spend his money on travelling rather than on buying more books: where would he have put additional books? Another reason appears in the lyric extravagance he is reported to have uttered to Muirhead: his preference for finding books in the running brooks or, indeed, for making them himself, was part of his mystique as a romantic poet, a mystique which his maid had presumably accepted without question and which she (along with his nephew) helped to perpetuate.

In fact Wordsworth himself, amusingly, put the maid's story in the proper perspective, when, relating the story, he gave its context. In a note to the second Ode to Lycoris, he wrote: "This [poem and three others with it] were composed in front of Rydal Mount and during my walks in the neighbourhood. Nine-tenths of my verses have been murmured out in the open air, and here let me repeat [the story about the maid]"—which he did and then continued: "After a long absence from home it has more than once happened that some one of my cottage neighbours has said 'Well, there he is: we are glad to hear him *booing* about again.' "[10]

Christopher's remark that Wordsworth was "a reader of nature rather than books" appears to have been overstated, for in another part of the *Memoirs* he phrased the same comparison thus: "Nature appears to have done more for Wordsworth than books...," then continued: "yet he was not remiss as a student. He read much of English literature, especially works of imagination. He knew a great deal of English poetry by heart...."[11] Even Isabella Fenwick's remark in 1845 that Wordsworth seldom read a book is to be explained by a reason other than a temperamental disinclination to read: Wordsworth for many years had been suffering from a disease of the eyes that often made it unwise, and at times impossible, for him to read.[12]

And what of "The Tables Turned" and "To My Sister"? About the first poem, Russell Noyes has reminded us that, in writing it, Wordsworth was responding specifically to the unreasonable attachment of Hazlitt to books of moral philosophy, especially those of the coldly intellectual Godwin. "No one should seriously suppose that Wordsworth was here or elsewhere declaring himself an enemy of book learning. He obviously did not mean that a person was to give up reading now and forever anymore than he was to sit in permanent passiveness on an old gray stone. He was protesting against the overbearing encroachment of the 'meddling intellect'."[13] About both poems it is well to remember that "the most notable stylistic feature," as Noyes remarks, "is exaggeration." And as Christopher himself cautioned us, "it is very unjust and erroneous to cite any one poem, or a few lines, composed in his earlier years, as a deliberate expression of his maturer judgement."[14]

The reasons for believing that Wordsworth read widely and avidly, however, do not rest on the qualifying of opposing evidence. They are found in various accounts of his reading, at all stages of his life.

Even as a boy, when he spent much of his time rambling the hills of Westmoreland and Cumberland, exulting in his glad animal movements, he read a prodigious amount. That he read Ovid "voraciously" we have already seen. In his father's library he read Shakespeare, Milton, Spenser, Fielding's novels, *Gil Blas, Don Quixote, Gulliver's Travels,* and *The Arabian Nights.*[15] At Hawkshead Grammar School, according to the son of Wordsworth's master (who remembered what his father had told him), Wordsworth wanted "all sorts of books; Tours and Travels, which my father was partial to, and Histories and Biographies, which were also favourites with him; and Poetry—that goes without saying. My father used to get the latest books from Kendal every month, and I remember him telling how he lent Wordsworth Cowper's *Task* when it first came out, and Burns' *Poems.*"[16] While at Hawkshead William also read Sandys' *Travels in the East,* Foxe's *Martyrs,* Evelyn's *Forest Trees,* Langhorne's *Poems,* Beattie's *Minstrel,* Percy's *Reliques,* "the poetry of Crabbe and Charlotte Smith, and the two Wartons." So immersed was he in reading, in fact, that, when he returned home from Hawkshead for holidays, he would often read—outdoors, admittedly, yet, nonetheless, not keeping himself open to the impulse from the neighbouring wood, but, rather, absorbed in his book. In *The Prelude* he described his memory of the circumstances:

> How often, in the course
> Of those glad respites, though a soft west wind
> Ruffled the waters to the Angler's wish
> For a whole day together, have I lain
> Down by thy side, O Derwent, murmuring stream!
> On the hot stones, and in the glaring sun,
> And there have read, devouring as I read,
> Defrauding the day's glory, desperate!
>   (5:482-89)

In fact, another passage from the same book of *The Prelude* puts "The Tables Turned" into another, proper, perspective:

> he, who, in his youth,
> A daily Wanderer among woods and fields,
> With living Nature hath been intimate,
> Not only in that raw unpractised time
> Is stirred to extasy, as others are,
> By glittering verse; but, further, doth receive,
> In measure only dealt out to himself,
> Knowledge and increase of enduring joy

> From the great Nature that exists in works
> Of mighty Poets. Visionary Power
> Attends the motions of the viewless winds
> Embodied in the mystery of words:
> There darkness makes abode, and all the host
> Of shadowy things work endless changes there,
> As in a mansion like their proper home.
> Even forms and substances are circumfused
> By that transparent veil with light divine;
> And, through the turnings intricate of verse,
> Present themselves as objects recognized,
> In flashes, and with glory not their own.
>
> (5:588-607)[17]

Wordsworth's reading at Cambridge Dorothy summed up thus: "He reads Italian, Spanish, French, Greek and Latin, and English"; he reads "a great deal and not only poetry and those languages he is acquainted with but history &c &c."[18] As one would expect from the time, he paid special attention to his reading in Spenser and Milton, and soon afterwards added Chaucer to the number.[19] While living at Racedown, Wordsworth was kept well supplied with books by his friends, who passed on even such a minor piece as *Lewesdon Hill*, a landscape poem by a local poet and parson.[20] At Grasmere, likewise, friends supplied him with books: Charles Lamb, in particular, took care to copy out for him three poems that had recently been published.[21] In 1807 Dorothy mentioned that Wordsworth was "greedily devouring" two of Dr. T. D. Whitaker's histories that a friend had sent him.[22] Lane Cooper has shown that, by about this time, Wordsworth had read literally dozens and dozens of travel books.[23] And once Wordsworth became well known as a poet, he began to receive a steady stream of unsought books, especially from other, junior poets. Literally scores of Wordsworth's letters are gracious acknowledgements of such gifts. It is then no wonder that in 1830 Dorothy was able to try to entice their brother Christopher away from his beloved Cambridge and into a lengthy visit with them by boasting of the library facilities available to them: "... you would have no want of Books ancient or modern—Lady Fleming allows William free access to her old library, and would really be proud of your making use of it. There is also the Hawkshead School Collection of Divinity and other Books—and Southey's large library—not to speak of the miscellaneous assemblage on our own shelves."[24] This "miscellaneous assemblage" by the time of Wordsworth's death numbered over 3,000 volumes.[25] And it should be added that many of these which Wordsworth would not have been able to read for himself, because of his recurring eye disease, he would have had read to him by various members of his family. As Edith Morley sums up in her edition of H. C. Robinson's *Correspondence with the Wordsworth Circle,* "we know from numerous references in the letters here published that it was for many years customary, in the evenings at Rydal Mount, for one or other of the party to read aloud to the assembled family."

That Wordsworth made good use of the library facilities and of his various opportunities to indulge in them is evident from his letters. In Appendix B: Wordsworth's Attitude Towards Cambridge Undergraduates, samples are presented of the courteous replies he made to writers of prize poems and the like who sent him copies of their work—replies which often incorporated painstaking analyses of selected passages. He appears to have been equally well acquainted with very minor and usually forgotten poets of earlier periods as well. He could almost casually ask a friend to get him a particular volume "of Bell's forgotten poetry," and in writing to another friend he could refer, just as casually, to certain "pleasing verses" by Richard Corbet, Bishop of Norwich, whose poems had been collected in 1647.[26] But it is in letters to two editors of English poetry, Dr. Robert Anderson and Alexander Dyce, that Wordsworth best revealed the amazing intimacy of his knowledge of obscure writers of the past.

Writing to Anderson in 1814, Wordsworth made suggestions for additions to Anderson's anthology, which already enjoyed an "unexampled comprehensiveness." Wordsworth had consulted with Coleridge and Southey, and among them they had made up a list of authors who should be added to Anderson's collection (going beyond, it should be noted, Chalmers' edition, likewise). Some of the names are familiar to specialists of the periods concerned: Skelton, Southwell, B. Googe, and N. Breton, for instance; but with many of them even specialists would be hard-pressed to provide more information: George Turberville, Thomas Watson, and Henry Willoughby; John Chalkhill, Abraham Fraunce, and Thomas May; William Chamberlayne, Thomas Randolph, and John Norris of Bemerton.[27] After suggesting the inclusion of these and similar original authors, Wordsworth then recommended some "old translations": Chapman and Fairfax as one would expect, but also "Goulding's Ovid, Phaer's

Virgil, May's Lucan, And as a curiosity the few books of Stanyhurst's Virgil." These writers, original and translators, were drawn from periods ranging from the fourteenth century to the early eighteenth.[28]

About little-read female authors of more recent times Wordsworth displayed an acute and sympathetic knowledge. Writing to Alexander Dyce, not only did he discuss the qualities of such women writers as Aphra Behn, Laetitia Pilkington, and Anne Killigrew; Jane Warton, Lady Winchilsea, and Lady Mary Wortley Montagu; he also displayed knowledge of poems by Lady Anne Lindsay, Jane Elliot, and Mrs. Katherine Fowler Philips—saying, by the way, that the first two had written the two best ballads of modern times.[29] Throughout his discussion of these minor writers, both male and female, Wordsworth showed a keen eye for specific detail and an acute feeling for quality in individual lines, even when he disliked the rest of the person's writings. With Anna Laetitia Barbauld, for instance, he felt that, in spite of her high powers of mind, she "was spoiled as a Poetess by being a Dissenter, and concerned with a dissenting Academy." Nonetheless he continued his appraisal by saying, "One of the most pleasing passages in her Poetry is the close of the lines upon life, written, I believe, when she was not less than 80 years of age: 'Life, we have been long together', etc."[30] Evidently he had persevered through much that displeased him, and at last had been rewarded with a gem.

When one multiplies this instance by the dozens of minor authors he discusses, one can begin to appreciate the vast extent of the reading he did, either on his own or through the eyes of his family, and the intensity with which he read and remembered.

B Wordsworth's Attitude Towards Cambridge Undergraduates

How likely was it that Wordsworth would borrow from the equivalent of a prize poem written by a Cambridge undergraduate? His attitude towards one Cambridge undergraduate is clearly shown in the letter he wrote to his nephew Christopher, at Cambridge, on 27 November 1828. After congratulating Christopher on his "success in college prizes" (including, presumably, the two Chancellor's Gold Medals he had won for prize poems), he concludes his letter with the postscript, referring to his own *Egyptian Maid*, "Last week I threw off a Romance of 360 verses or regular stanzas. I should like to read it to you, to know if it be good for any thing."[1]

Admittedly this was addressed to his nephew, and not to just any undergraduate author of a prize poem. The broader question remains: What was Wordsworth's attitude to young poets? Would he have made use of anything they wrote?

First should be noted the extraordinary degree of friendliness which Wordsworth displayed to those young writers who made his acquaintance—and that from the very first day of acquaintance. James Patrick Muirhead has described the visit he had with Wordsworth when, armed with a letter of introduction, he went, as a young writer with one book to his credit, to pay an unexpected call on the senior poet, who was then seventy-one. Wordsworth greeted him cordially, entertained him at dinner, and took him for a long walk in the hills, showing him the various objects which had prompted certain of his poems.[2] Altogether, apart from the initial greeting, Muirhead's reception was much like that accorded to Edward Quillinan twenty years earlier and described by him in a much better known passage.[3] In each account, Wordsworth's behaviour, though described by the young writer in an adulatory manner, could be seen by the cynic as pontificating, posturing, and showing off. But Muirhead's description contains evidence of a quality that cannot be discounted in this way. He noted the "friendly interest" which Wordsworth took in him, "such as I never could have expected or supposed possible to be shown by so great a man to so humble an admirer in so short a time."[4] "For the abundance of his kindness," Muirhead remarked, "I was not prepared; but it was so great, and so delightful, that I wished much that others could have witnessed it and shared in it. . . ." The high point came for Muirhead when, on their walk over the hills, Wordsworth "led me, hand in hand, 'linking down the braes together' [at a rattling pace], much to my amazement and ecstasy at finding my humble self admitted to such friendly freedom with such a being. . . ."

Muirhead and Quillinan were not the only young writers to whom Wordsworth showed instant friendship. When he met William Rowan Hamilton, who then was as much an aspiring young poet as a noted young astronomer, the two of them spent most of the night walking together under the stars, "absorbed in converse on high themes, and finding it almost impossible to part."[5] The fellow feeling, which was witnessed to by this nighttime perambulation, manifested itself in other forms as well. To Robert Pearce Gillies, a young poet who had seen an early draft of "Yarrow Visited," Wordsworth took care to explain that in a later draft he had made considerable changes so as to lighten the tone.[6] And the way in which Wordsworth communicated the news of the death of Arthur Henry Hallam likewise says much. To a friend he wrote, "A sad case was that of my young friend Hallam who was cut off at the age of 23—he was travelling with his father, the Author of the Middle Ages," and continued with the story of his unexpected death.[7] It is noteworthy that he said "my young friend Hallam" and not "the young son of my friend Hallam" or "the young son of the Author of the Middle Ages." He linked himself directly with the young Hallam, not indirectly through a person of his own generation.

This affinity for young writers was demonstrated in another way, which is even more pertinent to our purpose. In 1825, when Wordsworth was fifty-five, he wrote the equivalent of an undergradute prize poem. In his note to "The Pillar of Trajan," he explains: "I had observed in the Newspaper, that the Pillar of Trajan was given [at Oxford] as a subject for a prize-poem in English verse. I had a wish perhaps that my son, who was then an undergraduate at Oxford, should try his fortune, and I told him so; but he, not having been accustomed to write verse, wisely declined to enter on the task; whereupon I showed him these lines as a proof of what might, without difficulty, be done on such a subject."[8]

In view of this affinity for young writers, it is then not surprising that he took an interest in their writings, even when they were undergraduates or the equivalent. He wrote in 1825 to Thomas Kibble Hervey that the poem which that undergraduate had written for the Chancellor's Medal at Cambridge had given him "much pleasure."[9] About the undergraduate Francis Beaufort Edgeworth, Wordsworth wrote to Hamilton: "The Specimens of your young Friend's Genius are very promising. His poetical powers are there strikingly exhibited—nor have I any objections to make that are worthy of his notice...."[10] (The last clause was high praise indeed, for Wordsworth made many comments about the faults as well as the merits of the poetry of both Hamilton and his sister.)[11] About slightly later verses of Edgeworth's, Wordsworth wrote: "'While with the ashes of a light that was', and the two following lines are in the best style of dramatic writing.... 'This over-perfume of a heavy pleasure', etc is admirable—and indeed it would be tedious to praise all that pleases me."[12] He went out of his way to show interest in another young writer, as witnessed by what he wrote to Henry Crabb Robinson about John Moultrie, who had written for the literary magazine of Eton College and then for publications in Cambridge: Wordsworth praised "a Youngster who writes verses in the Etonian, to some of which our Cumberland Paper has introduced me, and some I saw at Cambridge. He is an Imp as hopeful I think as any of them...; if you should ever fall in with him tell him that he has pleased me much."[13] While visiting Cambridge he evidently inquired about writers there, for he wrote to Hamilton in 1830: "We have also a respectable show of blossom in poetry. Two brothers of the name of Tennyson in particular, are not a little promising."[14]

Not only was Wordsworth keenly interested in the writing of young poets, but he also, on occasion at least, valued what they wrote. This we have already seen in part, but more striking instances remain. When Lamb had introduced Edward Moxon to Wordsworth (by letter), the essayist had used what can only be described as very condescending language: "... pray pat him on the head, ask him a civil question or two about his verses, and favour him with your genuine autograph."[15] There was, however, no trace of condescension when Wordsworth wrote to Moxon about the title poem of his "little volume" of poetry; instead he showed keen appreciation: "Your poem I have read with no inconsiderable pleasure; it is full of natural sentiments and pleasing pictures.... Such lines as the latter of this Couplet

> Where lovely woman, chaste as Heaven above,
> Shines in the golden virtues of her love,

and many other passages in your Poem give proof of no commonplace sensibility."[16] About John Moultrie, as we have seen, Wordsworth wanted it to be known that his poetry had pleased him much. To R. P. Gillies he paid an amazing compliment. In the midst of citing virtues and defects in his poem *Exile*, Wordsworth wrote: "I was particularly charmed with the seventeenth stanza, first part. This is a passage which I shall often repeat to myself; and I assure you that, with the exception of Burns and Cowper, there is very little of recent verse, however much it may interest me, that sticks to my memory (I mean which I get by heart)."[17] As if being chosen to be memorized were not compliment enough, Wordsworth expressed even higher esteem for another passage from a young author and a willingness to do more even than memorize it. Bernard Barton, who was a bank clerk in Woodbridge, Suffolk, and who had written *Metrical Effusions* (1812), had sent Wordsworth a poem expressing pleasure in reading Wordsworth's poetry. In reply Wordsworth wrote: "I differ from you in thinking that the only poetical lines in your address are 'stolen from myself'. The best Verse, perhaps, is the following:

> Awfully mighty in his impotence,

which, by way of repayment, I may be tempted to steal from you on some future occasion."[18]

C Shenstone and Cowper

Reproduced below are two passages from the poetry of Shenstone and Cowper between which Wordsworth found "identity of thought" and "parallelisms" in phrasing. The first is from "Rural Elegance: An Ode to the late Duchess of Somerset" in William Shenstone, *Poetical Works*, ed. George Gilfillan (Edinburgh: James Nicol, 1854), 133:

> Her impulse nothing may restrain—
> Or whence the joy 'mid columns, towers,
>   Midst all the city's artful trim,
> To rear some breathless vapid flowers   [235]
>   Or shrubs fuliginously grim?
> From rooms of silken foliage vain,
> To trace the dun far distant grove,
> Where, smit with undissembled pain,
> The woodlark mourns her absent love,   [240]
> · Borne to the dusty town from native air,
> To mimic rural life, and soothe some vapour'd fair?
>
>   But how must faithless Art prevail,
>   Should all who taste our joy sincere,

195

>   To virtue, truth, or science, dear,   [245]
>   Forego a court's alluring pale,
>   For dimpled brook and leafy grove,
>   For that rich luxury of thought they love!
>   Ah, no! from these the public sphere requires
>   Examples for its giddy bands;   [250]
>   From these impartial Heaven demands
>   To spread the flame itself inspires;
>   To sift Opinion's mingled mass,
>   Impress a nation's taste, and bid the sterling pass.
>
>   Happy, thrice happy they,   [255]
>   Whose graceful deeds have exemplary shone
>   Round the gay precincts of a throne,
>   With mild effective beams!
>   Who bands of fair ideas bring,
>   By solemn grot, or shady spring,   [260]
>   To join their pleasing dreams!
>   Theirs is the rural bliss without alloy;
>   They only that deserve, enjoy.

Following are lines 743-801 of Book IV of *The Task*, in *Cowper: Poetical Works*, ed. H. S. Milford, 4th ed., corrections and additions by Norma Russell (London: Oxford University Press, 1967), 198-99:

>   It is a flame that dies not even there,
>   Where nothing feeds it: neither business, crowds,
>   Nor habits of luxurious city-life;   [745]
>   Whatever else they smother of true worth
>   In human bosoms; quench it, or abate.
>   The villas with which London stands begirt,
>   Like a swarth Indian with his belt of beads,
>   Prove it. A breath of unadult'rate air,   [750]
>   The glimpse of a green pasture, how they cheer
>   The citizen, and brace his languid frame!
>   Ev'n in the stifling bosom of the town,
>   A garden, in which nothing thrives, has charms
>   That soothe the rich possessor; much consol'd,
>   That here and there some sprigs of mournful mint,
>   Of nightshade, or valerian, grace the well   [757]

He cultivates. These serve him with a hint
That nature lives; that sight-refreshing green
Is still the liv'ry she delights to wear, [760]
Though sickly samples of th'exub'rant whole.
What are the casements lin'd with creeping herbs,
The prouder sashes fronted with a range
Of orange, myrtle, or the fragrant weed,
The Frenchman's darling? are they not all proofs
That man, immur'd in cities, still retains [766]
His inborn inextinguishable thirst
Of rural scenes, compensating his loss
By supplemental shifts, the best he may?
The most unfurnish'd with the means of life, [770]
And they that never pass their brick-wall bounds
To range the fields and treat their lungs with air,
Yet feel the burning instinct: over head
Suspend their crazy boxes, planted thick,
And water'd duly. There the pitcher stands [775]
A fragment, and the spoutless tea-pot there;
Sad witnesses how close-pent man regrets
The country, with what ardour he contrives
A peep at nature, when he can no more.

    Hail, therefore, patroness of health, and ease,
And contemplation, heart-consoling joys [781]
And harmless pleasures, in the throng'd abode
Of multitudes unknown! hail, rural life!
Address himself who will to the pursuit
Of honours, or emolument, or fame; [785]
I shall not add myself to such a chase,
Thwart his attempts, or envy his success.
Some must be great. Great offices will have
Great talents. And God gives to ev'ry man
The virtue, temper, understanding, taste, [790]
That lifts him into life; and lets him fall
Just in the niche he was ordain'd to fill.
To the deliv'rer of an injur'd land
He gives a tongue t'enlarge upon, an heart
To feel, and courage to redress her wrongs; [795]
To monarchs dignity; to judges sense;

To artists ingenuity and skill;
To me an unambitious mind, content
In the low vale of life, that early felt
A wish for ease and leisure, and ere long [800]
Found here that leisure and that ease I wish'd.

D Wordsworth's Attitude Concerning Acknowledgements

Wordsworth's attitude towards the practice of other authors in acknowledging or not acknowledging their sources was remarkably ambivalent. When referring, in a letter, to the borrowings which Peter Bayley had made from the *Lyrical Ballads* and from poets such as Akenside, Cowper, and Bowles, all unacknowledged, Wordsworth called such actions "verbal thefts."[1] Thomas Gray's practice of incorporating phrases from other poets Wordsworth described as "filching a phrase now from one author, and now from another."[2] And Byron, for his drawing "by wholesale" from his contemporaries without acknowledgement, deserved "severe chastisement."[3] But at the same time there could be, in his view, mitigating circumstances. The acknowledgement which Byron made of his borrowing from Coleridge, Wordsworth said, "takes very much from the reprehensibility of literary trespasses of this kind."[4] When his friend Coleridge passed off as his own certain passages which he had in fact translated from Schiller and Stolberg, Wordsworth wrote that this action was "excessive folly" and "silly if not worse," but, at the same time, he remarked that Coleridge, in translating these and other passages of the same German authors, "greatly excelled the original" and gave "50 times more than he took."[5]

What Wordsworth wrote to Scott about the latter's editing of Dryden generalizes the matter. Among the things which an editor has to provide, Wordsworth placed ("last" and "of less importance" than a correct text and explanatory notes) "notes pointing out passages or authors to which the Poet has been indebted, not in the piddling way of [a] phrase here and phrase there (which is detestable as a general practice) but where the Poet has really had essential obligations either as to matter or manner."[6] In seeing this pointing out of indebtedness as a function of an editor, Wordsworth must, of course, have presupposed that the author himself had not acknowledged his indebtedness. In fact Wordsworth appears, at least, to have taken such an absence of acknowledgement for granted, and in his letter to Scott there is no suggestion that Dryden really ought to have made acknowledgements.

Wordsworth's practice in his own poetry was likewise ambivalent. In *An Evening Walk* and *Descriptive Sketches* he made numerous acknowledgements of his borrowing from other writers (in prose as well as verse).[7] In "Tintern Abbey" Wordsworth dropped a note to line 106, saying "This line has a close resemblance to an admirable line of Young's, the exact expression of which I do not recollect."[8] Another such obligation he acknowledged in "The Brothers," when, to line 65, he dropped this note: "This description of the Calenture is sketched from an imperfect recollection of an admirable one in prose, by Mr. Gilbert, author of the *Hurricane.*"[9] He acknowledged using an old ballad, "The Rising of the North," in his *White Doe of Rylstone*, and he acknowledged borrowing from Shakespeare, Daniel, Southey, and Coleridge in *The Excursion.*[10] In fact in this same poem he went out of his way to remark that he had used a passage from the "Introduction to the Foundation-charter" of "the Abbey of St. Mary's Furness."[11]

At the same time Wordsworth left many borrowings unacknowledged. In fact, the number of unacknowledged borrowings noted in the standard edition of *An Evening Walk* exceeds the acknowledged ones, and the unacknowledged borrowings in *Descriptive Sketches* greatly outnumber the acknowledged ones, by something like sixteen to five.[12] A description of kissing leaves in his short lyric "Stray Pleasures" (1807) he owed to Drayton, but did not say so.[13] Seven lines of *The Waggoner* he borrowed from Sterne's *Tristram Shandy*, again without saying so.[14] And a passage in *The Excursion*, Christopher Wordsworth pointed out, was probably drawn from a scholarly note that Pope had written to his translation of *The Iliad*.[15]

It is virtually impossible to detect any pattern in Wordsworth's decisions, on the one hand to acknowledge his indebtedness, and on the other not to. He will acknowledge images from one travel book but not another. He will acknowledge using one old ballad but not another. He will note his indebtedness to Daniel but not to Drayton. He will acknowledge his use of Milton on some occasions but not on others. Not even with classical authors is there a pattern, for he will acknowledge indebtedness to Tasso and Virgil, but not to Caesar.[16] Sometimes the absence of acknowledgement may result from Wordsworth's not having been aware of the fact that he was borrowing, or he may have felt that a particular phrase borrowed was too trifling to acknowledge. But often the passage is so substantial that he had to be aware of what he was doing and is more substantial, in fact, than many phrases which he did acknowledge. It appears that Wordsworth could decide either way and for reasons known only to himself.

The Myth of Wordsworth's Total Originality

IN WORDSWORTHIAN SCHOLARSHIP, AN ASSUMPTION HAS repeatedly appeared that Wordsworth, in many important poems, was entirely original, that he owed nothing to any literary source or intermediary.

The reasons why and how such a scholarly fashion got started appear to be rather mixed. Evidently it arose, in part, from an ignorance, on the part of the scholars (until Robert Mayo), of Wordsworth's minor contemporaries, and from a practice of looking only to the major writers who preceded Wordsworth. We suspect, also, that another cause was a romantic assumption, dating at least from Edward Young, that true genius is entirely original. Since Wordsworth is a true genius, he must, then, have been entirely original.

A more legitimate reason for the fashion's getting started is a number of impressions which Wordsworth gave. On occasion, as when talking with Muirhead, for instance, Wordsworth would give the impression that he would much rather write a book than read one—so how could he possibly be influenced by other writers?[1] Yet he had, of course, acknowledged scores of literary debts in the many notes he published to his poems, and this fact should have served to counter the impression. In fact this very practice of acknowledging appears, paradoxically enough, to have been a further source for the scholarly fashion we are concerned with, this time as expressed in a less unknowing form. Since Wordsworth acknowledged what he borrowed (the belief appears to have run), then when he did not acknowledge, he had not borrowed. So certain poems, the *Lyrical Ballads* in particular, have been viewed as free of debt.

Whatever its origins, the scholarly fashion we are concerned with took as its form at the beginning of the century the assertion that Wordsworth was indebted, for his poetry, only to nature. John Morley said that Wordsworth "had no teachers nor inspirers save nature and solitude."[2] Georg Brandes asserted that "Wordsworth would never describe anything with which he was not perfectly familiar."[3] And Walter Raleigh wrote that Wordsworth's poetical career "shows us the genesis of poetry from its living material, without literary intermediary.... The dominant passion of Wordsworth's life owed nothing to books."[4] These three scholars Lane Cooper savaged thus, in 1907:

> In recounting the origin of the ballad now known as Coleridge's "Rime of the Ancient Mariner," Wordsworth tells us that the fateful death of the Albatross was a direct suggestion from him. He had been reading about this ominous bird in *Shelvocke's Voyages*, a book, he adds significantly, "which probably Coleridge never saw.".... Here is Wordsworth, who "would never describe anything with which he was not perfectly familiar," caught in the act of imaging for Coleridge, and for a poem in which the two were to be joint authors, a creature which neither of the ballad-makers could in all probability have seen in the flesh, sucking inspiration, not from "nature" or "solitude," but from a stirring narrative of adventure, and, in a capital instance, cruelly exhibiting the "genesis of poetry" out of dead(?) "material" with an eighteenth-century sea-captain for "literary intermediary."[5]

In spite of this attack, and Cooper's reminding the scholarly world of the vast amount of travel literature which lay behind many of Wordsworth's poems, the old fashion of assuming that Wordsworth was not indebted to literary antecedents re-emerged in the 1930s and continued into the 1950s. Various manifestations of this re-emergence were catalogued by Robert Mayo in his notes to his landmark essay of 1954, entitled "The Contemporaneity of the *Lyrical Ballads.*"[6] Many and prestigious are the scholars cited in the notes: Oliver Elton, H. Littledale, and Elsie Smith in the early 1930's; John Butt, H. V. D. Dyson, and J. R. Sutherland in the mid-1940s; and Douglas Bush, Helen Darbishire, George Mallaby, and Derek Patmore of the early 1950s. With varying degrees of circumspection, all these scholars made statements indicating their belief (or assumption) that the *Lyrical Ballads* burst upon the literary scene as something completely new, in both content and form. Implicit in this belief or assumption is, of course, the further belief or assumption that the *Lyrical Ballads* were in no way indebted to immediate predecessors, for either their form or content. Yet Mayo, in the body of his essay, proceeded to demonstrate that those *Ballads* were, in fact, heavily influenced, for both their contents and their forms, by (and to that extent, at least, indebted to) a host of poems appearing in British magazines in the decade or two preceding their publication. In no way were they new—except in their quality.

Once again the fallacy had been wrestled to the ground. And yet, twelve years later, in 1966, Margaret Drabble could write: "The *Lyrical Ballads* were, quite simply, different from anything that any English poet had published before 1798. They were different in language, in intention, and in subject matter."[7] Evidently the assumption of debt-free originality is like the character Maleger, Spenser's version of the classical Antaeus. Every time Prince Arthur defeated Maleger and drove him to the ground, the foul spectre sprang up again to renew its attack.[8] Like that spectre, the scholarly assumption that Wordsworth could not have had literary debts is a stubborn and resilient fallacy that has to be wrestled with repeatedly. It is for this reason that we have spent the time doing so.

F The Availability of Sources for the Hymn to Science

WITH SOME OF THE AUTHORS WHO, WE ARGUE IN Chapter 3, served as sources for Wordsworth's virtual Hymn to Science, there are difficulties. Not with Pope, Gray, and Shakespeare: there is no doubt at all that Wordsworth was well acquainted with them. Nor is there much difficulty with the availability to Wordsworth of Akenside's "Hymn to Science": it appeared in *Elegant Extracts,* and, since Christopher Wordsworth's Hawkshead notebook shows that that anthology was used as a text at the Grammar School, Wordsworth was probably acquainted with it through his brother, with whom he kept so close a communication that he even made some entries in that very notebook.[1]

But with Ramsay, Glover, and Mallet there *is* a difficulty. No mention is made, in any of the catalogues of Wordsworth's library, of his having owned copies of separate editions of those authors' works. The pertinent poems by Glover and Mallet did appear in the 1795 edition of Anderson's *British Poets,* and a copy of this edition was given to Wordsworth by his brother John in 1800.[2] But these dates pinpoint the difficulty. If 1794 really was the year when Wordsworth wrote his Hymn to Science, then we have argued that he borrowed and adapted from poems of Glover and Mallet one year before these appeared in

Anderson and six years before Wordsworth owned a copy of Anderson.

For those readers who agree with us that the close parallels between Wordsworth's lines and those of Ramsay, Glover, and Mallet point to Wordsworth's having borrowed from his predecessors (as he undoubtedly did from Fawkes at Hawkshead), there are two possible solutions to the difficulty facing us. Wordsworth may, in 1794, have owned copies of Ramsay, Glover, and Mallet, copies which did not remain in his library until it was catalogued.[3] He may, alternatively, have read borrowed copies and have memorized the pertinent passages. An attractive third solution, that Wordsworth may have written the Hymn to Science after he received his copy of Anderson in 1800, would appear to be all but ruled out by the dating of the MSS. provided by James Averill in his Cornell Wordsworth edition of *An Evening Walk*.[4] The passage that we have entitled the Hymn to Science is printed by de Selincourt from MS. "corrections and...new material" inserted in "a mutilated copy of the 1793 edition" of *An Evening Walk*.[5] The passage appears in Averill's edition in two parts (pages 138, 163). It would appear that de Selincourt, guided by the insertion into a passage in DC MS. 10 of lines that Averill numbers 205 and 206, pieced the two parts together in the manner Wordsworth intended.

G The Distinctive Cluster of Elements

THE CLUSTER OF ELEMENTS, REFERRED TO IN CHAPter 6, that can be found recurring in (at least) five major passages of Wordsworth's poetry consists of the following: solitariness, quiet or silence, stars, great height or depth, eternity, an exceptional perceiver, and something exceptional perceived.

In *The Excursion* (3:50-112)[1] there appears a description of "the hidden nook" (line 51), a "cabinet for sages" (line 74) which is indeed solitary, for clearly there is no human being there, apart from the visitors. There is extraordinary quiet or silence: there is no breeze (line 67); there is "no trace / Of motion, save the water that descended... softly creeping, like a breath of air" (lines 68-71); and even the stream is "voiceless" (line 92). The sky is "heaven's profoundest azure," "an abyss / In which the everlasting stars abide" and whose "boundless depth might tempt / The curious eye to look for them by day" (lines 94-100). Eternity is not only in the stars: it is also present as that into which time and nature will disappear (lines 111-12). The exceptional perceiver is found, in human terms, in the Wanderer himself, the "happy old Man" with "reverend lip" (line 76), and, more grandly, in "Contemplation," the power that does the greatest perceiving (lines 101-12). And what is it that is perceived? Rocks and stones that bear

> A semblance strange of power intelligent,
> And of design not wholly worn away...;
>
> (lines 83-84)

a chronicle

> Of purposes akin to those of Man,
> But wrought with mightier arm than now prevails...;
>
> (lines 89-91)

a "lodge" to which Contemplation may resort

> for holier peace,—
> From whose calm centre thou, through height or depth,
> Mayst penetrate, wherever truth shall lead;
> Measuring through all degrees, until the scale
> Of time and conscious nature disappear,
> Lost in unsearchable eternity!
>
> (lines 106-12)

In the early drafts of what was to become Book One of *The Excursion* there occurs another use of the same cluster, in the description of the influences at work on the pedlar (lines 202-59).[2] The pedlar's solitude is stressed:

> Yet with these lonesome sciences he still
> Continued to amuse the heavier hours
> Of solitude, and solitary thought.
>
> (lines 218-20)

Silence, too, is stressed: the winds are "silent" (line 226), the pedlar's "abstracted thought" has "stillness" (line 227—and cf. line 214), and especially (with Wordsworth's italicizing) his triangles were "The *silent* stars" (lines 210-11). Here, obviously, are the stars. Height is present, not only in them, but also in the pedlar's "altitudes," which were

> the crag
> Which is the eagle's birthplace; or some peak
> Familiar with forgotten years....
>
> (lines 211-12)

Eternity is implicit in the stars (line 211) and in the spirit and soul of Nature (lines 205, 238); it is also approached in that

>   peak
> Familiar with forgotten years, which shews,
> Inscribed, as with the silence of the thought,
> Upon its bleak and visionary sides,
> The history of many a winter storm,
> Or obscure records of the path of fire.
>   (lines 212-17)

(In a temporary addition to this passage, Wordsworth even had the peak witness to the Flood.) The pedlar is initially something of an exceptional perceiver and, under the tutelage of nature, becomes more of one. Appropriately, in view of the presence of all these elements belonging to the cluster, what he perceives is, as one would expect, the spiritual truth of life:

> He felt the sentiment of being, spread
> O'er all that moves, and all that seemeth still,
> O'er all which, lost beyond the reach of thought,
> And human knowledge, to the human eye
> Invisible, yet liveth to the heart,
> O'er all that leaps, and runs, and shouts, and sings,
> Or beats the gladsome air, o'er all that glides
> Beneath the wave, yea in the wave itself
> And mighty depth of waters.
>   In all things
> He saw one life, and felt that it was joy.
> One song they sang, and it was audible,
> Most audible then, when the fleshly ear
> O'ercome by grosser prelude of that strain,
> Forgot its functions, and slept undisturbed.
>   (lines 242-50, 251-56)

The passage in Book One of *The Prelude* beginning "Fair seed-time had my soul" (lines 301-475) is considerably longer, so long, in fact, that it might appear absurd to select seven elements from it.[3] But those elements are each repeated so many times that they virtually appear proportionately as often as do their counterparts in the hidden nook and in the pedlar's solitude. The perceiver is described four times as being alone (lines 315, 336, 421-22, 447-48), and the same solitariness is extended to the hills and cliffs (lines 322, 458). Similarly the perceiver's "calm existence" (line 349) is reflected in the "silent water" and the "silent bay" (lines 386, 448) in which he moves. The presence of the moon is mentioned twice (lines 314, 365) and that of stars four times (lines 314, 372, 405, 450). Height is implicit in the phrase "the sky seemed not a sky / Of earth" (lines 338-39) and explicit in the "high objects" (line 409) with which the perceiver's soul held converse. Eternity is likewise mentioned frequently: in the "immortal Spirit" (line 340), the "everlasting Motion" (line 404), the "enduring things" (line 409), and the "eternity of thought" (line 402). Not surprisingly, in view of the presence of all these elements, the perceiver himself is exceptional: he is a boy (cf. lines 306-7) in whom "the immortal Spirit grows" (line 340) and who enjoys "fellowship" with "high objects" (lines 408-15) and "intercourse," not only with them (line 422), but also with the "presences of Nature" (line 464). What, accordingly, he perceives is similar to what is perceived in the hidden nook and by the pedlar. Its strangeness is emphasized:

> While on the perilous ridge I hung alone,
> With what strange utterance did the loud dry wind
> Blow through my ears! the sky seemed not a sky
> Of earth....
>
> (lines 336-39)

The perceiver's brain

> Worked with a dim and undetermined sense
> Of unknown modes of being;...
> ... huge and mighty Forms, that do not live
> Like living men, moved slowly through the mind
> By day, and were a trouble to my dreams.
>
> (lines 391-93, 398-400)

He communed with "high objects, with enduring things, / With life and nature" (lines 409-10) and with those powers he addressed as

> Ye presences of Nature, in the sky,
> And on the earth! Ye visions of the hills!
> And Souls of lonely places!
>
> (lines 464-66)

These powers, he realized, reflected the "Wisdom and Spirit of the Universe," which he addressed, in turn, as

> Thou Soul that art the eternity of thought,
> That giv'st to forms and images a breath
> And everlasting Motion....
>
> (lines 401-4)

Wordsworth's "Ode: Intimations of Immortality from Recollections of Early Childhood"[4] provides an even closer parallel to the passage on Newton. The solitariness is in the "Child" addressed in the singular even though it is "Children" who "sport upon the shore" (lines 86, 109-11, 167). The silence is his as, "deaf and silent," he reads "the eternal deep" (line 113), and it is to be found also in "the eternal Silence" (line 156). "The Moon doth with delight / Look round her" (lines 12-13). Stars are present, with the moon (line 14) and as an image for our soul (line 59). So, too, is depth—explicitly in "the eternal deep" read by the child (line 113) and implicitly in "that immortal sea" (line 164) with its "mighty waters" (line 168). Eternity is present, not only in the "eternal deep" and the "eternal Silence" already seen (lines 113, 156), but also in "the eternal mind" (line 114), the "immortal sea" (line 164), the "waters rolling evermore" (line 168), and, especially, in the "Immortality" of the Child himself (line 119). That Child is, of course, the exceptional perceiver, a "six years' Darling of a pigmy size" (line 87) who is an "Eye among the blind" (line 112), who reads "the eternal deep" (line 113), and who is the "best Philosopher," a "Mighty Prophet! Seer blest!" (lines 111, 115)—qualities which, incidentally, further emphasize his solitariness. And what does he perceive? "... those truths... / Which we are toiling all our lives to find" (lines 116-17), those "truths that wake,/To perish never" (lines 156-57), those truths represented by the image of "that immortal sea / Which brought us hither" (lines 164-65)—a sea remarkably like that on which Newton is for ever voyaging.

The "Lines Composed a Few Miles above Tintern Abbey"[5] provide a parallel to the Newton passage that is closer still. The speaker is in the midst of "a wild secluded scene," where "the Hermit sits alone" and where the speaker himself has impressed on him "Thoughts of more deep seclusion" (lines 6-7, 22). His sister will likewise proceed in her "solitary walk" (line 135). She will feel, as he did, the "quietness" bestowed by nature (lines 125-27); her eye will presumably be "made," as his was, "quiet by the power / Of harmony" (lines 47-48). In the midst of light shone on them by the moon (lines 134-35), they feel the presence of something "Whose dwelling is the light of setting suns" (lines 93-97). This something is "far more deeply interfused" and is, presumably, productive of "the deep power of joy" felt by the speaker (lines 96, 48). Certainly it produces "elevated thoughts," as Nature feeds the mind with "lofty thoughts" (lines 95, 127-28). Eternity is likewise present, albeit implicitly, in the "motion" and "spirit" that "rolls through all things" (lines 100-102). The perceiver is the most exceptional yet recorded: he is "laid asleep / In body, and become[s] a living soul" (lines 45-46); through his eye and ear he creates as well as perceives (lines 106-7); and his mind (actually, in this instance, her mind) becomes "a mansion for all lovely forms" (lines 139-40). Not surprisingly, then, that which is perceived is the most magnificent yet encountered: "all lovely forms...all sweet sounds and harmonies" (lines 140-42), "the life of things" (line 49), and that "something far more deeply interfused" which "impels / All thinking things, all objects of all thought, / And rolls through all things" (lines 96-102).

Wordsworth's Poetic Expectations in Old Age

Both Wordsworth and his sister Dorothy regarded his sixtieth birthday anniversary as potentially marking a climacteric. Dorothy wrote to three correspondents in April of 1830, saying to each that, *although* William had now passed his sixtieth birthday, he continued in good health.[1] Wordsworth himself, in writing to his daughter Dora, said, "Thanks to Almighty God, though [your mother] is not many months short of the close of her sixtieth year and I have completed mine, we neither of us have yet felt, like the melancholy Cowper, that

'Threescore winters make a wintry breast'."[2]

Curiously, in quoting—or, rather, misquoting Cowper, Wordsworth has much improved on the original, making the phrasing more striking and thereby emphasizing the apprehension he apparently experienced that soon his own life would in fact prove that "Threescore winters make a wintry breast."[3] He continued to Dora: "Our affections are young and healthful. You rally me upon Hypochondriasis— but erringly—for I do gravely assure you that I have suffered much from headaches upon comparatively slight exertion. 'Non sum qualis eram' [I am not even as I was] and who ought to expect it?...I have given over writing verses till my head becomes stronger or my fancy livelier...."[4]

His sixtieth birthday, viewed with such foreboding, appears in fact to have proved to be the grand climacteric for Wordsworth, for two years later he was to write to Joseph Kirkham Miller, explaining why he would not undertake a writing project: "My sixty-second year will soon be completed, and though I have been favoured thus far in health and strength beyond most men of my age, yet I feel its effects upon my spirits; they sink under a pressure of apprehension to which, at an earlier period of my life, they would probably have been superior.... [The] years have deprived me of *courage* [i.e., heart], in the sense the word bears when applied by Chaucer to the animation of birds in spring time."[5] A little more than three years later, when writing to his friend Francis Wrangham and lamenting the recent passing of several contemporaries, Wordsworth wrote, "I cannot forget that Shakespeare, who scarcely survived 50—(I am now near the close of my 65th year) wrote

> In me that time of life thou dost behold
> When yellow leaves, or few or none, do hang
> Upon the bough."[6]

Wordsworth would, of course, have known that Shakespeare wrote that particular sonnet (73) early in his life, but the errors which Wordsworth made in quoting from memory speak even more revealingly of what had evidently become an obsession for him. As Wordsworth remembers the poem, the interlocutor is not simply *able* to behold the time of year in the speaker; he actually *does* behold the autumnal period. More obvious, of course, is the transposition of the phrase "in me": Shakespeare had tucked the words away in the most inconspicuous position in the first line, just before the concluding word "behold": Wordsworth transfers the phrase to the most prominent location in the line—indeed, in the whole poem. And even the reversal of the two units in the phrase "or none, or few" indicates a profound *malaise*. With Shakespeare the phrase "or none, or few" serves to make the number of yellow leaves so indefinite that the reader is not inclined to try to visualize the leaves.[7] Wordsworth, on the other hand, arranges the two units in the phrase so as to proceed from a sense of there being only a few leaves left to the utter desolation of there being none.

In November of the same year (1835), Wordsworth wrote, in a letter to Thomas Noon Talfourd, a passage which combined the sense of ageing despair with a hope for grand achievement in the face of old age. Talfourd, who had published *Poems on Various Subjects* in 1811, had just had his play *Ion* privately printed, and Wordsworth wrote to him the following: "I cannot help catching at the hope that, in the evening of life, you may realize those anticipations which you throw out. Chaucer's and Milton's great works were composed when they were far advanced in life. So, in times nearer our own, were Dryden's and Cowper's; and mankind has ever been fond of cherishing the belief that Homer's thunder and lightning were kept up when he was an old man and blind. Nor is it unworthy of notice that the leading interest attached to the name of Ossian is connected with grey hairs, infirmity, and privation."[8] But two years later (1837) Wordsworth wrote a letter to his family in which he indicated that he was past creating that kind of poetry which uses images. Writing to them from Salzburg and describing to them his journey through mountainous areas, Wordsworth said, "I have, however, to regret that this journey was not made some years ago,—to regret it, I mean, as a Poet; for... my mind has been enriched by innumerable images, which I could have turned to account in verse, and vivified by feelings which earlier in my life would have answered noble purposes, in a way they now are little likely to do."[9] It should be remembered, of course, that Wordsworth was far from feeble at this time: he was, after all, in the midst of making a most strenuous tour through mountainous areas of Germany. It was not his physical abilities which were impaired, but rather his poetic abilities which he felt had become enfeebled. Six months later, in January of 1838, the sense of enfeeblement had evidently increased. Writing to his friend William Rowan Hamilton, he lamented, "with so much before me that I could wish to do in verse,... the melancholy fact brought daily more and more home to my conviction that intellectual labour, by its action on the brain and nervous system, is injurious to the bodily powers, and especially to my eye-sight...."[10]

Especially since we know that later in this same year of 1838 Wordsworth was to undertake a major revision of parts of *The Prelude*, the question arises, "What kind of verse had he in mind?" We have the statement that he had so much before him that he could wish to do in verse and also the fact that he was indeed shortly to do much in verse. But we also have the statement made, when he wrote to his family from Salzburg in the full vigour of health, that he was little likely to be able to turn to account in verse the images with which his mind had become enriched as a result of his journey through the mountainous areas. The one way of reconciling these two apparently contradictory sets of facts and statements is to see Wordsworth as distinguishing the kinds of verse or poetry which he would be able to write. Much of the revision he was to undertake was to consist of clarifying the expression of meaning and revising harmonies: presumably he did not envisage being able to write the kind of poetry which required the use of grand and sublime imagery such as he had employed earlier in life.

In short, as Wordsworth sat down, in his sixty-ninth year, to make revisions to various passages in *The Prelude*, and in particular to the lines he had written on Roubiliac's statue of Sir Isaac Newton, he must have felt that, although he was in fact able to make revisions of a rather mundane sort, his time for creating truly great poetry had, alas, passed. And yet it was at precisely this time that he wrote lines which have been praised as being among the greatest and most sublime that he ever wrote.

I Dating the Last Two Lines on Newton's Statue

VARIOUS DATES HAVE APPEARED IN PRINT FOR THE TIME at which Wordsworth revised his lines on Newton's statue. Mary Moorman dates the addition of the last two lines as "early in 1832" but offers no evidence for doing so.[1] Presumably she has simply taken the first of the two dates which de Selincourt gave for revisions having been made to MS. D: the early months of 1832 and probably March of 1839.[2] (MS. E, which we have cited on occasion with regard to other revisions in which Wordsworth appears to have drawn on Hamilton, was written in May of 1839, and at least Book XIV of it was "reviewed" in July of 1839.) Reynold Siemens, in his *Catalogue* of the Wordsworth Collection, repeats de Selincourt's dates for the revision of MS. D: 1832 and 1839.[3] The three editors of the Norton Critical Edition of *The Prelude* in turn add a wrinkle, saying that the last two lines were added to the Newton passage "in 1838/39."[4]

De Selincourt offers formidable epistolary evidence for considerable revision having been made to the MS. in 1832. Dora Wordsworth, he notes,

> writes to Miss Kinnaird on February 17, 1832: "Father is particularly well and busier than 1000 bees. Mother and

he work like slaves from morning to night—an arduous work—correcting a long Poem written thirty years back and which is not to be published during his life—The Growth of his own Mind—the Ante-Chapel as he calls it to The Recluse..."; and on October 15, 1832, Dora reports her father as still correcting the old poem. Christopher Wordsworth senior writes to Christopher Wordsworth junior, April 18, 1832: "They were very loath to part with him [his son John] at Rydal for he has been of great value to all the family—more especially to your uncle—who having John to talk to in his walks, was very industrious through the whole winter at all other times of the day—and worked very hard, especially in the revising and finishing of his long autobiographic poem" [B.M. Add. MSS. 46137].[5]

At the same time, however, there is another letter, this one from Wordsworth himself, which suggests that he may not have accomplished as much revision to *The Prelude* as the other letters would indicate. Writing to William Rowan Hamilton on 8 February 1833, he remarked:

With regard to P[oetry] I must say that my mind has been [kept] this last year and more in such a state [of] anxiety that all harmonies appear to have been banished from it except those that reliance upon the goodness of God furnishes:

Tota de mente fugavi
Haec studia, atque omnes *delicias* animi.—[6]

The Latin quotation is from Catullus' 68th poem and is translated thus by F. W. Cornish: "I have banished from all my mind these thoughts and all the pleasures of my heart."[7] The underlining of "delicias" ("pleasures") was done by Wordsworth, and the whole quotation refers to the effects on Catullus of his brother's death. While it may be that Wordsworth still felt grief for his brother's death twenty-eight years after the event, it is of course much more likely that the primary allusion is to the fraternal relation to Dorothy and to the sad and shattered state, both physical and mental, of his beloved sister, "whose life," Wordsworth had commented at the beginning of the letter to Hamilton, "is but a struggle from day to day." Mary Moorman sums up the situation well when she says,

> Public and private anxiety had almost silenced William's muse throughout that sad year 1832; and it was not until Dorothy began to recover that he could even turn to reading. "A year has elapsed", he said to Quillinan [on 23 February 1833]..., "since I wrote any poetry but a few lines, and I have rarely even read anything in verse till within the last week, when I have begun to accustom my ear to blank verse in other [A]uthors with a hope they may put me in tune for my own."[8]

The "few lines" Wordsworth mentions, Mary Moorman ventures, may have been a poem in rhymed pentameter. Certainly Wordsworth seems to have implied that, whatever he wrote, little as it was, it was not in blank verse, since he was reading the blank verse of other authors "with a hope they may put me in tune for my own."

On the one hand there is attestation of great industry in revising *The Prelude* in 1832, and on the other hand there are assertions that, because of grief and anxiety, Wordsworth was not able for that year to write beyond a few lines of poetry, and those not in blank verse. Perhaps part of the seeming contradiction is resolved by what Dora added to her letter about Wordsworth's being busier than 1000 bees: "We can't be sufficiently thankful that his mind has been so much occupied during Aunt W's illness, had it not been so he would have been almost as ill as she."[9] In writing to his correspondents, Wordsworth may have made an unspoken distinction between writing new, independent poems and revising the old one. But such speculation leaves unresolved the matter of blank verse. At the very least, it would appear that one has some reason for assuming that the larger part of revision to MS. D was most likely done, not in 1832, but in 1838 and 1839.

Epistolary evidence for revision during August of 1838 is strong. On the 18th of that month Isabella Fenwick wrote Henry Taylor that Wordsworth "has been working hard this last month at this poem, that he may leave it in a state fit for publication so far as it is written.... He seems still to have a great power of working; he can apply himself five, six, or seven hours a day to composition, and yet be able to converse all the evening."[10] In the December and January following, however, it appears most unlikely that any revision would have been completed. On 20 January 1839, Wordsworth wrote to Hamilton: "... I have been prevented from writing by a succession of indispositions, one of which disabled me from either reading or writing, such was the state of my eyes, for upwards of two months."[11] And early in February Mary Wordsworth wrote to Quillinan: "I hold the pen for Mr W. who, you will be sorry to hear, is very unwell."[12] With the coming of March, however, work resumed. On the 28th of that month (in 1839) Isabella Fenwick wrote: "Our journey was postponed for a week, that the beloved old poet might accomplish the work that he had in hand, the revising of his grand autobiographical poem, and leaving it in a state fit for publication. At this he has been labouring for the last month, seldom less than six or seven hours a day, or rather one ought to say the whole day, for it seemed always in his mind—quite a possession, and much, I believe, he has done to it, expanding it in some parts, and perfecting it in all." In the evening he would walk over to Miss Fenwick's house at Ambleside, to tell her of his work, "of the difficulties he has had and how he had overcome them, of the *beautiful* additions he had made, and all the why and wherefore of each alteration."[13] As far as can be ascertained, then, either August of 1838 or March of 1839 appears to be the most likely time at which Wordsworth added the last two lines to his description of Newton's statue. May it be understood, accordingly, that when we say that Wordsworth made the revision in 1839, we mean in either August of 1838 or March of 1839 (at both of which times, incidentally, he was in his 69th year).

At the very least, it is clear that there is no compelling external evidence which would lead one to conclude that Wordsworth made his revisions to the Newton passage before he was able to read certain works produced by Hamilton in late 1832, late 1833, and the summer of 1835.

J The Availability of Bulwer's Poem

INFERENTIAL EVIDENCE INDICATES THAT, IN ALL LIKELIhood, Lytton Bulwer visited Wordsworth in the summer of 1824 and that, in consequence, he later sent him a copy of his prize poem "Sculpture."

The background is this. Lytton Bulwer gave an account, which his son repeated in his biography of his father, of the visit which Lytton Bulwer made to the Lake District in 1824, when he was a twenty-one-year-old undergraduate at Cambridge. From Penrith he "proceeded to travel on foot over the scenery of the English Lakes," staying for some time at Ambleside, which is very close to Rydal Mount.[1] During the summer of this year Wordsworth was at home in Rydal Mount, as we know from three letters of his wife, written in June and July.[2] In fact, Sara Hutchinson remarked about this time that "All the Robinsons from York are at Rydal—& they have gay *musical parties* & *what* not."[3] In other words, the opportunity existed for Bulwer to do what Edward Quillinan had done in 1821 and James Muirhead was to do in 1841—to drop in on the senior poet and pay his respects. The courteous thing for him to do, in consequence, would have been what Muirhead was later to do—send Wordsworth a copy of his latest book.[4] For Bulwer this would have been his prize-winning poem "Sculpture," which became available in three different forms: a separate publication in July of 1825, an extract (containing the lines on Newton's statue) reprinted in Bulwer's *Weeds and Wildflowers* of 1826, and the whole poem reprinted in *Cambridge Prize Poems* (1828), a copy of which we have suggested may have been sent by Christopher Wordsworth.[5]

Why neither Wordsworth nor Bulwer mentioned such a visit in any account that remains extant must certainly be considered. With Wordsworth and his family it is not surprising. No letters from Wordsworth or Dorothy survive from the summer of 1824, and none of the letters of Mary Wordsworth or Sara Hutchinson mentions Bulwer. But then the visit paid by Muirhead in 1841 is not mentioned in any letter from the circle, either, even though Wordsworth wrote a letter at the appropriate time to Isabella Fenwick, which was full of domestic trivia.[6] Not even the first visit paid by Quillinan is mentioned: only when he moved into the neighbourhood and began to see the Wordsworths on a regular basis does his name appear in their correspondence.[7] Presumably such visits were so much a matter of course that they did not merit mention.[8]

With the writings of Bulwer himself, the matter of omission is, admittedly, different. Presumably, however, the principal narrative purposes of Bulwer's account of his visit to the Lake District precluded the mention of a visit to Wordsworth. His account is taken up with the very sentimental visit he paid to the grave of his dead love, Viola, and with the Gothic terror of his narrowly escaping death at the hands of a landlord who tried to get into his room at night.[9] Describing the visit to Wordsworth would probably not have seemed in harmony with these main concerns.

Such a visit, however, like the ones made by Quillinan and Muirhead, seems to be implied in certain lines of the poem entitled "To Wordsworth" and contained in *The Siamese Twins* (1831), a copy of which Bulwer sent to Wordsworth with the inscription "To the Illustrious Wordsworth."[10] In the second stanza of that poem Bulwer describes Wordsworth walking "amid the mountains lone" while "Musing on Man." The stanza concludes with these lines:

> And from the full and silent Heart of Things,
> As o'er the hills thy unwatched footsteps trod,
>   Didst thou not draw the patriarchal springs
> Of love for Man and Nature, which the hues
> Of thy transparent verse all livingly suffuse?

We would ask that particular attention be paid to the second line quoted: "As o'er the hills thy unwatched footsteps trod." Does this mean simply that Wordsworth walked alone, or is it not more likely that this line reflects the amazement of Bulwer (at twenty-one) on seeing Wordsworth (at fifty-four) striding—"at a rattling pace," to use Muirhead's phrase—over the uneven hillside without ever watching where he put his feet, so intent was he on absorbing what Nature had to offer?

The themes of Wordsworth's poetry Bulwer proceeds to describe thus, in the fourth stanza:

> Man in his simple grandeur, which can take
>   From Power but poor increase; the Truth which lies
> Upshining in "the Well of homely Life;"
>   The Winds, the Waters, and their Mysteries—
> The Morn and moted Noon, the Stars which make
>   Their mirror in the heart; the Earth all rife
> With warnings and with wisdom; the deep lore
>   Which floateth air-like over lonely places—
> These made thy study and thy theme. . . .

These last three lines, especially, may refer to the many ancient legends which Wordsworth recounted, in his narrative poems particularly, as being associated with various deserted ruins, and yet, when one sets beside those lines this passage from Muirhead's description of his visit, another, more compelling possibility emerges:

> Near the lake, on the *old* road from Ambleside to Keswick, there was an opening in the storm dyke on the lake side of the road, with one of the loveliest views of the lake (Grasmere) to be had anywhere. Whether from the extreme beauty of the prospect, or from any consecration of the place in olden times to purposes of religion, and a preservation of its sanctity from the remembrance of the reward promised to faithful prayers there offered up, he said he did not know, but the rustic gate in this opening has always been called the *Wishing Gate,* and it is the belief of the people that a wish there breathed will find its accomplishment. He has already a poem upon it; but was made melancholy some time since by being told that the

gate had been removed, and the openings with the bright landscape shut up from passing eyes. On this he wrote another poem, regretting the ruthless change; but just the other day he heard that the report had been unfounded, and that the Wishing Gate was still in its proper and old abode. And he would go now with me to ascertain how the fact really was. Away we went, and, to our infinite joy, found the Wishing Gate *unharmed*, and standing in all its reverend rustic simplicity. You may conceive the interest with which I *then* heard him describe and point out all the manifold charms of the view, after doing which, he slowly, and with that musical emphasis which I never heard equally in any other recitation, repeated his *second* poem on the gate (yet unpublished), and enchanted at once my ear and mind.[11]

In the light of Muirhead's passage, do not Bulwer's lines, especially the ones about "the deep lore / Which floateth air-like over lonely places," seem more likely to reflect Bulwer's having listened to Wordsworth as, pausing by the various lonely objects (such as the Wishing Gate), he related the age-old lore associated with them—a lore which, because of the spell cast by his musical recitation, seemed then to float air-like over those objects in their lonely places?

This same kind of recitation in a deep bass voice which he reserved for poetical recitation[12]—coupled with his discussion of reviews and the unkind things that had been printed in them—again appears to be reflected, as having been heard in person, in the concluding lines of Bulwer's final stanza:

> Earth has no nobler, or more moral sight,
>   Than a Great Poet whom the world disowns,
> But stills not, neither angers;—from his height,
>   As from a star, float forth his sphere-like tones:
> He wits not whether the vex'd herd may hear
> The music wafted to the reverent ear;
> And far Man's wrath, or scorn, or heed, above,
> Smiles down the calm disdain of his majestic love!

After such a visit as appears to be reflected in this poem "To Wordsworth," the natural thing for Bulwer to do would certainly have been to send a complimentary copy of his prize-winning poem, and, judging by what Wordsworth demonstrated about other, similar works by promising young poets, he would have been keenly interested in reading it.

K Further Changes Due to Hamilton

IN THIS APPENDIX WE DISCUSS, PRINCIPALLY, A VARIETY of changes in *The Prelude* for which, we would argue, Hamilton was probably responsible.

A Comet's Course
In the thirteen-book version of *The Prelude*, when he began his list, in Book X, of entities that return to the same place, Wordsworth wrote (lines 70-71):

> "The horse is taught his manage, and the wind
> Of heaven wheels round and treads in his own steps...."

In MS. C (probably written sometime between 1817 and 1819), he replaced the second entity and made the opening lines read thus:

> The Horse is taught his manage, and the Stars
> Of wildest power wheel round in their own track.[1]

Then in MS. D he changed a key word in particular and made the lines read (lines 78-79 in the fourteen-book version):

> The Horse is taught his manage, & no Star
> Of wildest course but treads back his own steps. . . .[2]

Could Hamilton have contributed to the change from the vague "power" to the much more accurate "course"? (The *Oxford English Dictionary* makes it clear that it was not unusual in Wordsworth's day to use the word "star" for any celestial luminary, and, in view of its "wildest course," Wordsworth probably meant, by his word "star," a comet.) Halley's comet returned in 1835, and at least by 1832 a rumour had got abroad that the comet was to cross the Earth's orbit.[3] Consequently it is likely that Wordsworth and Hamilton talked about Halley's comet in either 1830 or 1834, during Hamilton's visit with Wordsworth. There would have been added reason for mentioning it, for Hamilton had been engaged (as early as 1830) in making calculations about the precise path the comet would take.[4] In the course of their conversation, Wordsworth would have had the opportunity of learning that "wildest power" was not particularly appropriate and that, if "orbit" were too scientific (though Young had used it), "course" would be more accurate.

There is even some evidence for conjecturing that a much more specific conversation took place, about the very phrasing that appeared in MS. C. During his stay with Wordsworth in 1830, Hamilton wrote to his sister, asking about his horse Comet: "How does the education of Comet proceed?"[5] The following year Hamilton wrote to Wordsworth about Comet: "I have lately got a mare whose countenance and character I like. I call it Planet, to distinguish it from a far more eccentric creature, Comet, whom I have degraded from the saddle to the car; in revenge for which Comet broke the shafts the other day. This morning Planet and I turned some neighbouring fields into an Ecliptic, and swept over enormous orbits, to the great amusement of some bystanders. . . ."[6] The familiar way in which Hamilton wrote about "degrading" Comet from the saddle to the car suggests that, when visiting Wordsworth, he had mentioned to him the question he had put to his sister in the letter he had sent her. It is here that we can conjecture that Wordsworth would have been struck with Hamilton's phrasing and could have said something like this: "How remarkable! You have just juxtaposed the education or manage of a horse with the career of a comet in the same way I have done in my autobiographical poem." He would then (our imagining continues) have taken out his MS. book and have read the relevant passage to Hamilton. We know that, in addition to Coleridge and the people who served as his amanuenses, Wordsworth either showed or read parts of his autobiographical poem to at least three or four people, and Hamilton, we know, he valued as highly as he did Coleridge.[7] Certainly, if Wordsworth did in fact read the passage to Hamilton, that reading would have provided Hamilton with the opportunity of repaying Wordsworth for the kindness he had shown in correcting some of the faulty diction Hamilton had used in various of his own poems.

Excited Spirits
Two other minor changes in wording offer even clearer evidence of Wordsworth's making use of something Hamilton wrote. In Book VII, lines 623-25, of the thirteen-book version, Wordsworth had written:

> Though rear'd upon the base of outward things,
> These, chiefly, are such structures as the mind
> Builds for itself.[8]

In MS. D Wordsworth changed the last two lines to read "Structures like these the excited Spirit doth mainly / Build for herself."[9] Hamilton in his Lecture of 1832 had emphasized the way in which the mind of the scientist abstracts from observed physical phenomena and then imaginatively postulates those laws and their operation that would account for the phenomena. So far his phrasing would simply parallel Wordsworth's, but in the rousing peroration to his Lecture he referred to the "spirits of Milton and Newton" which have been placed on kindred thrones and to the power of science to "lift" one above the stir of earth and to provide "enthusiasm" and "excitement."[10] "The excited spirit" neatly summarizes. In Book XIII, in speaking of the "higher minds," Wordsworth in the thirteen-book version had said (lines 91-92) that "This is the very spirit in which they deal / With all the objects of the universe...." *(P(deS)*, 484, corrected by collation with MS. A). In MS. D he changed "all the objects" to "the whole compass" *(P(O)*, 1127.) It is worth noting that Hamilton, in his Lecture of 1832, had written about "the mind of man" comprehending "all the scope, and character, and habits of those innumerable energies which...compose the material universe" (RPG 1:647). "Compass" is a good two-syllable synonym for "scope."

When "Or Are Caught" Was Added
When Wordsworth added a particularly significant phrase to his description of higher minds creating a "like existence," he may have been borrowing from his friend William Rowan Hamilton. Whenever that existence, Wordsworth wrote in the thirteen-book version of *The Prelude* (13:95-96), is "Created for them," those higher minds "catch it by an instinct." This wording he changed, in the fourteen-book version to (14:95-97):

> whene'er it dawns
> Created for them, catch it;—or are caught
> By its inevitable mastery....[11]

Since Hamilton, from whom Wordsworth was in the habit of borrowing ideas and phrases, had referred, in his address to the British Association, to "a human mind, possessing or possessed by some great truth,"[12] it would appear that Wordsworth could easily have helped himself to the alternating idea and have chosen to express it in a pair of terms synonymous with Hamilton's, one of which pair he had already used in his manuscript.

If we were able to know the actual year in which the phrase "or are caught" was added to Wordsworth's lines, we would have a better idea of its relationship to Hamilton. The phrase does not appear in the various versions of MSS. A and B, nor does it appear in the relevant passage in the notebook that de Selincourt identifies as MS. W. Since MS. C "stops abruptly at XII.187 (XIII.188)," the phrase presumably first appears in MS. D.[13] The original transcribing of MS. D, Owen is "inclined to suppose," occurred "during December 1831 and January 1832," and the Norton editors estimate "early in 1832."[14] Hamilton delivered his address to the British Association in 1835, and emendations were made to MS. D as late as 1839. The question is, of course, whether the phrase "or are caught" was written as part of the original transcribing or as a later emendation.

Two circumstances indicate that the original transcribing was probably done in response to dictation. On the page of the MS. on which our passage occurs, a partial line is written, crossed out, and then replaced with a line *below* it, as a person writing from dictation would do, not above it, as a person entering an emendation would do.[15] The second circumstance will emerge shortly.

On a first examination of the MS. and its printed transcript, the phrase "or are caught" appears to have been written as part of the original transcribing, especially since, in the printed transcription, it appears in the typeface used for the original transcription, a typeface which admittedly reflects the position and appearance of the phrase in the MS.[16] But a closer examination raises doubts. The lines immediately preceding appear to read thus in the original transcription:

> They, from their native selves, can send abroad
> Kindred infusions; for themselves create
> A like existence; &, wheneer it is created for them
> Catch it by instinct.

It will be noticed that the third line quoted has seven feet, while the fourth has three (this is the second circumstance indicating response to oral dictation); it could, accordingly, be that the third line was meant to end at "is" and that the fourth would have read (if transcribed accurately) "Created for them, catch it by instinct," thus leaving no room for further words. If so, the transcriber, becoming aware of her error, would have deliberately left a blank space on the page to the right of "instinct" and have begun the next line of text ("As angels stopped...") at the left-hand margin—as in fact she did.

Two sets of emendations appear in connexion with these lines. The first set proved temporary and was scored through, heavily, with the result that very little room (for further emendation) remained above "A like existence" and virtually none below it. So when the transcriber came to enter the second set of emendations, she had to erase the incomplete line "Catch it by instinct" in order to provide room for the new emendation.[17]

That second, and surviving, set of emendations allows the beginning of the third line ("A like existence;") to remain as it was, but substitutes a normal two and a half feet for the end of that line and a whole line for the phrase "Catch it by instinct" (which made up the original [partial] fourth line of the manuscript and which was erased to make room for the emendation), and continues, as an insertion, below the original fourth line. The emended version thus reads:

> A like existence; and if it appear
> Created for them, catch it,—or are caught

> By its inevitable mastery
> Like angels stopped....

If this reconstruction is accurate, the phrase "or are caught" was added as part of the emendation, and was slipped into the vacant space at the end of the line. In fact the "or" of the phrase overlaps the last two letters of something that was there before. Owen offers the tentative reading of "Each" for the word that was there before. For our purposes, fortunately, it does not matter what the word was: what matters is the fact that "or" was written over the ending of whatever was there before—and hence was written later than that previous word. Even if whatever was there before had been part of the original transcription, "or" was written later; and if "Each" (or whatever it was) was itself written as an emendation, "or" was written *still* later. In addition, it is difficult to see how the adverbial phrase "By its inevitable mastery" (which is clearly an emendation) could modify anything that had appeared in the original transcription: the only element that it can modify is the verb phrase "are caught." All of which would appear to indicate that the phrase "or are caught" was added as an emendation and so could easily have been entered after Wordsworth had read a copy of Hamilton's address to the British Association. If so, the phrase would probably, in fact, reflect another instance in which Wordsworth borrowed from Hamilton.

If, however, this reconstruction is not accurate, and the phrase "or are caught" was written before Hamilton made his address, we have a number of possible relationships for the phrase. In this particular instance it could be Hamilton who borrowed from Wordsworth; or each could have arrived at his phrase independently; or Hamilton could have communicated the phrase to Wordsworth orally before Wordsworth dictated the original transcription; or—and this is our sentimental favourite—a lively oral exchange between the two could have produced the concept which neither alone was likely to have produced.

Why A Certain Poem Was Promoted

There is possibly a further instance of the effect Hamilton had on Wordsworth's poetry, this one of a somewhat different kind. In 1827 Wordsworth published a short lyric addressed to "Poet" and with the first line reading "If thou indeed derive thy light from Heaven." It was probably written before 1827 and so before Wordsworth had met Hamilton. It makes use of star imagery in a particularly effective way, the imagery being aptly commented on by Wordsworth in the note he dictated to Isabella Fenwick: Rydal Mount, he said, is "backed and flanked by lofty fells, which bring the heavenly bodies to touch, as it were, the earth upon the mountain-tops, while the prospect in front lies open to a length of level valley, the extended lake, and a terminating ridge of low hills; so that it gives an opportunity to the inhabitants of the place of noticing the stars in both the positions here alluded to, namely, on the tops of the mountains, and as winter-lamps at a distance among the leafless trees" *(PW* 1:317). The poem itself reads as follows, with lines 2 and 14-16 having been added in 1837:

> If thou indeed derive thy light from Heaven,
> Then, to the measure of that heaven-born light,
> Shine, Poet! in thy place, and be content:—
> The stars pre-eminent in magnitude,
> And they that from the zenith dart their beams,
> (Visible though they be to half the earth,
> Though half a sphere be conscious of their brightness)
> Are yet of no diviner origin,
> No purer essence, than the one that burns,
> Like an untended watch-fire, on the ridge
> Of some dark mountain; or than those which seem
> Humbly to hang, like twinkling winter lamps,
> Among the branches of the leafless trees;
> All are the undying offspring of one Sire:
> Then, to the measure of the light vouchsafed,
> Shine, Poet! in thy place, and be content.
>
> *(PW* 1:1)

This poem was originally published as simply one of those in *Poems of Sentiment and Reflection*, but in 1845 Wordsworth had it placed at the beginning of his collected poems, because, he said, "I mean it to serve as a sort of Preface." The question arises, why was this particular poem elevated to such a significant position? Had it anything to do with Hamilton? Wordsworth wrote to Hamilton on 24 July 1829: "I like to see and think of you among the Stars...." (RPG 1:334; *LY* 2:97), and in his visit to Hamilton earlier in 1829 Wordsworth had urged him not to try to excel in poetry as well as in science, but to devote the major part of his energies to science, where his greater abilities lay, and to use his poetic gifts simply to provide "relief to personal feeling in the successive emergencies of life" (RPG 1:315). So the poem would have come to have added meaning for Wordsworth; in addition, it could well be that, because of Hamilton, Wordsworth had come to realize (more keenly than he had before), what very appropriate images stars make for those divine energies that support all the objects in the universe, including (and perhaps especially) poets in their varying degrees of ability.

L The Availability of Hunt's Review of Haydon's Painting

Some doubt may exist about whether Wordsworth would have read Hunt's review of Haydon's painting, especially since he is on record in his letters and conversation as having read few reviews. To his friend Francis Wrangham he wrote in 1807, "I am only a Chance-Reader of Reviews...."[1] His sister Dorothy observed in 1815, "We have seen none of the Reviews. The Eclectic, we are told, is highly encomiastic...."[2] Repeatedly in his letters there is the mention that he has not read this review or that, especially in the *Quarterly Review*.[3] With regard to the *Edinburgh Review*, he said that he would not pollute his fingers with touching it, and for a while he banned *Blackwood's Magazine* altogether from his house.[4] All this is, admittedly, true. At the same time, however, it should be noted that Dorothy asked their nephew Christopher Wordsworth to read *Blackwood's* criticism for them and to report on it, and in 1841 Wordsworth displayed an almost intimate understanding of Professor Wilson's writing in *Blackwood's*.[5] At various times Wordsworth and Dorothy remark on having read an article in the *Quarterly Review*, and, regardless of his earlier feelings against it, Wordsworth by 1819 was reading the *Edinburgh Review*.[6] More significantly, Wordsworth in 1825 wrote to Sir George Beaumont that "John Bull is very bitter against poor Haydon....": *John Bull* was a journal that had published a review severely criticizing Haydon's recent portraits, and Wordsworth's phrasing certainly suggests that he had read the review.[7] From another letter of his, in 1832, it is clear that he was still reading *John Bull*.[8]

There were particular reasons why Wordsworth would have read virtually all of the reviews of Haydon's painting—in addition to the fact that he himself figured in it. On the same day that he was occupied in considering revisions to *Peter Bell*, he talked with Henry Crabb Robinson about Haydon. Robinson recorded in his diary: "Wordsworth wants to have a large sum raised to enable him [Haydon] to continue in his profession. He wants £2,000 for his great picture (the produce of the Exhibition—the gross produce is £1,200) and he has suggested that part of this could be raised by subscription, so that the remainder could be advanced by way of purchase money for it, as an altar-piece to one of the new chambers."[9] What with his own keen awareness of the painting and what with his equally keen desire to see a subscription raised for its purchase, Wordsworth would have had every reason to be on the lookout for expressions of public response to the painting and so would likely have made a point of reading any potentially influential review.

In spite of Wordsworth's intense interest in the painting, however, there is some question as to how likely it would be that he would, in 1839, remember a review that had appeared in 1820.

His connexion with Haydon continued during those intervening years. Shortly after the showing of "Christ's Entry" Haydon asked Wordsworth for a loan. This Wordsworth declined, but evidently Haydon took the refusal in the proper spirit, for in December of that same year he visited Rydal Mount.[10] In 1821 Wordsworth wrote to Haydon, reporting praise for his painting of "The Raising of Lazarus."[11] From 1823 to 1831 there was, admittedly, an estrangement between the two, but it is significant that it was during this time, in 1825, that Wordsworth made his comment to Sir George Beaumont about *John Bull's* having been "very bitter against poor Haydon."[12] It should also be remembered that from late 1819 until his death Wordsworth continued to display in his dining room at Rydal Mount the chalk drawing of him which Haydon had made and sent to him.[13] By 1831 a reconciliation had taken place, Wordsworth sent Haydon a sonnet on his painting of Napoleon, the two exchanged friendly letters in June and July, and in the fall of 1831 Wordsworth would have heard the news that "Christ's Entry," to Haydon's sorrow, had been sold by its current owner to people who were going to ship it across the Atlantic Ocean to America.[14] Then in 1838, shortly before Wordsworth was to revise the Newton passage, Haydon sent him word that he was going to dedicate his public lectures to him, and Wordsworth sent two grateful letters in reply.[15] Almost always Wordsworth's letters to Haydon contain remarks about Haydon's paintings, and always in his dining room there hung, for him to see and be reminded, the chalk drawing done by Haydon. The chains of association were in place for Wordsworth whenever anything might occur to start them into action, and whether the chains proceeded through letters or the chalk drawing, they would encounter that other depiction Haydon had made of Wordsworth, the one in "Christ's Entry," and from there they could easily proceed to what Hunt had said in his review about the depiction of the person represented as standing beside Wordsworth—Sir Isaac Newton.

M Wordsworth's Acquaintance With Philo

WHILE AT CAMBRIDGE (1787-90) WORDSWORTH would have had a number of opportunities, and indeed occasions, to become acquainted with the writings of Philo Judaeus. His works had been published in 1742, in a handsome folio two-volume edition, complete with a Latin translation in columns parallelling the Greek text, by Thomas Mangey, who had studied at Wordsworth's own college, St. John's. Mangey had been, in fact, a most distinguished alumnus of the College, having been a fellow there for three years and having been awarded the degrees of Doctor of Laws and Doctor of Divinity.[1] Over the six-year period 1785-92, the German scholar Augustus Friedericus Pfeiffer produced his redaction (in five volumes) of the first half of Mangey's edition, and presumably the individual volumes would have arrived at St. John's College as they were published, some of them while Wordsworth was a student there, reading, among other subjects, Greek and Latin. As Mangey remarked in his Preface, there was a manuscript of Philo next door to St. John's, in Trinity College (in whose Antechapel stood the statue of Newton). In addition, Philo is mentioned frequently in Ralph Cudworth's book, *The True Intellectual System of the Universe*, which was recommended reading at Cambridge, and a copy of which Wordsworth at some time acquired for his own library.[2]

How well prepared would Wordsworth have been to read Philo's kind of Greek? He began his study of Greek at Hawkshead Grammar School and proceeded far enough there to read from Demosthenes, Homer, Lucian, and Xenophon.[3] He was also trained to compose poems, in English, in imitation of Greek and Latin poems, and, for two of his Greek exercises, he wrote "Anacreon (Imitation)" and "In part from Moschus—Lament for Bion," in each poem making use of ideas and phrases from the original.[4] When he was at Cambridge, Dorothy wrote that he was reading "in Italian, Spanish, French, Greek and Latin, and English"—not only poetry, but also "history &c &c."[5] About his reading in Greek one further aspect can be inferred from his use of Hederich's *Lexicon:* since this was a Greek-Latin / Latin-Greek word-book, he probably did much of his translation into and out of Greek by proceeding through Latin.[6] As a result, if he had any difficulty in reading Philo's Greek (and it can be very difficult in places), he would have been able to use Mangey's parallel Latin version as a guide; and if he had no difficulty with the original Greek, he would probably still have been interested in seeing how Mangey translated it into Latin.

After leaving Cambridge, Wordsworth would still have had several opportunities and occasions to pursue his acquaintance with Philo. In 1795 Caesar Morgan, who had strong Cambridge connexions, published a study on the concepts of the Trinity held by Plato and Philo, in which he was much concerned with the effects which their views had had on the Fathers of the Christian Church.[7] In 1797 Jacob Bryant published, through Cambridge University, his book *The Sentiments of Philo Judeus Concerning the Logos, or Word of God,* in which he argued that Philo had been greatly influenced by the early Christians. Since as late as 1792 Wordsworth had intended taking orders in the Church of England, his interest in such topics would have been keen.[8] Through his friendship with Coleridge, Wordsworth would have been reminded of Philo, for Coleridge had been impressed by him. Coleridge's father, who supervised the education of his children, in 1759 had contributed a note to the *Gentleman's Magazine* which was largely about Philo. Coleridge himself often referred to Philo's concept of "a Deus alter et idem," and in 1818 remarked that Philo was not "used half enough."[9] Another prompting from outside Cambridge would have come from the writings of Joseph Priestley. In 1782, in his controversial book *An History of the Corruptions of Christianity,* Priestley discussed Philo at length as an interpreter of Scripture and pointed out the extent to which he had influenced early Christian theologians. In 1784 he published an article (later republished in his collected works) on the Platonism of Philo.[10] While Wordsworth may not have been aware of either work at the time it was published, he could easily have been made aware of them through the connexions he established with several Unitarians, one of whose foremost leaders was Priestley. Moreover, Wordsworth and Priestley shared the same publisher, Joseph Johnson, and in a public letter to the Bishop of Llandaff, Wordsworth referred, approvingly, to "the philosophic Priestley."[11] In addition Priestley had become Coleridge's "hero," on whom he wrote a laudatory sonnet in 1794 and tributary lines in his "Religious Musings" of 1796.[12] So in all likelihood Wordsworth heard a fair amount about Priestley (and through him Philo) from Coleridge in his enthusiastic outpourings that lasted well into the night.

Why, especially in view of these recommendations, would Wordsworth not have acknowledged his use of Philo? In general, as discussed in Appendix D: Wordsworth's Attitude Concerning Acknowledgements, it is impossible to determine why Wordsworth chose, sometimes to acknowledge, and sometimes not to. But with regard to Philo in particular, there would have been persuasive reasons not to acknowledge. The entry for Philo in the *Encyclopaedia Britannica* of 1797 made for a pre-conditioned response to anyone adopting Philo's ideas as his own. Philo, said the article, "deduced the darkest meanings from the plainest words."[13] Who would regard Wordsworth's poetry seriously if they knew that he had drawn ideas from such a person? Philo also constituted a possibly more serious liability in view of what both Cudworth and Morgan had said about him. Cudworth had said that "We meet with no expression in any...Pagan Platonists, so Unhandsom and Offensive, as that of *Philo's*, in his Second Book of Allegories... *The [Word] is the Shadow of God...*," and Morgan had said, first in his Synopsis of Contents that "Origen [was] an admirer of Philo's system" and that the "controversy between Arius and Alexander [was] to be understood by a reference to the sophisticated doctrines of Philo," and then, in the Conclusion of his treatise, "The writings of Philo Judaeus furnished the Fathers of the Christian Church with the fatal means of deceiving themselves."[14] Clearly Philo had proved dangerously subversive, and Wordsworth had already been spied upon by the British government, which thought that he was likely a subversive.[15] Even the attention

Priestley had bestowed upon Philo would, ironically, have increased the desirability of keeping quiet about his own indebtedness to Philo, for Priestley was regarded, rightly or wrongly, as an enemy of orthodox Christianity as well as of the British Constitution.[16] Since Wordsworth was especially concerned about the money he could obtain by publishing his poetry, he would undoubtedly have felt that it was only prudent for him not to mention his association with Philo.[17] And the longer Wordsworth went without acknowledging, and the closer he moved towards orthodox Christianity, the less likely he would be to acknowledge his indebtedness to the Hellenistic Jew who had misled the early Christians.

Further Changes Due to Young

There is reason to believe that Wordsworth borrowed from Young in making a couple of changes at another place in *The Prelude*, at much the same time as he added to the passage on Newton's statue. In Book VIII of the 1805 version (lines 624-40), he celebrated "the time in which / The pulse of Being everywhere was felt" within him (lines 626-27). To illustrate the grandeur of this feeling, he turned to the stars and wrote:

> When all the several frames of things, like stars
> Through every magnitude distinguishable,
> Were half confounded in each other's blaze,
> One galaxy of life and joy.
>
> (lines 628-31)

Man's position in this grandeur he described thus:

> Then rose
> Man, inwardly contemplated, and present
> In my own being, to a loftier height;
> As of all visible natures crown....
>
> (lines 631-34)

Little wonder, then, that Wordsworth proceeded to climax this description of man's position by saying that he is "instinct / With Godhead" (lines 638-39).[1]

In the same time period, late in 1838 or early in 1839, as he added to his Newton passage, Wordsworth made two particularly noteworthy changes in this passage about feeling the "pulse of Being." The phrase "One galaxy of life and joy" he changed to "a galaxy / Of life & glory," and after the statement that man is the crown of all visible natures, he added "tho' born / Of dust & Kindred to the worm." This latter phrase the editors of the Norton edition refer to as "One of the most extreme of the Christian revisions of *The Prelude.*"[2] It certainly echoes Christian doctrine and it does so, admittedly, in a phrase whose content is a cliché. But the precise phrasing closely parallels two passages in Young's *Night Thoughts.* It is, of course, only appropriate that it should, for in his 1805 choice of stellar imagery and in his discussion of man's position in the universe, Wordsworth had already parallelled what Young had said, both in the passage on the voyaging planets we have examined and in the whole of Night IX, in which Young depicts himself as soaring through intergalactic space and drawing closer to the throne of God. As he approaches that throne, near the end of his poem, Young's persona asks God to look down, down "Through this wide waste of worlds; this vista vast, / All sanded o'er with suns," down "On a poor breathing particle in dust."[3] Closer still to Wordsworth's phrasing is a passage that occurs near the beginning of Young's entire poem, in a section where he describes the contrasting nature of man:

> An heir of glory! a frail child of dust!
> *Helpless* immortal! insect *infinite!*
> A worm! a god![4]

In 1805 Wordsworth had spoken of man's Godhead ("a god!" as Young had said) and had celebrated with galactic imagery. In 1838/39, at much the same time as he added the lines to his description of Newton's statue and also made a minor change to his description of Young as the Bard "With fancies thick as his inspiring stars,"[5] Wordsworth evidently wished to add the other, contrasting, side of man's nature. He retained his galactic imagery, which parallelled Young's and which indeed may have once again reminded him of Young; he changed "joy" to "glory" (Young's own word); and immediately after the statement that Man is "of all visible Natures crown," he inserted the contrasting clause "tho' born / Of dust & Kindred to the worm," which closely parallels Young's phrasing "a frail child of dust!... A worm!" What better model was there for Wordsworth to work from, when presenting the sublime contrasts of human nature, than the *Night Thoughts* of Edward Young?

On the Editing of the Lines on Newton's Statue

THE PASSAGE ON NEWTON'S STATUE IS FOUND IN FIVE manuscripts: following are printed transcripts and reconstructions, with textual commentary, of the various forms in which it appears in these manuscripts and also in the first printed edition of 1850. (We are particularly grateful to Mr. Jonathan Wordsworth and the Dove Cottage Trustees for permission to reproduce the passage from the various manuscripts.)

MS. A (Composed probably in 1804.[1] Transcribed in MSS. Verse 20 (DC MS. 52) by Dorothy Wordsworth in 1805. Revisions made by Wordsworth probably some time between 1816 and 1819.)[2]

> Her pealing Organ was my neighbour, too;
> And, from my Bed-room, I in moonlight nights
> Could see, right opposite, a few yards off,
> The Antechapel, where the Statue stood
> Of Newton, with his Prism & silent Face.

In the first line "Her" is crossed out and "Thy" is written above it. On the page opposite appears the beginning of a line "Then, from" and a single letter, possibly a "t," all of which is crossed out.

Above this appears the line "And in deep midnight when the Moon shone fair," which in turn is crossed out (curiously, this line appears in de Selincourt's notes as if it had not been crossed out). Beneath these lines crossed out appear the new lines of what is called MS. A^2.

MS. A^2

> Her pealing Organ was my neighbour, too;
> And, from my Pillow, when the Moon shone fair
> Or even by dimmer influence of the stars,
> In wakeful vision rapt I could behold
> Solemnly near and pressing on my sight
> The Antechapel, where the Statue stood
> Of Newton, with his Prism & silent Face.

The second line does not appear in de Selincourt's notes. The fourth line originally began, "I could behold, with unuplifted Head," which is crossed out, except for "Head." Evidently the line was replaced with the line written above *and* the line following it.

MS. B (A second copy of the original version composed, probably, in 1804. Transcribed in MSS. Verse 21 (DC MS. 53) by either Sara Hutchinson or Mary Wordsworth.[3] Revisions made by Wordsworth probably some time between 1816 and 1819.)

> Her pealing Organ was my neighbour, too,
> And, from my Bed-room, I in moonlight nights
> Could see, right opposite, a few yards off,
> The Antichapel, where the Statue stood
> Of Newton, with his Prism and silent Face.

The third of these lines is crossed out, and alternative lines are written (in Wordsworth's hand) between the first and second lines, between the second and third lines, and between the third and fourth lines. These alternative lines appear to read:

> And, in deep midnight, when the moon shone fair
> Then from my pillow [did I love] to mark
> Solemnly near & pressing on my sight

In the margin at the bottom of the page are added these lines:

> And from my pillow I had power to mark
> By glimmering starlight pressing on my sight
> In [darksome grandeur]

In the margin at the top of the page are added these lines:

> And from my pillow, I had power to mark
> Solemnly near & pressing on my sight
> In [darksome grandeur]—or with mellow gleams
> Of moonlight on her branchy windows playing
> [The Antechapel]

The first two words of the second line have a line running through them. On the left-hand page opposite, running vertically up the left-hand margin, appear the lines which de Selincourt, in his notes, designated B^2. We incorporate them in the reconstruction we offer below:

MS. B^2

> Her pealing Organ was my neighbour, too,
> And from my pillow I had power to mark
> Solemnly pressed upon my stedfast gaze
> By glimmering starlight, or with mellow gleams
> Of moonshine on the branchy windows playing
> The Antichapel, where the Statue stood
> Of Newton, with his Prism and silent Face.

MS. C (Copied from A, some time between 1816 and 1819, in MSS. Verse 22 (DC MS. 82), by John Carter, Wordsworth's clerk. Revisions made by Wordsworth.)[4]

> Her pealing Organ was my neighbour, too;
> And from my bed-room I in moonlight nights
> Could see, right opposite, a few yards off,
> The Antechapel where the Statue stood
> Of Newton, with his Prism and silent Face.

Emendations made by Wordsworth produced what we call C^2:

MS. C^2

> Her pealing Organ was my neighbour, too;
> And from my Pillow when the silver Moon
> Shone fair I could behold solemnly near
> The Antechapel where the Statue stood
> Of Newton, with his Prism and silent Face.

MS. D (Transcribed in MSS. Verse 23 (DC MS. 124) by Mary Wordsworth, possibly "during December 1831 and January 1832.")[5]

Until the publication of W.J.B. Owen's admirable edition, the original form of the Newton passage in MS. D was hidden under a wafer which had been pasted over it. Now that the wafer has been removed, it is evident that the original form closely parallelled that which we have called MS. C^2:

> Her pealing Organ was my neighbour too;
> And, from my Pillow, when the silver Moon
> Shone fair, I could behold, solemnly near
> The Antichapel, where the Statue stood
> Of Newton, with his prism, & silent face.[6]

At some time (we would argue in late 1838 or early 1839), certain changes were made in the original form of MS. D, with the changes being recorded (in Mary's hand) between the lines of the original. In the third line "Shone fair" was cancelled and had written above it "Or star-light," which presumably elaborated on the phrase at the end of the preceding line: "when the silver Moon." "Shone fair" itself is then struck out, and "behold" of the third line is struck out and replaced by "see," which then is also struck out. It would appear that these tentative revisions were then succeeded by the larger one of striking out the phrase "when the silver Moon" of the second line and all of what was left of the third line and replacing these with "looking forth by light" at the end of the second line and "My moon or favoring stars, I loved to mark" above the cancelled third line. What distraction or inattention (or Freudian slip) led to the inscribing

> A humming sound, less tuneable than bees,
> But hardly less industrious, with shrill notes
> Of sharp command and scolding intermixed.
> Near me was Trinity's loquacious Clock,
> Who never let the quarters, night or day,
> Slip by him unproclaimed, & told the hours
> Twice over, with a male & female voice.
> Her pealing Organ was my neighbour too;
> And from my pillow looking forth by light
> Of moon or favoring stars, I loved to mark
> The Antechapel, where the Statue stood
> Of Newton, with his prism, & silent face,
> The marble index of a Mind for ever
> Voyaging thro' strange seas of Thought, alone.
> Of College labors, of the Lecturer's room
> All studded round, as thick as chairs could stand,
> With loyal Students faithful to their books,
> Half & half Idlers, hardy Recusants,

The page on which occurs Wordsworth's enlargement of his lines on Newton's statue, in MS.D, from MSS. Verse 23; DC MS. 124. Reprinted with permission of Mr. Jonathan Wordsworth and the Dove Cottage Trustees from the Dove Cottage Papers Facsimiles, Special Collections Library, University of Alberta.

of "My moon" instead of "Of moon" it would be interesting to speculate on, but, alas, quite idle. Much more important is the insertion, between the last line of the passage on Newton's statue and the first line of the succeeding verse paragraph, of the couplet we have been so much concerned with. Evidently the period after "face" was changed to a dash and then the insertion made, the first line of which reads "The marble index of a Mind for ever" with a comma after "Mind" being struck out. The second line evidently began "Voyaging in": a change was then made, by writing over the "in" instead of above (there being no room above it) the "th" of "through," finishing the word "through," and completing the line: "strange Seas of Thought, alone." A transcription of the passage as it stood emended under the wafer would read thus:

> Her pealing Organ was my neighbour too;
> And, from my Pillow, looking forth by light
> My moon or favoring stars, I loved to mark
> The Antichapel, where the Statue stood
> Of Newton, with his prism, & silent face—
> The marble index of a Mind for ever
> Voyaging through strange Seas of Thought, alone.

Presumably the passage was judged too messy to be let stand; so it was transcribed (apart from the first line, which was allowed to stand) on to a wafer of fresh paper, which was then pasted over the original. On that wafer the passage reads thus (incorporating the untranscribed first line):

> Her pealing Organ was my neighbour too;
> And from my pillow, looking forth by light
> Of moon or favoring stars, I loved to mark
> The Antichapel, where the Statue stood
> Of Newton, with his prism, & silent face:
> The marble index of a Mind for ever
> Voyaging thro' strange seas of Thought, alone.[7]

At the end of the third line, after "mark," is added the word "see" in pencil. In the fourth line "Antichapel" might actually be spelled "Antechapel." The last line begins "Voyaging in thought"; the phrase "in thought" is struck out, "thro' strange" is written above it, and the rest of the line continues "seas of Thought, alone."

MS. E (Transcribed, in MSS. Verse 24 (DC MS. 145), by Dora Wordsworth and Elizabeth Cookson.)[8]

> Her pealing organ was my neighbour too,
> And from my pillow looking forth by light
> Of moon or favoring stars, I could behold
> The Antichapel where the Statue stood
> Of Newton with his prism, & silent face,
> The marble index of a Mind for ever
> Voyaging thro' strange seas of Thought, alone.

At the end of the third line, virtually in the margin and very faint, appears the word "mark." The word "behold" seems to be in a hand different from the rest of the passage and could possibly be Wordsworth's.

Version of 1850 printed by the publisher Moxon,[9] under the supervision of Christopher Wordsworth (the poet's nephew), Edward Quillinan (his son-in-law), and John Carter (his clerk).[10]

> Her pealing organ was my neighbour too;
> And from my pillow, looking forth by light
> Of moon or favouring stars, I could behold
> The antechapel where the statue stood
> Of Newton with his prism and silent face,
> The marble index of a mind for ever
> Voyaging through strange seas of Thought, alone.

Obviously the printed version of 1850 (what we shall call the Moxon version) differs from MS. E in a number of ways. At the end of the first line, a semicolon replaces the comma of MS. E (MS. D has a semicolon), thereby more noticeably separating the remaining lines from the first. In the second line the editors inserted a comma after "pillow," in effect restoring the punctuation of the MS. D pasteover and thereby dividing the modifying phrase into two parts, instead of allowing "looking" to be placed out of what would be a normal prosaic order. In the third line a "u" has been inserted into "favoring," which Wordsworth spelled without the "u," even though "neighbour," two lines above, has a "u." (Perhaps Wordsworth preferred that "favoring" should stay closer to the Latin form, "neighbour" being of Old English derivation.) The fourth line contains three differences, two of which are in "antechapel." In the second syllable an "e" has replaced "i": since the spelling of this syllable varied between the two forms in the earlier MSS., this change may be of little consequence. Much more important was the change from the upper-case "A" to the lower-case. In the context of the passage, "Antichapel" (or "Antechapel") appears to combine the functions of a common noun, referring to one member of the class of antechapels, and that of a proper noun, this being the name given that portion of Trinity College, just like the Chapel itself (and, indeed, the College). Since the function of a proper noun is present, and (we believe) dominant, the upper-case "A" should have been retained. The "Statue" of MS. E has likewise been reduced to "statue" in the Moxon version. Presumably the reason was a desire to modernize, but we who can compare MS. E with its predecessor, MS. D, can see that, although MS. E reduced the "O" of "Organ" (in MS. D) to lower case, it still retained the upper-case "S" of "Statue." Such a retention would consequently appear to reflect a special status for the word "Statue." In the fifth line, the Moxon version made two changes from MS. E. One was to substitute "and" for "&": as with "Antichapel" and "Antechapel," both forms appeared in the various MSS., and the change is probably stylistic only. But the removal of the comma after "prism" is of more consequence (even though it first appeared in MS. D), for the absence of the comma has led a noted scholar, always most meticulous, into reading "prism" as a noun modifier of "face."[11] In fact, since all the MSS. before MS. E place a comma after "Newton," a strong argument could be made for restoring it to that position, since its absence in MS. E is something that Wordsworth could have overlooked. In the sixth line, the Moxon version reduced "Mind" to "mind," even though it retained the upper-case "T" in the "Thought" of the next line. Consequently the peculiar, reciprocating relation between Newton's Mind and God's Thought is made more difficult to discern.[12] In addition, as with "Statue," we who have the earlier MSS. available, and so note that certain capitals were retained in MS. E even though others were removed, would conclude that in all likelihood the copyist, on instruction from Wordsworth, had a special reason to retain those capitals she did. In the final line the substitution of "through" in the Moxon version for "thro'" in MS. E follows Wordsworth's original spelling in MS. D and appears to be the result of a difference in stylistic convention, as with "&" and "and."

It should be noted that MS. E, though suspect in general (since it was a "hasty and inaccurate transcription of the final state of *D*"),[13] has strong authority for the particular passage on Newton's statue. In its third line it records the change from "I loved to mark" of the MS. D wafer to "I could behold"—presumably on Wordsworth's instruction. In fact, the word "behold" seems to be in a hand different from Dora's and is possibly Wordsworth's own. Since the entire Newton passage consists of only the one sentence, it would appear likely that, in changing the phrase "I loved to mark," Wordsworth would have gone on to review the rest of the sentence (overlooking, possibly, only the absence of the comma after "Newton"). Consequently the MS. E version of this passage, in all likelihood, represents the last MS. version to which Wordsworth gave his sanction.

Until de Selincourt's edition of *The Prelude*, editors and publishers had no version of the Newton passage available other than Moxon's: that version, consequently, is the one generally followed, except for occasional changes to accord with American spelling. De Selincourt, in 1926, had the opportunity of restoring the text of MS. E. Instead, he reproduced the Moxon text and in a note to the whole passage said, *"Stuck over in* D: D² *as* 1850," which is a condensed form of saying that the Newton passage has been completely rewritten on a piece of paper ("wafer") which has been pasted over the original passage in MS. D, and that the rewritten passage is identical with that in the first printed (Moxon) version. Such a statement, however, is simply not accurate, for, in addition to the numerous differences in spelling and punctuation, there is the matter that the Moxon version reads "I could behold" while the MS. D wafer reads "I loved to mark." MS. E is not even mentioned in de Selincourt's note, and the change (on the D wafer) in the last line of the passage, from "in thought" to "thro' strange seas of Thought" is likewise passed over in silence.

Following de Selincourt's edition (revised in 1959 by Helen Darbishire, but unchanged with regard to the Newton passage), it is understandable that editors and publishers continued to reproduce the Moxon version, with only occasional changes. With the publication of the Norton Critical Edition of *The Prelude* in 1979, another opportunity presented itself of restoring to the Newton passage the authentic text from MS. E. The editors of the Norton Edition were well aware of the deficiencies of the Moxon version of *The Prelude* in general: they rightly complained of "the alterations and intrusions" made by Wordsworth's executors in the Moxon version and say that their own version is "that of the first edition, refined by collation with *E*, and further checked against *D*."[14] We can only applaud their editorial principles (though we might ourselves prefer beginning with MS. E), and can only wish that they had applied those principles to the Newton passage, for they, too, have reproduced, unchanged, the Moxon version. One could be excused, in the light of this history, for wondering how many other passages have continued to appear as in the Moxon version in spite of their differences from MSS. E and D.

For this reason especially, we are delighted to note the recent (1985) publication of the Cornell Wordsworth *Fourteen-Book Prelude*, edited by W.J.B. Owen, complete with photographic reproductions of the MSS. and annotated transcriptions. Owen's edition, together with the forthcoming Cornell *Thirteen-Book Prelude*, to be edited by Mark Reed, should certainly meet the needs of Wordsworth scholars. Owen's "Reading Text" reproduces the MS. E version of the passage on Newton's statue, except for such accidental variants as an uppercase "O" in "Organ," a semicolon at the end of the first line, a comma after "pillow," an "e" in "Antechapel," a comma after "Newton," "and" for "&," a colon after "face," and "through" for "thro'."[15]

When it comes to providing a text, without variants, for use in the classroom and for other, more general, purposes, might we suggest a course of action particularly suited to the present situation in which there is considerable controversy over which version, "1805" or "1850," to reproduce. On one extreme there is the recent one-volume Oxford edition of Wordsworth's poems, by Stephen Gill, in which the reader would look in vain for the two lines of the Newton passage we have been so much concerned with—in fact, they will find reproduced (except for one or two differences in punctuation) the very first version of the passage, the one appearing in MS. A.[16] On the other extreme there is the recent one-volume Cambridge edition of Wordsworth's *Poetical Works*, by Paul D. Sheats, in which readers would look in vain for the haunting description of the "blue chasm," that "dark deep thoroughfare" in which Nature had "lodged / The Soul, the imagination of the whole"—because only the Moxon version is presented.[17]

As a final note, might we suggest that, when an editor presents the version of *The Prelude* of his choice, whether in whole or in selections, he devote something like ten percent of the total text to selections of the best poetry that appear in the other version? In this way all parties would gain: the editor, the readers, and the author himself.

Abbreviations Used in the Notes

For Wordsworth's Letters:

The location of the Wordsworth letters is indicated by the code listed below. The citation *LY* 4:431, for example, refers to page 431 of the fourth item listed under *LY* (for "Later Years"), viz., *The Letters: The Later Years, 1831–40*, ed. Ernest de Selincourt (unrevised vol. 2 of 1st ed.) (Oxford: Clarendon, 1939).

EY   *The Letters of William and Dorothy Wordsworth*, ed. Ernest de Selincourt, *The Early Years 1787–1805* (Vol. 1 of 2nd ed.), rev. Chester L. Shaver (Oxford: Clarendon, 1967).

LY   *The Letters of William and Dorothy Wordsworth*, ed. Ernest de Selincourt:

    LY 1   *The Letters: The Later Years, Part I, 1821–1828*, ed. Ernest de Selincourt (Vol. 3 [i.e., 4] of 2nd ed.), rev. Alan G. Hill (Oxford: Clarendon, 1978).

    LY 2   *The Letters: The Later Years, Part II, 1829–1834*, ed. Ernest de Selincourt (Vol. 5 of 2nd ed.), rev. Alan G. Hill (Oxford: Clarendon, 1979).

    LY 3   *The Letters: The Later Years, Part III, 1835–1839*, ed. Ernest de Selincourt (Vol. 6 of 2nd ed.), rev. Alan G. Hill (Oxford: Clarendon, 1982).

LY 4 *The Letters: The Later Years, 1831–40*, ed. Ernest de Selincourt (unrevised vol. 2 of 1st ed.) Oxford: Clarendon, 1939).

LY 5 *The Letters: The Later Years, 1841–50*, ed. Ernest de Selincourt (unrevised vol. 3 of 1st ed.) (Oxford: Clarendon, 1939).

MY *The Letters of William and Dorothy Wordsworth*, ed. Ernest de Selincourt:

MY 1 *The Letters: The Middle Years, Part I, 1806–1811*, ed. Ernest de Selincourt (Vol. 2 of 2nd ed.), rev. Mary Moorman (Oxford: Clarendon, 1969).

MY 2 *The Letters: The Middle Years, Part II, 1812–1820*, ed. Ernest de Selincourt (Vol. 3 of 2nd ed.), rev. Mary Moorman and Alan G. Hill (Oxford: Clarendon, 1970).

For Wordsworth's Poetry:

B William Wordsworth, *The Borderers*, ed. Robert Osborn (The Cornell Wordsworth) (Ithaca: Cornell University Press, 1982).

P *The Prelude* (used when no differentiation is required).

P(deS) William Wordsworth, *The Prelude, or Growth of a Poet's Mind*, ed. Ernest de Selincourt (Oxford: Clarendon, 1926); 2nd ed., rev. Helen Darbishire (Oxford: Clarendon, 1959).

P(N) William Wordsworth, *The Prelude: 1799, 1805, 1850*, ed. Jonathan Wordsworth, M. H. Abrams, and Stephen Gill (The Norton Critical Edition) (New York: W. W. Norton, 1979).

P(O) William Wordsworth, *The Fourteen-Book Prelude*, ed. W. J. B. Owen (The Cornell Wordsworth) (Ithaca: Cornell University Press, 1985).

P(P) William Wordsworth, *The Prelude, 1798–99*, ed. Stephen Parrish (The Cornell Wordsworth) (Ithaca: Cornell University Press, 1977).

P(1799) The two-part version of *The Prelude* completed in 1799.

P(1805) The thirteen-book version of *The Prelude* completed in 1805.

P(1850) The fourteen-book version of *The Prelude* published in 1850.

PTV William Wordsworth, *Poems, in Two Volumes, and Other Poems, 1800–1807*, ed. Jared Curtis (The Cornell Wordsworth) (Ithaca: Cornell University Press, 1983).

PW *The Poetical Works of William Wordsworth*, ed. Ernest de Selincourt and Helen Darbishire, 5 vols. (2nd ed. for Vols. 2 and 3) (Oxford:Clarendon, 1940–54).

For Manuscripts Containing Versions of "The Prelude"

The manuscripts are located in the Wordsworth archive at Dove Cottage, Grasmere, and photocopies of the manuscripts are on deposit in the libraries of Cornell University and the University of Alberta, as well as the Bodleian Library. For each manuscript the old classification number is given first, followed by the new. For dates and details of transcription, see Appendix O: On the Editing of the Lines on Newton's Statue.

MS. A   MSS. Verse 20; DC MS. 52.

MS. B   MSS. Verse 21; DC MS. 53.

MS. C   MSS. Verse 22; DC MS. 82.

MS. D   MSS. Verse 23; DC MS. 124.

MS. E   MSS. Verse 24; DC MS. 145.

Emended versions of the poetic text appearing in each manuscript are indicated by a superscript number affixed to the letter designation for the particular manuscript (e.g., D^2), with D^2 representing the first emendation, D^3 the second, and so on.

For Other Works Frequently Cited:

BRS   B. R. Schneider, Jr., *Wordsworth's Cambridge Education* (Cambridge: Cambridge University Press, 1957).

CW   Christopher Wordsworth, *Memoirs of William Wordsworth*, ed. Henry Reed, 2 vols. (Boston: Ticknor, Read, and Fields, 1851).

HCR   Henry Crabb Robinson, *The Correspondence of Henry Crabb Robinson with the Wordsworth Circle*, ed. Edith J. Morley, 2 vols. (Oxford: Clarendon, 1927).

HNF   Hoxie Neale Fairchild, *Religious Trends in English Poetry*, 6 vols. (New York: Columbia University Press, 1939–68).

HT   Sir Henry Taylor, *Correspondence of Henry Taylor*, ed. Edward Dowden (London: Longmans, 1888).

JW   Jonathan Wordsworth, "The Climbing of Snowdon," *Bicentenary Wordsworth Studies*, ed. Jonathan Wordsworth (Ithaca: Cornell University Press, 1970).

MHN   Marjorie Hope Nicolson, *Newton Demands the Muse* (1946; reprint, Hamden, Conn.: Archon, 1963).

MM   Mary Moorman, *William Wordsworth: A Biography* (London: Oxford University Press):

   MM 1 *William Wordsworth: A Biography: The Early Years, 1770–1803* (London: Oxford University Press, 1957).

   MM 2 *William Wordsworth: A Biography: The Later Years, 1803–1850* (London: Oxford University Press, 1965).

RPG   R. P. Graves, *Life of Sir William Rowan Hamilton*, 3 vols. (1882–89; reprint, New York: Arno, 1975).

Notes

Preface

1. Charles Tennyson, *Alfred Tennyson* (London: Macmillan, 1968), 490, quoting Collins where the punctuation indicates.

1 Elevating the Mind to God

1. That this is the passage referred to appears from the elaboration of ideas and phrases in it provided by Eliza Hamilton in her account of the discussion between her brother and Wordsworth (RPG 1:313). Her whole account of Wordsworth's meeting with the Hamilton family is exceptionally well written and of great interest to students of Wordsworth (RPG 1:311-14); it has been referred to in both MM 2:438-39 and Edith C. Batho, *The Later Wordsworth* (1933; reprint, New York: Russell and Russell, 1963), 28-32. The passage from *The Excursion* appears in *PW* 5:138-40.
2. Eliza Hamilton makes no record of Wordsworth's having referred to what he had said about Men of Science in his Preface to the *Lyrical Ballads*. Since in these passages, although he stressed the cooperation possible between the Poet and the Man of Science, he also pointed to the latter's being concerned with truths particular and remote (while the Poet is concerned with truths general and near), he may well have felt that what he had said there would help him but little. See *Literary Criticism of William Wordsworth*, ed. Paul M. Zall (Lincoln: University of Nebraska Press, 1966), 51-53.

3. From MS. E. On Book XIV of this MS. is written "Reviewed July 2, 1839," and the version in this MS. is, presumably, the last form of the poem seen and approved by Wordsworth. See Reynold Siemens, *The Wordsworth Collection: A Catalogue; Dove Cottage Papers Facsimiles of The University of Alberta* (Edmonton: The University of Alberta Press, 1971), 25. The version in W. J. B. Owen's reading text in *P(O)*, lines 57-63 of Book III, is identical, except for accidental variants: see Appendix O: On the Editing of the Lines on Newton's Statue.
4. See the letter from Wordsworth to his family, 5 July 1837 *(LY* 3:423). For a detailed discussion of Wordsworth's poetic expectations at this time, see Appendix H: Wordsworth's Poetic Expectations in Old Age.
5. *P(deS)*, 75, 527.
6. *P(N)*, 523.
7. MM 2:439.
8. *The Oxford Companion to English Literature*, ed. Sir Paul Harvey, 3rd ed. (Oxford: Clarendon, 1946), 555.
9. Alexander Pope, *An Essay on Man* (4:332), ed. Maynard Mack, *The Poems of Alexander Pope*, Twickenham Edition, 10 vols. (London: Methuen, 1939-67), 3 (pt. 1): 160.
10. RPG 1:313.
11. "Prospectus," lines 52-54, 69-70 *(PW* 5:4-5).
12. *P(1850)* 14:67, 71-72, 90, 93-95 *(P(O)* 259-60).
13. The concluding lines to the verses by Edmund Halley prefixed to the First Edition of Newton's *Principia*, in Isaac Newton, *Opera Quae Exstant Omnia*, ed. Samuel Horsley, 5 vols. (1779-85; reprint, Stuttgart-Bad Cannstatt: Friedrich Frommann Verlag, 1964), 2:8.
14. Canto 2, Stanza 11 of *The Castle of Indolence*, in James Thomson, *Poetical Works*, ed. J. Logie Robertson (London: Oxford University Press, 1908), 282; Pope, *Essay on Man* 2:81-82, Twickenham Edition, 3 (pt. 1): 64; Pope, *The Dunciad* (B 3:191; B 4:229-38), ed. James Sutherland, 3rd ed., Twickenham Edition, 5:329, 365-66; Book 1, Stanzas 49-51 of James Beattie, *The Minstrel*, in *The Poetical Works of Beattie, Blair, and Falconer*, ed. George Gilfillan (Edinburgh: James Nichol, 1854), 16-17.
15. *Paradise Lost* 11:500-501, 3:233, 6:851-52, 1:43, 6:869-70, in John Milton, *The Works of John Milton*, gen. ed. Frank Allen Patterson, Columbia University Edition, 18 vols. with 2-vol. index (New York: Columbia University Press, 1931-40), 2 (pt. 2): 363; 2 (pt. 1): 85; 2 (pt. 1): 208; 2 (pt. 1): 10; 2 (pt. 1): 209; "On the Morning of Christ's Nativity," line 123, in *Works of John Milton*, Columbia University Edition, 1 (pt. 1): 6; RPG 1:313.
16. MM 1:186.
17. See W. K. Thomas's note: *Explicator* 28 (Jan. 1970): no. 45.
18. William Blake, "The Tyger" (line 12) in William Blake, *The Poetry and Prose of William Blake*, ed. David V. Erdman, commentary by Harold Bloom (Garden City, N.Y.: Doubleday, 1965), 24. Wordsworth apparently owned a copy of *Songs of Innocence and of Experience* (see Chester L. Shaver and Alice C. Shaver, *Wordsworth's Library: A Catalogue* (New York and London: Garland, 1979), 28.
19. James Ussher, *A Body of Divinitie...* (London: Thomas Downes and

George Badger, 1645), 202-3. Bishop Ussher was the one responsible for determining the date 4004 B.C. which was printed opposite the beginning of Genesis in editions of the Bible for many generations.
20. Meanings verified in Johnson's *Dictionary* and the *OED*; "The Alley [in Imitation of Spenser]" (lines 35-36) in Alexander Pope, *Minor Poems*, ed. Norman Ault and John Butt, Twickenham Edition, 6:44; David Hartley, *Observations on Man*... (Part One, Prop. 61), ed. Theodore L. Huguelet, 2 vols. (1749; reprint, Gainesville, Fla.: Scholars' Facsimiles & Reprints, 1966), 1:213; Wordsworth, "The Farmer of Tilsbury Vale" (line 3) in *PW* 4:240; "Two Epigrams on Byron's *Cain*" (lines 1-2) in *PW* 4:378; "The Tables Turned" (lines 26-28) in *PW* 4:57.
21. Wordsworth to Walter Scott, 7 Nov. 1805 *(EY* 642).
22. *Sir Philip Sidney's Defense of Poetry*, ed. Lewis Soens (Lincoln: University of Nebraska Press, 1970), 8.
23. Samuel Taylor Coleridge, *Biographia Literaria*, ed. James Engell and W. Jackson Bate, being vol. 7 of *The Collected Works of Samuel Taylor Coleridge*, gen. ed. Kathleen Coburn (Princeton: Princeton University Press, 1983), 1:304 (end of Chap. 13).
24. John T. Graves to William Rowan Hamilton, 29 Dec. 1846 (RPG 2:549).
25. For Thomson and Pope see *MY* 1:507 and *Academy*, 23 Dec. 1905 (page 1334), as cited in Lane Cooper, "A Glance at Wordsworth's Reading," *Modern Language Notes* 22 (March 1907): 86.
26. *Henry James: Literary Criticism*, ed. Leon Edel & Mark Wilson (New York: Library of America, 1984), 52. For *rakes* see *Athenaeum*, No. 424 (12 Dec. 1835): 931; *The Inward Eye* (Ashington: Mid Northumberland Arts Group, 1970), 35.
27. Aubrey de Vere to Henry Taylor, 9 Mar. 1845 (HT 156).

2 The Sage As Hero

1. Quoted by Chantrey's secretary and superintendent of works, Allan Cunningham, in Cunningham's study *The Lives of the Most Eminent British Painters, Sculptors, and Architects*, 3 vols. (London: John Murray, 1830), 3:52-53.
2. G[eorge] Dyer, *History of the University and Colleges of Cambridge*, 2 vols. (London: Longmans, 1814), 2:327.
3. "Religious Musings, A Desultory Poem," lines 372-74, in his *Poems*, 2nd ed. (with poems by Charles Lamb and Charles Lloyd) (Bristol: Cottle; London: Robinson, 1797), 145.
4. W[illiam] S[elwyn], "Trinity College Chapel," in *Cambridge Portfolio*, ed. J[ohn] J[ames] Smith, 2 vols. (London: Parker; Cambridge: Deighton, 1840), 1:98.
5. Lucretius, *De Rerum Natura*, ed. & trans. W. H. D. Rouse, Loeb Classical Library (London: Heinemann; Cambridge, Mass.: Harvard University Press, 1959), 242 (3:1042-44).
6. Lucretius, *On Nature*, trans. Russel M. Geer (Indianapolis: Bobbs-Merrill, 1965), 112.

7. Frank E. Manuel, *The Religion of Isaac Newton* (Oxford: Clarendon, 1974), 65.
8. Perry Miller, "Bentley and Newton," in *Isaac Newton's Papers & Letters on Natural Philosophy and Related Documents*, ed. I. Bernard Cohen (Cambridge, Mass.: Harvard University Press, 1958), 274.
9. "And from his true dominion it follows that the true God is a living, intelligent, and powerful Being; and, from his other perfections, that he is supreme, or most perfect. He is eternal and infinite, omnipotent and omniscient; that is, his duration reaches from eternity to eternity; his presence from infinity to infinity; he governs all things, and knows all things that are or can be done." (Sir Isaac Newton, *Mathematical Principles of Natural Philosophy*, trans. Andrew Motte, rev. Florian Cajori (Chicago: Encyclopaedia Britannica, Inc., 1952), 370.)
10. Richard Bentley, *A Confutation of Atheism from the Origin and Frame of the World* (1693) in *Isaac Newton's Papers*, 332, 337, 320 (20, 25, and 8 of the 1693 edition of Bentley's eighth lecture).
11. On the base of the statue, at the rear, appears this inscription: "Posuit Robertus Smith S.T.P. Collegij hujus S. Trinitatis Magister, MDCCLV." For details concerning Robert Smith, D.D. (1689-1768), see *DNB* and Katharine A. Esdaile, *Roubiliac's Work at Trinity College, Cambridge* (Cambridge: Cambridge University Press, 1924), 3.
12. Marvell with his "Horatian Ode upon Cromwell's Return from Ireland" (1650) and Dryden with his "Heroic Stanzas on the Death of Oliver Cromwell" (1658).
13. See, for example, Bonamy Dobrée, *Restoration Tragedy, 1660-1720* (Oxford: Clarendon, 1929), Chap. I: "The Necessity for Heroism."
14. For a description of the poems see Robert D. Horn, *Marlborough: A Survey* (New York: Garland, 1975).
15. See *The History of Jonathan Wild*, Bk. I, Chaps. 1, 2, 5. For comparisons between military heroes and Newton, see Alan Dugald McKillop, "A Poem Sacred to the Memory of Sir Isaac Newton: Introduction," in James Thomson, *The Castle of Indolence and Other Poems*, ed. Alan Dugald McKillop (Lawrence: University of Kansas Press, 1961), 145-46.
16. "Lines Written as a School Exercise at Hawkshead," lines 53-56 *(PW* 1:260).
17. As quoted in Christopher Wren (the son), *Parentalia: or, Memoirs of the Family of the Wrens...* (London: Osborn, 1750), 343. Ensuing quotations are from 344 and 346.
18. The verses quoted by Wren are "Ex MS. D. Sprat." (344).
19. Wren, *Parentalia*, 343.
20. Francis Fawkes, "Will with a Wisp," in *The Works of the English Poets*, ed. Alexander Chalmers, 21 vols. (London: Johnson, 1810), 16:258.
21. William Whiston, *Sermons and Essays upon Several Subjects* (London, 1709), 208-9; cited by F.E.L. Priestley, in his essay "Newton and the Romantic Concept of Nature," *University of Toronto Quarterly* 17 (1947-48): 332-33.
22. James Thomson, "To the Memory of Sir Isaac Newton," lines 148-50, 137-43, in his *Poetical Works*, 440.
23. Allan Ramsay, "An Ode to the Memory of Sir Isaac Newton" (1728), in

The Poems of Allan Ramsay, new ed., 2 vols. (Paisley: Alex. Gardner, 1877), 1:147; Henry Jones, *Philosophy, a Poem* (Dublin: Powell, 1746), 6.
24. Richard Owen Cambridge, "On Seeing the Head of Sir Isaac Newton," in Chalmers, 18:296; Francis Fawkes, "An Eulogy on Sir Isaac Newton," in Chalmers, 16:253.
25. Wren, *Parentalia*, 345.
26. Elizabeth Tollet, "On the Death of Sir Isaac Newton" (1727), in *A Select Collection of Poems*, 8 vols. (London: J. Nichols, 1780-82), 6:69; biographical information on 6:64.
27. Richard Glover, "Poem on Sir Isaac Newton" (1728), in *The Works of the British Poets*, ed. Robert Anderson, 13 vols. (London: John and Arthur Arch, 1795), 11:546. Cf. Thomson, lines 91-93.
28. John Hughes, "The Ecstasy" (1720), lines 189-96, in *The Poetical Works of John Hughes* (Edinburgh: Apollo Press, 1779), 2:99-100; also in Anderson (1795), 7:331. The next quotation is from lines 128-29 (Hughes, 97; Anderson, 330). Cf. Thomson on Newton's measuring the speed of light: "Nor could the darting beam of speed immense / Escape his swift pursuit and measuring eye" (lines 94-95).
29. Thomson, lines 76-77.
30. David Mallet, "The Excursion" (1728), in Anderson, 9:694.
31. John Theophilus Desaguliers, *The Newtonian System of the World* (1728), quoted in HNF 1:357.
32. Hughes, lines 177-78.
33. MHN 40.
34. Tollet, 69.
35. Thomson, lines 57-58; Mallet, page 694.
36. Mallet, 693.
37. Ramsay, 1:148.
38. Mallet, 695.
39. Moses Browne, *Essay on the Universe* (1739), quoted in HNF 1:391.
40. Thomson, line 139; Ramsay, 1:148.
41. Desaguliers, in HNF 1:357; Glover, in Anderson, 11:545.
42. Desaguliers, in HNF 1:358; Mallet, in Anderson, 9:694; Thomson, lines 125, 128.
43. Tollet, in *Select Collection*, 6:70; Glover, in Anderson, 11:544.
44. Thomson placed on the title-page of his first edition, not the lines Smith was to allude to, but others by Lucretius praising Epicurus, with the implication, of course, that Newton was the rightful recipient. See McKillop, 135, 149.
45. Jane Brereton, *On the Bustoes in the Royal Hermitage* (1733), quoted in HNF 1:325.
46. Mark Akenside, *The Pleasures of the Imagination* (1757), Book I, in Chalmers, 14:83.
47. Mallet, in Anderson, 9:694.
48. E.A. Burtt, *The Metaphysical Foundations of Modern Physical Science* (New York: Harcourt, Brace, 1927), 236-37.
49. See Harold Bloom, *Blake's Apocalypse: A Study in Poetic Argument* (1963; reprint, Garden City, N. Y.: Doubleday, 1965), 171, where he refers to lines 4-8 of Plate 13 of *Europe: A Prophecy* (1794) and line 9 of plate 98

of Chap. 4 of *Jerusalem* (1804, 1820): see *The Poetry and Prose of William Blake*, ed. Erdman, 63-64, 254. Cf. also Donald D. Ault, *Visionary Physics: Blake's Response to Newton* (Chicago and London: University of Chicago Press, 1974), 45-50. It is worth adding that, in the plate 98 referred to, Blake appears to have prophesied a redemption for all three of Bacon, Locke, and Newton and to have placed them, so redeemed, in his pantheon.

50. Note to page 112, line 13, in *The Complete Works of Percy Bysshe Shelley*, ed. Roger Ingpen and Walter E. Peck, Julian Edition, 10 vols. (1926-30; reprint, New York: Gordian, 1965), 1:150.

51. For commendation, see Lecture 4 (1795) of his *Lectures on Revealed Religion* in *Lectures 1795: On Politics and Religion*, ed. Lewis Patton and Peter Mann, being vol. 1 of *The Collected Works of Samuel Taylor Coleridge*, gen. ed. Kathleen Coburn (London: Routledge & Kegan Paul; Princeton: Princeton University Press, 1971), 189-90 (see also note on page 190). For condemnation, see his note to *Joan of Arc* cited on 100-101 of the same volume: "It has been asserted that Sir Isaac Newton's philosophy leads in its consequences to Atheism; perhaps not without reason.... Sir Isaac Newton's Deity seems to be alternately operose and indolent; to have delegated so much power as to make it inconceivable what he can have reserved. He is dethroned by Vice-regent second causes." See also his notes (1817) cited in his *Biographia Literaria* (Chaps. 12 and 18), ed. Engell and Bate, 1:277-78n, and 2:75n.

52. *The Autobiography and Memoirs of Benjamin Robert Haydon, 1786-1846*, ed. A. P. D. Penrose (London: Bell, 1927), 231-32.

53. MHN 2.

54. *Shelley's Poetry and Prose*, ed. Donald H. Reiman and Sharon B. Powers, Norton Critical Edition (New York: W. W. Norton, 1977), 405.

55. Glover, in Anderson, 11:545.

56. Thomson, lines 96-102, 119-24.

57. Akenside, *The Pleasures of the Imagination* (1744), 2:103-20, in Chalmers, 14:66.

58. Lee M. Johnson, *Wordsworth's Metaphysical Verse: Geometry, Nature, and Form* (Toronto: University of Toronto Press, 1982), 50.

59. F. E. L. Priestley, 330.

60. Burtt's is not the only instance in the twentieth century of Newton's being misrepresented. A. J. Snow, in his *Matter and Gravity in Newton's Physical Philosophy* (London: Oxford University Press, 1926), insists, on page 209, that Newton said that God is the soul of the world, even though Newton plainly said the precise opposite. God, Newton said, "governs all things, not as the soul of the world, but as Lord over all": in fact, he dismissed the claim that God is the soul of the world as the work of fancy (see his "General Scholium," in *Math. Princs.*, page 370). At least two literary scholars have accepted Snow's misrepresentation of Newton (without going to Newton himself) and have based interpretations on it as if it were Newton's true position: S. G. Dunn, "A Note on Wordsworth's Metaphysical System," *Essays and Studies* 18 (1933): 107; Carl Grabo, *A Newton Among Poets* (Chapel Hill: University of North Carolina Press, 1930), 100. Even Melvin Rader, in his *Wordsworth: A Philosophical Ap-

proach (Oxford: Clarendon, 1967), comes perilously close, on page 45, to implying that Newton had referred to God as the soul of the world.
61. See *The Faerie Queene* 1.1.45-1.2.6.
62. MM 1:57; BRS 4-5; Eileen Jay, *Wordsworth at Colthouse* (Kendal: Titus Wilson & Son, 1970), 28-29.
63. For Wordsworth's oral loquacity consider the accounts of four observers. J. P. Muirhead could not have spent over five hours with Wordsworth, and yet the number of topics Wordsworth discussed (many at length) is staggering: no wonder Muirhead "listened to the uninterrupted stream of his eloquence" (James Patrick Muirhead in a letter to his mother, 1 Sept. 1841, published in *Blackwood's Magazine* 221 (June 1927): 730). Isabella Fenwick remarked, concerning Wordsworth's talking about his attack of sciatica: "You may easily imagine how copiously he would talk on the subject, and how minute he would be in his description of its rise and fall, &c...." (to Henry Taylor, 18 Aug. 1838, in HT 93). Miss Fenwick wrote in the same letter: "He seems still to have a great power of working; he can apply himself five, six, or seven hours a day to composition, and yet be able to converse all the evening" (HT 97). Aubrey de Vere wrote to Taylor, 9 Mar. 1845: "We have toiled up the mountain sides, and he has murmured like a young pine-grove for hours together, and not been the least tired" (HT 156). Christopher Wordsworth described his uncle's conversation as a "copious river-like flow of words, sweeping along with a profusion of imagery, reflections, and incidents, in a majestic tide" (CW 2:477).
64. Referring to Jean Sylvain Bailly, a French astronomer who was guillotined, Wordsworth wrote, "Not Newton's Genius could have saved his head/ From falling by the *Mouvements* he had led" (Wordsworth to John Wordsworth, 7 Dec. 1832 (LY 2:573)).
65. Zall, *Literary Criticism*, 61.
66. *P(O)*, 141, 68.
67. Muirhead, 741.
68. RPG 1:311-14.
69. *P(1850)* 3:269-76 in *P(O)*, 68.
70. See Queries 18-24 of his *Opticks* and the final paragraph of the General Scholium in his *Principia*.
71. The passage appears on page 250 of vol. 3 of Thomas Birch's *History of the Royal Society of London*, as reprinted in *Isaac Newton's Papers & Letters*, ed. Cohen, 180.
72. The passage appears in Thomas Birch, "The Life of the honourable Robert Boyle," in *The Works of the Honourable Robert Boyle*, new ed., 6 vols. (1772; reprint, Hildesheim: Georg Olm, 1965-66), 1:cxviii.
73. Fawkes, "An Eulogy on Sir Isaac Newton," in Chalmers, 16:252; Mallet, in Anderson, 9:695.
74. Hughes, lines 114-16, 123-25.
75. Mallet, in Anderson, 9:693. The next quotation is from 9:694.
76. MM 1:101.
77. *PW* 1:260.
78. *The Pleasures of the Imagination* (1744), 2:126-31, in Chalmers, 14:66.
79. *PW* 1:13n.

80. BRS 219.
81. *PW* 5:385.
82. We quote the wording, and cite the line numbering, of the 1850 version, as in *P(O)*, 95. The dream "is in fact a brilliantly imaginative transformation of a dream experienced by the philosopher Descartes in 1619." (See *P(N)*, 158n.)
83. *P(O)*, 96.
84. BRS 257. Lines 115-28 of Book VI of *The Prelude* also testify to the same kind of relation, for Wordsworth, between geometry and the heavens.
85. See note 9.
86. Joseph Warren Beach, *The Concept of Nature in Nineteenth-Century English Poetry* (1936; reprint, New York: Pageant, 1956), 80-81. The next reference is to 84-85.
87. BRS 258-61; Geoffrey Durrant, *Wordsworth and the Great System* (Cambridge: Cambridge University Press, 1970), 101-02.
88. BRS 252.
89. RPG 1:314.
90. RPG 3:171 (Hamilton to Miss Alcock, 29 Apr. 1864).
91. The poems are nos. XXXIV and XXXV of "Poems on Sentiment and Reflection" *(PW* 4:107-14, 426-28). The line quoted (line 60 of the second poem) addresses the same "Babe" described in the first poem. See also MM 2:494.
92. *P(O)*, 234.
93. William Tasker's Ode appeared in the *Gentleman's Magazine* for Oct., 1799, on pages 884-85. The lines quoted appear in Stanza I. Also interesting is the difference between the 1805 version and the 1850 version of Wordsworth's lines (see *P(N)*, 418-19). In the earlier version he had written "Sage, patriot, lover, hero." In the later version, "Warrior" replaced "lover": the reader of the twentieth century is reminded of those Flower Children of the 1960s who, becoming disenchanted in the 1970s, embraced Star Wars in the 1980s.
94. Joseph Spence, *Anecdotes, Observations, and Characters, of Books and Men*, ed. S. W. Singer (London: Carpenter, 1820), 54.
95. The article, running 400-434 in vol. 23, was concerned with the versions by Singer and Malone, along with *The Invariable Principles of Poetry* by W. L. Bowles. In 1826 Wordsworth could well have been reminded (or informed) of Newton's simile by its inclusion in a note ("q") which Elizabeth Barrett wrote to a passage on Newton in the First Book of her poem *An Essay on Mind* (see Elizabeth Barrett Browning, *Poetical Works*, ed. Alice Meynell (London: Ward, Lock, n.d.), 14, 28-29). As will be seen later on, Wordsworth was extraordinarily conversant with the poetry of female authors, both preceding and contemporary.
96. James Foster, *Discourses on All the Principal Branches of Natural Religion and Social Virtue* (London: 1749-52), 183, 56-57, 58, 68, cited in F. E. L. Priestley, 334.
97. *PW* 2:261-62.

3 What Oft Was Thought

1. Louis Trenchard More, *Isaac Newton: A Biography* (1934; reprint, New York: Dover, 1962), 127. The following remark by Bishop Atterbury appears on the same page.
2. The Popean passages may be found, in the order cited, as follows: Alexander Pope, *The Iliad of Homer*, Books X-XXIV, Twickenham Edition, 8:153; *The Odyssey of Homer*, Books XIII-XXIV, Twickenham Edition, 10:150; "The Capon's Tale," *Minor Poems*, Twickenham Edition, 6:256.
3. "An Expostulation with Inigo Jones," in *The Poems of Ben Jonson*, ed. Bernard H. Newdigate (Oxford: Shakespeare Head, 1936), 296.
4. Twickenham Edition, 2:258.
5. See Allardyce Nicoll, *A History of English Drama, 1660-1900* (Cambridge: Cambridge University Press, 1955), 57-59, 82.
6. See M. L. Clarke, *Classical Education in Britain, 1500-1900* (Cambridge: Cambridge University Press, 1959), 46-60; W. A. L. Vincent, *The Grammar Schools: Their Continuing Tradition, 1660-1714* (London: John Murray, 1969); Foster Watson, *The Old Grammar Schools* (Cambridge: Cambridge University Press, 1916). As for Elizabeth Tollet, it would appear from her literary productions that her education, probably acquired at home (her father was a commissioner of the navy, and they lived in an apartment in the Tower—*Select Collection*, 6:64n), was modelled on that of her male counterparts.
7. MHN 40.
8. In HNF 1:325.
9. 2:257-58.
10. 2:242.
11. Quoted in MHN 136.
12. MHN 11-13.
13. Ramsay, 1:147, 149; Hughes, lines 176-78.
14. Thomson, lines 187-89.
15. Thomson, line 126.
16. In Chalmers, 14:66.
17. Thomson, lines 122, 124.
18. *Gentleman's Magazine* 1 (April 1731): 169.
19. *The Early Wordsworthian Milieu: A Notebook of Christopher Wordsworth with a few entries by William Wordsworth*, ed. Z. S. Fink (Oxford: Clarendon, 1958), 104-18.
20. W. J. B. Owen, "Literary Echoes in *The Prelude*," *The Wordsworth Circle* 3 (Winter, 1972): 13.
21. *PW* 1:260.
22. Tollet, in *Select Collection*, 6:69; Hughes, lines 177, 180, 186.
23. Ramsay, 1:148.
24. Thomson, lines 57-58, 76-77, 193-94. Succeeding quotations from Thomson are from lines 73-75, 196-98.
25. BRS 5-7.
26. This poem appeared in vol. 1 (1775) of the magazine, page 4 *(Correspondence and Papers of Edmond Halley*, ed. E. F. MacPike (Oxford:

Clarendon, 1932), 207). Information concerning the *European Magazine* appears in Fink, page 25.
27. Chalmers, 16:234; Jay, 28.
28. In Chalmers, 16:252. The poem extends to page 253. Wordsworth is clearly echoing Fawkes more than Halley, for the latter had written simply "Quae... Obvia conspicimus, nubem pellente Mathesi" (things which we see clearly exposed, mathematical reason having expelled the cloud). Halley's poem appears in Newton, *Opera Quae Exstant Omnia*, ed. Horsley, 2:7-8.
29. In the original the lines concerning the superior powers read:

> Talia monstrantem mecum celebrate camaenis,
> Vos ô caelicolûm gaudentes nectare vesci...
> Newtonum Musis charum....   (Newton, *Opera*, 2:8).

These lines Leon J. Richardson, Professor of Latin in the University of California, has translated thus:

> Then ye who now on heavenly nectar fare,
> Come celebrate with me in song the name
> Of Newton, to the Muses dear....

(In *Sir Isaac Newton's Mathematical Principles...*, trans. Andrew Motte, rev. Florian Cajori (Berkeley: University of California Press, 1934), xv.)

Fawkes appears to have acquired his "Elysian bowers" from Hughes's poem "The Ecstasy," where the earlier poet asked Newton's spirit to

>   lead me on thro' all th' unbeaten wilds of day:
> As when the Sibyl did Rome's father guide
> Safe thro' the downward roads of night,
> And in Elysium bless'd his sight
> With views till then to mortal eyes deny'd.
>
>   (lines 180-84)

For an argument that much of what is in Wordsworth's lines derives from Pope, see Abbie Findlay Potts, *Wordsworth's "Prelude": A Study of Its Literary Form* (1953; reprint, New York: Octagon, 1966), 35-38.
30. Akenside's Hymn appears in Chalmers, 14:132-33.
31. *PW* 1:13n.
32. In Anderson, 11:547.
33. In Anderson, 9:695.
34. *Evening Walk* A146 and *Descriptive Sketches* B314, for instance, appear to be influenced by Milton's "gulf profound" *(Paradise Lost* 2:592).
35. Ramsay, 1:149.
36. *An Essay on Man*, 3:152, ed. Maynard Mack, Twickenham Edition, 3 (pt. 1): 108.
37. *The Tempest*, 1.1.23; 5.1.2; 1.2.372.
38. *Windsor Forest, Pastoral Poetry and an Essay on Criticism*, Twickenham Edition, 1:153.
39. CW 2:480.

40. *PW* 4:285.
41. Quoted in *PW* 4:467.
42. Evidence of the interchangeability appears in Appendix G: The Distinctive Cluster of Elements.
43. Quoted in HNF 1:325.
44. In Anderson, 11:544, 545, 547.
45. There is potentially a problem with the dates at which Wordsworth could have secured copies of some of the poems we have argued he used as building blocks. See Appendix F: The Availability of Sources for the Hymn to Science.
46. Wordsworth to Anne Taylor, 9 April 1801 *(EY* 327-28).

4 A Prevailing Practice

1. Owen, "Literary Echoes in *The Prelude,*" 13.
2. Dorothy Wordsworth to Jane Marshall, 18 Oct. 1807 *(MY* 1:167).
3. Dorothy Wordsworth to Lady Beaumont, 3 Jan. 1808 *(MY* 1:187).
4. Dorothy Wordsworth to Lady Beaumont, 25 Dec. 1805 *(EY* 664).
5. Dorothy Wordsworth to Sara Hutchinson, 18 Feb. 1815 *(MY* 2:200).
6. Wordsworth to James Webbe Tobin, 6 Mar. 1798 *(EY* 212).
7. Wordsworth to Catherine Clarkson, [Jan. 1815] *(MY* 2:191).
8. Wordsworth to Alexander Dyce, 5 Jan. 1844 *(LY* 5:1196).
9. Samuel Johnson, *Lives of the English Poets,* World's Classics Edition, 2 vols. (London: Oxford University Press, 1949), 2:343-44.
10. Wordsworth to Walter Scott, 7 Nov. 1805 *(EY* 642).
11. Wordsworth to H. C. Robinson, Dec. 1838 (HCR 1:374).
12. Frederick A. Pottle, "The Eye and the Object in the Poetry of Wordsworth," in *Wordsworth: Centenary Studies,* ed. Gilbert T. Dunklin (Princeton: Princeton University Press, 1951), 27.
13. See Appendix A: The Myth of Wordsworth's Reading But Little.
14. See Appendix B: Wordsworth's Attitude Towards Cambridge Undergraduates.
15. Wordsworth to Sir George Beaumont, 29 July 1805 *(EY* 611).
16. Wordsworth to Alexander Dyce, 11 Mar. 1835 *(LY* 3:31-32).
17. The album was printed in facsimile by Henry Frowde in London in 1905. The Preface is by J. Rogers Rees, and the Introduction by Harold Littledale.
18. Wordsworth's misquotation of the last two lines of Shakespeare's Sonnet 64 (63) is slight, but his misquotation of Waller is more interesting. Where Waller, in line 7 of "Go, Lovely Rose," wrote "And shuns to have her graces spied," Wordsworth dictated "And loves to have her graces spied" (72). And where Waller, in lines 11-12 of "To the Young Lady Lucy Sidney" ("To A Very Young Lady"), wrote

> And then what wonders shall you do,
> Whose dawning beauty warms us so?

Wordsworth improved it to read

> If such thy dawning beauty's power
> Who shall abide its noon-tide hour? (73).

Cf. *The Poems of Edmund Waller*, ed. G. Thorn Drury (London: Lawrence and Bullen; New York: Scribner's, 1893), 57, 128.
19. Page iv of the album.
20. Wordsworth to B. R. Haydon, 16 Jan. 1820 *(MY* 2:577).
21. Wordsworth to John Kenyon, 23 Sept. 1833 *(LY* 2:640).
22. Wordsworth to R. P. Gillies, 9 June 1817 *(MY* 2:385).
23. Wordsworth to S. T. Coleridge, 9 Dec. 1803 *(EY* 425-26). Wordsworth's misidentifying Sonnet 69 as Sonnet 70 could be explained by mistaken looking rather than not looking, but his misidentifying Canzone 18A as Canzonet 31 cannot be explained on these grounds.
24. H. A. L. Fisher, "Winchester in the Eighteenth Century," in *Winchester College, 1393-1893*, by Old Wykehamists (London: Arnold, 1893), 84-85. Definitions of "vulgus" and "varying" are derived from the *OED*; a "varying" may also have been longer, filling a small exercise book.
25. Wordsworth to W. S. Landor, 20 Apr. 1822 *(LY* 1:125); CW 1:34; 2:480.
26. CW 2:492; *LY* 5:1334n.
27. Wordsworth to Alexander Dyce, 22 June 1830 *(LY* 2:292).
28. *Journals of Dorothy Wordsworth*, ed. Mary Moorman (London: Oxford University Press, 1971), 110.
29. Wordsworth may well have encountered Davies' poem again after that original incident, for in 1810 his son John asked that he might be given a copy of Enfield's *Speaker*. But the way Wordsworth phrased his comment to Dyce suggests that he was going back in memory to the original event. (For John's request see *The Love Letters of William and Mary Wordsworth*, ed. Beth Darlington (Ithaca: Cornell University Press, 1981), 96.)
30. Wordsworth to John Peace, 19 Jan. 1841 *(LY* 5:1063); *Cowper: Poetical Works*, ed. H. S. Milford, 4th ed., corrections and additions by Norma Russell (London: Oxford University Press, 1967), 198-99; *The Poetical Works of William Shenstone*, ed. George Gilfillan (Edinburgh: James Nicol, 1854), 133.
31. We have substituted parentheses for the two semicolons Cowper used.
32. Russell Noyes says of the painter Richard Wilson (1713-82) that "he was before his time and therefore at the mercy of patrons who were wedded to the 'brown tree' and the classical tradition." See Noyes, *Wordsworth and the Art of Landscape* (Bloomington: Indiana University Press, 1968), 50.
33. CW 2:476. In view of Wordsworth's obvious comfort with Milton and the rich benefit he received from reworking Milton's phrases, we find it difficult to be sympathetic towards the thesis Harold Bloom has argued, that Wordsworth sought to avoid being influenced by him and even sought to "overcome" him. See Harold Bloom, *The Anxiety of Influence: A Theory of Poetry* (New York: Oxford University Press, 1973), 125-26.
34. *Paradise Lost* 6:233-36, cited in *PW* 3:460.

35. Wordsworth to Thomas Powell, Mar. 1841 (*LY*, 5:1071).
36. E.g., *PW* 3:485, concerning line 21 of "Processions," and *PW* 4:418, concerning "Ode to Duty."
37. *PW* 1:358, 3:472, 5:460-61.
38. *PW* 2:506, 3:523.
39. "Characteristics of a Child Three Years Old" (lines 15-16) in *PW* 1:229.
40. *PW* 3:16. For biographical details see MM 2:212.
41. *Paradise Lost* 11:263-64; *Comus*, line 564; *Paradise Lost* 10:921-22; as found in Milton, *Works*, Columbia Edition, 2 (pt. 2): 355, 337; 1 (pt. 1): 106.
42. Cowper, *Table Talk* (lines 724-25), in *Poetical Works*, 16.
43. David Hartley, *Observations on Man...*, 1:21-24; *PW* 2:260.
44. Wordsworth to William Mathews, 3 Aug. 1791 (*EY* 56); *The Waggoner* 2:128-34 (*PW* 2:498-99).
45. Laurence Sterne, *The Life and Opinions of Tristram Shandy, Gentleman*, ed. Ian Watt (1760-67; reprint, Boston, Mass.: Houghton Mifflin, 1965), 240.
46. Laurence Sterne, *A Sentimental Journey Through France and Italy and Letters*, new ed. (London: Thomas Tegg et al., 1823), 19-20 ("The Remise Door: Calais").
47. *PW* 4:464.
48. Wordsworth to Catherine Clarkson, Jan. 1815 (*MY* 2:191). The spelling "heigth," incidentally, was an acceptable variant at the time.
49. See Joseph Addison, *The Evidences of the Christian Religion* (Edinburgh: William Darling, 1776). In its section entitled "Immortality of the Soul and a Future State" (pages 245, 235), it reprinted the two passages mentioned. Cf. Shaver, *Wordsworth's Library*, 4.
50. MM 1:15. Pupils at the dame school were required to memorize parts of the Bible, and the *Spectator* was yoked with the Bible—especially, one would think, the essay on the immortality of the soul.
51. *Spectator* No. 635 (20 Dec. 1714) in *The Spectator*, ed. Donald F. Bond, 5 vols. (Oxford: Clarendon, 1965), 5:170-71. The Newton passage appears on page 236 of *Evidences of the Christian Religion*.
52. Joseph Addison, *Cato*, in *Bell's British Theatre*, 20 vols. (London: John Bell, 1776-78), 3:59. Not only this speech in English, but also its translation into Latin (appearing on the opposite page), can be found in the section "Immortality of the Soul and a Future State" in *The Evidences of the Christian Religion*, 244-45.
53. Curiously the *OED* does not list the meaning "immortality" for "eternity," in spite of that meaning's appearance in this line. It does cite the word as it appears in the next line following ("Eternity! thou pleasing, dreadful thought!") as illustrating the meaning "The future eternity: time without end," and it does offer a meaning close to immortality: "the condition into which the soul enters at death; the future life." In the Latin version of Cato's speech, not only "eternity" of line 9 but also "immortality" of line 3 are translated by *Aeternitatis*, for good reason, since *aeternitas* meant both "eternity" and "immortality." For people conversant with Latin, the English "eternity" meant "immortality" as well.

54. *P(O)*, 102; Owen, 9-10. The other two passages are discussed on pages 10-12.
55. Milton, *Works*, Columbia Edition, 2 (pt. 1): 221-22. The next quotation is from 2 (pt. 2): 401. *P(deS)*, 480, 2.
56. *P(O)*, 72-73; Cooper, 112-13. The quotation from Bartram's *Travels* (1794) is from 47-48.
57. The information about authorship appears on page 1199, the poem itself runs from 1200 to 1204, and the passage quoted appears on 1202-3. The statue was erected on Friday, 4 July 1755 *(Gentleman's Magazine* 25 (1755): 328).
58. Hughes, line 191; Tollet, *Select Collection*, 6:70.
59. John Bell, *Bell's Classical Arrangement of Fugitive Poetry*, 14 vols. (London: Bell, 1789-91), 13:8-11. The passage we are concerned with appears on page 10.
60. Wordsworth to William Mathews, 24 Oct. 1795 *(EY* 154); Dyer, *History of Cambridge*, 328.
61. MS. A; date of 1803 for completion suggested by Mark L. Reed, *Wordsworth: The Chronology of the Middle Years* (Cambridge, Mass.: Harvard University Press, 1975), 12.
62. The second line of this revision was quickly changed to read "And, from my Pillow, when the Moon shone fair," after what was apparently the antecedent version of the line, "And in deep midnight when the Moon shone fair," had been deleted.
63. *Spectator* 5:171.
64. MS. B. See Appendix O: On the Editing of the Lines on Newton's Statue for details.
65. MS. C. De Selincourt's date in *P(deS)*, xxii.
66. For details see Appendix D: Wordsworth's Attitude Concerning Acknowledgements.
67. For a discussion of the myth, see Appendix E: The Myth of Wordsworth's Total Originality.

5 Linking Together

1. *PW* 3:444-45.
2. Coe, *Wordsworth and the Literature of Travel*, 32-33.
3. JW 449-74.
4. JW 454. For the text of "A Night-Piece," see Beth Darlington, "Two Early Texts: *A Night-Piece* and *The Discharged Soldier*," *Bicentenary Wordsworth Studies*, 431. For the *Prelude* text see *P(deS)*, 480-82.
5. See Chapter 4.
6. JW 452.
7. JW 453.
8. See Darlington, 431, and JW 454.
9. JW 462.
10. See JW 453, citing page 73 of Clarke's *Survey*, published in 1787.
11. JW 462.

12. S. G. Dunn, "A Note on Wordsworth's Metaphysical System," *Essays and Studies* 18 (1933): 74-109, esp. 108-9; Newton P. Stallknecht, *Strange Seas of Thought* (Bloomington: Indiana University Press, 1958), 131-37, 280-81.
13. Newton wrote of "certain active Principles, such as is that of Gravity," which move all particles (Bk. 3, Pt. 1, of his *Opticks*, ed. I. Bernard Cohen et al. (New York: Dover, 1952), 401; Shaftesbury argued for one active and vital Principle determining all others *(The Moralists* (1732), Pt. 3, sec. 1, page 365, as cited in Stallknecht, 135). In his *General Scholium* Newton remarked: "In bodies,...we touch only their outward surfaces...; but their inward substances are not to be known either by our senses, or by any reflex act of our minds: much less, [then], have we any idea of the substance of God." The cause of gravity, he said further, "penetrates to the very centres of the sun and planets." *(Mathematical Principles of Natural Philosophy* (Chicago: Encyclopaedia Britannica, 1952), 371.)
14. *Moralists*, cited in Stallknecht, 136.
15. *General Scholium*, in *Math. Princs.*, 370.
16. Stallknecht, 132-33; cf. 125-28.
17. *Aeneid*, 6:724-32; Cicero, *De Natura Deorum*, Bk. 2, secs. 10-11 (suggested by Jane Worthington Smyser, in her *Wordsworth's Reading of Roman Prose*, and reproduced in Stallknecht, 280-81).
18. *Spring*, lines 849-66, in Thomson, *Works*, ed. Robertson, 35-36; *Essay on Man*, 1:267-80, in Pope, *Poems*, Twickenham Edition, 3 (pt. 1): 47-49.
19. *PW* 3:562 (cf. 3:350).
20. John Robert Moore, "Wordsworth's Unacknowledged Debt to Macpherson's *Ossian*," *PMLA* 40 (1925): 372.
21. Douglas Bush, *Mythology and the Romantic Tradition in English Poetry* (1937; reprint, New York: W. W. Norton, 1963), 58-59.
22. *PW* 2:216-17.
23. Frederick Garber, *Wordsworth and the Poetry of Encounter* (Urbana: University of Illinois Press, 1971), 159-62.
24. For Dorothy and Mary, see *PW* 2:507. See also the entry for 15 April 1802 in *Journals of Dorothy Wordsworth*, ed. Mary Moorman (London: Oxford University Press, 1971), 109-10.
25. See Moore, 371-72, and Coe, 31-32, who points out that Bartram describes daffodils as being "tossed about" by "the mountain breezes."
26. Hanspeter Schelp, "Wordsworth's 'Daffodils' Influenced by a Wesleyan Hymn?" *English Studies* 42 (1961): 307-9.
27. Garber, 160.
28. Garber, 162; *Comus*, lines 104-19.
29. *Plato, With an English Translation: Timaeus, Critias, Cleitophon, Menexenus, Epistles*, ed. and trans. R. G. Bury, Loeb Classical Library, 12 vols. (London: Heinemann, 1914-35), 9:85-87.
30. Ralph Cudworth, *The True Intellectual System of the Universe* (1678; reprint, Stuttgart-Bad Cannstatt: Friedrich Frommann Verlag, 1964), 122; see Christopher Wordsworth, *Scholae Academicae* (1877; reprint, London: Frank Cass, 1968), 130; Shaver, 71.

31. *De Opificio Mundi* (hereafter abbreviated to *Op.*) in *Philo*, trans. F. H. Colson and G. H. Whitaker, Loeb Classical Library, 10 vols. (Cambridge, Mass.: Harvard University Press, 1929-62), 1:7-137. For man in the elements, see sec. 147 (1:116-17); dance in the sky, secs. 54, 70 (1:40-41, 54-55); other elements associated with dance, sec. 78 (1:62-63); dance in the human observer, sec. 70 (1:54-55).
32. *Op.* 70, 77-78 (1:54-55, 60-63).
33. See Appendix M: Wordsworth's Acquaintance with Philo.
34. Wordsworth could have used either the huge folio edition in two volumes, published in 1742 by William Bowyer in London or the smaller-sized five-volume redaction of Mangey's first volume prepared by Pfeiffer in Germany between 1785 and 1792. We shall cite page numbers in the folio edition of 1742.
35. All four elements are described in *Op.* 147 (1:116-17); Mangey I, 35. We reproduce the Greek characters printed in the Loeb text.
36. *Journals of Dorothy Wordsworth*, ed. Moorman, 109-10.
37. *Rape of the Lock* 2:71, in Pope, *Poems*, Twickenham Edition, 2:164; Dryden's translation of Virgil's *Pastorals*, 2:61-62, in *The Poems of John Dryden*, ed. James Kinsley, 4 vols. (Oxford: Clarendon, 1958), 2:879.
38. *Op.* 78 (1:62-63); Mangey I, 18.
39. *PTV* 330-31.
40. Philo's χορηγίαι καὶ ἀφθονίαι and Mangey's *copia ubertasque* in *Op.* 77 (1:60-61); Mangey I, 18.
41. *Op.* 78 (1:62-63); Mangey I, 18.
42. Philo's γυμνικοὺς ἀγῶνας and ἀγωνιστῶν... πλῆθος; Mangey's *athletarum spectacula* and *copiam concertatorum* in *Op.* 78 (1:62-63); Mangey I, 18.
43. Mangey I, 18.
44. *Op.* 78 (1:62-63); Mangey I, 18.
45. *Op.* 77 (1:60-61); Mangey I, 18.
46. *Op.* 77 (1:60-63); Mangey I, 18.
47. *Op.* 70 (1:54-55); Mangey I, 15.
48. *P(1850)* 12:45, and see *P(N)*, 418n; lines 39-40 of "Tintern Abbey" in *PW* 2:260.
49. Henry More, *Apocalypsia Apocalypeos; or, the Revelation of St. John the Divine unveiled* (London: J. Martyn and W. Kettilby, 1680), 5. We have used italics to indicate what More put in Gothic, the words of the original on which he was elaborating.
50. *Op.* 53 (1:40-41); 70 (1:54-55).
51. Cudworth, 123.
52. Lines 284-85 of "An Hymne of Heavenly Beavtie," in Edmund Spenser, *The Works of Edmund Spenser*, ed. Edwin Greenlaw et al., A Variorum Edition, 10 vols. with index (Baltimore: Johns Hopkins Press, 1932-57), 7 (Minor Poems 1): 230. At line 60 of the other poem, "An Hymne of Heavenly Love" (page 215), Wordsworth could well have found the line to which he appears to allude in both versions of his poem. Spenser described the stars as "ten thousand gemmes of shyning gold." In the version of 1807, line 4 read "A host of dancing Daffodils," and line 6 read "Ten thousand dancing in the breeze": together, and relying implicitly on the colour of the daffodils, they appear to have alluded to Spenser's

line and thereby have made an implicit comparison between the daffodils and the stars. The version of 1815 supplied the colour "golden" (line 4), introduced the "stars" explicitly (line 7), and moved the "Ten thousand" down to line 11, thereby making the allusion and comparison less implicit and spreading the process over two stanzas.

53. Lines 31 and 40 of *Il Penseroso* in Milton, *Works*, Columbia Edition, 1 (pt. 1): 41.
54. Lines 65-66, 73, 126 of *Il Penseroso* and lines 18, 94-96, 129, 69 of *L'Allegro*, in Milton, *Works*, Columbia Edition, 1 (pt. 1): 42, 44, 35, 37, and 39.
55. Lines 165-66 of *Il Penseroso* in Milton, *Works*, Columbia Edition, 1 (pt. 1): 45; *Op.* 54 (1:40-41); lines 285-87 of "An Hymne of Heavenly Love," in Spenser, *Works*, Variorum Edition, 7 (Minor Poems 1): 221.
56. Line 120 of *Il Penseroso*, in Milton, *Works*, Columbia Edition, 1 (pt. 1): 44.
57. *Op.* 70-71 (1:54-57); 153 (1:120-21). "Life of solitude" translates Philo's μονήρη βίον and Mangey's *solitariam vitam* (Mangey I, 37). Presumably Mary was aware of the delicious irony arising from this passage in Philo: that it was she, the woman, in fact the wife of little more than a year, who supplied the lines about "the bliss of solitude."
58. See *PTV* 330-31. Johnson observed in his *Dictionary* that *sprightly* should be spelled *spritely*, "but custom has determined otherwise."
59. Garber, 160; Pottle, 33. Strangely, Coleridge recorded a most unenlightened response to the final stanza of the poem when he said, "Assuredly we seem to sink most abruptly, not to say burlesquely, and almost as in a *medly*," from the couplet about the inward eye to the last two lines *(Biographia Literaria*, ed. Engell and Bate, 2:137).
60. Preface of 1802 in *Literary Criticism of William Wordsworth*, ed. Zall, 42, 46, 44.
61. *PTV* 419.
62. Preface of 1802, in *Literary Criticism*, 57-58.
63. See *PW* 4:463.
64. *PW* 4:396-97.

6 Strange Seas

1. For a discussion of the date at which the final two lines were added, see Appendix I: Dating the Last Two Lines on Newton's Statue.
2. William Wordsworth, *Prose Works*, ed. W.J.B. Owen and Jane Worthington Smyser, 3 vols. (Oxford: Clarendon, 1974), 3:295. The speech was made in 1836.
3. See the "Dedication" to *The Elements of Sir Isaac Newton's Philosophy*, by Mr. Voltaire, trans. John Hanna (London: Stephen Austen, 1738), iii-viii, esp. v.
4. The text is that of MS. E.
5. *P(deS)*, 73n.
6. Lines 199-204, *PW* 5:271.

7. Lines 155-56 of *Il Penseroso* in *Works*, Columbia Edition, 1 (pt. 1): 45.
8. Lines 51-54 of "A Song for St. Cecilia's Day, 1687," in *The Works of John Dryden*, gen. eds. Edward Niles Hooker and H. T. Swedenberg, Jr. (Berkeley and Los Angeles: University of California Press, 1956-), 3:203.
9. Edward A. Armstrong, *Shakespeare's Imagination: A Study of the Psychology of Association and Inspiration* (London: Drummond, 1946), 147-49.
10. Page references for the passages noted: *PW* 5:76-78; 5:384-85; *P(O)* 36-41; *PW* 4:279-85; 2:259-63.
11. See Appendix G: The Distinctive Cluster of Elements.
12. John Jones, *The Egotistical Sublime: A History of Wordsworth's Imagination* (London: Chatto & Windus, 1954), 54-110.
13. Herbert Lindenberger, *On Wordsworth's "Prelude"* (Princeton: Princeton University Press, 1963), 211-12.
14. A. C. Bradley, *Oxford Lectures on Poetry* (1909; reprint, Bloomington: Indiana University Press, 1961), 142.
15. Raymond Dexter Havens, *The Mind of a Poet*, 2 vols. (Baltimore: Johns Hopkins University Press, 1941), 1:57-58. The quotation is from lines 25-28 of "Star-gazers," *PW* 2:220.
16. Havens, 1:58.
17. In the light of the gloss provided by these parallel passages, the statement made about the pedlar, that "he scann'd the laws of light / With a strange pleasure of disquietude" takes on added meaning *(PW* 5:385).
18. *P(O)*, 88.
19. Wordsworth to W. E. Gladstone, 21 Mar. 1841 *(LY* 5:1201).
20. Wordsworth to George Crabbe, Feb. 1834 *(LY* 2:691-92).
21. Emile Legouis, *The Early Life of William Wordsworth*, trans. J. W. Matthews, 2nd rev. ed. (1897; reprint, New York: Russell and Russell, 1965), 79n.
22. *P(deS)*, 527; *P(N)*, 95n.
23. Wordsworth to A. Dyce, 12 Jan. 1829; 16 Oct. 1829 *(LY* 2:3; 157).
24. *PW*, 1:21; *P(deS)*, 185 (6:180-82).
25. Doughty compared 3:516-19 of *The Prelude* with Thomson's *Castle of Indolence* 1:30. Cited by de Selincourt in *P(deS)*, 531, and by Havens, 2:352.
26. De Selincourt compares *The Prelude* 1:559-61 with Thomson's *Winter*, lines 106-7, and *The Prelude* 8:266 with *Autumn*, lines 726-30 *(P(deS))*, 519, 580); Havens compares *The Prelude* 6:650-52 with *Spring*, lines 522-23, and *The Prelude* 8:229-30 with *Winter*, line 16 (2:429, 461).
27. Abbie Findlay Potts, *Wordsworth's "Prelude": A Study of Its Literary Form* (1953; reprint, New York: Octagon, 1966), 98-131.
28. Thomson, *Poetical Works*, ed. Robertson, 440 (lines 125-31 of the elegy).
29. More, 615. For a description of the chronology see pages 612-21.
30. A third and no small reason for identifying the subject of these lines as Newton's *Chronology* is the fact that Alan Dugald McKillop does so, too. (See McKillop, 212.) Perhaps Thomson's passage should be further explicated. Time is like an ebb tide which bears everyone down to eternity, which in turn is like a vast sea, still subject to time, for "the green islands of the happy" (where the gods allow those they have rescued from death to live in joy) were subject to the sovereignty of Chronos (Hesiod, *Works*

and Days, lines 168-73, in *Hesiod: Theogony, Works and Days, Shield*, trans. Apostolos N. Athanassakis (Baltimore: Johns Hopkins University Press, 1983), 71.) Time bears all down to the sea, all except Newton, who alone makes headway against it and even "ascends" it to its source. The lights were raised (or "hung out" as the first edition reads—McKillop, 153n) as a signal whereby whoever was uncertain about the way could follow the navigator's ship as it led the way up the river. The detail of the lights being raised "at equal distances"—presumably from the deck—reflects the practice of flotillas signalling by night. Captain Edward Cooke recorded one such signal—"In case of losing Company, and meeting in the Night..., to know each other by three Lights of an equal Height"—and another, even closer in parallel—"*To weigh*, the Admiral will, besides his usual Lights, put out two Lights at his Main Top-Mast Shrouds, of equal Height..." (Capt. Edward Cooke, *A Voyage to the South Sea, and Round the World, Perform'd in the Years 1708, 1709, 1710, and 1711* (1712; reprint, Amsterdam and New York: Israel and Da Capo, 1969), 1:159; 2:81).

31. See Appendix J: The Availability of Bulwer's Poem.
32. E. G. Lytton Bulwer, "Sculpture," in *Cambridge Prize Poems* (Cambridge: W. P. Grant, 1840), 179. Later quotations are from this page and the preceding. Bulwer later added the surname of Lytton. By the time he was created Baron Lytton (in 1866) his full name and title were Edward George Earle Lytton Bulwer-Lytton, 1st Baron Lytton of Knebworth.
33. Most striking of the direct parallels between Bulwer's lines and those of Scott's Ode (pages 10-11) are the following. For Scott's line "He trac'd the wonders of the sky," Bulwer has "Stands the immortal Wanderer of the sky." Scott's phrases (appearing separately) "The chambers of the sun explor'd" and the "bright ethere[a]l guest" appear combined in Bulwer's phrase "ethereal sunshine." Scott's references to "sage," "mighty Mind," and being "taught on eagle-wings to fly" reappear in Bulwer's line "The sage who, borne on Thought's sublimest car." More interesting, and more persuasive also, are two elegant variations made by Bulwer. In writing "Hence, where the organ full and clear, / With loud hosannas charms the ear," Scott had alluded to lines in Milton's *Il Penseroso*, to which Wordsworth himself was later to allude: "There let the pealing Organ blow, / To the full voic'd Quire below" (lines 161-62). Bulwer, by way of variation, looked to those lines of Milton's that immediately preceded the ones alluded to ("To walk the studious Cloysters pale, /... With /...storied Windows richly dight, / Casting a dimm religious light"—lines 156-60) and in his turn referred to them: "Lo! where, through cloister'd aisles, the soften'd day / Throws o'er the form a 'dim religious' ray...." (Milton, *Works*, Columbia Edition, 1 (pt. 1): 45.) The other variation involves Newton's discoveries. Scott, apart from referring generally to Newton's having "trac'd the wonders of the sky," referred specifically to Newton's discoveries in optics, focussing on the "prism" and "the chambers of the sun." Bulwer, apart from adapting the general reference, chose to fasten on the other discoveries Newton had made (the moon's effects on the tides of the earth and the gravitational laws which kept the stars in place) and wrote that Newton "Track'd the vague moon, and read the mystic star."

34. Muirhead (quoting Wordsworth), 733.
35. Isabella Fenwick to Henry Taylor, 9 June 1839, in HT 123.
36. Sara Hutchinson to Mrs. Hutchinson, 4 March 1834, in *The Letters of Sara Hutchinson from 1800 to 1835*, ed. Kathleen Coburn (London: Routledge & Kegan Paul, 1954), 404.
37. Dorothy Wordsworth to Lady Beaumont, 14 August 1810 *(MY* 1:422). When writing to Wordsworth about the same incident, she added another dimension: "The silent face gave me feelings that were I am sure sublime—though dear Mr Clarkson did now and then disturb me by pointing out the wrinkles in the silk stockings, the buckles etc etc—all which etceteras are in truth worthy of admiration." *(MY* 1:426)
38. Quoted in Cunningham, *Lives of the Most Eminent British Painters, Sculptors, and Architects,* 3:52-53.
39. "Religious Musings" (1796), lines 366-68, in Samuel Taylor Coleridge, *The Complete Poetical Works*, ed. Ernest Hartley Coleridge, 2 vols. (Oxford: Clarendon, 1912), 1:123.
40. Selwyn, 1:98.
41. Cunningham, 3:51-52.
42. MM 2:442-43.
43. Spence, *Anecdotes,* 54.
44. Frances Blanshard, *Portraits of Wordsworth* (London: Allen, 1959), 52.
45. See Haydon, *Autobiography and Memoirs,* ed. Penrose, 239-48.
46. *PW,* 2:377 and 530. See Warren U. Ober, "Nature, the Imagination, and the Conversion of Peter Bell," *Yearbook of English Studies* 3 (1973): 175.
47. He had arrived by June 2. See *HCR on Books and Their Writers,* 1:240.
48. *Examiner,* 7 May 1820, page 300.
49. Some questions may well exist about whether Wordsworth would have read the review in the first instance and, if he did, whether he would have remembered it nineteen years later. These questions are discussed in Appendix L: The Availability of Hunt's Review of Haydon's Painting.
50. *De Somnis* (hereafter abbreviated to *Som.)* i.42-44 (5:316-19).
51. Philo: ἀποδημίαν στελλόμενον ἀπὸ τοῦ ἀορίστου καὶ ἀπειρομεγέθους ἐπιστήμης χωρίου *(Som.* i.42 (5:316)); Mangey's translation: *peregre proficiscitur ab amplissima optimaque regione scientiae* (Mangey I, 627).
52. Key phrases: a fair voyage with the sovereign mind: πρὸς τόν ἡγεμόνα νοῦν εὐπλοῆσαι; *navigatio...prima...ad mentem principem*; having got out of its fleshly body: σωματικὸν ὄγκον ἐκδῦσα; *egressa è domo corporeâ*; to ascertain by the mind alone: (put negatively in the Greek) ὁμιλεῖν εἰσάπαν ἀδυνατεῖ διανοίᾳ μόνῃ ; *sola mente persequi*; The soul... apprehends the intelligible only in its unencumbered movement: (referring to ψυχὴ) γυμνὴν κίνησιν αὐτῆς τὰ νοήσει μόνῃ καταληπτὰ ἔλαχε; *Anima...nudo ipsius motu tantum intelligibilia comprehendit* (all phrases from *Som.* i.43-44 (5:316-18); Mangey I, 627).
53. *Night Thoughts,* 6:176-80 in Edward Young, *Complete Works,* ed. James Nichols, 2 vols. (1854; reprint, Hildesheim: Olms, 1968), 1:98.
54. In line 106 (and note) of "Tintern Abbey" *(PW* 2:262); referring to *Night Thoughts* 6:427.
55. See Appendix N: Further Changes Due to Young.

7 A Kindred Spirit

1. RPG 1:154. The rest of the paragraph is drawn from the same volume, pages 103, 228, 231, 234, and 194. Hamilton was to continue his breadth of scholarship: in 1830 he insisted that a young nobleman whom he was about to accept as a student in mathematics "should be able, when [he took] up any Greek or Latin book..., to open at any page and read it aloud as if it were an English one—an attainment which Mr. Pitt is said to have possessed in an eminent degree, and which must have contributed much to his subsequent parliamentary success." (Hamilton to Viscount Adare, 4 Feb. 1830 (RPG 1:357).)
2. Two more recent biographies of Hamilton summarize what Graves has to say about the relationship between Wordsworth and Hamilton: these are Thomas L. Hankins' *Sir William Rowan Hamilton* (Baltimore and London: Johns Hopkins University Press, 1980), esp. 102-3, and Sean O'Donnell's *William Rowan Hamilton: Portrait of a Prodigy* (Dublin: Boole, 1983), esp. 77-78. Three further studies of that relationship have been published: Charles L. Pittman, "A Biographical Note on Wordsworth," *Bulletin of Furman University*, 29.3 (May 1946): 31-53; Charles L. Pittman, "An Introduction to a Study of Wordsworth's Reading in Science," *Furman Studies*, 33.5 (Spring 1950): 27-60; George Dodd, "Wordsworth and Hamilton," *Nature*, 228 (26 Dec. 1970): 1261-63.
3. RPG 1:264. The next quotation is from 1:262.
4. Wordsworth to Hamilton, 24 Sept. 1827 *(LY* 1:546-47).
5. RPG 1:260.
6. "It Haunts Me Yet," RPG 1:265.
7. Edmund Turnor, *Collections for the History of the Town and Soke of Grantham. Containing Authentic Memoirs of Sir Isaac Newton...* (London: William Miller, 1806), 179.
8. Wordsworth to Hamilton, 24 Sept. 1827 (RPG 1:267; *LY* 1:545).
9. "General Scholium" in *Mathematical Principles of Natural Philosophy* by Sir Isaac Newton... (Chicago: Encyclopaedia Britannica, 1952), 371.
10. "Four Letters from Sir Isaac Newton to Doctor Bentley; containing Some Arguments in Proof of a Deity," in Newton, *Opera Quae Exstant Omnia*, ed. Horsley, 4:429. Presumably by "considering" Newton meant "thoughtful, reflective," a meaning common at the time *(OED)*.
11. *Opticks*, introd. Whittaker, 370 (Bk. 3, Pt. 1, Qu. 28). The "first Cause" Newton had described in the preceding sentence as "a Being incorporeal, living, intelligent, omnipresent, who in infinite Space, as it were in his Sensory, sees the things themselves intimately, and throughly perceives them, and comprehends them wholly by their immediate presence to himself...."
12. *An Essay on Man*, 4:332, Twickenham Edition, 3 (pt. 1): 160.
13. Rough draft for lecture of 11 Dec. 1832 (RPG 1:657-58).
14. Hamilton to Miss Lawrence, 1825 (RPG 1:193-94); Newton, "General Scholium" in *Mathematical Principles* by Newton, 369.
15. Introductory Lecture on Astronomy, 1831 (RPG 1:503); the next quotation is from the same page.
16. Introductory Lecture on Astronomy, 1832 (RPG 1:648).

17. Hamilton to Wordsworth, 8 Dec. 1827 (RPG 1:284). In the Lecture of 1831 Hamilton said that he felt "a sense of arduous responsibility when thus invited to direct the thoughts and feelings and desires of a brother-man in their goings-forth from earth to heaven" (RPG 1:500).
18. "Farewell Verses to William Wordsworth at the Close of a Visit to Rydal Mount in 1830" (RPG 1:369).
19. RPG 1:503. If Hamilton did not derive his golden chain from Pope's Great Chain of Being, he may have derived it from Milton's own "golden chain" by which the "pendant world" is suspended from heaven's floor *(Paradise Lost* 2:1051-52) or from the "invisible chain" which Adam Smith asserted astronomers sought to find which would connect the rapid motion and the natural inertness of the planets. See Adam Smith, *Essays on Philosophical Subjects* (1795; reprint, New York: Garland, 1971), 104-5.
20. "Recollections" (RPG 2:276).
21. RPG 2:141-47, 695-97.
22. RPG 1:637. The next two quotations are from the same page.
23. Draft of letter to Coleridge (not sent), 3 Oct. 1832 (RPG 1:592).
24. As observed and recorded by the American author George Ticknor, and as quoted in RPG 2:158.
25. RPG 2:159. In 1705 Newton was persuaded to stand for election to Parliament from Cambridge. Since he faced fierce competition, Halifax arranged for the Queen to make the detour from Newmarket and the races, so as to strengthen his chances. Richard S. Westfall comments: "The queen's 'great Assistance' to Newton's election was his knighting, an honor bestowed, not for his contributions to science, not for his service [as master of] the Mint, but for the greater glory of party politics in the election of 1705. Halifax, who had organized the visit, orchestrated it as a political rally. Besides Newton, the queen also knighted Halifax's brother and mandated the university to confer an honorary doctorate on Halifax himself. In a nonpartisan gesture, he allowed her also to knight Newton's old friend, John Ellis, a mere academic then vice-chancellor of the university." In the event, Newton finished, in a field of four candidates, a distant fourth. (Richard S. Westfall, *Never at Rest: A Biography of Isaac Newton* (Cambridge: Cambridge University Press, 1980), 624-26.) It should perhaps be added that the bust of Professor Whewell now graces the same Antechapel in which stands the statue of Newton.
26. Wordsworth to Hamilton, 20 Jan. 1839 (RPG 2:292; *LY* 3:655).
27. Isabella Fenwick to Henry Taylor, 18 Aug. 1838 (HT 97).
28. RPG 1:269.
29. Aubrey De Vere to Hamilton, 25 July 1855 (RPG 3:30); 5 Dec. 1846 (RPG 2:541).
30. RPG 1:642, 652, 654.
31. RPG 1:645-46.
32. RPG 1:641, 653-54. The lines quoted from *The Excursion* are 1:280-86; those from the Immortality Ode are lines 62-77.
33. RPG 2:276. The poem "Recollections" is found on 2:275-77.
34. Letter from R. P. Graves in the Memoir, by Thomas Woodward, of the

life of William Archer Butler, in Butler's *Sermons Doctrinal and Practical*, 2nd American ed. (Philadelphia: Parry & McMillan, 1859), 29.
35. Quoted in *PW* 4:430.
36. *PW* 4:125-26.
37. Wordsworth to Hamilton, 25 June 1832 (*LY* 2:535-36). See Ernest de Selincourt, *Dorothy Wordsworth: a Biography* (Oxford: Clarendon, 1933), 67-69; and Lawrence Hanson, *The Life of S. T. Coleridge: The Early Years* (1938; reprint, New York: Russell & Russell, 1962), 182-91.
38. Wordsworth to Hamilton, 25 June 1832 (*LY* 2:535-36).
39. RPG 1:646.
40. *Athenaeum*, No. 407 (15 Aug. 1835): 622.
41. RPG 1:349-50.
42. RPG 1:350.
43. Hamilton visited Wordsworth at Rydal Mount for a few hours in September of 1827, three weeks in August of 1830, a few hours in September of 1834, and on August 19th, 1838 (RPG 1:262-64, 368; 2:110, 266-67).
44. Coleridge to Wordsworth, 30 May 1815, in *Collected Letters of Samuel Taylor Coleridge*, ed. Earl Leslie Griggs, 6 vols. (Oxford: Clarendon, 1956-71), 4:575.
45. RPG 3:223; cf. 2:35.
46. RPG 1:499-503.
47. Hamilton wrote to Wordsworth, for example, on 1 Feb. 1830, that he was enclosing a "large... quantity of prose extracts from former writings of my own, on subjects upon which we have conversed" (RPG 1:354).
48. Hamilton's address to the British Association, 10 Aug. 1835 (RPG 2:151).
49. Hamilton's Introductory Lecture on Astronomy, 1833 (RPG 2:70-71).
50. Memorandum of notes for a letter, [Nov.] 1829 (RPG 1:350).
51. RPG 1:320.
52. RPG 2:203. Wordsworth later in the year acknowledged receipt of two sonnets from Hamilton (Wordsworth to Hamilton, 21 Dec. 1837 (*LY* 3:499-500)).
53. Date in MM 2:592; note in *PW* 4:424-25; poem in *PW* 4:102.
54. *P(deS)*, 182, corrected by collation with MS. A.
55. *P(O)*, 659.
56. RPG 1:646. The next quotation is from the same page.
57. The original phrasing is "immaterial Creatures." "Agents" is inserted in Wordsworth's hand above "Creatures," which, however, is not deleted. *P(O)*, 659.
58. Helen Darbishire, *The Poet Wordsworth* (Oxford: Clarendon, 1950), 139.
59. RPG 1:647. The next quotation is from the same page.
60. The particular form of expression given to the thought may have derived from lines in Bulwer's "Sculpture." In talking about Newton's mastery of the laws of Nature, Bulwer phrased the relation this way:

> Sway'd from the planet, or the desert cloud,
> To him the Spirits of the Night were bow'd.
> *(Cambridge Prize Poems,* 178.)

The parallel in phrasing is, of course, far from being conclusive evidence of borrowing. Wordsworth had used the picture of bowing the head a number of times before; in fact he had even used the picture of a spirit (an immortal agent) bowing her head, when he had lamented that in Scotland "lessons" then were taught "That make the Patriot-spirit bow her head / Where the all-conquering Roman feared to tread." (Poem VIII, "Composed in the Glen of Loch Etive," lines 12-14, in *Yarrow Revisited and Other Poems* (1835) *(PW* 3:268).) The curious thing about this passage, however, is that it was written in 1831, not long after Wordsworth could well have read a copy of Bulwer's "Sculpture."

61. *P(O)*, 659.
62. The same account of Grantham which recorded the story of Newton's frustrated love quoted Newton's son-in-law Conduitt as having said, about Newton: "He seemed to doubt whether there were not intelligent beings superior to us, who superintended [the] revolutions of the heavenly bodies, by the direction of the Supreme Being." (Edmund Turnor, ed., *Collections for the History of the Town and Soke of Grantham*, 172-73; cited by Gale E. Christianson in his study *In the Presence of the Creator: Isaac Newton and His Times* (New York: Free Press; London: Collier Macmillan, 1984), 574.)
63. RPG 1:640-41.
64. The flight is described in Night IX, lines 1715-2434. Particularly relevant lines include "Orb above orb ascending without end!" (1097), "Ye borderers on the coasts of bliss, what are you? / A colony from heaven?" (1762-63), and for the content: "Through this wide waste of worlds; this vista vast, / All sanded o'er with suns...." (2311-12) (Young, *Works*, ed. Nichols, 1:226-44, 212).
65. For Young's "system," see, e.g., Night IX, lines 1730, 1750, 1912, 2217 (Young, *Works* 1:227, 231, 238). As for Hamilton's "kindred," in addition to the "kindred impulses" already quoted, Hamilton used the word three times in two pages: "kindred thrones," "kindred enthusiasm," and "kindred genius" (RPG 1:649, 652-53).
66. Wordsworth had used the word twice in two lines in *The Excursion*: "kindred love" and "kindred joy" (4:1216-17) *(PW* 5:148).
67. From Eliza Hamilton's account (RPG 1:314).
68. *P(deS)*, 480-82, corrected by collation with MS. A.
69. *P(O)*, 1121.
70. *P(O)*, 1215.
71. See the *OED* under "star."
72. *P(O)*, 1125.
73. RPG 1:649, 650-51. The next quotation is from 1:640.
74. RPG 2:151-52. Also in *Athenaeum* No. 407 (15 Aug. 1835): 622.
75. Darbishire, *The Poet Wordsworth*, 139.
76. *P(deS)*, 483.
77. Lines 44-48 of "The Eolian Harp" (1795) in *The Poems of Samuel Taylor Coleridge*, ed. E. H. Coleridge, 1:102.
78. As reported by R. P. Graves in his Lecture "Recollections of Wordsworth and the Lake Country," in *The Afternoon Lectures on Literature & Art De-*

livered in the Theatre of the Royal College of Science, S. Stephen's Green, Dublin, in the Years 1867 & 1868 (Dublin: William McGee; London: Bell and Daldy, 1869), 282.
79. *P(O)*, 1215.
80. All quotations from this Lecture appear in RPG 2:71. The "[intellectual]" appearing below picks up a phrase from 2:70.
81. RPG 2:152.
82. *P(deS)*, 484-85; *P(O)*, 1127-29. The likelihood of Wordsworth's having borrowed from Hamilton admittedly depends, in part, on when the phrase "or are caught" was added to the poem. For a discussion of this matter, see Appendix K: Further Changes Due to Hamilton.
83. Thomas Gray and William Collins, *Poetical Works*, ed. Roger Lonsdale (Oxford: Oxford University Press, 1977), 35.
84. See Frank H. Ellis, "Gray's *Elegy:* the Biographical Problem in Literary Criticism," *PMLA* 66 (1951): 971-1008.
85. For a further discussion of Wordsworth's private and public voices in *The Prelude*, see Lindenberger, 3-9.
86. Jonathan Wordsworth, *William Wordsworth: The Borders of Vision* (Oxford: Clarendon, 1982), 331. (Next reference 329).
87. See Appendix K: Further Changes Due to Hamilton.
88. Our observations on the various MSS. are drawn from de Selincourt's notes in *P(deS)*, 74-75, from Owen's edition in *P(O)*, 471, and from facsimiles of the Dove Cottage MSS. A-E.
89. RPG 1:640. We do not argue, of course, that Wordsworth was influenced by Hamilton to *use* the image of the moon and stars in the first place. Wordsworth had used those luminaries, separately and together, many times before: what we argue for is the influence of Hamilton in moving Wordsworth to *restore* the combined image in this particular instance and to add to it the peculiar epithet "favoring."
90. RPG 1:645-46.
91. RPG 1:650-51.
92. Memorandum of notes incorporated in a letter to F. B. Edgeworth in 1829 (RPG 1:350).
93. *Athenaeum*, No. 407 (15 Aug. 1835): 624.
94. Hamilton to Viscount Adare, 26 Dec. 1830 (RPG 1:411).
95. RPG 2:71.
96. RPG 2:151-52, and *Athenaeum*, No. 407 (15 Aug. 1835): 622.
97. Wordsworth to Hamilton, 8 Feb. 1833 *(LY* 2:589-90).

8 But Ne'er So Well Exprest

1. *Som.* i.250-51 (5:426-29); Mangey I, 657-58. Mangey's full phrase: *mens accipit vim & robur insuperabile.*
2. *Som.* i.247 (5:426-29); Mangey I, 657. Mangey's full phrase: *ita ut anima quasi mortua, velut columna, defixa haereat.* Both Philo and Mangey go on to say that, with Lot's wife, the pillar was of salt, but we are con-

cerned with the effect that the image of the soul *defixa* (one of whose principal meanings was "petrified") could have had on Wordsworth's imagination.
3. *Som.* i.242 (5:424); Mangey I, 657.
4. See *A Concordance of Ovid*, 2 vols. (1939; reprint, Hildesheim: Georg Olms, 1968), 2:1102.
5. *Oxford Dictionary of English Proverbs*, ed. F.P. Wilson, 3rd ed. (Oxford: Clarendon Press, 1970), 237.
6. Lines 51-52, in *Complete Poetical Works*, ed. E. H. Coleridge, 1:14. This version was not published in Wordsworth's day: he may, of course, have seen it in manuscript.
7. Samuel Lover, *Rory O'More* (1837; reprint, London: Routledge, Warne, and Routledge, 1864), chap. 42, page 371. So popular was the novel that it was reprinted in 1839.
8. William Selwyn, in his description of the statue, writes as if it were the statue itself, "this outward form," which "enshrined a spirit full of immortality," the soul of Newton (Selwyn, 1:98). The statue of the Commendatore in Mozart's *Don Giovanni* also comes to mind.
9. Cunningham, 3:52.
10. *P(deS)*, 482-83; *P(O)*, 1123, 1125, 1215.
11. Wordsworth consulted Johnson's *Dictionary* regularly. See, e.g., Wordsworth to Barron Field, 24 Oct. 1828 *(LY* 1:644); Wordsworth to George Huntly Gordon, 15 Dec. 1828 *(LY* 1:689).
12. RPG 1:646.
13. *P(1805)* 8:399-416, in *P(deS)*, 284-86; *P(1850)* 8:262-81, in *P(O)*, 167. Owen's reading text is quoted here.
14. Thomas Love Peacock, *Melincourt* (1817), chap. 32, in *The Novels of Thomas Love Peacock*, ed. David Garnett (London: Rupert Hart-Davis, 1948), 283.
15. That Newton accepted as fact God's intervention in human history can be seen most clearly in what he has to say about the prophets: see his *Observations upon the Prophecies of Holy Writ*, Pt. 1, Chap. 1, in Newton, *Opera Quae Exstant Omnia*, ed. Horsley, 5:304.
16. Lines 125-31 of the elegy, in *Poetical Works*, ed. Robertson, 440. Further meanings of "index" can be seen to have an appropriate application, either in connotation or through association: index of power in algebra, index of refraction, prelude, and (in Latin) a touchstone for gold.
17. Lines 19-20 *(PTV* 234).
18. RPG 2:151; *Athenaeum*, No. 407 (15 Aug. 1835): 622, 624.
19. RPG 1:646, 651.
20. Spence, 54.
21. Cooper, 87-88, 112-13; Coe, *passim*.
22. These books, for example, were listed in the sale catalogue of Wordsworth's library: Captain Cooke's *Two First Voyages round the World*, 1809 (lot 104); Alexander Mackenzie's *Voyages from Montreal to the Frozen and Pacific Oceans in 1780-1793*, 1801 (lot 124); Mavor's *Collection* (as mentioned), 1796 (lot 139); George Shelvocke's *A Voyage Round the World by way of the Great South Sea*, 1726 (lot 159); and *Voyages and Travels...with Introductory Discourse... by Mr. Locke*, 1744 (lot

172). *Transactions of the Wordsworth Society*, 6 (1884): passim.
23. For Mallet, see Anderson, 9:693; for Young, see *Night Thoughts* 6:178-80 *(Complete Works*, ed. Nichols, 1:98); for Philo, *Som.* i.42-44 (5:316-19), Mangey I, 627.
24. RPG 2:71.
25. *P(O)*, 470-71.
26. RPG 1:645-48.
27. RPG 1:646. The next quotation is from 1:647.
28. HNF 1:325.
29. Anderson, 11:545.
30. Anderson, 9:694.
31. Chalmers, 14:133, 83.
32. Samuel Boyse, "Deity," in Chalmers, 14:546; also HNF 1:410.
33. Qu. 28 of Book 3, Pt. 1, of *Opticks* (introd. Whittaker), 370.
34. *Cambridge Prize Poems* (1840), 179.
35. "Religious Musings," lines 366-68 *(Complete Poetical Works*, ed. E. H. Coleridge, 1:123).
36. Selwyn, 1:98. Although Selwyn's description was printed in the book form of the *Cambridge Portfolio* in 1840, it may well have appeared earlier, for the book as a whole was first "issued in 14 numbers, No. I. being published about Nov. 1838" (Robert Bowes, *A Catalogue of Books Printed at or Relating to the University Town & County of Cambridge*... (Cambridge: Macmillan & Bowes, 1894), 356 (item no. 1993)).
37. Cunningham, 3:52.
38. RPG 1:503.
39. See W. J. Bate, ed., *Criticism: the Major Texts* (New York: Harcourt Brace, 1952), 363, 387.
40. RPG 1:647.
41. RPG 1:350.
42. RPG 1:648.
43. *P(1805)* 1:428-31, in *P(deS)*, 26; *P(1850)* 1:401-04, in *P(O)*, 39. Owen's reading text is quoted here.
44. George Gordon, Lord Byron, *Don Juan*, 14:101, ed. Leslie A. Marchand (Boston: Houghton Mifflin, 1958), 403.
45. Admittedly the speaker does not actually see the statue: he sees, instead, the outside of the Antechapel, inside of which stands the statue. But the effect of the expression is so strong that one responds as if the speaker could behold the statue itself.
46. Line 128 of Daniel's "Complaynt of Rosamund" and Chap. 38 of Scott's *Ivanhoe*, both as cited in the *OED*.
47. Lines 86-89 of *Samson Agonistes* and *Paradise Lost* 9:1063-64, in Milton, *Works*, Columbia Edition, 1 (pt. 2): 340 and 2 (pt. 2): 298.
48. *OED*, citing Newton's *Daniel*, I.xi.
49. For Philo: *Op.* 53 (1:40-41). A passage in another classical author could well have helped to confirm Wordsworth in his use of "silent" and also in his use of "favoring." The passage, which could readily have been in Milton's mind as well, is in Virgil's *Aeneid* and has to do with the Greek ships as they returned at night to the shores of Troy so that their hosts could join the group about to be released from the huge wooden statue

they had left behind. They sailed, Virgil wrote (2:255), *tacitae per amica silentia lunae*, which can be translated as "through the favouring silence of the hidden moon." For Milton's blind Samson, the connotation of being at the mercy of enemies would have fitted with exquisite nicety. For Wordsworth, an inversion in the judgement value of the phrase would have been required, but he was accustomed to that in his borrowing. Yet has he not also inverted the role of the moon? While he made the statue's face "silent," it was by the light of the moon that he was able to see the Antechapel. Actually, in a sense he had precedents for both uses of the moon and was thereby able to secure his paradox. Both Stanyhurst and Pitt misread the meaning of *tacitae* and presented the moon as fully present and shining. Stanyhurst wrote, "shinings of Moone most freendlye doe guide them," and Pitt followed suit: "By silent Cynthia's friendly beams convey'd." Dryden appears to have read the Latin correctly, for he wrote, "Safe under Covert of the silent Night." All of which reinforces what we have observed about both "index" and "vacant": when a word continues current but its more usual meanings shift, one must be most careful when reading it in work of a preceding age. (References: *Virgil, with an English Translation*, ed. and trans. H. Rushton Fairclough, Loeb Classical Library, 2 vols. (London: Heinemann, 1965), 1:310; Richard Stanyhurst, *The First Foure Bookes of Virgils Aeneis* (London: Henrie Bynneman, 1583), 28; "Pitt's Translation of Virgil's Aeneid" in Chalmers 19:541; [John] Dryden, *The Works of Virgil Translated into English Verse*, 3 vols. (London: Jacob Tonson, 1721), 2:499 (line 334 of Bk. II).)

50. *A General and Bibliographical Dictionary of the Fine Arts*, ed. James Elmes (London: Thomas Tegg, 1826), under "Expression" and column 3 of "Painting."
51. See Charles Le Brun, *A Method To Learn To Design The Passions*, [trans. John Williams,] ed. Alan T. McKenzie (1734; reprint, Los Angeles: University of California, William Andrews Clark Memorial Library Publication Numbers 200-201, 1980); J. J. Engel, *Ideen zu einer Mimik*, 2 vols. (Berlin: Manlius, 1785-86); J. J. Engel, *Idées sur le Geste et L'Action Théâtrale*, 2 vols. (Paris: Barrois, 1788-89); Henry Siddons, *Practical Illustrations of Rhetorical Gesture and Action; adapted to the English drama: from a work on the subject by M. Engel* (London: Phillips, 1807): we use the "Second Edition, Improved" of 1822, reprinted in New York by Benjamin Blom, 1968.
52. See the reproduction in Blanshard, *Portraits of Wordsworth*, Plates 6a and 6b; Le Brun, 27.
53. Le Brun, 24-28. For Engel the voluptuous kind of rapture was characterized by the eye appearing to hide itself behind the eyelid and a mysterious smile playing on the half-open lips (Engel, *Idées*, 1:204). It is worth noting that in the engraving of Newton's statue made by J. Le Keux, the uplifted eyes and the half-open lips are made to stand out strikingly (*Memorials of Cambridge: A Series of Views... Engraved by J. Le Keux [with text by] Thomas Wright and H. Longueville Jones*, 2 vols. (London: Bogue, 1845), opp. 1:65).
54. Le Brun, 28; for a reproduction of Bernini's work, see Robert Wallace et al., *The World of Bernini, 1598-1680* (New York: Time-Life Books, 1970),

55. In the *Cambridge Portfolio*, to which William Selwyn contributed his description of Newton's statue, there also appears an unsigned anecdote in which it is claimed that the statue, "when first completed, had the mouth closed." When a friend and connoisseur pointed to this closing as a defect, Roubiliac reworked the mouth so as to open it *(Cambridge Portfolio*, 1:204). If accurate, the story points to a code, accepted by both the connoisseur and the sculptor, which required that the mouth be open so as to indicate the kind of emotion being portrayed.
56. See the *OED* under "ecstasy," "rapture," and "transport."
57. William Selwyn appears to have taken rapture quite seriously and to have thought of it in Christian terms. See the discussion of his description of the statue in the next section.
58. See MSS. Verse 20 (DC MS. 52). The original lines were composed probably in 1804 and transcribed by Dorothy Wordsworth in 1805; revisions were made by Wordsworth some time between 1816 and 1819 *(P(deS)*, xx; Siemens, 21; *P(N)*, 508-509).
59. Lines 2:24-25 in Cowper's translation, in *The Works of William Cowper, Esq.*, ed. Robert Southey, 15 vols. (London: Baldwin and Cradock, 1835-37), 11:32; Geo[rge] Chapman, *Homer Prince of Poets*... (London: Samuel Macham, [1610]), 19.
60. Homer, *The Iliad*, trans. A. T. Murray, Loeb Classical Library, 2 vols. (1924; reprint, London: Heinemann, 1960), 1:54; Cowper, 2:67; Chapman, 19; Alexander Pope, *The Iliad of Homer*, Twickenham Edition, 7:127-30 (lines 10-11, 24, 42, 72-73 of Book II).
61. *The Iliad of Homer*, trans. Richmond Lattimore (Chicago: University of Chicago Press, 1951), 77 (2:57); Homer, *The Iliad*, trans. E. V. Rieu (Harmondsworth, England: Penguin, 1950), 41; Homer, *The Iliad*, trans. Robert Fitzgerald (New York: Anchor Press / Doubleday, 1974), 37. Fitzgerald even parallels Wordsworth's pillow by having his vision stand above Agamemnon's pillow.
62. As late as 1829, Southey used the noun form *rapt*, meaning "rapture" or "ecstasy" when he wrote "In one of his rapts the Angels, who conducted his spirit...bade him look down upon the earth." (Cited in the *OED*.)
63. *De Migratione Abrahami* (The Migration of Abraham, hereafter abbreviated to *Mig.*), 190 (4:242-43).
64. *Mig.* 190 (4:242). The Loeb translators write "in waking hours": the word in both Philo, ἐγρηγόρσεσιν and Mangey, *vigilantes* (Mangey I, 466), can also be translated "wakeful."
65. *Mig.* 191 (4:242-45).
66. Lines 25-28 *(PTV* 234-35).
67. *Mig.* 191 (4:242-43).
68. Cf. Mangey's phrasing: *impetum...propulsare... oculos claudunt, et aures obturant* (I, 466).
69. *Quis Rerum Divinarum Heres* (Who Is the Heir of Divine Things), 3 (4:284-85). The word Liddell and Scott translate as "silenced" (ἐπιστομίζουσι), the Loeb editors translate as "tongue-tied": it is an extension of the word's basic meaning of "curbed" or "bridled." The two phrases Philo uses for "joy" are περιχαρεῖ and ὑπερβάλλουσαι χαραί.

70. The conjunction of silence and the divine is made even clearer in the comment Philo wrote on Gen. 24.21: "...he stood silent a long while, giving place to that which spoke in him without mouth or tongue or instruments or voice, (namely) the divine Logos...." Unfortunately this particular passage would not have been available to Wordsworth. *(Philo: Supplement,* trans. and ed. Ralph Marcus, Loeb Classical Library, 2 vols. (Cambridge, Mass.: Harvard University Press, 1961), 1:391.)
71. *Som.* i.43 (5:316): αἰσθήσεων ὄχλον ἀποδρᾶσα with Philo, *turba sensuum* with Mangey (I, 627).
72. Parallels to the elements in this kind of allegorical reading can be found in Wordsworth's description of the crowd at Bartholomew Fair in *P(1850)* 7:675-771.
73. *The Excursion* 4:959-68.
74. In view of the way Wordsworth used many of his sources, it is appropriate to quote the citation, by the *OED*, of another meaning of "silent": "His quotations are what have been called 'Silent,' without any mention of the source."
75. See *DNB*, 18:517-19; Robert Smith, *Harmonics, Or The Philosophy of Musical Sounds* (1749; reprint, New York: Da Capo Press, 1966), 3-5, 8-9; *Traité D'Optique, par M. Smith..., Traduit De L'Anglais...* (Brest: Romain Mallassis, 1767), xi.
76. Philo, *Legum Allegoria* (Allegorical Interpretations) iii.100-101 (1:368-69); Mangey I, 107. Mangey's wording continues: *manifeste increatum contemplatur, ita ut ex ipsos ipsum comprehendat, & umbram ejus: hoc est verbum ejus, & mundum hunc universum.* Cf. *P(1850)* 2:413.
77. *Som.* i.36 (5:314-15); *Leg. All.* iii.102-3 (1:368-71).
78. *Paradise Lost* 3:380, in Milton, *Works,* Columbia Edition, 2 (pt. 1): 91.
79. Selwyn, 1:98.
80. Biographical details from *DNB* 17:1171-72 and *Alumni Cantabrigienses, Part II: From 1752 to 1900,* comp. John Venn and J. A. Venn, 6 vols. (Cambridge: Cambridge University Press, 1940-54), 5:462). At the time of writing his description, Selwyn was rector of Bramstone, Leics. He later became Lady Margaret Professor of Divinity and a Fellow of the Royal Astronomical Society, having photographs of the sun made at Ely, 1863-73. He was also a religious poet and in 1860 edited Book I of Origen's treatise, and in 1876 Books I-IV. It is a curious fact that Origen in his treatise refers to the very two works of Philo in which appears the claim that Moses rose above the created universe and saw God clearly (Origen, *Contra Celsum,* trans. and ed. Henry Chadwick (Cambridge: Cambridge University Press, 1965), 226 (IV:51-52) and 334 (VI:22)).
81. *Paradise Lost* 3:1-6, in Milton, *Works,* Columbia Edition, 2 (pt. 1): 77.
82. Cf. Origen, 333 (VI:21), and Philo, *Som.* ii.189 (5:529) and *De Vita Mosis* ii.3 (6:451-53).
83. Lines 232-33, *Complete Poetical Works,* ed. E. H. Coleridge, 1:196.
84. *The Excursion,* 6:217-18 *(PW* 5:193).
85. Lines 21-22 of "Tintern Abbey," in *PW* 2:260. "Alone," though technically in the middle of a line, ends a whole verse paragraph.
86. "Goody Blake and Harry Gill," line 36 *(PW* 4:174).
87. "Alice Fell," lines 19-20 *(PW* 1:233).

88. "The Last of the Flock," lines 3-4 *(PW* 2:43).
89. Wordsworth to Hamilton, 12 Feb. 1829 *(LY* 2:31). Presumably Wordsworth, and not Edgeworth, underlined the *alone.*
90. *The Borderers,* 3:1515-19 *(B* 213).
91. "Sonnet XI: Suggested at Tyndrum in a Storm," in *Yarrow Revisited (PW* 3:269).
92. *B* 212-13, 609.
93. As can be seen from the photographs appearing in [R. Robson and R. H. Glauert], *Trinity College* (Cambridge: Trinity College, 1967), [15] and [16]. Interestingly, Selwyn provided an aural equivalent when he said about those who would follow in Newton's steps, "after listening to the solemn strains of the Evening Chant, let them gaze awhile before they depart on the sculptured form of the best and wisest of British Philosophers" (Selwyn, 1:98).

Appendix A: The Myth of Wordsworth's Reading But Little

1. Dorothy Wordsworth to Lady Beaumont, 5 Jan. 1805 *(EY* 525).
2. *MY* 1:190, citing De Selincourt quoting Hutchinson: *MY* 1:458c, 1st ed.
3. Wordsworth to H. C. Robinson, April 1836, in HCR 1:298; Muirhead, 740.
4. Isabella Fenwick to H. C. Robinson, 29 Jan. 1845, in HCR 2:589.
5. Isabella Fenwick to Henry Taylor, 29 June 1838, in HT 87. Miss Fenwick added a comment about the maid, saying that she illustrated all of Wordsworth's domestic servants: "They all seem to derive some cultivation from him."
6. CW 2:98.
7. *PW* 4:57.
8. *PW* 4:59-60.
9. Muirhead, 739-40.
10. *PW* 4:423. In a note to two sonnets of 1838, Wordsworth said that they "were composed on what we call the 'Far Terrace' at Rydal Mount, where I have murmured many thousands of verses" *(PW* 3:501).
11. CW 1:43.
12. As Wordsworth explained to Walter Savage Landor in a letter dated 20 Apr. 1822, saying that the disease (now diagnosed as trachoma) began in 1805 and was so bad that it "makes me so dependent on others, abridges my enjoyments by cutting me off from the power of reading, and causes me to lose a great deal of time: and the worst of it is, that from the long standing of the complaint, I cannot encourage a hope of getting rid of it" *(LY* 1:123).
13. Russell Noyes, *William Wordsworth* (New York: Twayne, 1971), 62-63.
14. CW 1:5.
15. MM 1:9.
16. Jay, 28-29, quoting notes made by Thomas Bowman, son of the Thomas Bowman who was Wordsworth's master, for the Tercentenary of Hawkshead Grammar School in 1885. The next quotation is from the same source.

17. *P(O)*, 109-10.
18. Dorothy Wordsworth to Jane Pollard, 26 June 1791 *(EY* 52).
19. MM 1:99-101.
20. MM 1:290.
21. MM 1:513.
22. Dorothy Wordsworth to Jane Marshall, 18 Oct. 1807 *(MY* 1:167).
23. Cooper, "A Glance at Wordsworth's Reading," 88.
24. Dorothy Wordsworth to Christopher Wordsworth, 27 Apr. 1830 *(LY* 2:252).
25. Cf. HCR 2:867. The following quotation is from the same page.
26. Wordsworth to William Mathews, 20 Oct. 1795 *(EY* 154); Wordsworth to Sir George Beaumont, 29 July 1805 *(EY* 611).
27. Wordsworth to Dr. Robert Anderson, 17 Sept. 1814 *(MY* 2:151-55). The editors of the letters courteously provide footnote information about the authors cited.
28. Mary Moorman has commented that Wordsworth was well read "even in the less distinguished literature of the eighteenth century" *(MY* 1:166n). We would agree, but would also extend the range backwards a few centuries.
29. Wordsworth to Alexander Dyce, c. 19 Apr. 1830, 10 May 1830, 4 Dec. 1833 *(LY* 2:236-39, 259-60, 664).
30. Wordsworth to Alexander Dyce, 10 May 1830 *(LY* 2:260). Since Henry Reed, in his edition of the *Memoirs*, provides a note to this sentence of Wordsworth's, in which he cites and then quotes the wrong poem by Anna Laetitia Barbauld, we quote the conclusion to the one to which Wordsworth was actually referring. Entitled "Life" (as Wordsworth indicated), it is a modified dialogue between the body and the soul, which ends thus:

> Life! we've been long together,
> Through pleasant and through cloudy weather;
>   'Tis hard to part when friends are dear;
>   Perhaps 't will cost a sigh, a tear;
>   Then steal away, give little warning,
>   Choose thine own time;
>   Say not Good night, but in some brighter clime
>   Bid me Good morning.

(*The Works of Anna Laetitia Barbauld*, with a memoir by Lucy Aikin, 2 vols. (London: Longmans, 1825), 2:261-62.)

Appendix B: Wordsworth's Attitude Towards Cambridge Undergraduates

1. Wordsworth to Christopher Wordsworth, Jnr., 27 Nov. 1828 *(LY* 1:670-71).
2. Muirhead, 730, 733-43.
3. Reprinted as Appendix 1 in *LY* 1:701-2.

4. Muirhead, 742-43. The next two quotations are from pages 730 and 741.
5. RPG 1:260.
6. Wordsworth to Robert Pearce Gillies, 12 Nov. 1814 *(MY* 2:167-68).
7. Wordsworth to Robert Jones, 29 Oct. 1833 *(LY* 2:651).
8. *PW* 3:502.
9. Wordsworth to Thomas Kibble Hervey, late 1825 *(LY* 1:419).
10. Wordsworth to Hamilton, 12 Feb. 1829 *(LY* 2:30).
11. E.g., Wordsworth to Hamilton, 24 Sep. 1827 *(LY* 1:545-46), 12 Feb. 1829 *(LY* 2:30), 23 Dec. 1829 *(LY* 2:183-84).
12. Wordsworth to Hamilton, 12 Feb. 1829 *(LY* 2:31).
13. Wordsworth to H.C. Robinson, c. March 1821 *(LY* 1:45 and n.).
14. Wordsworth to Hamilton, 26 Nov. 1830 *(LY* 2:354).
15. *LY* 1:497n.
16. Wordsworth to Edward Moxon, c. 7 Dec. 1826 *(LY* 1:497-98).
17. Wordsworth to R. P. Gillies, 22 Dec. 1814 *(MY* 2:179).
18. Wordsworth to Bernard Barton, 12 Jan. 1816 *(MY* 2:269).

Appendix C: Shenstone and Cowper

no notes

Appendix D: Wordsworth's Attitude Concerning Acknowledgements

1. Wordsworth to S. T. Coleridge, 9 Dec. 1803 *(EY* 424-25).
2. Wordsworth to R. P. Gillies, 15 Apr. 1816 *(MY* 2:301).
3. Wordsworth to Henry Taylor, 26 Dec. 1823 *(LY* 1:237).
4. Wordsworth to Henry Taylor, 26 Dec. 1823 *(LY* 1:237).
5. Wordsworth to H. C. Robinson, 10 Mar. 1840 (HCR 1:401-2).
6. Wordsworth to Walter Scott, 7 Nov. 1805 *(EY* 642).
7. See *PW* 1:320-23, 326-29.
8. *PW* 2:262.
9. *PW* 2:2.
10. For *The White Doe* see notes for 2:515, 3:716-17, 3:796 *(PW* 3:299, 304, 307); for *The Excursion* see *PW* 5:372, 424, 444, 465.
11. *The Excursion* 7:980-82 *(PW* 5:468).
12. See *PW* 1:320-23, 326-29.
13. *PW* 2:494 (re: lines 33-35).
14. *The Waggoner* 2:128-34 *(PW* 2:498-99).
15. *PW* 5:427 (re: 4:745-50).
16. Wordsworth acknowledged indebtedness, in his *Descriptive Sketches*, for "most of the images in...sixteen verses" (lines 307-22) to "M. Raymond's interesting observations annexed to his translation of Coxe's Tour in Switzerland" *(PW* 1:65), but he did not acknowledge a debt in "The Egyptian Maid" (lines 47-48) to a travel book by Sir T. Herbert *(PW* 3:502). He did not acknowledge a debt, in "Strange fits of passion have I known" (line 6) to Percy's *Reliques (PW* 2:472). Examples concerning Milton are legion in the notes to *PW.* Tasso was acknowledged

in *An Evening Walk*, line 129 *(PW* 1:16), and Virgil in *Descriptive Sketches*, lines 636-37 *(PW* 1:80 and 328), but Wordsworth used Caesar without acknowledgement in "Guilt and Sorrow," lines 122-23 *(PW* 1:336).

Appendix E: The Myth of Wordsworth's Total Originality

1. Muirhead, 740.
2. John Morley, *Studies in Literature*, 1904, quoted by Cooper, 83.
3. Georg Brandes, *Main Currents*, Vol. IV, quoted by Cooper, 83.
4. Walter Raleigh, *Wordsworth*, 1903, 44, 45, quoted by Cooper, 83.
5. Cooper, 87-88.
6. This essay first appeared in *PMLA* 69 (1954): 486-522, and is reprinted in Alun Jones and William Tydeman, *Wordsworth, "Lyrical Ballads": A Casebook* (London: Macmillan, 1972), 79-126. The catalogue referred to appears in notes 1, 6, 9, 10, 21, 28.
7. Margaret Drabble, *Wordsworth* (London: Evans Brothers, 1966), 21.
8. *Faerie Queene*, 2.11.20-46 (lines 172-414).

Appendix F: The Availability of Sources for the Hymn to Science

1. *Elegant Extracts* was first published in 1789. The third, Dublin, edition (1789) is the one referred to in Christopher's notebook (Fink, 75). In the 1791 edition Akenside's "Hymn to Science" appears in 1:460-61.
2. MM 1:101.
3. Ramsay's *Poems* had been reprinted frequently since their first publication in 1720; the edition of 1780 or 1793, for instance, could easily have come to Wordsworth's attention. Mallet's *Works* had been printed in 1748 and 1759; his poems also appeared in Johnson's *English Poets*, Vol. 53, which had been in print for some years by 1794. Glover's poem on Newton had been prefixed to *A View of Newton's Philosophy* by Henry Pemberton (1728) and had, apparently, not been reprinted till its inclusion in Anderson's *British Poets*, Vol. 11. The books which appeared in the sales catalogue of Wordsworth's library "were only those which remained after the members of the Wordsworth family chose the books they respectively wished to retain;...a very large number — and those the most valuable — *were* retained" *(Transactions of the Wordsworth Society* 6 (1884): iv).
4. William Wordsworth, *An Evening Walk*, ed. James Averill (Ithaca and London: Cornell University Press, 1984), 129-30, 158.
5. *PW* 1:13n, 320

Appendix G: The Distinctive Cluster of Elements

1. *PW* 5:76-78.
2. *PW* 5:384-85.

3. *P(O)*, 36-41. These elements are already present in the original version of the lines (27-201), in *P(P)*, 43-48. It is interesting to note, however, that, even though "high objects, with eternal things" (line 136, page 46), are conspicuously present, along with references to "Powers of earth," "Genii of the springs," and "Familiars of the lakes" (lines 186-88, page 47), there is no mention of the "Wisdom and Spirit of the Universe."
4. *PW* 4:279-85.
5. *PW* 2:259-63.

Appendix H: Wordsworth's Poetic Expectations in Old Age

1. Dorothy Wordsworth to Christopher Wordsworth, Jnr., 13 April 1830; to Henry Crabb Robinson, 22 Apr. 1830; to Catherine Clarkson, ended 27 Apr. 1830 *(LY* 2:229, 242, 246).
2. Wordsworth to Dora Wordsworth, late Apr. 1830 *(LY* 2:257).
3. Cowper wrote "at my birth / (Since which I number three-score winters past)" and proceeded to describe an oak tree as "A shatter'd veteran, hollow-trunk'd." See "Yardley Oak," lines 2-4, in Cowper, *Poetical Works*, 410.
4. *LY* 2:257.
5. Wordsworth to Joseph Kirkham Miller, 17 Dec. 1831 *(LY* 2:464).
6. Wordsworth to Francis Wrangham, 2 Feb. 1835 *(LY 3:19).*
7. As Hallett Smith, in effect, observed in his *Elizabethan Poetry: A Study in Conventions, Meaning, and Expression* (Cambridge, Mass.: Harvard University Press, 1952), 183.
8. Wordsworth to Thomas Noon Talfourd, 28 Nov. 1835 *(LY* 3:126).
9. Wordsworth to his family, 5 July 1837 *(LY* 3:423).
10. Wordsworth to William Rowan Hamilton, 4 Jan. 1838 *(LY* 3:509).

Appendix I: Dating the Last Two Lines on Newton's Statue

1. MM 2:439.
2. *P(deS)*, xxiii. The reference for MS. E, following, is to page xxiv.
3. Siemens, 24.
4. *P(N)*, 95n.
5. *P(deS)*, xxiii.
6. Wordsworth to Hamilton, 8 Feb. 1833 *(LY* 2:590).
7. "The Poems of Gaius Valerius Catullus," trans. F. W. Cornish, in *Catullus, Tibullus, and Pervigilium Veneris*, Loeb Classical Library (London: Heinemann; Cambridge, Mass.: Harvard University Press, 1962), 140-41.
8. MM 2:493-94; *LY* 2:595.
9. MM 2:501, citing Dora to Miss Kinnaird, MS. *DCP.* (copy).
10. In HT 97.
11. *LY* 3:655.
12. Mary Wordsworth to Edward Quillinan, early Feb. 1839 *(LY* 3:659).
13. Isabella Fenwick to Henry Taylor, 28 Mar. 1839 (HT 117).

Appendix J: The Availability of Bulwer's Poem

1. E. R. Bulwer, Earl of Lytton, *The Life... of Edward Bulwer, Lord Lytton*, 2 vols. (London: Kegan Paul, 1883), 1:273, 288-92.
2. Mary Wordsworth to Thomas Monkhouse, 25 June, 14 July, and (undated but) July, 1824 (Mary Wordsworth, *Letters*, 108-16).
3. Sara Hutchinson to Thomas Monkhouse, June-July 1824 (Sara Hutchinson, *Letters*, 285).
4. "I am to send a copy of my book to Wordsworth" (Muirhead, p. 743). The editor believes that the book was probably Muirhead's translation of Arago's *Eloge historique de James Watt* (728-29).
5. The separate edition of 1825 was published, presumably, by the authorities of the University of Cambridge; *Weeds and Wildflowers* (1826) was printed in Paris by A. Coniam; and in *Cambridge Prize Poems* of 1828 "Sculpture" runs from page 207 to page 226.
6. Wordsworth to Isabella Fenwick, 30 Aug. 1841 *(LY* 4:1088-89).
7. Quillinan's first visit occurred on 1 May 1821 *(LY* 1:701); the first reference to him in an extant letter is in Wordsworth's to John Kenyon, 23 July 1821: "... I have held out expectations to an Irish Gentleman [Quillinan] who has lately taken lodgings in this neighbourhood that I might accompany him on a Tour through a considerable part of his country..." *(LY* 1:68).
8. That visits by people other than poets likewise often went unnoticed in letters is suggested by the scene described by Quillinan, dated 1 May 1821: "Saw Mr Wordsworth come out of his Cottage with a party of visitors among whom were some lovely young ladies.... Was pleased with finding the retirement of the Poet so respectably invaded. It seemed to be the homage paid to Genius by wealth and Beauty." *(LY* 1:701) Presumably Henry Crabb Robinson's reference to "Literary Dandies whom Wordsworth (alluding to Litton [sic] Bulwer) declared to be the worst" concerns a time considerably later than 1824 (Robinson to Thomas Robinson, 19 Mar. 1852—HCR 2:787).
9. Bulwer's whole account of his visit to the Lake District runs pages 273-300. Of these, pages 275-85 are concerned with his dead love, and pages 297-98 with the happenings at the inn.
10. The title page reads: "The Siamese Twins. A Satirical Tale of the Times. With Other Poems. By the Author of 'Pelham,' &c. &c. London: Henry Colburn and Richard Bentley, New Burlington Street. MDCCCXXXI." "To Wordsworth" appears on pages 371-73.
11. Muirhead, 742.
12. Muirhead, 736. Isabella Fenwick described Wordsworth's reading from his MS. by quoting "that 'song divine of high and passionate thoughts, to their own music chanted'" (to Henry Taylor, 18 Aug. 1838, in HT 95). Cf. Eliza Hamilton's description of Wordsworth's reading: "Wordsworth first finished the passage, in a very low, impressive tone, moving his finger under every line as he went along, and seeming as he read to be quite rapt out of this world. I felt a tear gathermg in my eye as I looked at him, and at that moment, I cannot exactly define why, he seemed to me sublime..." (RPG 1:313). Wordsworth's little grandson called such

recitations "Grandpapa reading without a book" (Isabella Fenwick to Henry Taylor, 29 June 1838, in HT 87).

Appendix K: Further Changes Due to Hamilton

1. P(deS), 370.
2. P(O), 941.
3. RPG 1:656.
4. RPG 1:372-73.
5. Hamilton to his sister Sydney, 30 July 1830 (RPG 1:386).
6. Hamilton to Wordsworth, 14 Oct. 1831 (RPG 1:470-71).
7. Speaking of *The Prelude*, Dorothy wrote to Lady Beaumont (25 May 1804): "You will rejoice to hear, that he has gone on regularly, I may say rapidly, with the poem of which Coleridge shewed you a part..." *(EY 477)*; Wordsworth himself wrote to Thomas Noon Talfourd (c. 10 Apr. 1839): "... I will mention that, in the year 1805, I concluded a long poem upon the formation of my own mind, a small part of which you saw in manuscript, when I had the pleasure of a visit from you at Rydal" *(LY 3:680)*; Isabella Fenwick to Henry Taylor (9 June 1839): "I remembered the description of [Wordsworth's room in St. John's] in his autobiographical poem..." (HT 123); Henry Crabb Robinson in writing to Thomas Robinson (18 June 1847) implied first-hand knowledge of the poem when he wrote: "Of that knot of great men, only Wordsworth lingers—And he will not write any more—But there is an unpublished poem of great value" (HCR 2:650); and what Dorothy said, in writing to Lady Beaumont (29 Nov. 1805), implied that Wordsworth intended inviting responses from his friends: "I am now engaged in making a fair and final transcript of the Poem on his own Life. I mean *final*, till it is prepared for the press, which will not be for many years. No doubt before that time he will, either from the suggestions of his Friends or his own or both have some alterations to make, but it appears to us at present to be finished." *(EY 650)*. In addition Thomas De Quincey "read *The Prelude* in manuscript during the period, approximately 1809-15, while he was a neighbor of Wordsworth in the Lake Country" *(P(N), 545n)*.
8. P(deS), 256.
9. P(O), 801.
10. RPG 1:652-53.
11. P(deS), 484-85; P(O), 260 (Owen's reading text); cf. 1126-29.
12. RPG 2:152.
13. See P(deS), xxii, xxiii, 484-85, 623ff.
14. P(O), 8; P(N), 509.
15. P(O), 1128-29: following the line "By sensible impressions not enthralled," and located in the position normal for the next line to be transcribed in, is the partial line "But quickened, & thereby made." This partial line is scored through, and below it (and with less intervening space than usual) appears the line "But, by their quickening Virtue, made more apt." This in turn is followed by its completion "To hold communion with the invisible world." A later emendation has crossed out "Virtue" and placed the word "impulse" above it—and actually above the original, scored-through line as well.

16. *P(O)*, 1126-29.
17. That Owen was able to decipher what had been erased speaks highly of his editorial skills.

Appendix L: The Availability of Hunt's Review of Haydon's Painting

1. Wordsworth to Francis Wrangham, 4 Nov. 1807 *(MY* 1:174).
2. Dorothy Wordsworth to Priscilla Wordsworth, 27 Feb. 1815 *(MY* 2:206).
3. E.g., Wordsworth to Henry Crabb Robinson, 24 June 1817 *(MY* 2:394); Wordsworth to Benjamin Dockray, 2 Dec. 1828 *(LY* 1:678); Wordsworth to Lady Beaumont, 8 July 1831 *(LY* 2:405).
4. Wordsworth to Catherine Clarkson, Jan. 1815 *(MY* 2:190-91); *MY* 2:522n; and Dorothy Wordsworth to Henry Crabb Robinson, 24 Nov. 1821 *(LY* 1:94-95).
5. Dorothy Wordsworth to Christopher Wordsworth, Jnr., 13 Apr. 1830 *(LY* 2:230); Wordsworth declared to James Patrick Muirhead that in "his quality both as a prose and as a verse writer...diffuseness [was Wilson's] fault, and cheerful, natural, warm-hearted vigour his excellence" (Muirhead, 738).
6. Re: *Quarterly Review* see c. 8 May 1819 *(MY* 2:541), 26 Dec. 1823 *(LY* 1:237), 12 Apr. 1825 *(LY* 1:337), 15 Dec. 1828 *(LY* 1:691), 24 Jan. 1831 *(LY* 2:364); re: *Edinburgh Review* see 1 May 1819 *(MY* 2:538), 16 June 1819 *(MY* 2:545). In 1841 Wordsworth insisted that he "neither reads nor sees" the *Edinburgh Review* (Muirhead, 737).
7. Wordsworth to Sir George Beaumont, 28 May 1825 *(LY* 1:350 and n.).
8. Wordsworth to Lord Lonsdale, c. 17 Mar. 1832 *(LY* 2:514).
9. *HCR on Books,* 1:241-42 (entry for 11 June 1820).
10. Wordsworth to B.R. Haydon, late Apr. 1820 *(MY* 2:593 and *LY* 1:70n).
11. Wordsworth to Haydon, 18 Aug. 1821 *(LY* 1:70).
12. *LY* 2:377n; Wordsworth to Sir George Beaumont, 28 May 1825 *(LY* 1:350).
13. Wordsworth to Haydon, 16 Jan. 1820 *(MY* 2:577); *LY* 2:400n.
14. Wordsworth to Haydon, 23 Apr. 1831 *(LY* 2:377); Wordsworth to Haydon, 11 June 1831 *(LY* 2:396); Wordsworth to Haydon, c. 8 July 1831 *(LY* 2:407); *The Diary of Benjamin Robert Haydon,* ed. Willard Bissell Pope, 5 vols. (Cambridge, Mass.: Harvard University Press, 1960-63), 3:555-56.
15. Wordsworth to Haydon, 25 June 1838 *(LY* 3.612), 28 July 1838 *(LY* 3.619-20).

Appendix M: Wordsworth's Acquaintance with Philo

1. *DNB* 20:917.
2. Christopher Wordsworth, *Scholae Academicae* (1877; reprint, London: Frank Cass, 1968), 130; Shaver, 71.

3. T. W. Thompson, *Wordsworth's Hawkshead*, ed. Robert Woof (London: Oxford University Press, 1970), 91.
4. See *PW* 1:261-62, 286-87, 366, 370.
5. Dorothy Wordsworth to Jane Pollard, 26 June 1791 *(EY* 52).
6. See Benjamin Hederich, *Graecum Lexicon Manuale* (Lipsiae: Gleditschi; London: Nourse, 1767).
7. Caesar Morgan graduated from Trinity College, Cambridge, in 1773, became a Fellow of that College for two years, had an essay (which had won an international prize) published by Cambridge University Press in 1787, and received the degree of Doctor of Divinity in 1793. See "Advertisement" to Caesar Morgan, *An Investigation of the Trinity of Plato and of Philo Judaeus* (1795; reprint, Cambridge: Cambridge University Press, 1853), v.
8. See Jacob Bryant, *The Sentiments of Philo Judeus Concerning the Logos, or Word of God* (Cambridge: John Burges (Printer to the University), 1797), 14-22 and *passim*; MM 1:213.
9. *Gentleman's Magazine* 29 (1759): 57-58; *Collected Letters of Samuel Taylor Coleridge*, ed. Griggs, 4:632 (e.g.), 803.
10. Joseph Priestley, *An History of the Corruptions of Christianity*, 2 vols. (1782; reprint, New York: Garland, 1974), 1:23, 30-31, 34; Pelagius [presumed to be Priestley's pseudonym], "Of the Platonism of Philo," in J. Priestley, *The Theological Repository* (Birmingham) 4 (1784): 408-20, reprinted in his *Theological and Miscellaneous Works*, 25 vols. (1817-32; reprint, New York: Kraus Reprint, 1972), 6:186-95.
11. See H. W. Piper, *The Active Universe* (London: Athlone Press, 1962), 63-67; *Prose Works of William Wordsworth*, ed. Alexander B. Grosart, 3 vols. (1876; reprint, New York: AMS Press, 1967), 1:10.
12. Lawrence Hanson uses the word "hero" in his *Life of S. T. Coleridge*, 50. The sonnet, published first in the *Morning Chronicle* in Dec. 1794, appears in Coleridge's *Complete Poetical Works*, ed. E. H. Coleridge, 1:81-82, and the lines (371-76) of "Religious Musings" appear on page 123 of the same volume.
13. *Encyclopaedia Britannica* (Edinburgh: Bell and MacFarquhar, 1797), 14:483-84.
14. Cudworth, 581-82; Morgan, xi, 158.
15. MM 1:331.
16. Harper, *William Wordsworth*, 1:197.
17. See MM 1:347.

Appendix N: Further Changes Due to Young

1. *P(deS)*, 298-300.
2. The changes appear on a wafer stuck over MS. D *(P(O)*, 863). The editors of the Norton edition date this passage "1838/39" *(P(N)*, 301n). The fourteen-book version runs from line 476 to line 494 *(P(O)*, 172-73.
3. 9:2311-14 (1:241).
4. 1:79-81 (1:5).

5. According to de Selincourt's note *(P(deS)*, 252), MSS. A and B read simply "Doctor Young," with no further description; changes made to MS. A, and consequently MSS. C and D, read: "and the Bard / Of night who spangled o'er a gloomy theme / With fancies thick as his inspiring stars." An emendation made to MS. D then changed "Of night who" to "Whose genius" *(P(O)*, 797). (An interesting intermediate version, unnoticed by De Selincourt, appears in MS. B: "That Bard / Who spangled oer a dark and gloomy theme / With fancies bright ["bright" is deleted, and "thick" substituted] as his inspiring stars.") See *P(O)*, 152 (7:566).

Appendix O: On the Editing of the Lines on Newton's Statue

1. Reed, *Chronology, Middle Years*, 12.
2. *P(deS)*, xx; Siemens, 21; *P(N)*, 508-9.
3. De Selincourt *(P(deS)*, xx) and Siemens (22) say Sara; the Norton editors say Mary *(P(N)*, 509).
4. *P(deS)*, xxii; Siemens, 23; *P(N)*, 509.
5. *P(O)*, 8. The Norton editors say "early in 1832" *(P(N)*, 509).
6. *P(O)*, 470-71. The differences from MS. C are in the use of commas, the "&" for "and" and certain spellings: "Antichapel" for "Antechapel," "prism" for "Prism," and "face" for "Face."
7. *P(O)*, 470-71.
8. *P(O)*, 8.
9. William Wordsworth, *The Prelude, or Growth of a Poet's Mind* (London: Edward Moxon, 1850), 57-58.
10. *P(deS)*, xxiv.
11. "The face has something of the shape of a 'prism'...." David Perkins, ed., *English Romantic Writers* (New York: Harcourt, Brace, 1967), 227.
12. The reciprocating relation is discussed in Chapter 8.
13. *P(N)*, 509.
14. *P(N)*, xii and 512. On the latter page the editors add the statement: "on very exceptional occasions it has been necessary to go back a stage further to see if *D* itself perpetuated an error."
15. *P(O)*, 62.
16. Stephen Gill, ed., *William Wordsworth*, The Oxford Authors (Oxford and New York: Oxford University Press, 1984), 406.
17. Paul D. Sheats, ed., *The Poetical Works of Wordsworth*, Cambridge Edition (Boston: Houghton Mifflin, 1982), 217.

Bibliography

Abrams, M. H., ed. *English Romantic Poets: Modern Essays in Criticism.* New York: Oxford University Press, 1960.
Addison, Joseph, and Sir Richard Steele. *Addison and Steele.* Ed. R. J. Allen. New York: Rinehart, 1957.
———. *The Spectator.* Ed. Donald F. Bond. 5 vols. Oxford: Clarendon, 1965.
Alumni Cantabrigienses, Part II: From 1752 to 1900. Comp. John Venn and J. A. Venn. 6 vols. Cambridge: Cambridge University Press, 1940-54.
Anderson, Robert, ed. *The Works of the British Poets.* 13 vols. London: John and Arthur Arch, 1795.
Armstrong, Edward A. *Shakespeare's Imagination: A Study of the Psychology of Association and Inspiration.* London: Drummond, 1946.
Athenaeum. No. 407 (15 Aug. 1835): 617-24 ("Original Papers—Fifth Meeting of the British Association for the Advancement of Science").
———. No. 408 (22 Aug. 1835): 640-50 ("Original Papers—Fifth Meeting of the British Association for the Advancement of Science").
———. No. 424 (12 Dec. 1835): 930-31 (William Wordsworth's

"Extempore Effusion, upon reading, in the Newcastle Journal, the notice of the Death of James Hogg" and his note).

Ault, Donald D. *Visionary Physics: Blake's Response to Newton.* Chicago and London: University of Chicago Press, 1974.

Bailey, Nathaniel. *An Universal Etymological English Dictionary.* 6th ed. London: Knapton et al., 1733.

Barbauld, Anna Laetitia. *The Works of Anna Laetitia Barbauld.* With a memoir by Lucy Aikin. 2 vols. London: Longmans, 1825.

Bate, W. J., ed. *Criticism: The Major Texts.* New York: Harcourt, Brace, 1952.

Batho, Edith C. *The Later Wordsworth.* 1933. Reprint. New York: Russell and Russell, 1963.

Beach, Joseph Warren. *The Concept of Nature in Nineteenth-Century English Poetry.* 1936. Reprint. New York: Pageant, 1956.

Bell, John. *Bell's Classical Arrangement of Fugitive Poetry.* 14 vols. London: Bell, 1789-91.

Bell's British Theatre, Consisting of the Most Esteemed English Plays. 20 vols. London: John Bell, 1776-78.

Blake, William. *The Poetry and Prose of William Blake.* Ed. David V. Erdman. Commentary by Harold Bloom. Garden City, N. Y.: Doubleday, 1965.

Blanshard, Frances. *Portraits of Wordsworth.* London: Allen and Unwin, 1959.

Bloom, Harold. *The Anxiety of Influence: A Theory of Poetry.* New York: Oxford University Press, 1973.

———. *Blake's Apocalypse: A Study in Poetic Argument.* 1963. Reprint. Garden City, N. Y.: Doubleday, 1965.

Bowes, Robert. *A Catalogue of Books Printed at or Relating to the University Town & County of Cambridge...* Cambridge: Macmillan & Bowes, 1894.

Boyle, Robert. *The Works of the Honourable Robert Boyle.* New ed. 6 vols. 1772. Reprint. Hildesheim: Georg Olm, 1965-66.

Bradley, A. C. *Oxford Lectures on Poetry.* 1909. Reprint. Bloomington: Indiana University Press, 1961.

Browning, Elizabeth Barrett. *Poetical Works.* Ed. Alice Meynell. London: Ward, Lock, n. d.

Bryant, Jacob. *The Sentiments of Philo Judeus [sic] Concerning the Logos, or Word of God.* Cambridge: John Burges (Printer to the University), 1797.

Burtt, E. A. *The Metaphysical Foundations of Modern Physical Science.* New York: Harcourt, Brace, 1927.
Bush, Douglas. *Mythology and the Romantic Tradition.* 1937. Reprint. New York: W. W. Norton, 1963.
Butler, William Archer. *Sermons Doctrinal and Practical.* 2nd American ed. Philadelphia: Parry and McMillan, 1859.
Byron, George Gordon, Lord. *Don Juan.* Ed. Leslie A. Marchand. Boston: Houghton Mifflin, 1958.
Cambridge Portfolio. Ed. Rev. J[ohn] J[ames] Smith. 2 vols. London: John W. Parker; Cambridge: J. and J. J. Deighton, 1840.
Cambridge Prize Poems. Cambridge: W. P. Grant, 1840.
Catullus, Tibullus, and Pervigilium Veneris. Trans. F. W. Cornish. Loeb Classical Library. London: Heinemann; Cambridge, Mass.: Harvard University Press, 1966.
Chalmers, Alexander, ed. *The Works of the English Poets.* 21 vols. London: Johnson, 1810.
Chapman, Geo[rge]. *Homer Prince of Poets...* London: Samuel Macham, [1610].
Christianson, Gale E. *In the Presence of the Creator: Isaac Newton and His Times.* New York: Free Press; London: Collier Macmillan, 1984.
Clarke, M. L. *Classical Education in Britain, 1500-1900.* Cambridge: Cambridge University Press, 1959.
Coe, Charles Norton. *Wordsworth and the Literature of Travel.* New York: Bookman Associates, 1953.
Coleridge, Samuel Taylor. *Biographia Literaria.* Ed. James Engell and W. Jackson Bate. 2 vols. Vol. 7 of *The Collected Works of Samuel Taylor Coleridge.* Gen. ed. Kathleen Coburn. Princeton: Princeton University Press, 1983.
———. *Collected Letters of Samuel Taylor Coleridge.* Ed. Earl Leslie Griggs. 6 vols. Oxford: Clarendon, 1956-71.
———. *The Complete Poetical Works.* Ed. Ernest Hartley Coleridge. 2 vols. Oxford: Clarendon, 1912.
———. *Lectures 1795: On Politics and Religion.* Ed. Lewis Patton and Peter Mann. Vol. 1 of *The Collected Works of Samuel Taylor Coleridge.* Gen. ed. Kathleen Coburn. London: Routledge and Kegan Paul; Princeton: Princeton University Press, 1971.
———. *Poems.* 2nd ed. With poems by Charles Lamb and Charles Lloyd. Bristol: Cottle; London: Robinson, 1797.

Concise Oxford Dictionary of Current English. 6th ed. Oxford: Clarendon, 1976.

A Concordance of Ovid. 2 vols. 1939. Reprint. Hildesheim: Georg Olms, 1968.

Cooke, Capt. Edward. *A Voyage to the South Sea, and Round the World, Perform'd in the Years 1708, 1709, 1710, and 1711.* 2 vols. 1712. Reprint. Amsterdam and New York: Israel and Da Capo, 1969.

Cooper, Lane. "A Glance at Wordsworth's Reading." *Modern Language Notes* 22 (1907): 83-89; 110-17.

Cowper, William. *Cowper: Poetical Works.* Ed. H. S. Milford. 4th ed. Corrections and additions by Norma Russell. London: Oxford University Press, 1967.

———. *The Works of William Cowper, Esq.* Ed. Robert Southey. 15 vols. London: Baldwin and Cradock, 1835-37.

Cudworth, Ralph. *The True Intellectual System of the Universe.* 1678. Reprint. Stuttgart-Bad Cannstatt: Friedrich Fromman Verlag, 1964.

Cunningham, Allan. *The Lives of the Most Eminent British Painters, Sculptors, and Architects.* 3 vols. London: John Murray, 1830.

Curme, George D. *English Grammar.* New York: Barnes and Noble, 1947.

Darbishire, Helen. *The Poet Wordsworth.* Oxford: Clarendon, 1950.

De Selincourt, Ernest. *Dorothy Wordsworth: A Biography.* Oxford: Clarendon, 1933.

Dictionary of National Biography.

Dobrée, Bonamy. *Restoration Tragedy, 1660-1720.* Oxford: London: Oxford University Press, 1917—. Clarendon, 1929.

Dodd, George. "Wordsworth and Hamilton." *Nature* 228 (26 Dec. 1970): 1261-63.

Drabble, Margaret. *Wordsworth.* London: Evans Brothers, 1966.

Dryden, John. *The Poems of John Dryden.* Ed. James Kinsley. 4 vols. Oxford: Clarendon, 1958.

———. *The Works of John Dryden.* Gen. eds. Edward Niles Hooker and H. T. Swedenberg, Jr. Berkeley and Los Angeles: University of California Press, 1956—.

———. *The Works of Virgil Translated into English Verse.* 3 vols. London: Jacob Tonson, 1721.

Dunklin, Gilbert T., ed. *Wordsworth: Centenary Studies.* Princeton: Princeton University Press, 1951.

Dunn, S. G. "A Note on Wordsworth's Metaphysical System." *Essays and Studies* 18 (1933): 74-109.
Durrant, Geoffrey. *Wordsworth and the Great System*. Cambridge: Cambridge University Press, 1970.
Dyer, G[eorge]. *History of the University and Colleges of Cambridge*. 2 vols. London: Longmans, 1814.
Edinburgh Review 11 (Oct. 1807): 214-31 (Review of *Poems, in Two Volumes*, by William Wordsworth).
Ellis, Frank H. "Gray's *Elegy:* the Biographical Problem in Literary Criticism." *PMLA* 66 (1951): 971-1008.
Elmes, James, ed. *A General and Bibliographical Dictionary of the Fine Arts*. London: Thomas Tegg, 1826.
Encyclopaedia Britannica. Edinburgh: Bell and MacFarquhar, 1797.
Engel, J. J. *Ideen zu einer Mimik*. 2 vols. Berlin: Manlius, 1785-86.
———. *Idées sur le Geste et L'Action Théâtrale*. 2 vols. Paris: Barrois, 1788-89.
Esdaile, Katharine A. *Roubiliac's Work at Trinity College, Cambridge*. Cambridge: Cambridge University Press, 1924.
Examiner, 7 May 1820: 297-300 (Review of B. R. Haydon's "Christ's Triumphant Entry into Jerusalem").
Fairchild, Hoxie Neale. *Religious Trends in English Poetry*. 6 vols. New York: Columbia University Press, 1939-68.
Fielding, Henry. *The Works of Henry Fielding*. Ed. Leslie Stephen. 10 vols. London: Smith, Elder, 1882.
Fink, Z. S., ed. *The Early Wordsworthian Milieu: A Notebook of Christopher Wordsworth with a few entries by William Wordsworth*. Oxford: Clarendon, 1958.
Garber, Frederick. *Wordsworth and the Poetry of Encounter*. Urbana: University of Illinois Press, 1971.
Gentleman's Magazine 1 (April 1731): 169 ("Verses Design'd for the Monument of Sir Isaac Newton").
———. 25 (1755): 328 (Note on the erection of Roubiliac's statue of Newton at Trinity College, Cambridge).
———. 29 (1759): 57-58 ("Observations on the Mosaic Account of the Creation" by John Coleridge).
———. 69 (Oct. 1799): 884-85 ("Stanzas from Tasker's Ode to the Spirit of Alfred...").
———. 69 (Nov. 1799): 964 (Review of Jacob Bryant's *The Sentiments of Philo Judaeus...*).

Gilfillan, George, ed. *The Poetical Works of Beattie, Blair, and Falconer.* Edinburgh: James Nichol, 1854.

Grabo, Carl. *A Newton Among Poets.* Chapel Hill: University of North Carolina Press, 1930.

Graves, R. P. *Life of Sir William Rowan Hamilton.* 3 vols. 1882-89. Reprint. New York: Arno, 1975.

———, et al. *The Afternoon Lectures on Literature & Art Delivered in the Theatre of the Royal College of Science, S. Stephen's Green, Dublin, in the Years 1867 & 1868.* Dublin: William McGee; London: Bell and Daldy, 1869.

Gray, Thomas, and William Collins. *Poetical Works.* Ed. Roger Lonsdale. Oxford: Oxford University Press, 1977.

Halley, Edmond. *Correspondence and Papers of Edmond Halley.* Ed. E. F. MacPike. Oxford: Clarendon, 1932.

Hankins, Thomas L. *Sir William Rowan Hamilton.* Baltimore and London: Johns Hopkins University Press, 1980.

Hanson, Lawrence. *The Life of S. T. Coleridge: The Early Years.* 1938. Reprint. New York: Russell and Russell, 1962.

Harper, George McLean. *William Wordsworth: His Life, Works, and Influence.* 2 vols. 1929. Reprint. New York: Russell and Russell, 1960.

Hartley, David. *Observations on Man....* Ed. Theodore L. Huguelet. 2 vols. 1749. Reprint. Gainesville, Fla.: Scholars' Facsimiles & Reprints, 1966.

Hartman, Geoffrey H. *Wordsworth's Poetry, 1787-1814.* New Haven and London: Yale University Press, 1964.

Havens, Raymond Dexter. *The Mind of a Poet.* 2 vols. Baltimore: Johns Hopkins Press, 1941.

Haydon, Benjamin Robert. *The Autobiography and Memoirs of Benjamin Robert Haydon, 1786-1846.* Ed. A. P. D. Penrose. London: Bell, 1927.

———. *The Diary of Benjamin Robert Haydon.* Ed. Willard Bissell Pope. 5 vols. Cambridge, Mass.: Harvard University Press, 1960-63.

Hederich, Benjamin. *Graecum Lexicon Manuale.* Lipsiae: Gleditschi; London: Nourse, 1767.

Hesiod. *Theogony, Works and Days, Shield.* Trans. Apostolos N. Athanassakis. Baltimore: Johns Hopkins University Press, 1983.

Homer. *The Iliad.* Trans. A. T. Murray. Loeb Classical Library. 2 vols. 1924. Reprint. London: Heinemann, 1960.

———. *The Iliad.* Trans. E. V. Rieu. Harmondsworth, England: Penguin, 1950.
———. *The Iliad.* Trans. Robert Fitzgerald. New York: Anchor Press / Doubleday, 1974.
———. *The Iliad of Homer.* Trans. Richmond Lattimore. Chicago: University of Chicago Press, 1951.
Horn, Robert D. *Marlborough: A Survey.* New York: Garland, 1975.
Hughes, John. *The Poetical Works of John Hughes.* 2 vols. Edinburgh: Apollo Press, 1779.
Hutchinson, Sara. *The Letters of Sara Hutchinson from 1800 to 1835.* Ed. Kathleen Coburn. London: Routledge and Kegan Paul, 1954.
The Inward Eye: A Celebration of Wordsworth (1770-1970). Ashington, Northumberland: Mid Northumberland Arts Group, 1970.
James, Henry. *Literary Criticism.* Ed. Leon Edel and Mark Wilson. New York: Library of America, 1984.
Jay, Eileen. *Wordsworth at Colthouse.* Kendal: Titus Wilson and Son, 1970.
Johnson, Lee M. *Wordsworth's Metaphysical Verse: Geometry, Nature, and Form.* Toronto: University of Toronto Press, 1982.
Johnson, Samuel. *A Dictionary of the English Language.* 2 vols. 1755. Reprint. New York: AMS, 1967.
———. *A Dictionary of the English Language.* 3 vols. London: Longmans, 1827.
———. *Lives of the English Poets.* World's Classics Edition. 2 vols. London: Oxford University Press, 1949.
———. *Rasselas, Poems, and Selected Prose.* Ed. B. H. Bronson. New York: Holt, Rinehart, and Winston, 1958.
Jones, Alun, and William Tydeman, ed. *Wordsworth, "Lyrical Ballads": A Casebook.* London: Macmillan, 1972.
Jones, Henry. *Philosophy, a Poem.* Dublin: Powell, 1746.
Jones, John. *The Egotistical Sublime: A History of Wordsworth's Imagination.* London: Chatto and Windus, 1954.
Jonson, Ben. *The Poems of Ben Jonson.* Ed. Bernard H. Newdigate. Oxford: Shakespeare Head, 1936.
Keats, John. *The Poems of John Keats.* Ed. Jack Stillinger. Cambridge, Mass.: Harvard University Press, 1978.
Le Brun, Charles. *A Method to Learn to Design The Passions.* Trans. John Williams. Ed. Alan T. McKenzie. 1734. Reprint. Los

Angeles: University of California, William Andrews Clark Memorial Library Publication Numbers 200-201, 1980.
Legouis, Emile. *The Early Life of William Wordsworth, 1770-1798.* Trans. J. W. Matthews. 2nd rev. ed. 1897. Reprint. New York: Russell and Russell, 1965.
Liddell, Henry George, and Robert Scott, comps. *A Greek-English Lexicon.* Rev. ed. Oxford: Clarendon, 1968.
Lindenberger, Herbert. *On Wordsworth's "Prelude."* Princeton: Princeton University Press, 1963.
Locke, John. *An Essay Concerning Human Understanding.* Ed. Peter H. Nidditch. Oxford: Clarendon, 1975.
Lover, Samuel. *Rory O'More.* 1837. Reprint. London: Routledge, Warne, and Routledge, 1864.
Lucretius. *De Rerum Natura.* Ed. and trans. W. H. D. Rouse. Loeb Classical Library. London: Heinemann; Cambridge, Mass.: Harvard University Press, 1959.
―――. *On Nature.* Trans. Russel M. Geer. Indianapolis: Bobbs-Merrill, 1965.
Lytton, Edward Robert Bulwer, Earl of. *The Life, Letters, and Literary Remains of Edward Bulwer, Lord Lytton.* 2 vols. London: Kegan Paul, Trench, 1883.
Lytton Bulwer, E. G. *Sculpture.* Cambridge: Cambridge University [?], 1825.
―――. *The Siamese Twins: A Satirical Tale of the Times.* London: Henry Colburn and Richard Bentley, 1831.
―――. *Weeds and Wildflowers.* Paris: A. Coniam [printer], 1826.
Manuel, Frank E. *The Religion of Isaac Newton.* Oxford: Clarendon, 1974.
Mayo, Robert. "The Contemporaneity of the *Lyrical Ballads.*" *PMLA* 69 (1954): 486-522.
Memorials of Cambridge: A Series of Views... Engraved by J. Le Keux [with text by] Thomas Wright and H. Longueville Jones. 2 vols. London: Bogue, 1845.
Meyer, George W. "A Note on the Sources and Symbolism of the *Intimations Ode.*" *Tulane Studies in English* 3 (1952): 33-45.
Milton, John. *The Works of John Milton.* Gen. ed. Frank Allen Patterson. Columbia University Edition. 18 vols. with 2-vol. index. New York: Columbia University Press, 1931-40.
Moore, John Robert. "Wordsworth's Unacknowledged Debt to Macpherson's *Ossian.*" *PMLA* 40 (1925): 362-78.

Moorman, Mary. *William Wordsworth: A Biography: The Early Years, 770-1803*. London: Oxford University Press, 1957.
——. *William Wordsworth: A Biography: The Later Years, 1803-1850*. London: Oxford University Press, 1965.
More, Henry. *Apocalypsia Apocalypeos; or, the Revelation of St. John the Divine unveiled*. London: J. Martyn and W. Kettilby, 1680.
More, Louis Trenchard. *Isaac Newton: A Biography*. 1934. Reprint. New York: Dover, 1962.
Morgan, Caesar. *An Investigation of the Trinity of Plato and of Philo Judaeus*. 1795. Reprint. Cambridge: Cambridge University Press, 1853.
Muirhead, James Patrick. "A Day With Wordsworth." *Blackwood's Magazine* 221 (June 1927): 728-43.
Newton, Sir Isaac. *Isaac Newton's Papers & Letters on Natural Philosophy and Related Documents*. Ed. I. Bernard Cohen. Cambridge, Mass.: Harvard University Press, 1958.
——. *Mathematical Principles of Natural Philosophy*.... Trans. Andrew Motte. Rev. Florian Cajori. Berkeley: University of California Press, 1934.
——. *Mathematical Principles of Natural Philosophy*.... Trans. Andrew Motte. Rev. Florian Cajori. Chicago: Encyclopaedia Britannica, Inc., 1952.
——. *Opera Quae Exstant Omnia*. Ed. Samuel Horsley. 5 vols. 1779-85. Reprint. Stuttgart-Bad Canstatt: Friedrich Frommann Verlag, 1964.
——. *Opticks*. Introd. Sir Edmund Whittaker. New York: Dover, 1952.
Nicoll, Allardyce. *A History of English Drama, 1660-1900*. Cambridge: Cambridge University Press, 1955.
Nicolson, Marjorie Hope. *Newton Demands The Muse*. 1946. Reprint. Hamden, Conn.: Archon, 1963.
Noyes, Russell. *William Wordsworth*. New York: Twayne, 1971.
——. *Wordsworth and the Art of Landscape*. Bloomington: Indiana University Press, 1968.
Ober, Warren U. "Nature, the Imagination, and the Conversion of Peter Bell." *Yearbook of English Studies* 3 (1973): 170-80.
O'Donnell, Sean. *William Rowan Hamilton: Portrait of a Prodigy*. Dublin: Boole, 1983.
Origen. *Contra Celsum*. Trans. and ed. Henry Chadwick. Cambridge: Cambridge University Press, 1965.

Owen, W. J. B. "Literary Echoes in *The Prelude*." *The Wordsworth Circle* 3 (Winter 1972): 3-16.
The Oxford Companion to English Literature. Ed. Sir Paul Harvey. 3rd ed. Oxford: Clarendon, 1946.
Oxford English Dictionary. Compact edition. 2 vols. [New York]: Oxford University Press, 1971.
Oxford Latin Dictionary. Oxford: Clarendon, 1968-82.
Peacock, Thomas Love. *The Novels of Thomas Love Peacock.* Ed. David Garnett. London: Rupert Hart-Davis, 1948.
Perkins, David, ed. *English Romantic Writers.* New York: Harcourt, Brace, 1967.
[Philo Judaeus.] *Philo.* Trans. F. H. Colson and G. H. Whitaker. Loeb Classical Library. 10 vols. Cambridge, Mass.: Harvard University Press, 1929-62.
Φίλωνος τοῦ Ἰουδαίου τὰ εὑρισκόμενα ἅπαντα. *Philonis Judaei opera quae reperiri potuerunt omnia.* Ed. Thomas Mangey. 2 vols. London: Bowyer, 1742.
———. *Opera Omnia. Graece et Latine.* Ed. Thomas Mangey. Rev. Augustus Friedericus Pfeiffer. 2nd ed. 5 vols. Erlangae: Libraria Heyderiana, 1820.
———. *Philo: Supplement.* Trans. and ed. Ralph Marcus. Loeb Classical Library. 2 vols. Cambridge, Mass.: Harvard University Press, 1961.
Piper, H. W. *The Active Universe.* London: Athlone Press, 1962.
Pittman, Charles L. "A Biographical Note on Wordsworth." *Bulletin of Furman University* 29.3 (May 1946): 31-53.
———. "An Introduction to a Study of Wordsworth's Reading in Science." *Furman Studies* 33.5 (Spring 1950): 27-60.
Pope, Alexander. *The Poems of Alexander Pope.* Twickenham Edition. 10 vols. London: Methuen, 1939-67.
Potts, Abbie Findlay. *Wordsworth's "Prelude": A Study of Its Literary Form.* 1953. Reprint. New York: Octagon, 1966.
Priestley, F. E. L. "Newton and the Romantic Concept of Nature." *University of Toronto Quarterly* 17 (1947-48): 323-36.
Priestley, Joseph. *An History of the Corruptions of Christianity.* 2 vols. 1782. Reprint. New York: Garland, 1974.
———. *Theological and Miscellaneous Works.* 25 vols. 1817-32. Reprint. New York: Kraus Reprint, 1972.
Quarterly Review 23 (1820): 400-434 (Review of Joseph Spence's

Anecdotes... and W. L. Bowles's *Invariable Principles of Poetry...*).
Rader, Melvin. *Wordsworth: A Philosophical Approach.* Oxford: Clarendon, 1967.
Ramsay, Allan. *The Poems of Allan Ramsay.* New ed. 2 vols. Paisley: Alex. Gardner, 1877.
Reed, Mark L. *Wordsworth: The Chronology of the Early Years 1770-1799.* Cambridge, Mass.: Harvard University Press, 1967.
——. *Wordsworth: The Chronology of the Middle Years.* Cambridge, Mass.: Harvard University Press, 1975.
Robinson, Henry Crabb. *The Correspondence of Henry Crabb Robinson with the Wordsworth Circle.* Ed. Edith J. Morley. 2 vols. Oxford: Clarendon, 1927.
——. *Henry Crabb Robinson on Books and Their Writers.* Ed. Edith J. Morley. 3 vols. London: Dent, 1938.
[Robson, R., and R. H. Glauert.] *Trinity College.* Cambridge: Trinity College, 1967.
Schelp, Hanspeter. "Wordsworth's 'Daffodils' Influenced by a Wesleyan Hymn?" *English Studies* 42 (1961): 307-9.
Schneider, B. R., Jr. *Wordsworth's Cambridge Education.* Cambridge: Cambridge University Press, 1957.
A Select Collection of Poems. 8 vols. London: J. Nichols, 1780-82.
S[elwyn], W[illiam]. "Trinity College Chapel," in *Cambridge Portfolio.* Ed. Rev. J[ohn] J[ames] Smith. 2 vols. London: John W. Parker; Cambridge: J. and J. J. Deighton, 1840. Pages 87-98.
Shakespeare, William. *The Complete Works of Shakespeare.* Ed. George Lyman Kittredge. Boston: Ginn, 1936.
Shaver, Chester L., and Alice C. Shaver. *Wordsworth's Library: A Catalogue.* New York and London: Garland, 1979.
Shelley, Percy Bysshe. *The Complete Works of Percy Bysshe Shelley.* Ed. Roger Ingpen and Walter E. Peck. Julian Edition. 10 vols. 1926-30. Reprint. New York: Gordian, 1965.
——. *Shelley's Poetry and Prose.* Ed. Donald H. Reiman and Sharon B. Powers. Norton Critical Edition. New York: W. W. Norton, 1977.
Shenstone, William. *The Poetical Works of William Shenstone.* Ed. George Gilfillan. Edinburgh: James Nicol, 1854.
Siddons, Henry. *Practical Illustrations of Rhetorical Gesture and Action; adapted to the English drama: from a work on the subject by M. Engel.* 2nd ed. 1822. Reprint. New York: Benjamin Blom, 1968.

Sidney, Sir Philip. *Defense of Poetry.* Ed. Lewis Soens. Lincoln: University of Nebraska Press, 1970.
Siemens, Reynold. *The Wordsworth Collection: A Catalogue; Dove Cottage Papers Facsimiles of The University of Alberta.* Edmonton: University of Alberta Press, 1971.
Smith, Adam. *Essays on Philosophical Subjects.* 1795. Reprint. New York: Garland, 1971.
Smith, Hallett. *Elizabethan Poetry: A Study in Conventions, Meaning, and Expression.* Cambridge, Mass.: Harvard University Press, 1952.
Smith, Robert. *Harmonics, Or the Philosophy of Musical Sounds.* 1749. Reprint. New York: Da Capo Press, 1966.
———. *Traité D'Optique, par M. Smith..., Traduit De L'Anglais....* Brest: Romain Mallassis, 1767.
Snow, A. J. *Matter and Gravity in Newton's Physical Philosophy.* London: Oxford University Press, 1926.
Spence, Joseph. *Anecdotes, Observations, and Characters, of Books and Men.* Ed. S. W. Singer. London: Carpenter, 1820.
Spenser, Edmund. *The Works of Edmund Spenser.* Ed. Edwin Greenlaw, Charles Grosvenor Osgood, Frederick Morgan Padelford, and Ray Heffner. A Variorum Edition. 10 vols. with index. Baltimore: Johns Hopkins Press, 1932-57.
Stallknecht, Newton P. *Strange Seas of Thought.* Bloomington: Indiana University Press, 1958.
Stanyhurst, Richard. *The First Foure Bookes of Virgils Aeneis.* London: Henrie Bynneman, 1583.
Sterne, Laurence. *The Life and Opinions of Tristram Shandy, Gentleman.* Ed. Ian Watt. 1760-67. Reprint. Boston: Houghton Mifflin, 1965.
———. *A Sentimental Journey Through France and Italy and Letters.* New ed. London: Thomas Tegg et al., 1823.
Taylor, Sir Henry. *Correspondence.* Ed. Edward Dowden. London: Longmans, 1888.
Tennyson, Charles. *Alfred Tennyson.* London: Macmillan, 1968.
Thomas, W. K. "Mouths and Eyes in Lycidas." *Milton Quarterly* 9 (May 1975): 39-42.
———. Note on Sir Philip Sidney's "Leave Me, O Love, Which Reachest But to Dust." *Explicator* 28 (Jan. 1970): no. 45.
———. "The Vanishing God." *College English* 31 (1970): 738.

Thompson, T. W. *Wordsworth's Hawkshead.* Ed. Robert Woof. London: Oxford University Press, 1970.
Thomson, James. *The Castle of Indolence and Other Poems.* Ed. Alan Dugald McKillop. Lawrence: University of Kansas Press, 1961.
——. *Poetical Works.* Ed. J. Logie Robertson. London: Oxford University Press, 1908.
Transactions of the Wordsworth Society 6 (1884): iii-iv; 195-257 ("Preface" and "The Rydal Mount Library Catalogue").
Turnor, Edmund. *Collections for the History of the Town and Soke of Grantham. Containing Authentic Memoirs of Sir Isaac Newton. . . .* London: William Miller, 1806.
Ussher, James. *A Body of Divinitie. . . .* London: Thomas Downes and George Badger, 1645.
Vincent, W. A. L. *The Grammar Schools: Their Continuing Tradition, 1660-1714.* London: John Murray, 1969.
Virgil. *Virgil, with an English Translation.* Ed. and trans. H. Rushton Fairclough. Loeb Classical Library. 2 vols. London: Heinemann, 1965.
Voltaire [François-Marie Arouet]. *The Elements of Sir Isaac Newton's Philosophy.* Trans. John Hanna. London: Stephen Austen, 1738.
Wallace, Robert, et al. *The World of Bernini, 1598-1680.* New York: Time-Life Books, 1970.
Waller, Edmund. *The Poems of Edmund Waller.* Ed. G. Thorn Drury. London: Lawrence and Bullen; New York: Scribner's, 1893.
Watson, Foster. *The Old Grammar Schools.* Cambridge: Cambridge University Press, 1916.
Westfall, Richard S. *Never at Rest: A Biography of Isaac Newton.* Cambridge: Cambridge University Press, 1980.
Wilson, F. P., ed. *Oxford Dictionary of English Proverbs.* 3rd ed. Oxford: Clarendon, 1970.
Winchester College, 1393-1893. "By Old Wykehamists." London: Arnold, 1893.
Wordsworth, Christopher. *Memoirs of William Wordsworth.* Ed. Henry Reed. 2 vols. Boston: Ticknor, Read, and Fields, 1851.
——. *Scholae Academicae.* 1877. Reprint. London: Frank Cass, 1968.
Wordsworth, Dorothy. *Journals of Dorothy Wordsworth.* Ed. Mary Moorman. London: Oxford University Press, 1971.
Wordsworth, Dorothy, and William Wordsworth. *The Letters: The*

Early Years, 1787-1805. Ed. Ernest de Selincourt. Vol. 1 of 2nd ed. Rev. Chester L. Shaver. Oxford: Clarendon, 1967.

———. *The Letters: The Middle Years, Part I, 1806-1811.* Ed. Ernest de Selincourt. Vol. 2 of 2nd ed. Rev. Mary Moorman. Oxford: Clarendon, 1969.

———. *The Letters: The Middle Years, Part II, 1812-1820.* Ed. Ernest de Selincourt. Vol. 3 of 2nd ed. Rev. Mary Moorman and Alan G. Hill. Oxford: Clarendon, 1970.

———. *The Letters: The Later Years, Part I, 1821-1828.* Ed. Ernest de Selincourt. Vol. 3 [i.e.., 4] of 2nd ed. Rev. Alan G. Hill. Oxford: Clarendon, 1978.

———. *The Letters: The Later Years, Part II, 1829-1834.* Ed. Ernest de Selincourt. Vol. 5 of 2nd ed. Rev. Alan G. Hill. Oxford: Clarendon, 1979.

———. *The Letters: The Later Years, Part III, 1835-1839.* Ed. Ernest de Selincourt. Vol. 6 of 2nd ed. Rev. Alan G. Hill. Oxford: Clarendon, 1982.

———. *The Letters: The Later Years, 1831-40.* Ed. Ernest de Selincourt. Unrevised vol. 2 of 1st ed. Oxford: Clarendon, 1939.

———. *The Letters: The Later Years, 1841-50.* Ed. Ernest de Selincourt. Unrevised vol. 3 of 1st ed. Oxford: Clarendon, 1939.

Wordsworth, Jonathan, ed. *Bicentenary Wordsworth Studies.* Ithaca: Cornell University Press, 1970.

Wordsworth, Mary. *The Letters of Mary Wordsworth, 1800-1855.* Ed. Mary E. Burton. Oxford: Clarendon, 1958.

Wordsworth, Mary, and William Wordsworth. *The Love Letters of William and Mary Wordsworth.* Ed. Beth Darlington. Ithaca: Cornell University Press, 1981.

Wordsworth, William. *The Borderers.* Ed. Robert Osborn. The Cornell Wordsworth. Ithaca: Cornell University Press, 1982.

———. *An Evening Walk.* Ed. James Averill. The Cornell Wordsworth. Ithaca and London: Cornell University Press, 1984.

———. *The Fourteen-Book Prelude.* Ed. W. J. B. Owen. The Cornell Wordsworth. Ithaca: Cornell University Press, 1985.

———. *Literary Criticism of William Wordsworth.* Ed. Paul M. Zall. Lincoln: University of Nebraska Press, 1966.

———. *Poems, in Two Volumes, and Other Poems, 1800-1807.* Ed. Jared Curtis. The Cornell Wordsworth. Ithaca: Cornell University Press, 1983.

———. *The Poetical Works*. Ed. Ernest de Selincourt and Helen Darbishire. 5 vols. 2nd ed. for vols. 2 and 3. Oxford: Clarendon, 1940-54.

———. *The Poetical Works of Wordsworth*. Ed. Paul D. Sheats. Cambridge Edition. Boston: Houghton Mifflin, 1982.

———. *The Prelude, or Growth of a Poet's Mind*. London: Edward Moxon, 1850.

———. *The Prelude, or Growth of a Poet's Mind*. Ed. Ernest de Selincourt. 2nd ed. Rev. Helen Darbishire. Oxford: Clarendon, 1959.

———. *The Prelude, 1798-99*. Ed. Stephen Parrish. The Cornell Wordsworth. Ithaca: Cornell University Press, 1977.

———. *The Prelude: 1799, 1805, 1850*. Ed. Jonathan Wordsworth, M. H. Abrams, and Stephen Gill. Norton Critical Edition. New York: W. W. Norton, 1979.

———. *The Prelude*, MS. A: MSS. Verse 20; Dove Cottage MS. 52.

———. *The Prelude*, MS. B: MSS. Verse 21; Dove Cottage MS. 53.

———. *The Prelude*, MS. C: MSS. Verse 22; Dove Cottage MS. 82.

———. *The Prelude*, MS. D: MSS. Verse 23; Dove Cottage MS. 124.

———. *The Prelude*, MS. E: MSS. Verse 24; Dove Cottage MS. 145.

———. *Prose Works*. Ed. Alexander B. Grosart. 3 vols. 1876. Reprint. New York: AMS Press, 1967.

———. *Prose Works*. Ed. W.J.B. Owen and Jane Worthington Smyser. 3 vols. Oxford: Clarendon, 1974.

———. *William Wordsworth*. Ed. Stephen Gill. Oxford Authors. Oxford and New York: Oxford University Press, 1984.

———, comp. *Poems and Extracts Chosen by William Wordsworth for an Album Presented to Lady Mary Lowther, Christmas, 1819*. Preface J. Rogers Rees. Introd. Harold Littledale. London: Henry Frowde, 1905.

The World No. 200 (28 Oct. 1756): 1199-1204 ("An Ode to Sculpture").

Wren, Christopher. *Parentalia: or, Memoirs of the Family of the Wrens*. . . . London: Osborn, 1750.

Young, Edward. *The Complete Works*. Ed. James Nichols. 2 vols. 1854. Reprint. Hildesheim: Georg Olms, 1968.

Index

Acknowledgements, Wordsworth's attitude towards 79-80, 199-201
Addison, Joseph: *The Campaign* 21; *Cato* 73-74
"Admiration" in visual code of expression 165-66
Agamemnon 168-70
Akenside, Mark: "Hymn to Science" 52-54, 57-58, 79, 157, 205; *On the Pleasures of the Imagination* 28, 31, 36, 38, 48-49, 157; other references 45, 63, 97, 146, 199
Alfred, King 40-41
"Alone" in Wordsworth's lines on Newton's statue *(P* 3:57-63) 177-80
Anderson, Robert 35, 61, 183, 185, 189, 205-6, 292
Annual Register (Dodsley) 106
Aristotle 46, 47
Armstrong, Edward A. 102
Armstrong, John 63
Atterbury, Bishop Francis 44
Averill, James 206

Bacon, Sir Francis 27, 29, 158, 264
Bailly, Jean Sylvain 265
Barbauld, Anna Laetitia 190, 290
Barton, Bernard 194
Bartram, William 69, 76, 85, 273
Bastille 111
Bayley, Peter 199
Beattie, James: *The Minstrel* 8, 82, 187; other references 63, 97
Beaumont, Francis 62
Beaumont, Sir George 62, 234, 235
Beaumont, Sir John 63
Beaumont, Lady Margaret 112, 129, 295, 296
Beaupuy, Michel 103
Bede 83
Behn, Aphra 190
Bell's Classical Arrangement of Fugitive Poetry 61, 77, 189
Bentley, Richard 20, 121
Berkeley, George (bishop of Cloyne) 143
Bernini 166
Bible, The Holy 69, 146; I Corinthians 71; Exodus 176;

315

Lord's Prayer 161; Luke 175-76; I Peter 176; Psalm 88, 9; Psalm 139, 9; Revelation 91
Birch, Thomas 34
Blackwood's Magazine 234
Blake, William 10, 29, 260, 263-64
Bloom, Harold 263-64, 270
Boehme, Jakob 83
Book of Common Prayer 9-10
Bowles, William Lisle 199
Bowman, Thomas (Wordsworth's Hawkshead master) 51, 187, 289
Bowman, Thomas (son of Wordsworth's Hawkshead master) 187, 289
Boyle, Robert 27, 34
Boyse, Samuel 157
Bradley, A. C. 103
Brandes, Georg 203
Brereton, Jane 28, 45, 57, 157
Breton, N. 189
Brinkley, John 130
British Association for the Advancement of Science 123
Browne, Moses 27
Browning, Elizabeth Barrett 266
Bryant, Jacob 238
Bulwer, E. G. Lytton *see* Lytton Bulwer, E. G. [etc.]
Bulwer-Lytton, E. G. *see* Lytton Bulwer, E. G. [etc.]
Burns, Robert 187, 194
Burtt, E. A. 28, 31
Bush, Douglas 84, 204
Butler, Archer 126
Butt, John 204
Byron, George Gordon, Lord 63, 161, 199

Caesar, Julius 201, 292
Cambridge, Richard Owen 24, 44
Cambridge Portfolio 285, 287
Cambridge Prize Poems 109
Cambridge University 32-34, 62, 76, 79, 87, 102, 109, 111, 124, 180, 188, 189, 191, 193, 221, 237-38, 297; *see also* St. John's College *and* Trinity College
Carew, Thomas 63
Carter, John 246, 250
Catullus 218
Chalkhill, John 189
Chalmers, Alexander 189
Chamberlayne, William 189
Chantrey, Sir Francis 17, 112-13
Chapman, George 168-69, 189
Chaucer, Geoffrey 46, 188, 214, 215
Churchill, Charles 69
Cicero 64, 83
Clarke, James 83
Clarkson, Catherine 72-73
Clarkson, Thomas 278
Cluster of seven images recurrent in Wordsworth's poetry 102-4, 116, 154, 160, 161, 207-12
Code of literary allusion, verbal 19-20, 164, 172-73
Code of gesture and expression, visual 164-68, 172-73
Coe, Charles Norton 81, 153
Coleridge, John (Samuel Taylor Coleridge's father) 238
Coleridge, Samuel Taylor: *Biographia Literaria* 13, 29, 264, 275; "The Eolian Harp" 138-39; *Joan of Arc* 13, 264; "Kubla Khan" 82; *Lectures on Revealed Religion* 13, 264; "Monody on the Death of Chatterton" 149; "Religious Musings" 18, 112-13, 157, 239; "The Rime of the Ancient Mariner" 177-78, 203; other references 103, 123, 125, 128-29, 138, 158, 189, 199-200, 228, 238-39, 295
Collins, Churton vii-viii
Concise Oxford English Dictionary 149
Conduitt, John 44, 108, 282
Cook, Captain James 115, 160
Cooke, Captain Edward 277, 284
Cookson, Elizabeth 250

Cooper, Lane 75-76, 153, 188, 203
Corbet[t], Bishop Richard 62, 189
Cornell Wordsworth, The 253
Cornish, F. W. 218
Corpus of poetical tribute to Newton, reworked 43-49
Cowper, William: *The Iliad* (Cowper's translation) 168-69; *Table Talk* 70; *The Task* 65-68, 187, 195-98; "Yardley Oak" 213, 293; other references 63, 172, 194, 215
Coxe, William 291
Crabbe, George 106, 187
Cromwell, Oliver 20-21
Crowe, William (author of *Lewesdon Hill*) 188
Cudworth, Ralph 87, 92, 94, 237, 239
Cunningham, Allan 113, 150, 158

Daniel, Samuel 63, 162, 201
Darbishire, Helen 69, 133, 138, 204, 252
Davies, Sir John 85
Davies, Sneyd 65, 270
Depth (or height) as an element in the cluster of seven images recurrent in Wordsworth's poetry 102-3, 116-17, 207-12
De Quincey, Thomas 295
Desaguliers, John T. 26-27, 46
De Selincourt, Ernest 5, 56, 60, 69, 79, 100, 107, 206, 217, 245, 246, 252, 298
De Vere, Aubrey 15, 125, 265
Doddridge, Philip 63
Doughty, Oswald 107
Dove Cottage Trustees 244
Drabble, Margaret 204
Drayton, Michael 200-201
Dryden, John: "Heroic Stanzas on the Death of Oliver Cromwell" 20; "A Song for St. Cecilia's Day, 1687" 101; Virgil (Dryden's translation) 74, 89, 286; other references 12, 33, 60, 63, 64, 200, 215

Dunn, S. G. 83, 264
Durrant, Geoffrey 39
Dyce, Alexander 60, 65, 189, 190
Dyer, George 17-18, 78
Dyer, John 63

Eclectic Review 234
"Ecstasy" in visual code of expression 165-68, 287
Edgeworth, Francis 130, 143, 158, 178, 193, 289
Edinburgh Review 234, 296
Elegant Extracts 73, 205
Elliott, Jane 190
Ellis, John 280
Elmes, James 164
Elton, Oliver 204
Encyclopaedia Britannica (1797) 239
Enfield, William 65, 270
Engel, J. J. 164, 286
Epicurus 19-20, 45, 175, 176, 263
"Esteem" in visual code of expression 165
Eternity as an element in the cluster of seven images recurrent in Wordsworth's poetry 102-4, 116, 154-55, 161, 207-12
Ether 32-35
"Ethereal" ("Etherial") 32-35
European Magazine 51
Evelyn, John 22, 187
Examiner, The 114-16, 234-36

Fairfax, Edward 332
Fawkes, Francis 23-24, 35, 44, 47, 51-52, 146, 152, 268
Fenwick, Isabella 72, 97, 111, 125, 131, 145, 183, 186, 219, 220, 222, 232, 265, 289, 294, 295
Finch, Anne, Countess of Winchilsea 63, 190
Fink, Z. S. 49
Fitzgerald, Robert 169, 287
Fleming, Lady Ann le 188

Fontenelle, Bernard Le Bovier, Sieur de 24
"For Ever" in Wordsworth's lines on Newton's statue (P 3:57-63) 154-55
Foster, James 41-42
Foxe, John 187
Fraunce, Abraham 189
Furness Abbey (Abbey of St. Mary's Furness), Introduction to the Foundation-Charter of 200

Garber, Frederick 85-86, 95
Geer, Russel M. 19
General Magazine of Arts and Science 51
Gentleman's Magazine 45, 49, 238, 266
Gilbert, William 200
Gill, Stephen 253
Gillies, R. P. 192, 194
Gladstone, W. E. 106
Glauert, R. H. 289
Glover, Richard 25, 27-28, 30, 44-45, 47, 53, 57-58, 156, 205-6, 292
Godwin, William 186
Golding, Arthur 189
Googe, B. 189
Grabo, Carl 264
Graves, Rev. Charles 129
Graves, John T. 13
Graves, R. P. 119, 125, 126, 130
Gray, Thomas: "Elegy Written in a Country Churchyard" 140; "Ode on the Pleasure arising from Vicissitude" 56; other references 63, 69, 199, 205
Grove, Henry 73-74, 78

Halifax, Charles Montague, Earl of 280
Hall, Joseph 60
Hallam, Arthur Henry 192-93
Halley, Edmund 7, 24, 47, 51, 268
Hamilton, Eliza 6, 9, 33, 259, 282, 294

Hamilton, Sydney 227, 295
Hamilton, Sir William Rowan:
—attitude towards Newton: admiration for 32; Newton's sacrifice of love for achievement 120-21; Newton's "one great stride of thought" 134, 156; Newton's image of ocean of truth 143, 153; as "favoured discoverer" 153; Newton's mind for ever voyaging 153-54; Newton's thought 156; relation of Newton's mind to God's Thought 158-61; possible visit to Newton's statue and concept of rapture 167
—attitude towards Newtonian science: provides evidence of God 121-23, 280; imagination in it analogous to artistic imagination 125, 128-32; principles derived from observed facts 132-34
—breadth of interests and scholarship 118, 279
—career: training 118; Professor of Astronomy 118; pioneer in algebra 123, in optics 123; knighted 123-24
—major motifs in writings and conversation: analogy between beauty and science 125, 128-32; belief that beings more intelligent than humans exist somewhere 134-35; golden chain from earth to heaven 123, 137, 280
—relations with Wordsworth: changes Wordsworth's attitude towards science 7, 98; correspondence with 119-20, 122, 124-25, 129-30, 131, 215, 218-20; first meeting 118-19, 192; friendship 118-44; influence on elevation of "If thou indeed derive thy light from Heaven" 231-33; influence on Wordsworth's revision of lines on Newton's statue 141-44, 147-48,

150, 156, 158-59, 161, 166-68, 283, and of other *Prelude* passages 132-35, 135-42, 226-31; major influence on Wordsworth 33, 121-22, 125-28, 137-38, 140-41; paraphrases lines from "Tintern Abbey" 125, 153; prompts writing of "So fair, so sweet, withal so sensitive" 126-28; says Wordsworth claimed descent from Alfred 40; sends Wordsworth copies of his writings 119-20, 122-23, 125-26, 129, 281; visits from Wordsworth 3, 130-31; visits to Wordsworth 125-30, 281
—works: poetry: "Botany" (sonnet) 131-32; "Farewell Verses to William Wordsworth at the Close of a Visit to Rydal Mount in 1830" 122-23; "It Haunts Me Yet" (poem on his severe disappointment in love) 119-21; "Recollections" (poem to Wordsworth) 123, 124-25; prose: "Address to the British Association" (10 Aug. 1835) 128-29, 130, 137-38, 139-40, 143-44, 152-53, 166-67, 229, 231; "Introductory Lecture on Astronomy" (1831) 122-23, 129, 158; "Introductory Lecture on Astronomy" (1832) 122, 125, 134-35, 137, 142-43, 144, 153, 158-59, 228; "Introductory Lecture on Astronomy" (1833) 130, 139, 144; "Metaphysical Remarks on Algebra as the Science of Pure Time" 123
Hanson, Lawrence 297
Hare, Julius C. 126
Hartley, David 10-11, 71-72, 93, 95
Harvey, Sir Paul 6
Havens, R. D. 104, 107
Hawkshead 21, 32, 49-50, 64, 73, 147, 187-88, 205, 238; *see also* Wordsworth, William, works,
poetry, "Lines Written as a School Exercise at Hawkshead"
Haydon, Benjamin R. *(Christ's Entry)* 29, 63, 99, 114-15, 164-65, 168, 234-36
Hazlitt, William 114, 186
Hederich, Benjamin 238
Height (or depth) as an element in the cluster of seven images recurrent in Wordsworth's poetry 102-3, 116-17, 207-12
Hemans, Felicia Dorothea 68
Herbert, Sir T. 291
Heroes, English 20-24
Heron, Robert 81
Hervey, Thomas Kibble 193
Hill, Alan G. 194
Hobbes, Thomas 20, 31
Homer, 64, 168-70, 201, 215, 238
Hughes, John 25-26, 35, 45, 47-49, 77, 152, 268
Hunt, John 115
Hunt, Leigh 115
Hunt, Robert 115-16, 146-47, 152, 156, 234-36
Hutchinson, Sara 63, 112, 221-22, 245
Hutchinson, Thomas 183

Imagination, Wordsworth's 13-16, 146-48
"Index" in Wordsworth's lines on Newton's statue *(P* 3:57-63) 148-52, 284
"Inward eye" in Daffodils poem 92-93

James, Henry 15
James, Captain Thomas 63
John the Baptist 176
John Bull 234-35
Johnson, Joseph 239
Johnson, Lee M. 31
Johnson, Samuel 60, 150, 162, 275, 284, 292
Jones, Henry 24, 44
Jones, Inigo 44

Jones, John 103
Jonson, Ben 44

Keats, John 29-30, 69, 114, 154
Kepler, Johannes 130
Killigrew, Anne 63, 190

Lamb, Charles 29-30, 32, 114, 188, 194
Landor, W. S. 289
Langhorne, John 63, 187
Lattimore, Richmond 169
Le Brun, Charles 111, 164-67, 172
Legouis, Emile 106-7
Le Keux, J. 286
Liddell, Henry George 169, 287
"Light" 173-76
Lindenberger, Herbert 103
Lindsay, Lady Anne 190
Littledale, H. 204
Locke, John 29, 32, 264, 284
Loeb Classical Library, editors and translators of 169, 171, 287
Lot's wife 146, 283
Lover, Samuel 149, 284
Lowther, Lady Mary 63
Lucretius 19-20, 27, 45, 47, 64, 263
Lytton Bulwer, E. G., later Edward George Earle Lytton Bulwer-Lytton, 1st Baron Lytton of Knebworth: "Sculpture" 109-10, 150, 152, 154, 156-57, 159, 221-25, 277; *Siamese Twins and Other Poems* 109, 222; "To Wordsworth" 222-25; *Weeds and Wildflowers* 222; other references 109, 221-25, 294

McKillop, A. D. 276
Macpherson, James 84
Mallaby, George 204
Mallet, David 25-28, 35, 43, 53, 153, 156-57, 205-6, 292
Mangey, Thomas 88-90, 145-46, 149, 153, 172-73, 237-38, 274, 283, 287; *see also* Philo

"Marble" in Wordsworth's lines on Newton's statue *(P* 3:57-63) 149-50
Marlborough, John Churchill, Duke of 21, 23
Martin, Benjamin 51
Marvell, Andrew 12, 63
Mavor, Rev. W. 153, 284
May, Thomas 189
Mayo, Robert 202-4
Memory, Wordsworth's use of in appropriating his sources viii, 14-16, 59-62, 68-80, 81-97, 105-17, 144-80, 193-94
Mickle, William Julius 63-64
Miller, Joseph Kirkham 214
Milton, John: *Comus* 84, 86; "Il Penseroso" 92–94, 100–101, 277; "L'Allegro" 93; "Ode on the Morning of Christ's Nativity" 9; *Paradise Lost* 8-9, 54, 68-70, 75, 81-82, 83-84, 125, 163, 173, 175, 268, 280; *Paradise Regained* 69; *Samson Agonistes* 83, 162-63, 285; other references 33, 60, 63-64, 68-69, 74, 85, 103, 125, 157, 188, 201, 215, 228, 270, 291
"Mind" in Wordsworth's lines on Newton's statue *(P* 3:57-63) 149-51, 154-56
Monkhouse, Thomas 29
Montagu, Lady Mary Wortley 190
Moore, John Robert 84
Moorman, Mary 5, 32, 217, 219, 290
More, Henry 91-92
Morgan, Caesar 238-39, 297
Morley, Edith 189
Morley, John 203
Moses 173-76, 288
Moultrie, John 193-94
Moxon, Edward 194, 250
Muirhead, James P. 33, 183, 185, 191-92, 202, 221-24, 265, 294, 296

Newton, Sir Isaac. *See also* Newton, Sir Isaac, Roubiliac's statue of
—attitudes towards: as English hero 7, 23-24, 24-28, 263; in 18th century 44-49, 73, 98-99, 156-57; by English Romantics 28-32, 114-15, 263-64; by Hamilton 129-30, 134, 143, 154, 156, 158-59, 161; by Wordsworth 5-7, 32-40, 41-42, 50-58, 83, 139-41, 159-64, 168-72, 251
—image of boy by the shore 41, 113-15, 143, 148, 152-53
—life: appearance 43-44; disappointed in love 120-21; knighted 124, 280; stands for Parliament 280; refers to "silent moon" 163; refers to early and full light 174-75
—mind voyaging 16, 152-61
—view of God and creation: "aether" 33-34; beings more intelligent than man 134, 282; Christian beliefs 20, 39, 41-42, 262; God not soul of the world but its Lord 264-65; God seen through science 121-22, 279-80; God's intervention in history 284; seen as atheist 29, 264; space as God's sensorium 157, 279
—works: *Chronology of Antient Kingdoms Amended* 56, 108, 152; "General Scholium" (of *Philosophiae Naturalis Principia Mathematica*) 31, 45, 121-22, 173, 264; *Opticks* 32, 45, 121; *Principia (Philosophiae Naturalis Principia Mathematica)* 31, 38-39, 41, 47, 51; "Second Paper on Light & Colours" 34
Newton, Sir Isaac, Roubiliac's statue of: Latin inscription on pedestal of 112, 146; "rapture" expressed by 165-68, 286-87; Le Brun and Williams as possible sources for depiction of rapture by 165-67; "admiration and sublimity" expressed by 166-67; possibly seen by Hamilton 167-68; apparent anomaly in 168; descriptions of 174-77, 286-87; portrays Newton as pre-eminent in philosophy and superior to Moses 173-77; story of Roubiliac's reworking mouth 287; other references 5-6, 12, 15-16, 17-20, 41-42, 46-47, 76-80, 98-117, 272; for Wordsworth's lines on *see under* Wordsworth, William: works: *Prelude* 3:57-63
Newtonian science, shifting views of 24-32
Nicolson, Marjorie H. 26, 30, 47
Norris, John 189
Norton Critical Edition of *The Prelude*, editors of 5, 107, 217, 229, 253, 298
Noyes, Russell 186, 270

Oakley, Richard 23
Old age, Wordsworth's poetic expectations in 5, 213-16, 219-20
Origen 175, 239, 288
Originality, Wordsworth's 13-16, 79-80, 202-4
Ossian 84-85, 215
Ovid 61, 64, 149, 186
Owen, W. J. B. 49, 59, 74-76, 82, 229, 231, 247, 253, 296
Oxford English Dictionary 33, 44, 91, 96, 160-63, 227, 270-71, 285, 287

Patmore, Derek 204
Paul, Saint 71
Peace, John 65
Peacock, Thomas Love 151
Pemberton, Henry 292
Perceiver, the exceptional, as an element in the cluster of seven images recurrent in

Wordsworth's poetry 102-4, 116, 154, 158, 207-12
Percy, Bishop Thomas 187, 291
Perkins, David 251, 298
Petrarch 64, 270
Pfeiffer, Augustus Friedericus 237
Phaer, Thomas 189-90
Philips, Katherine Fowler 190
Philo of Alexandria, *aka* Philo Judaeus: *De Migratione Abrahami* 169-71, 287; *De Opificio Mundi* 87-97, 163-64, 285; *De Somnis* 115-16, 145-46, 148-49, 153, 171, 173, 176, 283-84; *De Vita Mosis* 176; *Legum Allegoria* 173; *Quis Rerum Divinarum Heres* 171, 287; *Supplement* (Loeb Classical Library) 288; other references 87-88, 171-73, 175, 237-40, 288
Pilkington, Laetitia 63, 190
Pitt, Christopher 286
Plato 74, 84-86, 238-39
Pope, Alexander: "The Alley" 11; "The Capon's Tale" 44; *The Dunciad* 7; *An Essay on Man* 6-7, 55, 83, 122; *The Iliad* (Pope's translation) 44, 168-69, 201; *The Odyssey* (Pope's translation) 44; *The Temple of Fame* 44, 46-47; *Windsor Forest* 55; other references 21, 33, 56, 60, 63-64, 89, 205, 268, 280
Pottle, Frederick A. 61, 95
Potts, Abbie F. 83, 107, 268
Priestley, F. E. L. 31
Priestley, Joseph 238-40, 297
"Prism" in Wordsworth's lines on Newton's statue *(P* 3:57-63) 161-62, 168-69, 177
Private experience and meaning *versus* public meaning and statement in Wordsworth's poetry 69-72, 84-97, 126-28, 135-41, 171-72, 177
Proclus 84
Public meaning and statement *versus* private experience and meaning in Wordsworth's poetry *see* Private experience and meaning *versus* public meaning and statement in Wordsworth's poetry

Quarterly Review 41, 234, 296
Quiet as an element in the cluster of seven images recurrent in Wordsworth's poetry: *see* Silence
Quillinan, Edward 192, 219-22, 250, 294

Rader, Melvin 264-65
Raleigh, Walter 203
Ramsay, Allan 24, 26-27, 43-44, 47-50, 54-55, 152, 156, 205-6, 292
Randolph, Thomas 189
"Rapture" in visual code of expression 165-69, 172, 286-87
Raymond, Louis 291
Reading, Wordsworth's viii, 59-80, 81-97, 105-10, 112-17, 183-90, 193-94, 266, 290
Reed, Henry 290
Reed, Mark 253
Richardson, Leon J. 268
Rieu, E. V. 169
"Rising of the North, The" 200
Robinson, Henry Crabb 61, 189, 193, 235, 294-95
Robson, R. 289
Roubiliac, Louis François *see* Newton, Sir Isaac, Roubiliac's statue of
Rydal Mount 183, 185, 189, 221, 232, 235, 295

Sages, English 40-42, 128-32, 135-41
St. John's College (Cambridge) 99-101, 111, 151, 175, 237, 295
Samson 163, 285
Sandys, George 187
Schelling, Friedrich Wilhelm Joseph von 83

Schelp, Hanspeter 85
Schiller, Johann Christoph Friedrich von 199
Schneider, B. R., Jr. 37-39
Science and scientists, right and wrong kinds of 3-13, 128-32
Scott, James (author of the "Ode to Sculpture") 76-80, 105-6, 110, 120, 146, 152, 154, 156, 161, 277
Scott, Robert 169, 287
Scott, Sir Walter 12, 60, 106, 162, 185, 200
Selwyn, William 18, 113, 157, 174-76, 284, 285, 287, 288, 289
Shaftesbury, Anthony Ashley Cooper, Third Earl of 83, 273
Shakespeare, William: *King John* 62; "Sonnet 64" 63, 269; "Sonnet 73" 214; *The Tempest* 55-56; other references 63-64, 69, 200, 205
Sheats, Paul D. 253
Shelley, Percy B. 29-30, 32
Shelvocke, George 203, 284
Shenstone, William: "Rural Elegance: An Ode to the Late Duchess of Somerset" 65-68, 195-98
Siddons, Henry 164, 166
Sidney, Sir Philip 10, 13
Siemens, Reynold 217, 298
Silence as an element in the cluster of seven images recurrent in Wordsworth's poetry 102-4, 112-13, 116, 207-12
"Silent" in Wordsworth's lines on Newton's statue *(P* 3:57-63) 161-64, 170-72, 177, 285-86, 288; in "Star Gazers" 171-72
Simmias Rhodius 86, 92, 94
Skelton, John 60, 189
Smart, Christopher 63
Smith, Adam 280
Smith, Charlotte 187
Smith, Elsie 204
Smith, Hallett 293

Smith, Robert, Master of Trinity 20, 27, 46-47, 77, 146, 164, 167, 172-73, 262-63
Smyser, Jane Worthington 273
Snow, A. J. 264
Solitariness as an element in the cluster of seven images recurrent in Wordsworth's poetry 102-4, 112-13, 116, 207-12
Something exceptional perceived, as an element in the cluster of seven images recurrent in Wordsworth's poetry 102-4, 112-13, 116, 157-61, 207-12
Sources used and possibly used by Wordsworth *see* Addison, Joseph; Akenside, Mark; Bartram, William; Beattie, James; Bede; Bible, the Holy; Blake, William; Boehme, Jakob; *Book of Common Prayer;* Boyse, Samuel; Brereton, Jane; Browne, Moses; Caesar, Julius; Cambridge, Richard Owen; Chantrey, Sir Francis; Chapman, George; Churchill, Charles; Cicero; Coleridge, Samuel Taylor (esp. "Eolian Harp," "Kubla Khan," "Monody on... Chatterton," "Religious Musings," "The Rime of the Ancient Mariner"); Cowper, William (esp. *The Iliad, Table Talk,* "Yardley Oak"); Cudworth, Ralph; Cunningham, Allan; Davies, Sir John; Desaguliers, John T.; Drayton, Michael; Dryden, John (esp. "Song for St. Cecilia's Day," "Virgil"); Dyer, George; *Elegant Extracts; Examiner, The;* Fawkes, Francis; Foster, James; Furness Abbey...; Gilbert, William; Glover, Richard; Gray, Thomas (esp. "Ode on the Pleasure arising from Vicissitude");

Grove, Henry; Halley, Edmund; Hamilton, Sir William Rowan; Hartley, David; Haydon, Benjamin R.; Herbert, Sir T.; Heron, Robert; Homer; Hughes, John; Hunt, Robert; Jones, Henry; Keats, John; Lytton Bulwer, E. G. (esp. "Sculpture"); Macpherson, James; Mallet, David; Mangey, Thomas; Milton, John (esp. *Comus*, "Il Penseroso," "L'Allegro," "Ode on the Morning of Christ's Nativity," *Paradise Lost, Paradise Regained, Samson Agonistes*); More, Henry; Newton, Sir Isaac (esp. "aether," "image of boy by the shore"); Oakley, Richard; Ossian; Percy, Bishop Thomas; Philo of Alexandria; Pitt, Christopher; Plato; Pope, Alexander (esp. "The Alley," *The Dunciad, An Essay on Man, Iliad, Windsor Forest)*; Proclus; Ramsay, Allan; Raymond, Louis; "Rising of the North, The"; Roubiliac, Louis François *(see* "Newton, Sir Isaac, Roubiliac's statue of "*)* Schelling, Friedrich Wilhelm Joseph von; Scott, James; Selwyn, William; Shaftesbury, Anthony Ashley Cooper, Third Earl of; Shakespeare, William; Simmias Rhodius; Southey, Robert; *Spectator, The*; Spence, Joseph; Spenser, Edmund; Stanyhurst, Richard; Sterne, Laurence; Tasker, William; Tasso, Torquato; Taylor, Thomas; Thomson, James; Tollet, Elizabeth; Virgil; Voltaire; Walton, Izaak; Wesley, Charles; Whitaker, T. D.; Wilkinson, Thomas; Wordsworth, Dorothy; Wordsworth, Mary; Young, Edward

Southey, Robert 65, 106, 188, 200, 287
Southwell, Robert 189
Spectator, The 73, 78, 271
Spence, Joseph 41
Spenser, Edmund: "Colin Clout's come home again" 84; *Faerie Queene* 32, 63, 84, 204; "Hymn of Heavenly Beauty" 92, 274; "Hymn of Heavenly Love" 92, 94, 274-75; other references 63-64, 74, 188
Stallknecht, Newton P. 83
"Standing-up" 64, 73
Stanyhurst, Richard 190, 286
Stars as an element in the cluster of seven images recurrent in Wordsworth's poetry 102-3, 116, 207-12
Sterne, Laurence: *A Sentimental Journey through France and Italy* 71-72; *Tristram Shandy* 71, 200
Stolberg, Friedrich Leopold 199
"Strange seas" in Wordsworth's lines on Newton's statue *(P* 3:57-63) 160-61, 177
"Sublimity" in visual code of expression 166
Sutherland, J. R. 204
Swinburne, A. C. 141

Talfourd, Thomas Noon 215, 295
Tasker, William 40
Tasso, Torquato 201, 291
Taylor, Sir Henry 111, 219
Taylor, Thomas 84
Taylor, William 32, 103
Tennyson, Alfred, Lord vii-viii, 13-14, 194
Tennyson, Charles (Alfred's brother) 194
Tennyson, Charles (Alfred's grandson) vii
Thomson, James: *Autumn* 276; *The Castle of Indolence* 7, 276; *Spring*

83, 276; "To the Memory of Sir Isaac Newton" 24-27, 30-31, 38, 47-48, 50, 106-9, 113-14, 148, 152, 158, 263, 276-77; *Winter* 276; other references 39, 45, 63, 97, 177
"Thought" in Wordsworth's lines on Newton's statue *(P* 3:57-63) 155-61
Ticknor, George 280
Tollet, Elizabeth 25-27, 44-45, 50, 77, 152, 156, 177
"Transport" in visual code of expression 165-66, 286-87
Trinity College (Cambridge) 77-78, 99-101, 112, 124, 151, 167, 172, 175, 180, 237-38, 251, 288, 297
Turberville, George 189

Ussher, Bishop James 10, 260-61

"Vacant" in Daffodils poem 91-93, 163, 169
Vallon, Annette 121
"Varying" 64, 270
"Veneration" in visual code of expression 164-65
Vincent, Mrs. (Newton's early love) 121
Virgil 64, 74, 83, 201, 285-86, 292
Voltaire (François-Marie Arouet) 29, 99, 114
"Voyaging" in Wordsworth's lines on Newton's statue *(P* 3:57-63) 152-61
"Vulgus" 64, 270

Waller, Edmund 63, 269-70
Walton, Izaak 59
Warton, Jane 63, 190
Warton, Joseph 187
Warton, Thomas 187
Watson, Richard (bishop of Llandaff) 239
Watson, Thomas 189
Webster, John 63

Wesley, Charles 85, 95
Westfall, Richard S. 280
Whewell, William 124, 280
Whiston, William 23-24
Whitaker, T. D. 59, 188
Wilkinson, Thomas 81
Williams, John 164-65, 167
Willoughby, Henry 189
Wilson, John 234, 296
Wilson, Richard 270
Wither, George 63
Winchester College 64
Winchilsea, Anne Finch, Countess of 63, 190
Wordsworth, Catherine (Wordsworth's daughter) 69-71
Wordsworth, Christopher (Wordsworth's brother) 49, 51, 188, 205, 218
Wordsworth, Christopher (Wordsworth's nephew) 183-84, 186, 191, 200, 218, 222, 234, 250, 265
Wordsworth, Dora (Wordsworth's daughter) 213, 217-19, 250, 252
Wordsworth, Dorothy (Wordsworth's sister) 48, 59-61, 65, 82, 85, 88-90, 103, 112, 128, 183-85, 188, 213, 218-19, 222, 234, 238, 244, 273, 278, 281, 287, 295
Wordsworth, Jane (Wordsworth's granddaughter) 40
Wordsworth, John (Wordsworth's brother) 35, 218
Wordsworth, John (Wordsworth's nephew) 218
Wordsworth, John (Wordsworth's son) 265
Wordsworth, Jonathan 81-83, 141, 244
Wordsworth, Mary (Wordsworth's wife) 85, 92, 155, 183, 220-22, 245, 247, 275
Wordsworth, William
—attitudes: towards machinery 100-1; towards Newton 32-34,

36-40, 41-42, 158-61, 170-72; towards Newton's statue 111-14, 145; towards science 3-7, 49-58, 128-44
—characteristics as an author: ability to write in old age 5, 213-16, 217-20; acknowledging indebtedness 79-80, 199-201; cluster of seven images 102-4, 116, 154, 160-61, 207-12; composing 15-16, 183-84, 185-86, 289; double meaning (private and public) 69-72, 84-87, 126-28, 135-41, 171-72, 177; imagination 13-16, 146-48; influenced by Coleridge, Dorothy, and/or Hamilton 125, 128, 138-40, 238; memory, use of viii, 14-16, 17-18, 59-62, 68-80, 81-97, 105-17, 144-80, 193-94; originality 13-16, 79-80, 202-4; reading viii, 59-80, 81-97, 105-10, 112-17, 183-90, 193-94; revising 132-35, 135-42, 142-44, 148-52, 152-55, 155-61, 177-80, 226-33, 283, and see subheading "works"; showing MSS. 228, 295; sources, use of viii, 14-16, 59-62, 68-80, 81-97, 105-17, 144-80, 193-94, and see "Sources used and possibly used by Wordsworth"
—characteristics as a private person: health 186, 289; languages, command of 61, 188, 238; library 183-84, 185-86, 188-89, 206, 237, 292; quoting from memory 14, 62-65, 83, 186, 213-14; reading, range of 61, 183-90, 266, 290; reciting 224, 294-95; re-enacting of moving bed 111, 145; response to beauty 111; talking non-stop 32, 265
—portrait in Haydon's *Christ's Entry* 29, 164-65, 168, 234-36
—relations with contemporary writers: at Haydon's dinner 29-30; editors 12, 65, 189-90, 195-98; nephew 191; views them as "thieves" 61; young writers 192-94, 221-25
—relations with William Rowan Hamilton see Hamilton, Sir William Rowan, relations with Wordsworth
—works: letters: Recipients of Wordsworth's letters appear as main index entries, and the subjects of his letters likewise appear as main index entries and also as entries within the various subheadings under Wordsworth, William
—works: poetry (apart from *Prelude):* "Alice Fell" 178, 288; "Anacreon (Imitation)" 238; "Apology" 83; *Benjamin the Waggoner* 200; *The Borderers* 178-80; "The Brothers" 200; "Characteristics of a Child three years old" 69, 271; "Composed in the Glen of Loch Etive" 282; "The Daffodils" *see* "I wandered lonely as a cloud"; *Descriptive Sketches* 82, 200, 291-92; "Ecclesiastical Sonnet XVIII, Apology" 83; "The Egyptian Maid" 191, 291; *An Evening Walk* 5, 12, 37, 52-58, 107, 200, 205-6, 292, and *see* ["Hymn to Science"]; *The Excursion:* (1:202-59) 102-4, 208-9; (1:229-35) 37-38; (1:254) 126; (3:50-112) 102-4, 160, 207-8; (3:82-83) 104; (4:334-38) 105; (4:941-78) 3-4, 8-11; (6:217-18) 178; (6:1005) 69; (8:199-204) 100; (9:1-20) 83; other references 6, 60, 69, 72, 125-26, 129, 200, 276; "The Farmer of Tilsbury Vale" 11; "Goody Blake and Harry Gill" 178; "Guilt and Sorrow" 292; ["Hymn to Science"] in Wordsworth's MS. revisions to

An Evening Walk 12, 52-58, 146, 152, 154, 205-6; "If thou indeed derive thy light from Heaven" ("Poet") 231-33; "In a Carriage, Upon the Banks of the Rhine" 69; "I wandered lonely as a cloud" 84-97, 116, 163, 170; "Laodamia" 13; "The Last of the Flock" 178, 289; "Lines Written as a School Exercise at Hawkshead" 5, 12, 21, 36, 49-52, 152, 154; "Lucy" poems 103; *Lyrical Ballads* 58, 199, 203-4; "Moschus: Lament for Bion, In Part from" 238; "A Night Piece" 82; "Ode: Intimations of Immortality" 72-74, 97, 102-4, 114, 125, 211; "Ode to Duty" 39; "Ode to Lycoris, the Second" 185-86; *Peter Bell* 114, 235; "The Pillar of Trajan" 193; "Poems of Sentiment and Reflection" 232; "Poems of Sentiment and Reflection XXXIV and XXXV" 40, 266; *The Recluse* 6, 59-60, 218; *River Duddon* sonnet no. XXIV 69; "She was a Phantom of delight" 69; "So fair, so sweet, withal so sensitive" 125-28; "The Solitary Reaper" 81; "Spanish Guerillas" 68; "The Sparrow's Nest" 69; "Star Gazers" 152, 170-72; "Strange fits of passion have I known" 291; "Stray Pleasures" 200; "Suggested at Tyndrum in a Storm" 179, 289; "Surprised by joy—impatient as the Wind" 69-71; "The Tables Turned" 11, 131, 184-87, 261; "The world is too much with us; late and soon" 84; "This Lawn, a carpet all alive" 131-32; "Tintern Abbey, Lines Composed a Few Miles Above" 42, 71-72, 91, 94, 102-4, 125, 142, 153, 178, 200, 212; "To —— Upon the Birth of Her First-Born Child, March, 1833" ("Poems of Sentiment and Reflection XXXIV") 40, 266; "To B. R. Haydon, on Seeing his Picture of Napoleon Buonaparte on the Island of St. Helena" 235; "To My Sister" 184-86; "Two Epigrams on Byron's *Cain*" 11; *The Waggoner* 200; "The Warning" ("Poems of Sentiment and Reflection XXXV") 40, 266; *The White Doe of Rylstone* 59, 200; "The World is too much with us" 84; *Yarrow Revisited and Other Poems* 179, 282, 289; "Yarrow Visited" 192

—works: *The Prelude:* (1:6-18) *(P 1805)* 75; (1:301-475) 102-4, 160, 209-11; (1:337-38) 104; (1:559-61) 107, 276; (**3:57-63**) *(P 1850* and equivalent lines in other versions) 5-6, 12, 27-28, 33, 37, 76-80, 98-117, 141-44, 145-80 (esp. 150, 153-56, 159-64, 168-70, 172, 177-80), 216-20, 236, 244-54, 285, 298; (3:62-63) 102-3, 217-20; (3:269-70) 33; (3:431-44) 75-76; (3:516-19) 107, 276; (4:334-38) 104-5; (5:50-140) 102; (5:65-67, 104-6) 38, 41; (5:339-42) 74; (5:482-89) 187; (5:588-607) 187-88; (6:115-28) 266; (6:123-28) 132-34; (6:143-49) *(P 1805)* 132-34; (6:180-82) 107, 276; (6:650-52) 107, 276; (7:162-67) 32-33; (7:566) 242, 298; (7:623-25) *(P 1805)* 228; (7:675-771) 288; (8:229-30) 107, 276; (8:262-81) 151; (8:266) 107, 276; (8:476-94) 241-43; (8:624-40) *(P 1805)* 241-43; (9:75-80) 111; (10:70-71) *(P 1805)* 226; (10:78-79) 226-27; (12:61-64) 40, 266; (13:36-65) *(P 1805)* 81-83; (13:40-96) *(P 1805)* 135-42; (13:42-46) *(P 1805)* 75; (13:54-59) *(P 1805)* 253; (13:91-92) *(P 1805)* 228; (13:95-96) *(P 1805)* 229;

(14:39-97) 135-42, 150-51, 160; (14:67, 71-72, 90, 93-95) 6-7; (14:95-97) 229-31; MSS. 244-54, 298; MS. A 228, 229, 244-45, 298; MS. A² 245; MS. B 229, 245-46, 298; MS. B² 246; MS. C 226-27, 229, 246, 298; MS. C² 247; MS. D 217, 219, 226, 228, 229, 247-53, 298; MS. D² 252; MS. E 217, 250-53; MS. W 229; other references 7, 71, 107, 111, 128, 147, 215-16, 217-19

—works: prose: Fenwick note to "If thou indeed derive thy light from Heaven" 232; Fenwick note to "Ode: Intimations of Immortality" 72, 97; Fenwick note to "This Lawn, a carpet all alive" 131-32; "A Letter to the Bishop of Landaff" 239; "Preface" to *Lyrical Ballads* 32, 96, 259; "Speech on laying the Foundation-stone of the New School in the Village of Bowness, Windermere, 1836" 98

World, The 76

Wrangham, Francis 214, 234

Wren, Sir Christopher 22-23, 26, 76

Wren, Christopher (the younger) 24

Young, Edward: *Night Thoughts* 116-17, 135, 153-54, 159-60, 241-43; other references 39, 117, 200, 202

Zacharias 176